BATMAN KNIGHTSEND

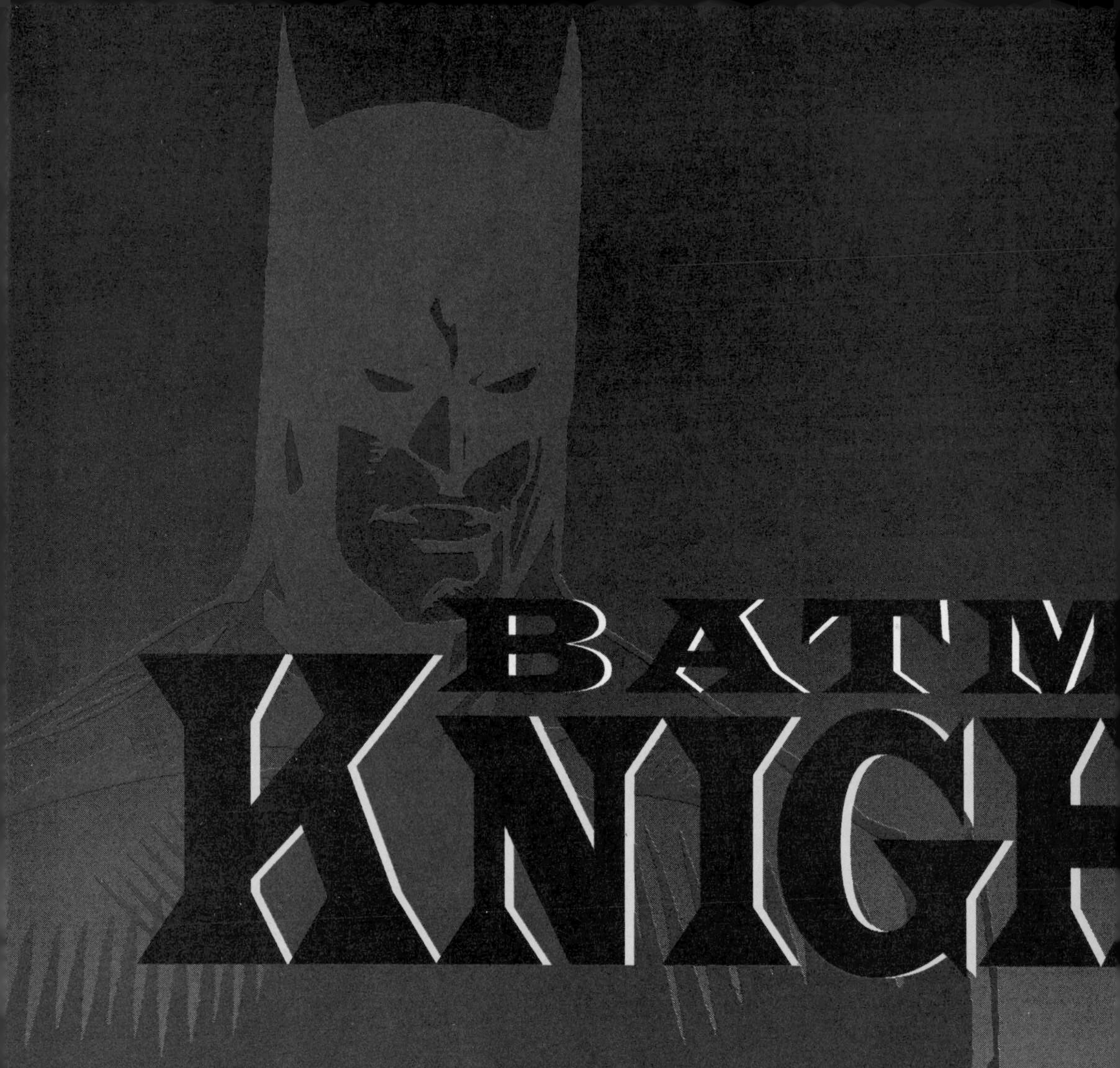
BATM
KNIG

WRITTEN BY

Chuck Dixon
Jo Duffy
Alan Grant
Doug Moench
Dennis O'Neil

ILLUSTRATED BY

Jim Balent
Bret Blevins
Rick Burchett
Dick Giordano
Tom Grummett
Scott Hanna
Barry Kitson
Ray Kryssing
Mike Manley
Ron McCain
Graham Nolan
Josef Rubinstein
Bob Smith
Ron Wagner

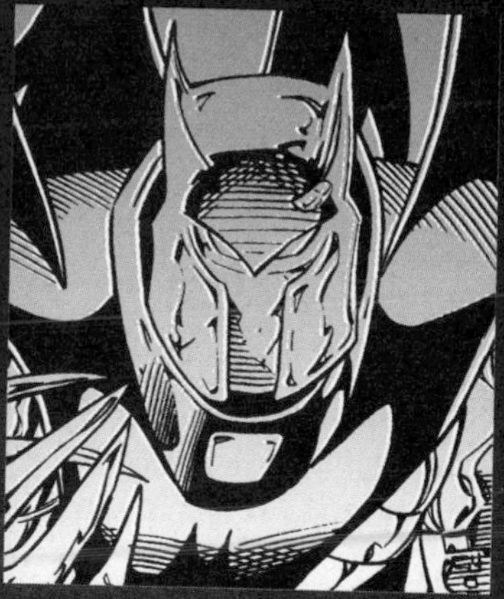

N
TSEND

COLORED BY

Adrienne Roy
Digital Chameleon
Buzz Setzer

LETTERED BY

Ken Bruzenak
Todd Klein
John Costanza
Willie Schubert
Albert DeGuzman
Bob Pinaha

COVERS BY

Kelley Jones & John Beatty
Brian Stelfreeze
Tom Grummett &
Ray Kryssing
Jim Balent
Kelley Jones
Barry Kitson &
Scott Hanna
Mike Mignola

BATMAN CREATED BY BOB KANE

BATMAN: KNIGHTSEND

Published by DC Comics. Cover and compilation
copyright © 1995 DC Comics. All Rights Reserved.

Originally published in single magazine form in BATMAN 509-510, BATMAN: SHADOW OF THE BAT 29-30,
DETECTIVE COMICS 676-677, BATMAN: LEGENDS OF THE DARK KNIGHT 62-63,
ROBIN 8-9 and CATWOMAN 12.
Copyright © 1994 DC Comics.
All Rights Reserved. All characters, their distinctive
likenesses and related indicia featured in this publication are trademarks of DC Comics.
The stories, characters, and incidents featured in this
publication are entirely fictional.

DC Comics, 1325 Avenue of the Americas,
New York, NY 10019
A division of Warner Bros. - A Time Warner Entertainment Company
Printed in Canada. First Printing.
ISBN: 1-56389-191-3
Cover by Graham Nolan and Brian Stelfreeze.

H

ere's how my grandmother told it to me: **"There's a hero in Gotham City who dresses like a bat. He fights against the bad men, but he never, ever kills them."**

I was six years old, and I was hooked.

That was 40 years ago. I'd just seen my first Batman comic, sent by a relative who'd emigrated to America at the end of World War II. I don't remember the particular story, but I can still recall my grandmother asking several times as she read it to me: "And what do you think happens next?"

INTRODUCTION BY ALAN GRANT

The question has haunted all of my comic-reading years. "What happens next?" came to define my feelings for comics — not out of impatience with plot or characters, but as a sign of the intrigue and sheer heat that a good comic generates.

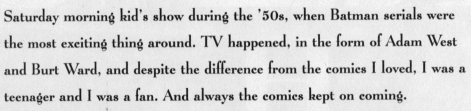

"What happens next?" For Batman, a lot stayed the same — he still dressed like a bat, fought the bad men, and never killed them. But also, much happened. Like movies...I was a regular at the Saturday morning kid's show during the '50s, when Batman serials were the most exciting thing around. TV happened, in the form of Adam West and Burt Ward, and despite the difference from the comics I loved, I was a teenager and I was a fan. And always the comics kept on coming.

At some forgotten age I started to worry. Surely there was only a finite number of Batman stories possible before the character lost his magic and was retired to the Great Comics Graveyard? After all, as well

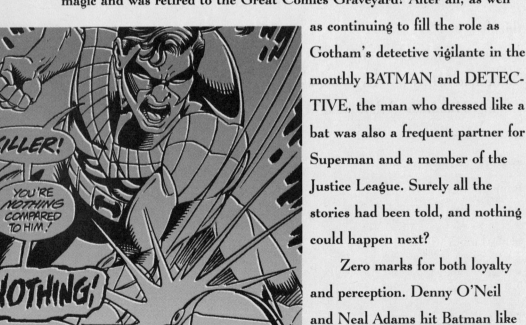

KILLER!

YOU'RE NOTHING COMPARED TO HIM!

NOTHING!

as continuing to fill the role as Gotham's detective vigilante in the monthly BATMAN and DETECTIVE, the man who dressed like a bat was also a frequent partner for Superman and a member of the Justice League. Surely all the stories had been told, and nothing could happen next?

Zero marks for both loyalty and perception. Denny O'Neil and Neal Adams hit Batman like a tornado, whisking away the boring old bits and reinventing the characters for a new generation of

readers (and me: I was still there).

The legend proceeded. Dick Grayson, the original Robin, grew up and began to question his role, eventually moving away to become Nightwing and his own man. Bruce Wayne dallied with pretty girls. Always the four constants remained — the bat-hero, the bad men, the vow never to kill...and that knife-edge feeling of "What happens next?"

Denny returned, this time as Batman Editor, and the question became — what couldn't possibly happen next? Frank Miller, for a start. A new Robin, a smart-mouthed delinquent more in keeping with the times — although the fault lines he created among fans showed that they preferred Dick Grayson's more traditional heroics. A deadlier Joker who, responding to readers' telephone votes, murdered the brash young Robin.

The Batman juggernaut rolled on: Marv Wolfman and Jim Aparo's third Robin, Tim Burton's movie, and Sam Hamm's masterful spell as a comics writer sent circulations soaring. Hundreds of thousands of new readers joined us, their voices swelling to a crescendo: "What happens next, Denny?"

Expand the creative pool, bring longtime Bat-chronicler Doug Moench back to the fold, sign up the singular writing talents of Chuck Dixon. Lock them in a room with a half-dozen artists and editorial wunderkind in upstate New York, and don't let them out until they've

created a new villain, Bane, who will truly prove to be Batman's equal. Let Denny and burgeoning superstar Joe Quesada introduce an intriguing new character — avenging angel Azrael — to the Gotham City mythos.

And then...? Well, try lighting the blue touchpaper and retiring to a safe distance as the conventions of 50 years of Batman stories explode around you.

Bane not only penetrates to the very heart of Batman's security, but breaks his back. No longer able to function as Gotham's Dark Knight, Bruce Wayne has his own reasons for not calling in his old friend and ex-partner, Dick Grayson, to fill his boots. Instead, he hands over the Mantle of the Bat to Azrael, alias Jean Paul Valley, a brilliant student whose life has been turned upside down by the discovery that he's been programmed by his own father to fill the role of assassin for the mysterious Order of St. Dumas. When Bruce's therapist, Shondra Kinsolving, and new Robin's father Jack Drake are kidnapped, Bruce pursues their captors 'round the world — leaving the safety of Gotham City in the hands of Azrael.

This is one of the few mistakes Bruce has made since that fateful night when he first became the Batman. The hypnotic conditioning induced by Jean Paul's father runs far deeper than anyone supposed; "the System," as he calls it, has a way of imposing itself and its demands on whatever conscious decisions he might make. In his hands,

the role of Batman becomes less of a detective, less a true hero, more a brutal vengeance machine. The flowing lines of the Bat-costume give way to the metallic angles of a suit of armor. Commissioner Gordon, a linchpin of the Bruce Wayne Batman's war on crime, is left out of the loop entirely. The stalwart Alfred resigns. The role of Boy Wonder is sidelined until Robin is little more than a spectator at what he perceives to be fast becoming the death of the Batman legend.

Azrael disobeys orders to match himself against the might of Bane — and when he wins, it seems as if he may have rid Gotham of one tyrant only to replace him with another...Azrael himself. As the excesses of the System become greater, and harder for him to bear, so Azrael's own behavior plunges towards the criminal...culminating in the awful night when he turns his back and allows the serial killer Abattoir to perish, thereby condemning Abattoir's innocent captive to a slow and painful death.

If my grandmother were still alive, this is how she might put it today: "There's a man in Gotham City who dresses in a suit of armor. He fights against the bad men, and sometimes he kills them. He used to be a hero." And, I hope, there would be a twinkle in her eye as she teased: "But Bruce Wayne's better now. He's coming back to Gotham. And what do you think will happen next?"

I'm forty-six years old, and I'm still hooked.

How about it, Denny? What happens next?

Alan Grant

12-18-94

KnightsEnd Part 1
SPIRIT of the BAT

YOUR SCENT, SWEET *JASMINE*-- YOUR EYES, COLD *STONE*. YOU ARE *LADY SHIVA*... WHOSE LIFE IS LIVED ONLY FOR *VIOLENCE*.

MY LIFE IS LIVED FOR *SKILL*.

I CRAVE *CHALLENGE*.

YOU SLEEP *LITTLE*, AND YOU WAKE UP CRAVING *BLOOD*.

YOU ARE A *VAMPIRE*, PERVERTING A *GIFT* WHICH COULD MAKE YOU *IMMORTAL*.

DOUG MOENCH
Story

MIKE MANLEY
Pencils

DICK GIORDANO
Ink

ADRIENNE ROY
Colors

KEN BRUZENAK
Letters

JORDAN B. GORFINKEL
Assistant Editor

DENNIS O'NEIL
Editor

BATMAN created by Bob Kane

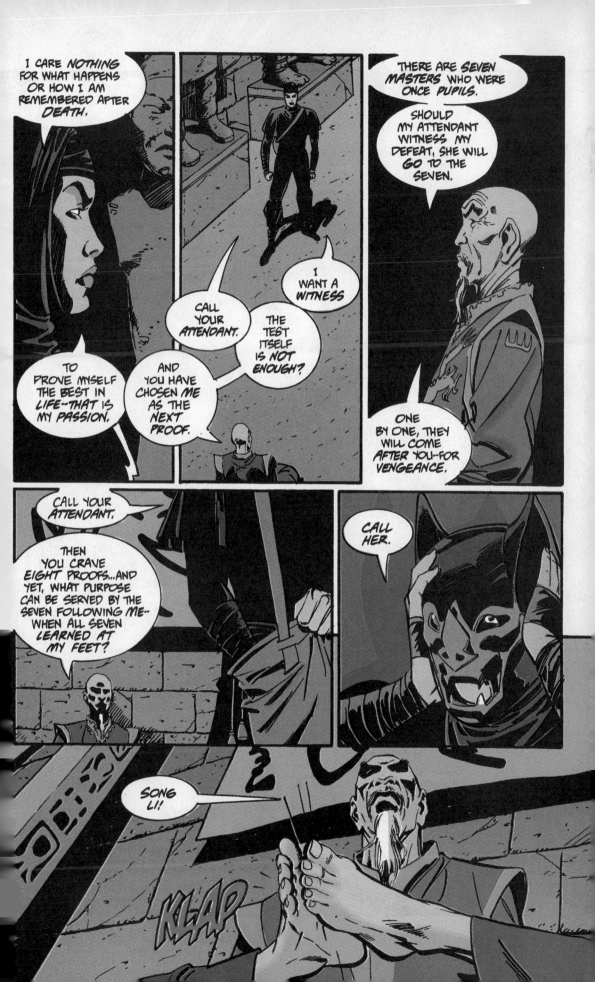

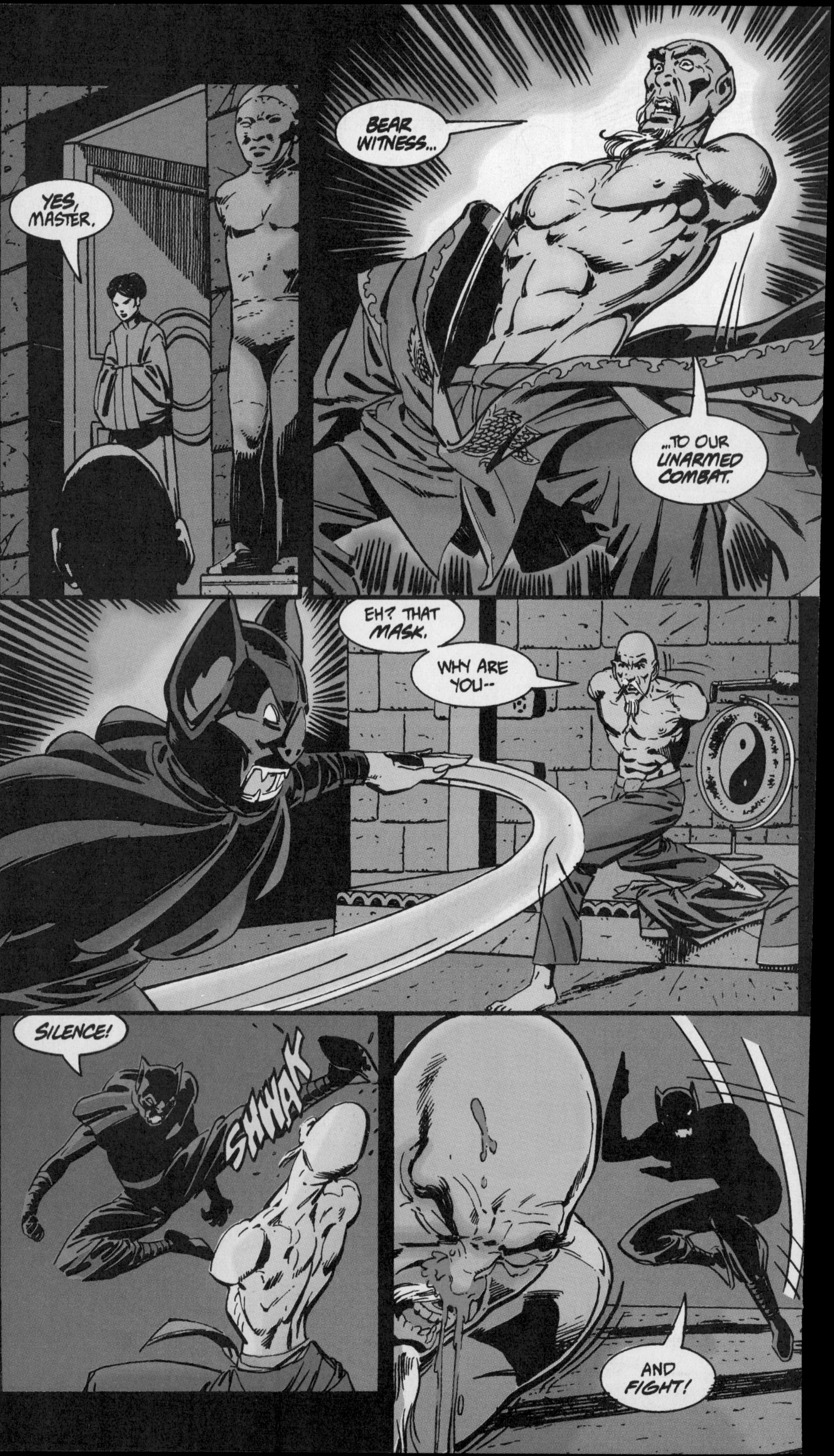
YES, MASTER.
BEAR WITNESS...
...TO OUR UNARMED COMBAT.
EH? THAT MASK.
WHY ARE YOU--
SILENCE!
SHWAK
AND FIGHT!

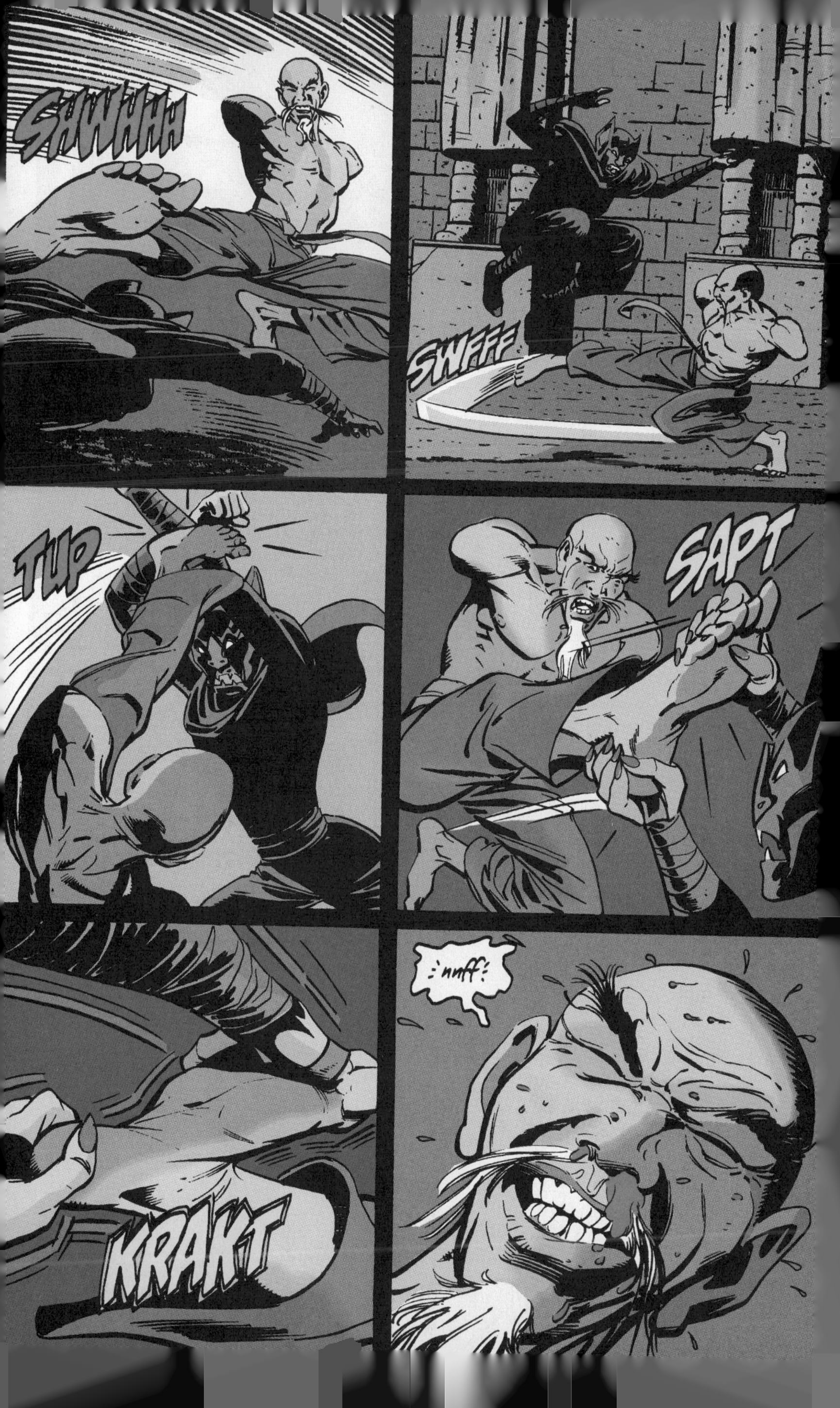
SHWHHH
SWFFF
TUP
SAPT
KRAKT
:nnff:

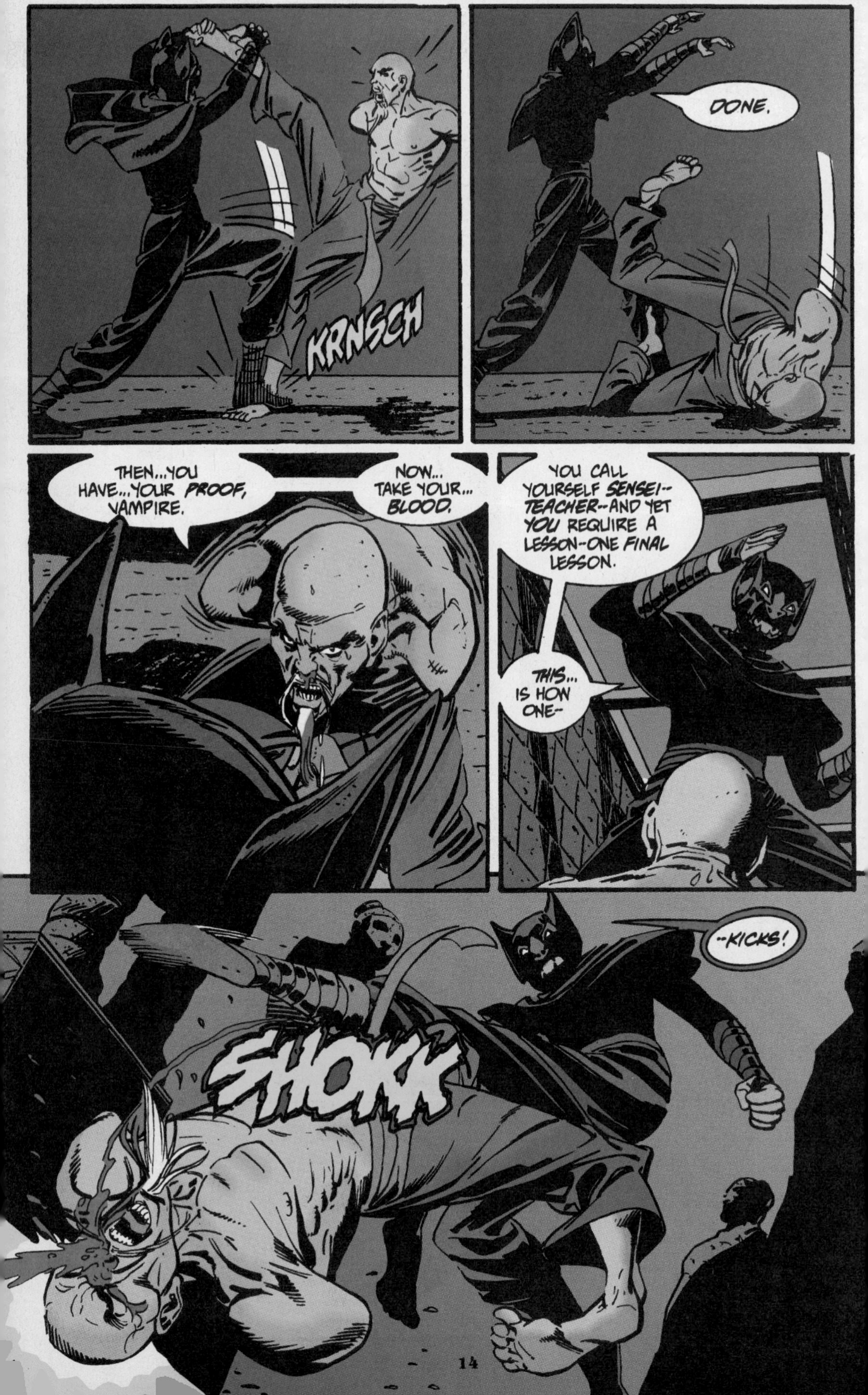
KRNSCH
DONE.
THEN...YOU HAVE...YOUR PROOF, VAMPIRE.
NOW... TAKE YOUR... BLOOD.
YOU CALL YOURSELF SENSEI-- TEACHER--AND YET YOU REQUIRE A LESSON--ONE FINAL LESSON.
THIS... IS HOW ONE-
--KICKS!
SHOKK

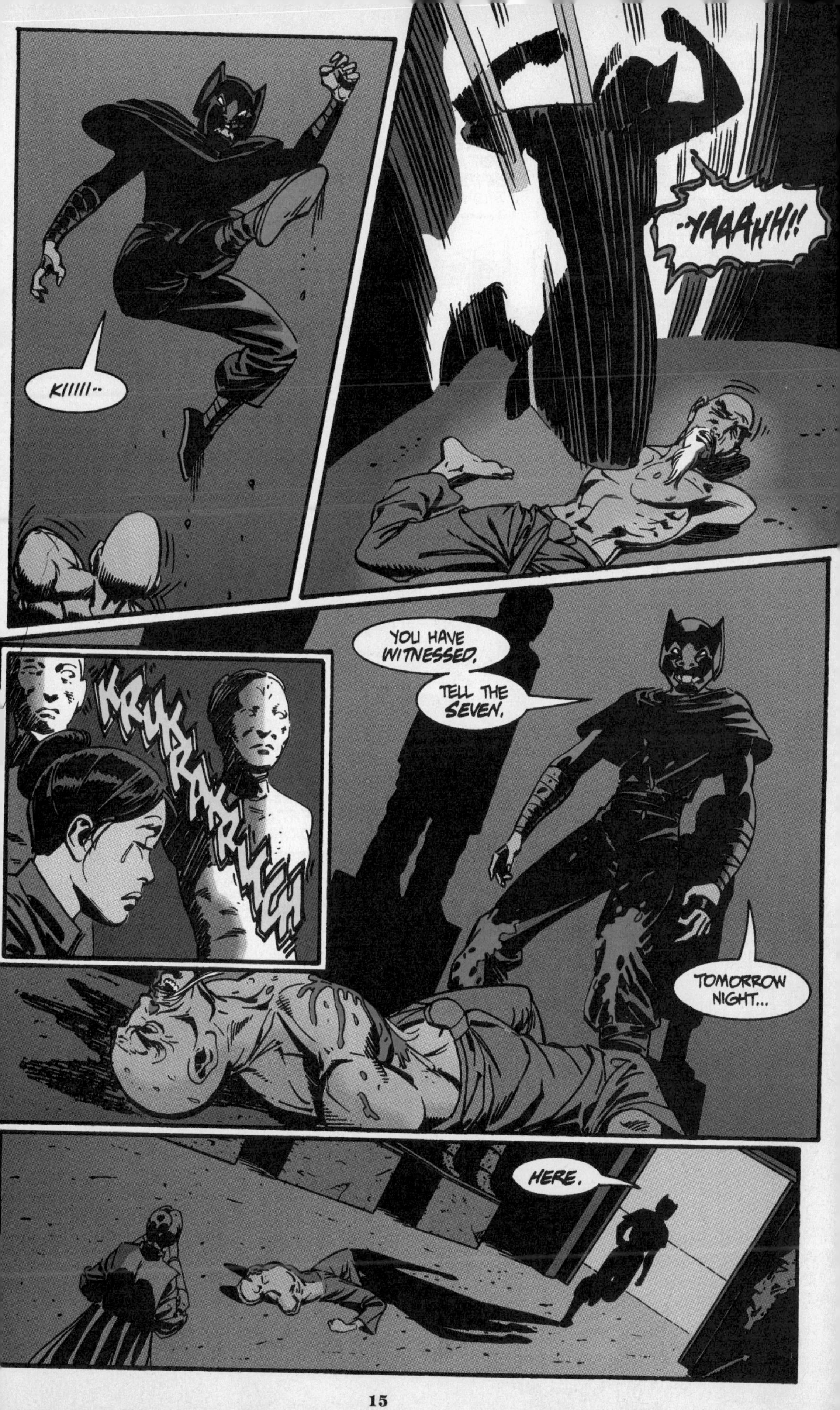
KIIIII--
--YAAAHH!!
KRUKRAKRUNCH
YOU HAVE WITNESSED,
TELL THE SEVEN,
TOMORROW NIGHT...
HERE.

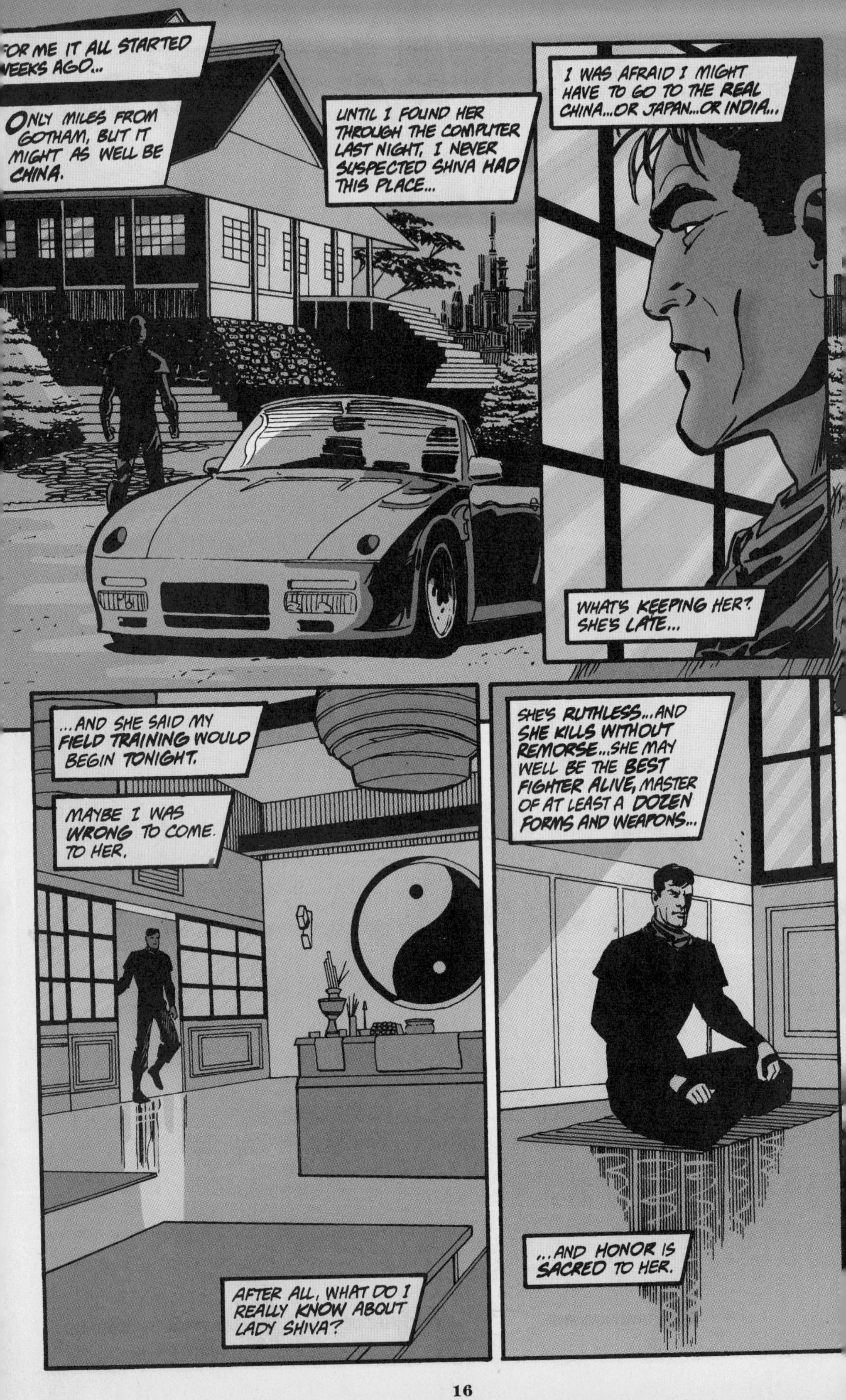
FOR ME IT ALL STARTED WEEKS AGO...
ONLY MILES FROM GOTHAM, BUT IT MIGHT AS WELL BE CHINA.
UNTIL I FOUND HER THROUGH THE COMPUTER LAST NIGHT, I NEVER SUSPECTED SHIVA HAD THIS PLACE...
I WAS AFRAID I MIGHT HAVE TO GO TO THE REAL CHINA...OR JAPAN...OR INDIA...
WHAT'S KEEPING HER? SHE'S LATE...
...AND SHE SAID MY FIELD TRAINING WOULD BEGIN TONIGHT.
MAYBE I WAS WRONG TO COME TO HER.
AFTER ALL, WHAT DO I REALLY KNOW ABOUT LADY SHIVA?
SHE'S RUTHLESS...AND SHE KILLS WITHOUT REMORSE...SHE MAY WELL BE THE BEST FIGHTER ALIVE, MASTER OF AT LEAST A DOZEN FORMS AND WEAPONS...
...AND HONOR IS SACRED TO HER.

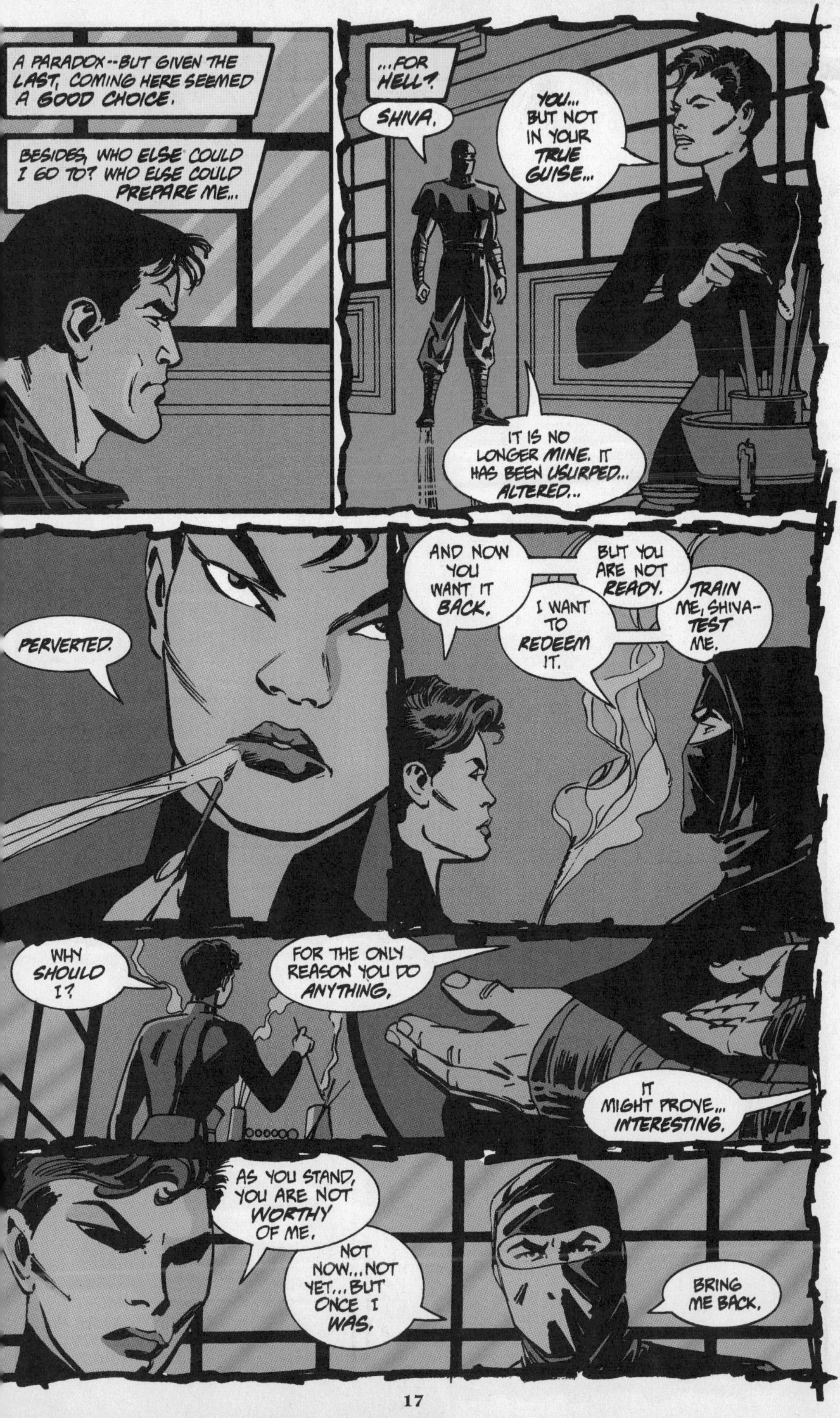
A PARADOX--BUT GIVEN THE LAST, COMING HERE SEEMED A GOOD CHOICE.
BESIDES, WHO ELSE COULD I GO TO? WHO ELSE COULD PREPARE ME...
...FOR HELL?
SHIVA.
YOU... BUT NOT IN YOUR TRUE GUISE...
IT IS NO LONGER MINE. IT HAS BEEN USURPED... ALTERED...
PERVERTED.
AND NOW YOU WANT IT BACK.
I WANT TO REDEEM IT.
BUT YOU ARE NOT READY.
TRAIN ME, SHIVA--TEST ME.
WHY SHOULD I?
FOR THE ONLY REASON YOU DO ANYTHING.
IT MIGHT PROVE... INTERESTING.
AS YOU STAND, YOU ARE NOT WORTHY OF ME.
NOT NOW... NOT YET... BUT ONCE I WAS.
BRING ME BACK.

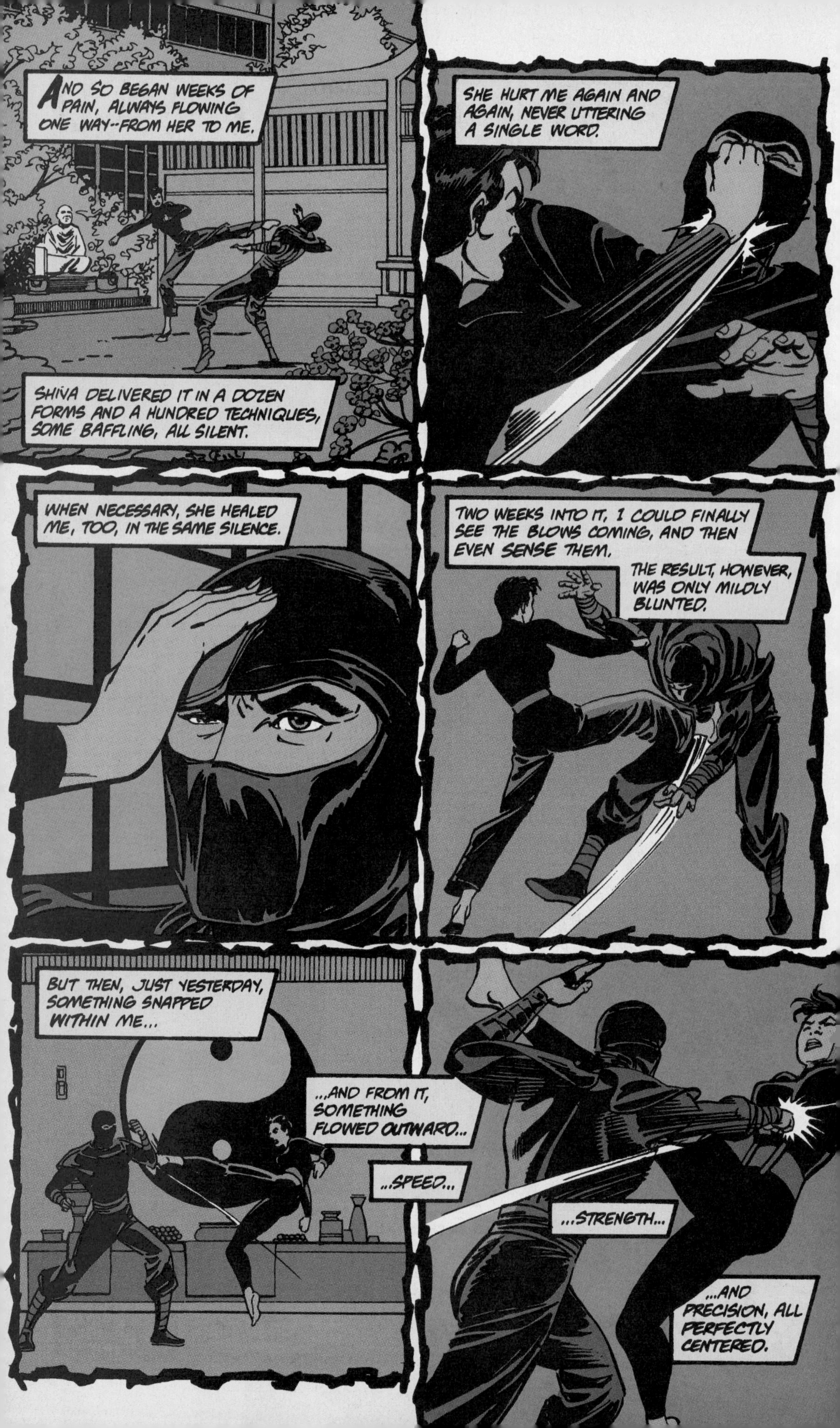
AND SO BEGAN WEEKS OF PAIN, ALWAYS FLOWING ONE WAY--FROM HER TO ME.
SHIVA DELIVERED IT IN A DOZEN FORMS AND A HUNDRED TECHNIQUES, SOME BAFFLING, ALL SILENT.
SHE HURT ME AGAIN AND AGAIN, NEVER UTTERING A SINGLE WORD.
WHEN NECESSARY, SHE HEALED ME, TOO, IN THE SAME SILENCE.
TWO WEEKS INTO IT, I COULD FINALLY SEE THE BLOWS COMING, AND THEN EVEN SENSE THEM.
THE RESULT, HOWEVER, WAS ONLY MILDLY BLUNTED.
BUT THEN, JUST YESTERDAY, SOMETHING SNAPPED WITHIN ME...
...AND FROM IT, SOMETHING FLOWED OUTWARD...
...SPEED...
...STRENGTH...
...AND PRECISION, ALL PERFECTLY CENTERED.

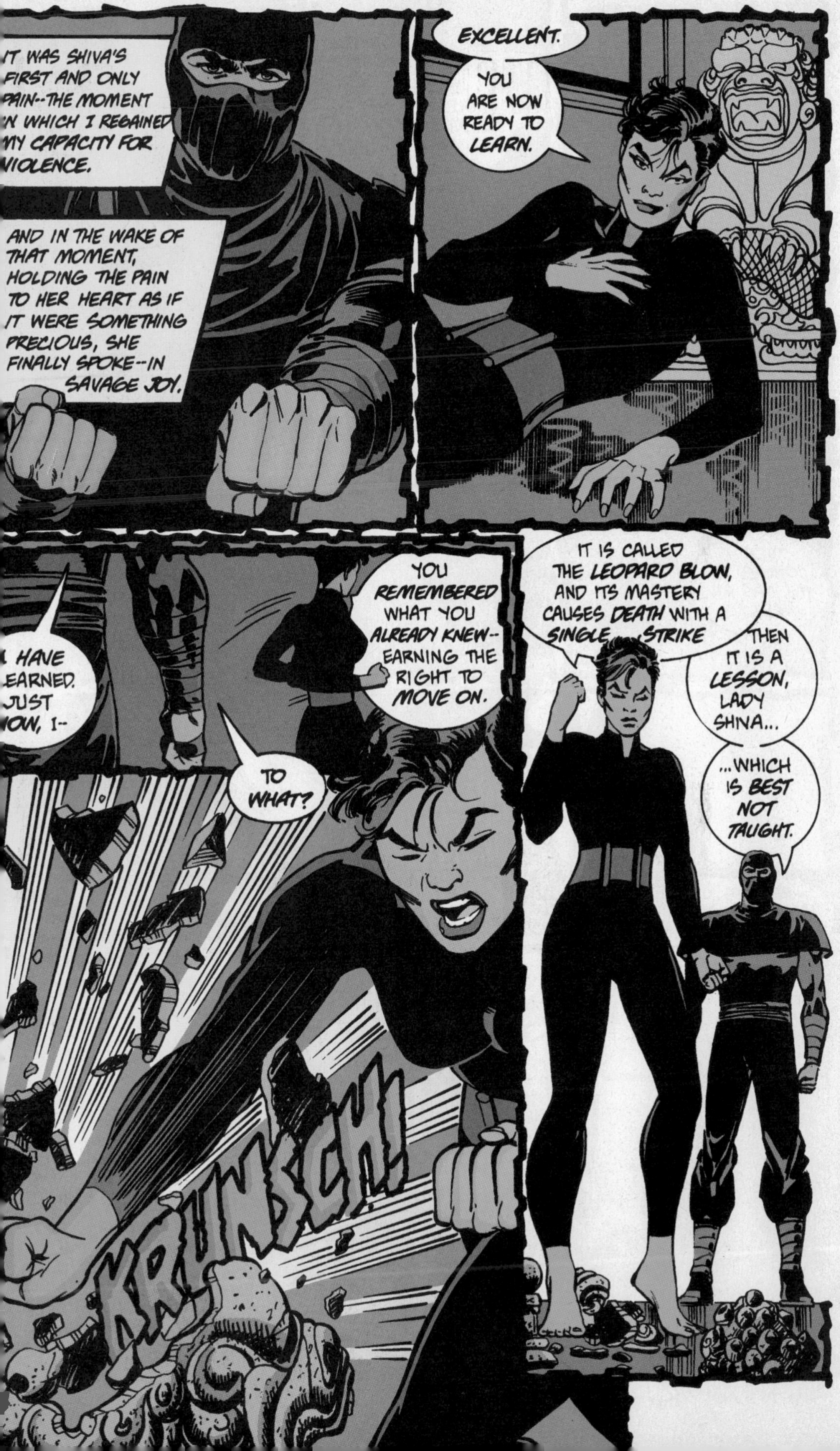
IT WAS SHIVA'S FIRST AND ONLY PAIN--THE MOMENT IN WHICH I REGAINED MY CAPACITY FOR VIOLENCE.
AND IN THE WAKE OF THAT MOMENT, HOLDING THE PAIN TO HER HEART AS IF IT WERE SOMETHING PRECIOUS, SHE FINALLY SPOKE--IN SAVAGE JOY.
EXCELLENT.
YOU ARE NOW READY TO LEARN.
I HAVE LEARNED. JUST NOW, I--
YOU REMEMBERED WHAT YOU ALREADY KNEW--EARNING THE RIGHT TO MOVE ON.
TO WHAT?
KRUNSCH!
IT IS CALLED THE LEOPARD BLOW, AND ITS MASTERY CAUSES DEATH WITH A SINGLE STRIKE
THEN IT IS A LESSON, LADY SHIVA...
...WHICH IS BEST NOT TAUGHT.

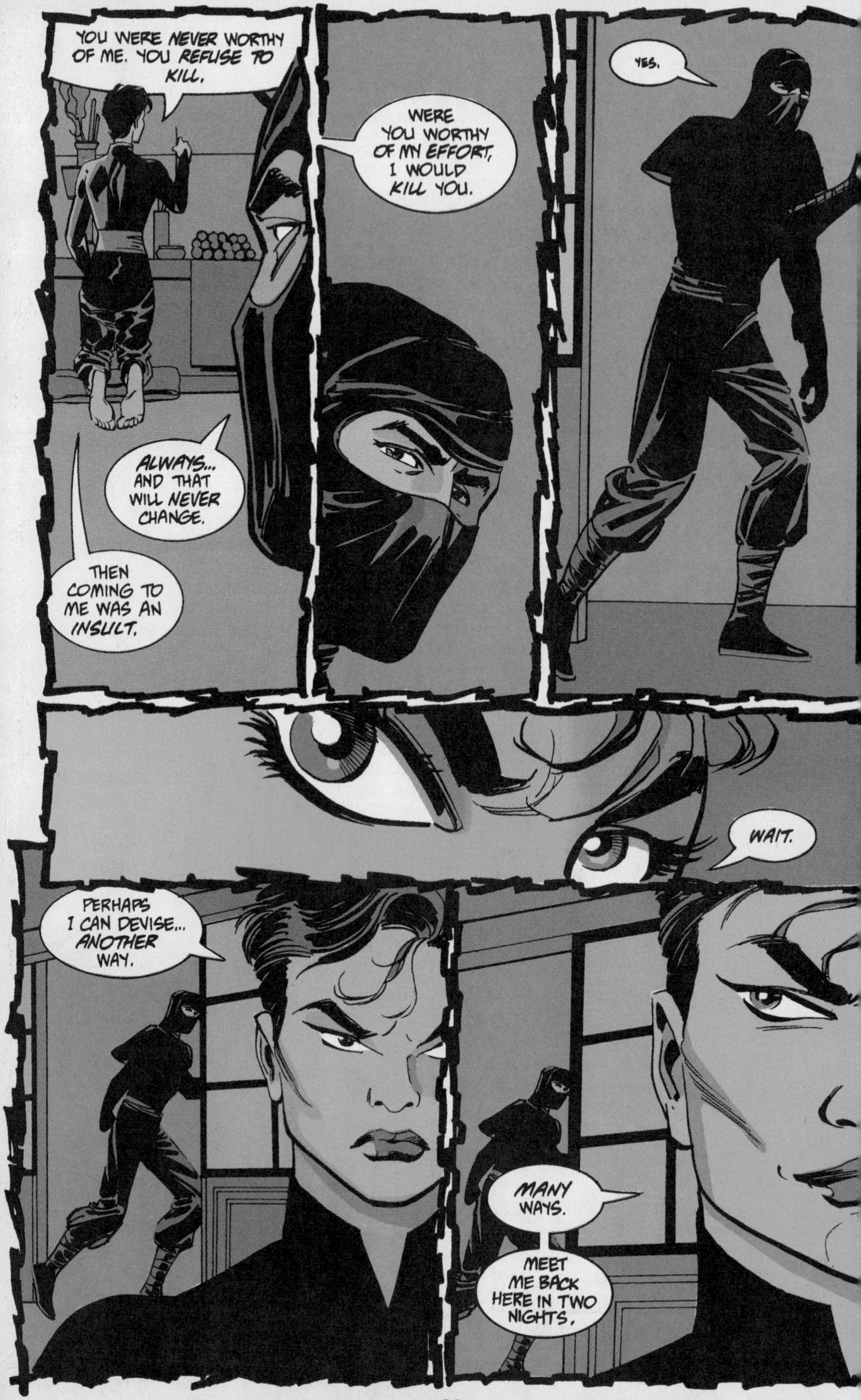
YOU WERE NEVER WORTHY OF ME. YOU REFUSE TO KILL.
WERE YOU WORTHY OF MY EFFORT, I WOULD KILL YOU.
YES.
ALWAYS... AND THAT WILL NEVER CHANGE.
THEN COMING TO ME WAS AN INSULT.
WAIT.
PERHAPS I CAN DEVISE... ANOTHER WAY.
MANY WAYS.
MEET ME BACK HERE IN TWO NIGHTS.

SO HERE I AM. AND WHATEVER SHE PLANNED TO DEVISE, SHE SAID IT WOULD BEGIN TONIGHT... SO WHERE IS--

HERE.

AS SILENT AS A SLEEPING BREATH...

...BUT I SHOULD HAVE SENSED HER.

I'VE LOST EVERY EDGE.

TAKE IT.

THE... MASK OF TENGU...SYMBOLIC OF THE BAT SPIRIT...

IF YOU ARE NOT YET READY TO WEAR YOUR TRUE MASK...THEN AT LEAST ASSUME YOUR TOTEM.

AND THE FIELD TRAINING?

WITH ACCEPTANCE OF THE MASK, IT BEGINS TOMORROW NIGHT...

...WHEN YOU DON THE MASK...

...AT THIS ADDRESS.

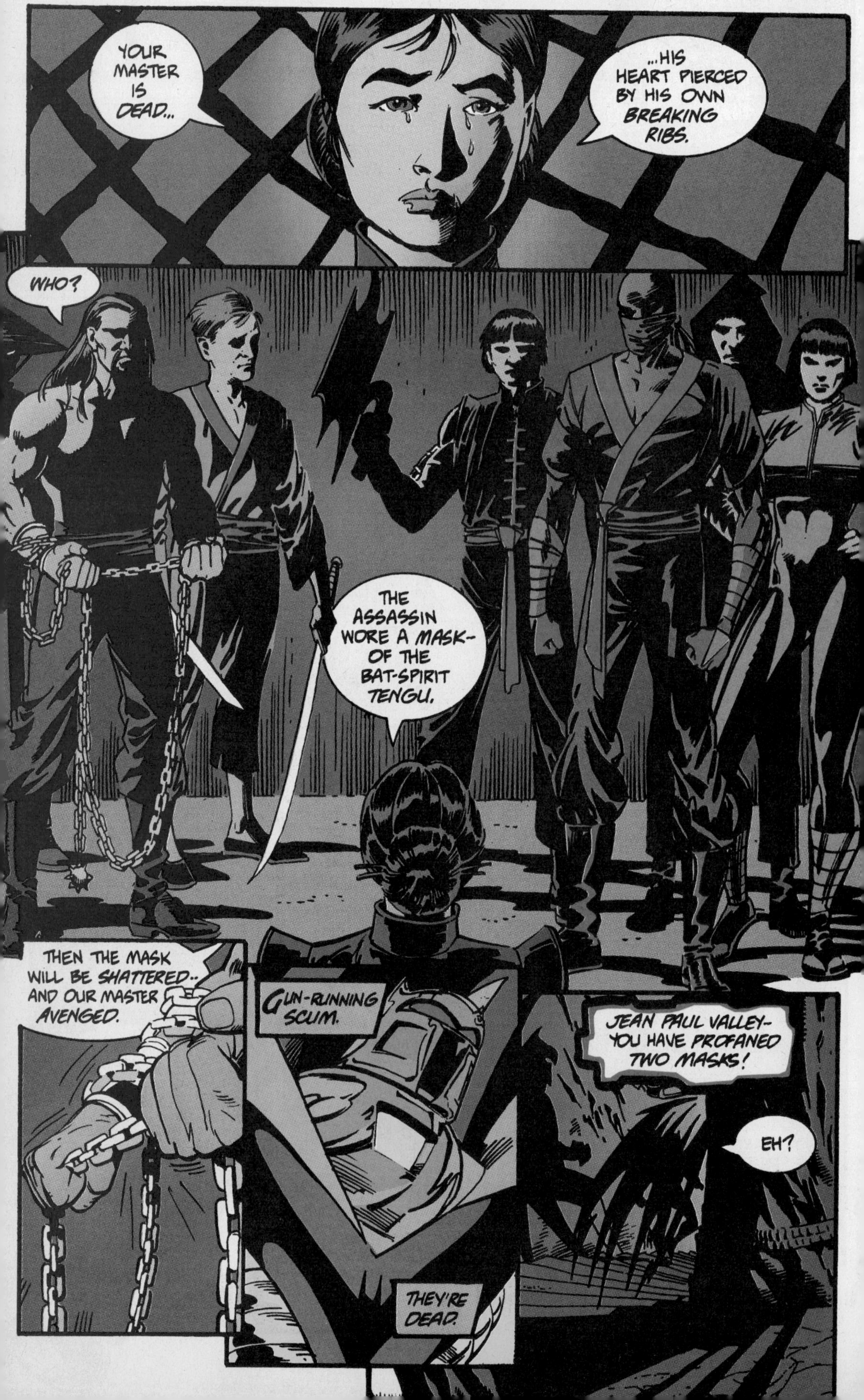
YOUR MASTER IS DEAD...
...HIS HEART PIERCED BY HIS OWN BREAKING RIBS.
WHO?
THE ASSASSIN WORE A MASK-OF THE BAT-SPIRIT TENGU.
THEN THE MASK WILL BE SHATTERED... AND OUR MASTER AVENGED.
GUN-RUNNING SCUM.
JEAN PAUL VALLEY-YOU HAVE PROFANED TWO MASKS!
EH?
THEY'RE DEAD.

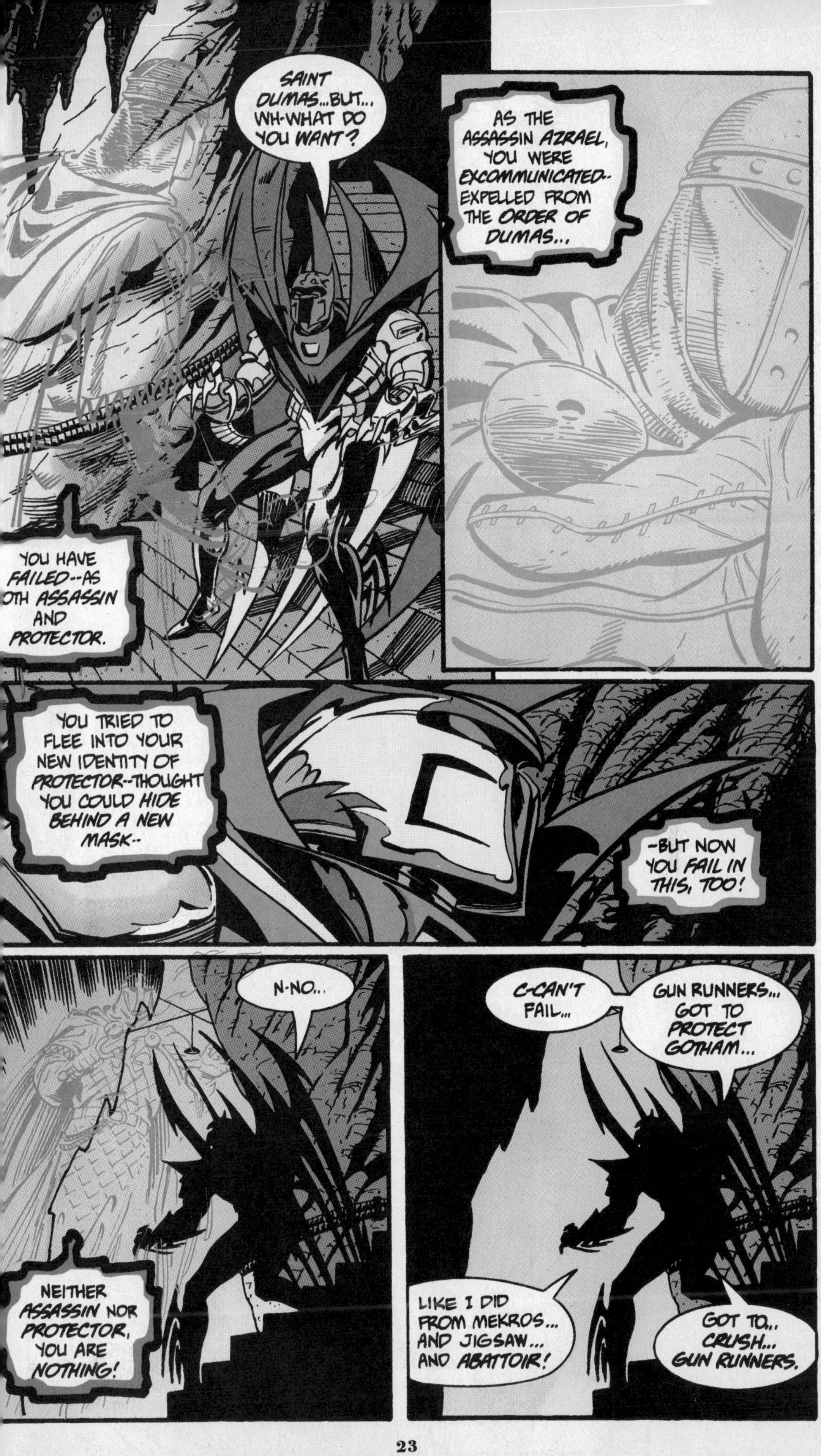
SAINT DUMAS...BUT... WH-WHAT DO YOU WANT?
AS THE ASSASSIN AZRAEL, YOU WERE EXCOMMUNICATED-- EXPELLED FROM THE ORDER OF DUMAS...
YOU HAVE FAILED--AS OTH ASSASSIN AND PROTECTOR.
YOU TRIED TO FLEE INTO YOUR NEW IDENTITY OF PROTECTOR--THOUGHT YOU COULD HIDE BEHIND A NEW MASK--
--BUT NOW YOU FAIL IN THIS, TOO!
N-NO...
NEITHER ASSASSIN NOR PROTECTOR, YOU ARE NOTHING!
C-CAN'T FAIL...
GUN RUNNERS... GOT TO PROTECT GOTHAM...
LIKE I DID FROM MEKROS... AND JIGSAW... AND ABATTOIR!
GOT TO... CRUSH... GUN RUNNERS.

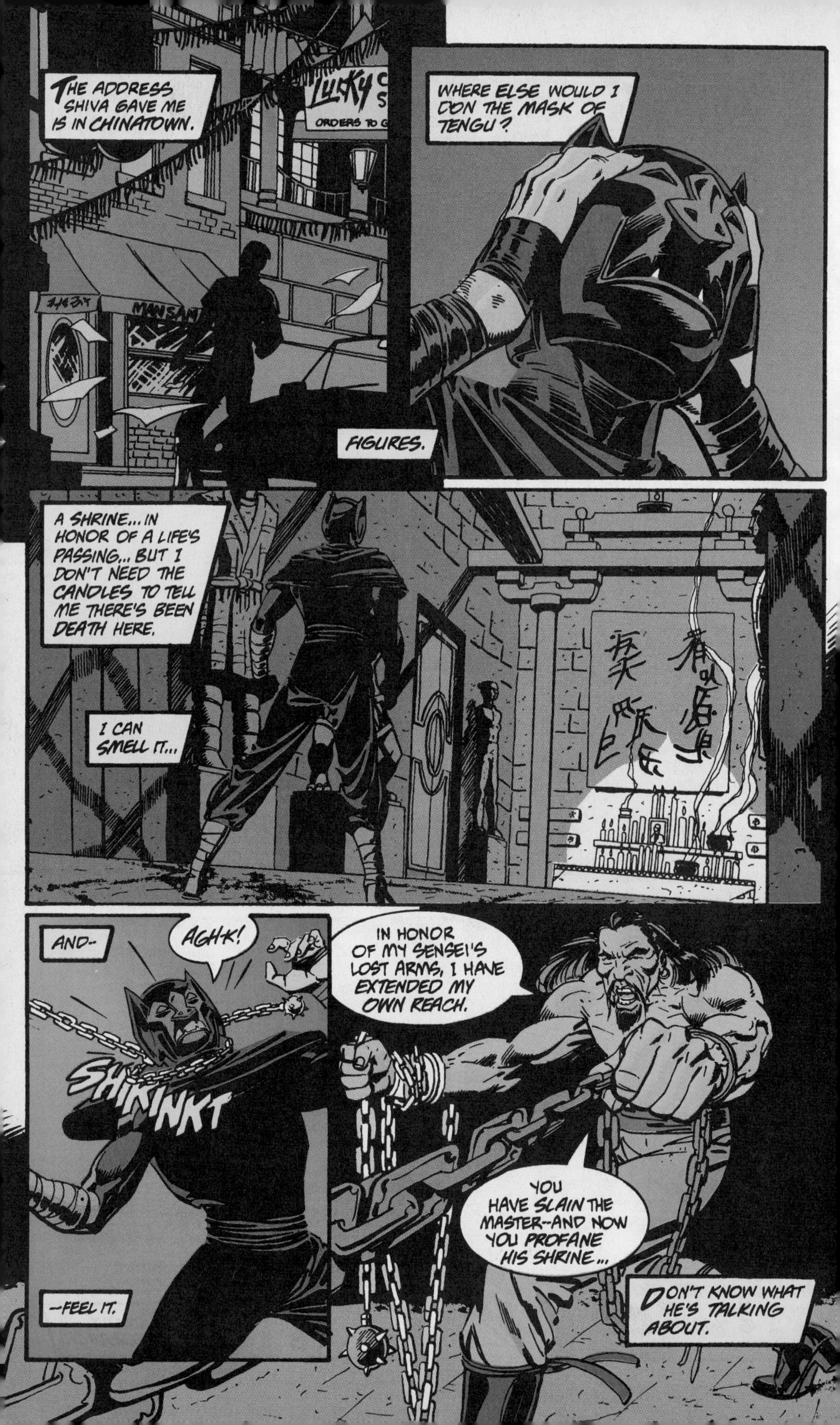
THE ADDRESS SHIVA GAVE ME IS IN CHINATOWN.
LUCKY
ORDERS TO G
WHERE ELSE WOULD I DON THE MASK OF TENGU?
FIGURES.
A SHRINE... IN HONOR OF A LIFE'S PASSING... BUT I DON'T NEED THE CANDLES TO TELL ME THERE'S BEEN DEATH HERE.
I CAN SMELL IT...
AND--
AGH-K!
IN HONOR OF MY SENSEI'S LOST ARMS, I HAVE EXTENDED MY OWN REACH.
SHHKINKT
YOU HAVE SLAIN THE MASTER--AND NOW YOU PROFANE HIS SHRINE...
--FEEL IT.
DON'T KNOW WHAT HE'S TALKING ABOUT.

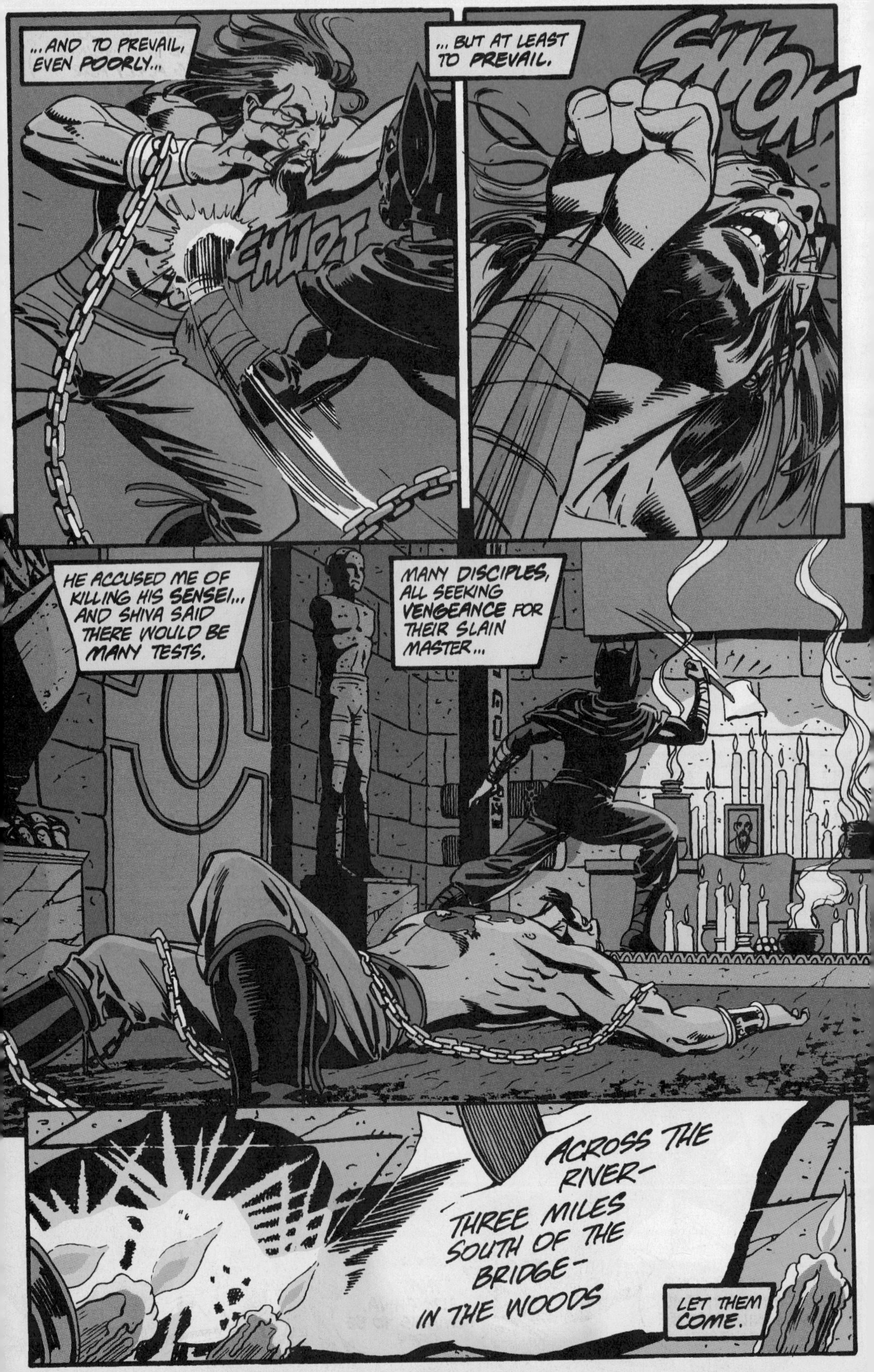
...AND TO PREVAIL, EVEN POORLY...
CHUDT
...BUT AT LEAST TO PREVAIL.
SMOK
HE ACCUSED ME OF KILLING HIS SENSEI... AND SHIVA SAID THERE WOULD BE MANY TESTS.
MANY DISCIPLES, ALL SEEKING VENGEANCE FOR THEIR SLAIN MASTER...
ACROSS THE RIVER-
THREE MILES SOUTH OF THE BRIDGE-
IN THE WOODS
LET THEM COME.

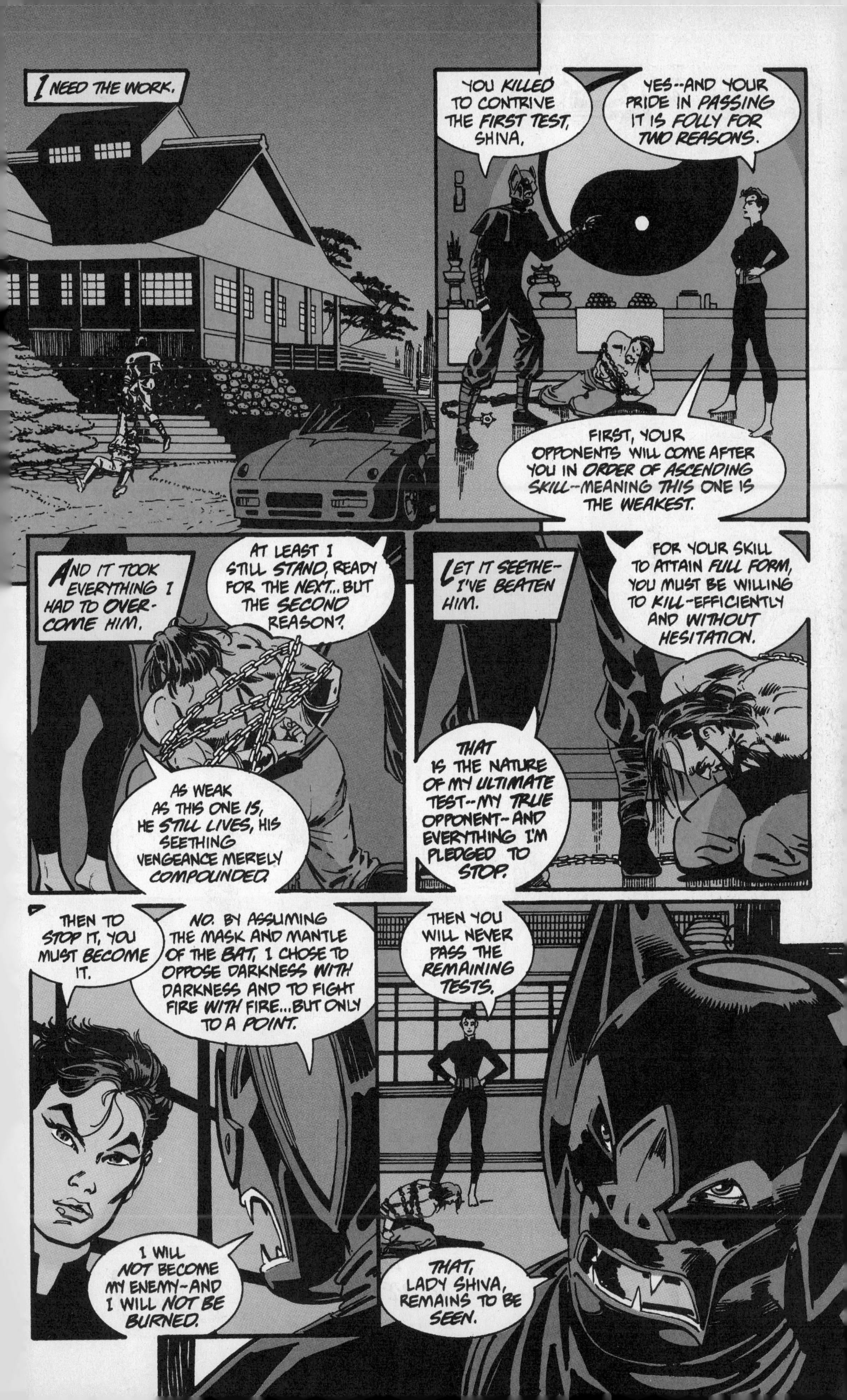
I NEED THE WORK.
YOU KILLED TO CONTRIVE THE FIRST TEST, SHIVA.
YES--AND YOUR PRIDE IN PASSING IT IS FOLLY FOR TWO REASONS.
FIRST, YOUR OPPONENTS WILL COME AFTER YOU IN ORDER OF ASCENDING SKILL--MEANING THIS ONE IS THE WEAKEST.
AND IT TOOK EVERYTHING I HAD TO OVER-COME HIM.
AT LEAST I STILL STAND, READY FOR THE NEXT... BUT THE SECOND REASON?
AS WEAK AS THIS ONE IS, HE STILL LIVES, HIS SEETHING VENGEANCE MERELY COMPOUNDED.
LET IT SEETHE-- I'VE BEATEN HIM.
FOR YOUR SKILL TO ATTAIN FULL FORM, YOU MUST BE WILLING TO KILL--EFFICIENTLY AND WITHOUT HESITATION.
THAT IS THE NATURE OF MY ULTIMATE TEST--MY TRUE OPPONENT--AND EVERYTHING I'M PLEDGED TO STOP.
THEN TO STOP IT, YOU MUST BECOME IT.
NO. BY ASSUMING THE MASK AND MANTLE OF THE BAT, I CHOSE TO OPPOSE DARKNESS WITH DARKNESS AND TO FIGHT FIRE WITH FIRE... BUT ONLY TO A POINT.
I WILL NOT BECOME MY ENEMY--AND I WILL NOT BE BURNED.
THEN YOU WILL NEVER PASS THE REMAINING TESTS.
THAT, LADY SHIVA, REMAINS TO BE SEEN.

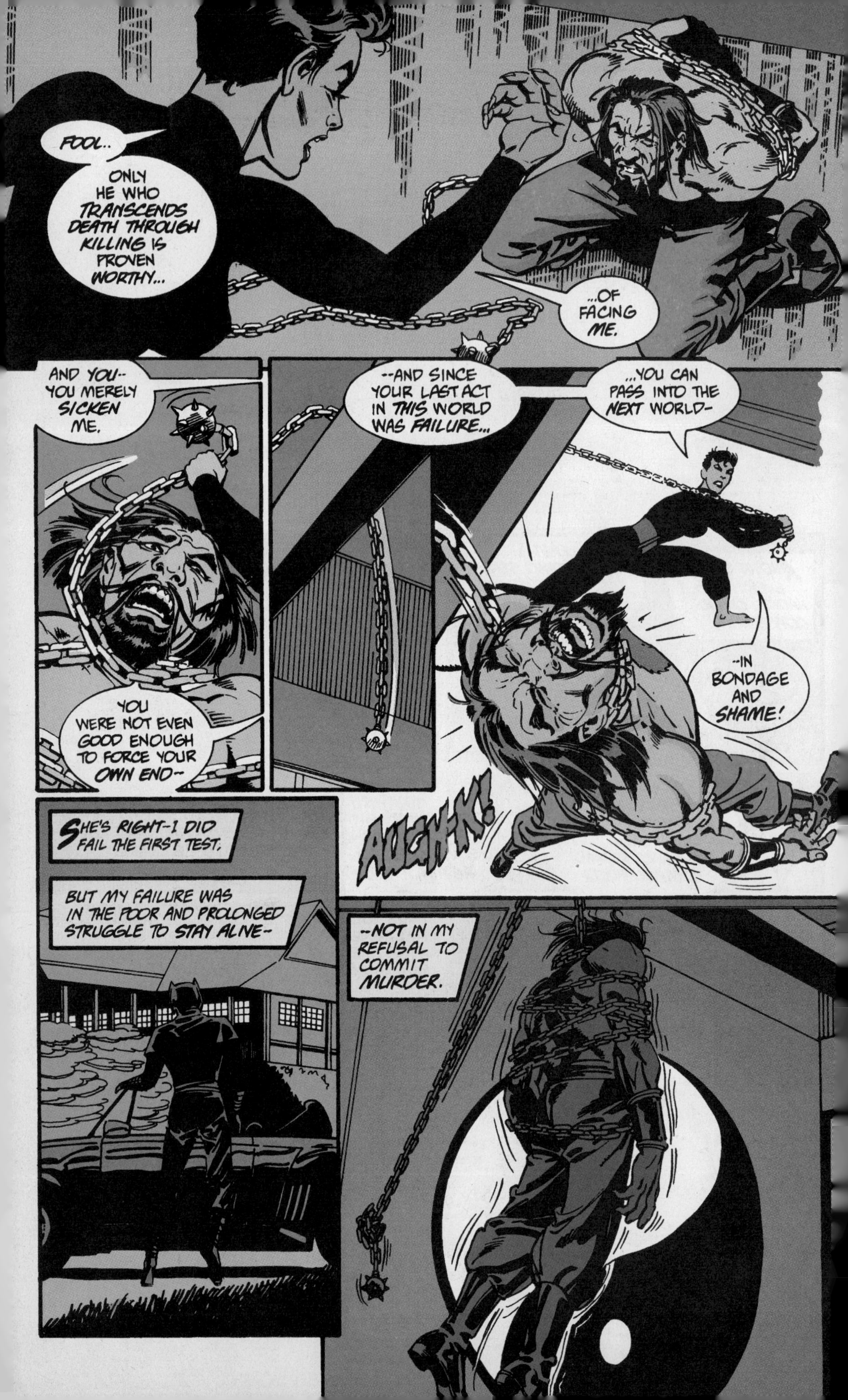
FOOL..
ONLY HE WHO TRANSCENDS DEATH THROUGH KILLING IS PROVEN WORTHY...
...OF FACING ME.
AND YOU-- YOU MERELY SICKEN ME.
YOU WERE NOT EVEN GOOD ENOUGH TO FORCE YOUR OWN END--
--AND SINCE YOUR LAST ACT IN THIS WORLD WAS FAILURE...
...YOU CAN PASS INTO THE NEXT WORLD-
--IN BONDAGE AND SHAME!
AUGH-K!
SHE'S RIGHT--I DID FAIL THE FIRST TEST.
BUT MY FAILURE WAS IN THE POOR AND PROLONGED STRUGGLE TO STAY ALIVE--
--NOT IN MY REFUSAL TO COMMIT MURDER.

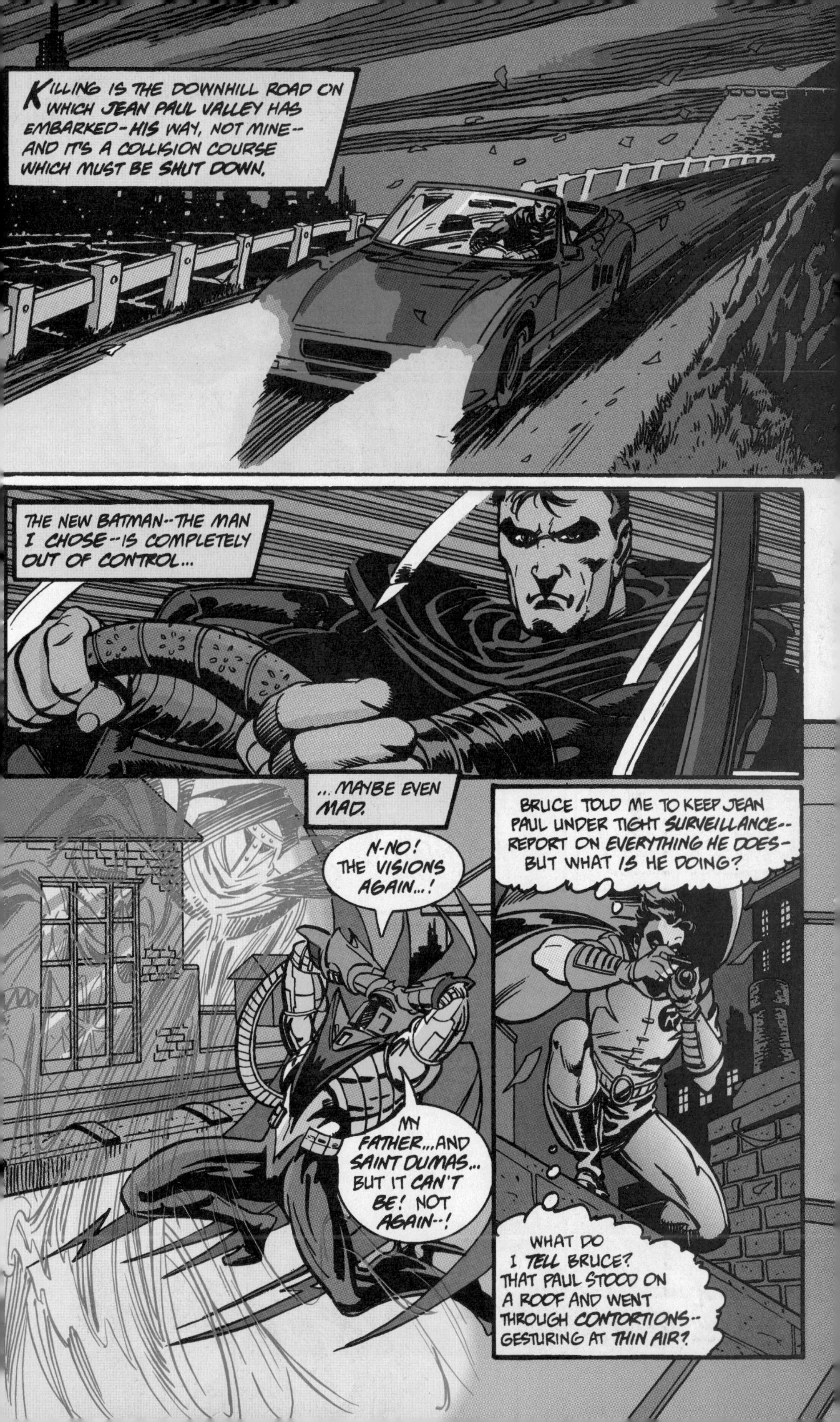
KILLING IS THE DOWNHILL ROAD ON WHICH JEAN PAUL VALLEY HAS EMBARKED--HIS WAY, NOT MINE--AND IT'S A COLLISION COURSE WHICH MUST BE SHUT DOWN.
THE NEW BATMAN--THE MAN I CHOSE--IS COMPLETELY OUT OF CONTROL...
...MAYBE EVEN MAD.
N-NO! THE VISIONS AGAIN...!
MY FATHER...AND SAINT DUMAS... BUT IT CAN'T BE! NOT AGAIN--!
BRUCE TOLD ME TO KEEP JEAN PAUL UNDER TIGHT SURVEILLANCE--REPORT ON EVERYTHING HE DOES-BUT WHAT IS HE DOING?
WHAT DO I TELL BRUCE? THAT PAUL STOOD ON A ROOF AND WENT THROUGH CONTORTIONS--GESTURING AT THIN AIR?

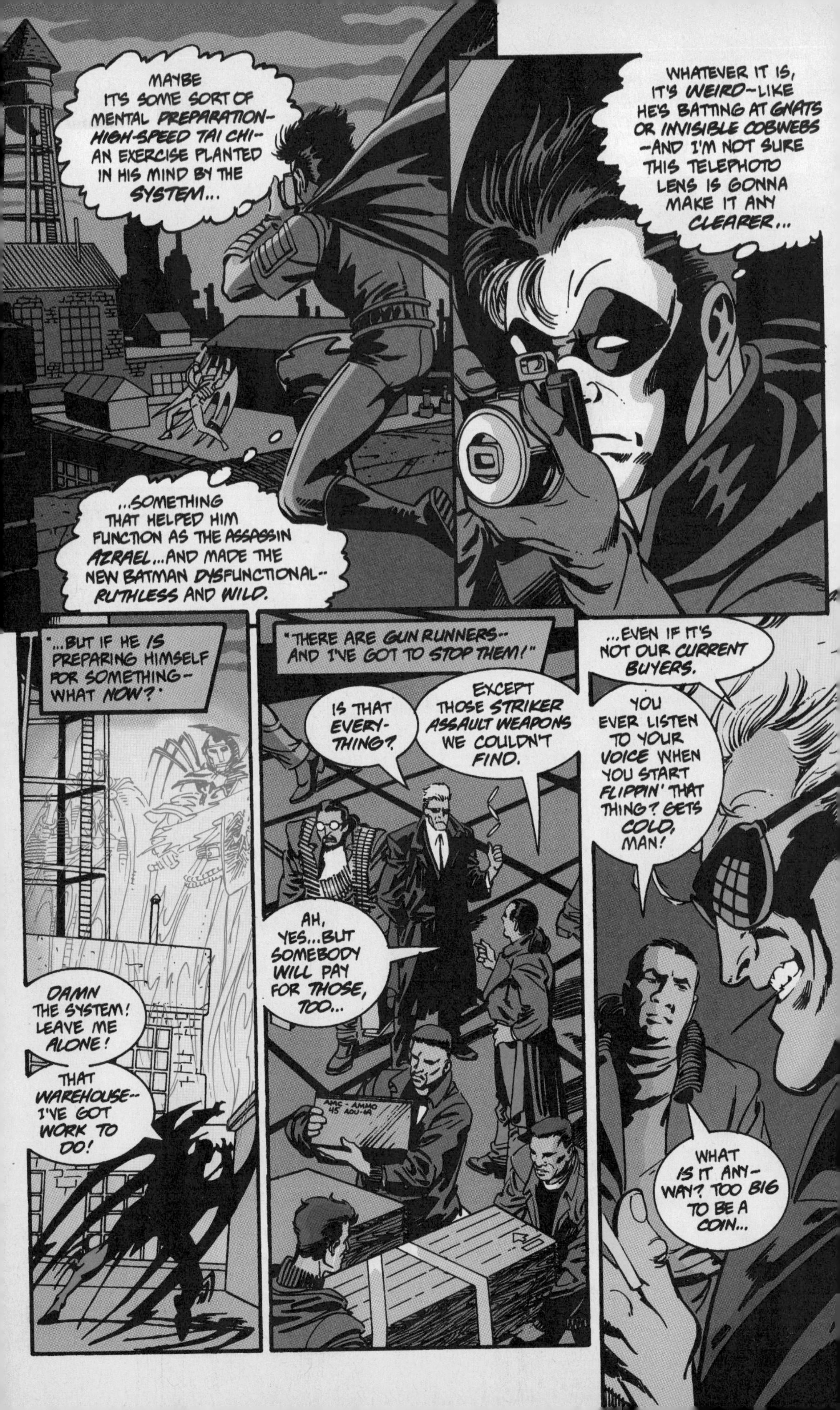
MAYBE IT'S SOME SORT OF MENTAL PREPARATION-HIGH-SPEED TAI CHI-AN EXERCISE PLANTED IN HIS MIND BY THE SYSTEM...
...SOMETHING THAT HELPED HIM FUNCTION AS THE ASSASSIN AZRAEL...AND MADE THE NEW BATMAN DYSFUNCTIONAL--RUTHLESS AND WILD.
WHATEVER IT IS, IT'S WEIRD--LIKE HE'S BATTING AT GNATS OR INVISIBLE COBWEBS--AND I'M NOT SURE THIS TELEPHOTO LENS IS GONNA MAKE IT ANY CLEARER...
"...BUT IF HE IS PREPARING HIMSELF FOR SOMETHING-WHAT NOW?"
DAMN THE SYSTEM! LEAVE ME ALONE!
THAT WAREHOUSE--I'VE GOT WORK TO DO!
"THERE ARE GUN RUNNERS--AND I'VE GOT TO STOP THEM!"
IS THAT EVERY-THING?
EXCEPT THOSE STRIKER ASSAULT WEAPONS WE COULDN'T FIND.
AH, YES...BUT SOMEBODY WILL PAY FOR THOSE, TOO...
AMC - AMMO 45 ACU-49
...EVEN IF IT'S NOT OUR CURRENT BUYERS.
YOU EVER LISTEN TO YOUR VOICE WHEN YOU START FLIPPIN' THAT THING? GETS COLD, MAN!
WHAT IS IT ANY-WAY? TOO BIG TO BE A COIN...

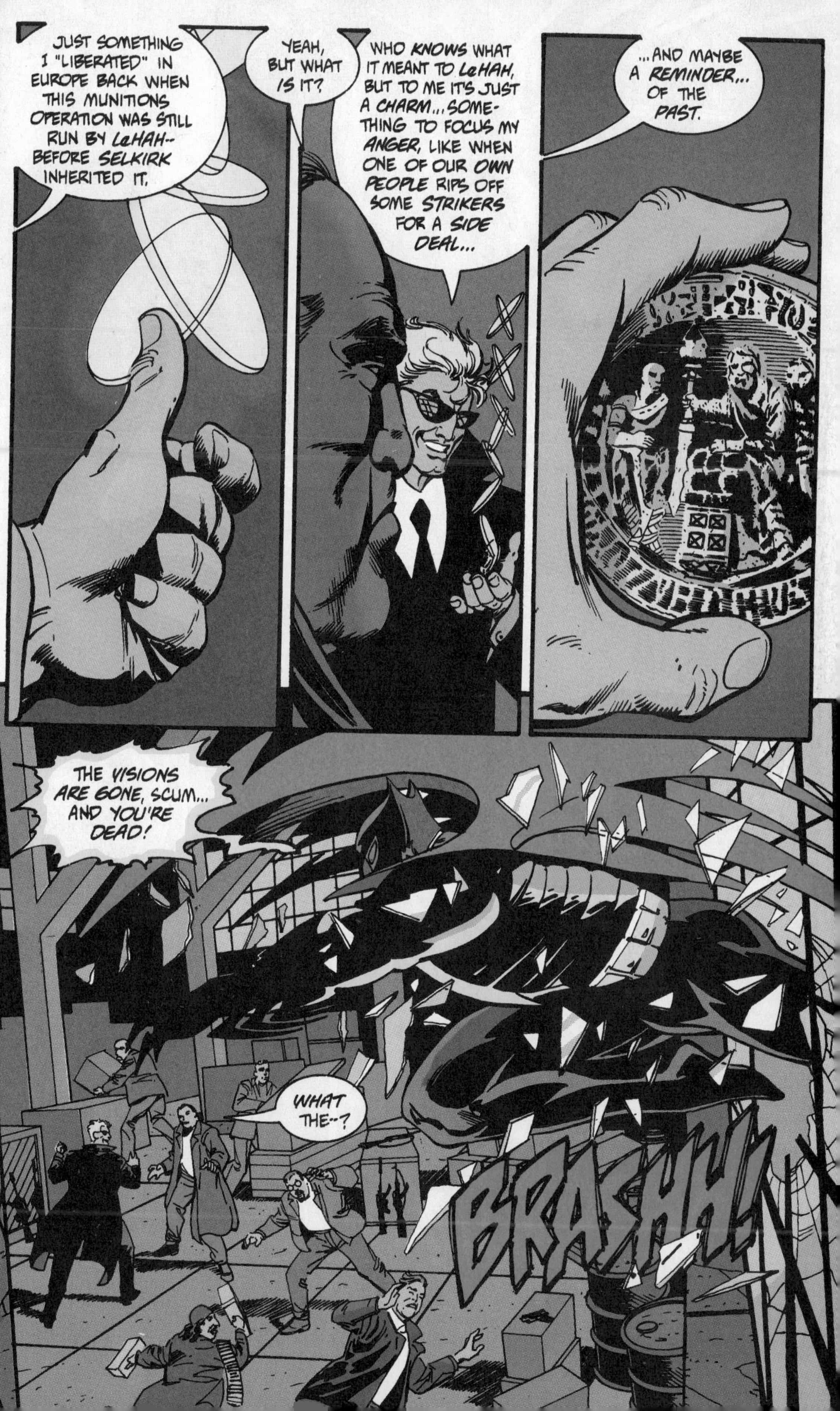
JUST SOMETHING I "LIBERATED" IN EUROPE BACK WHEN THIS MUNITIONS OPERATION WAS STILL RUN BY LeHAH-- BEFORE SELKIRK INHERITED IT.
YEAH, BUT WHAT IS IT?
WHO KNOWS WHAT IT MEANT TO LeHAH, BUT TO ME IT'S JUST A CHARM... SOMETHING TO FOCUS MY ANGER, LIKE WHEN ONE OF OUR OWN PEOPLE RIPS OFF SOME STRIKERS FOR A SIDE DEAL...
...AND MAYBE A REMINDER... OF THE PAST.
THE VISIONS ARE GONE, SCUM... AND YOU'RE DEAD!
WHAT THE--?
BRASHH!

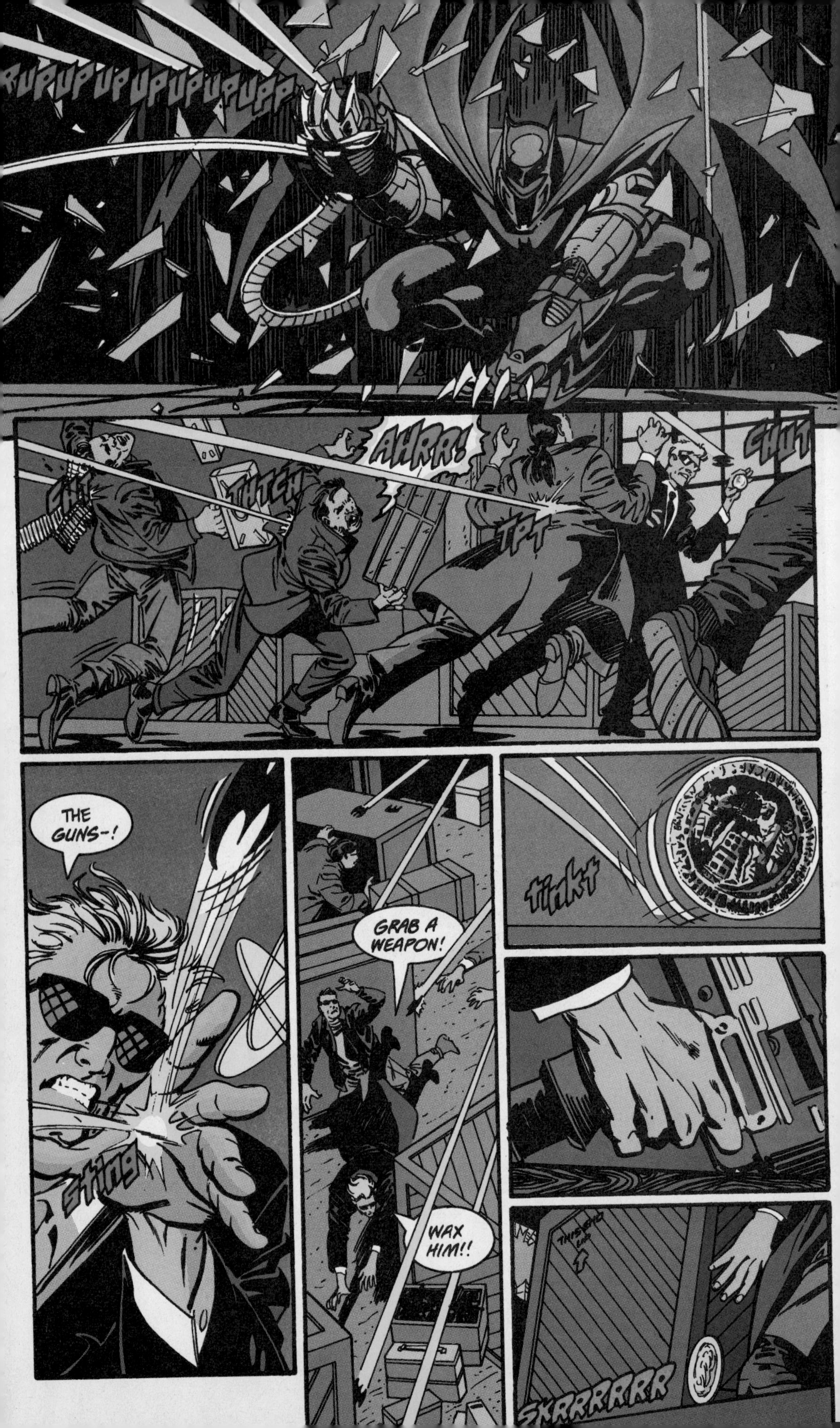
RUPUPUPUPUPUPUPP
CHT
THTCH
AHRR!
TPT
CHUT
THE GUNS-!
sting
GRAB A WEAPON!
WAX HIM!!
tinkt
SKRRRRRRR

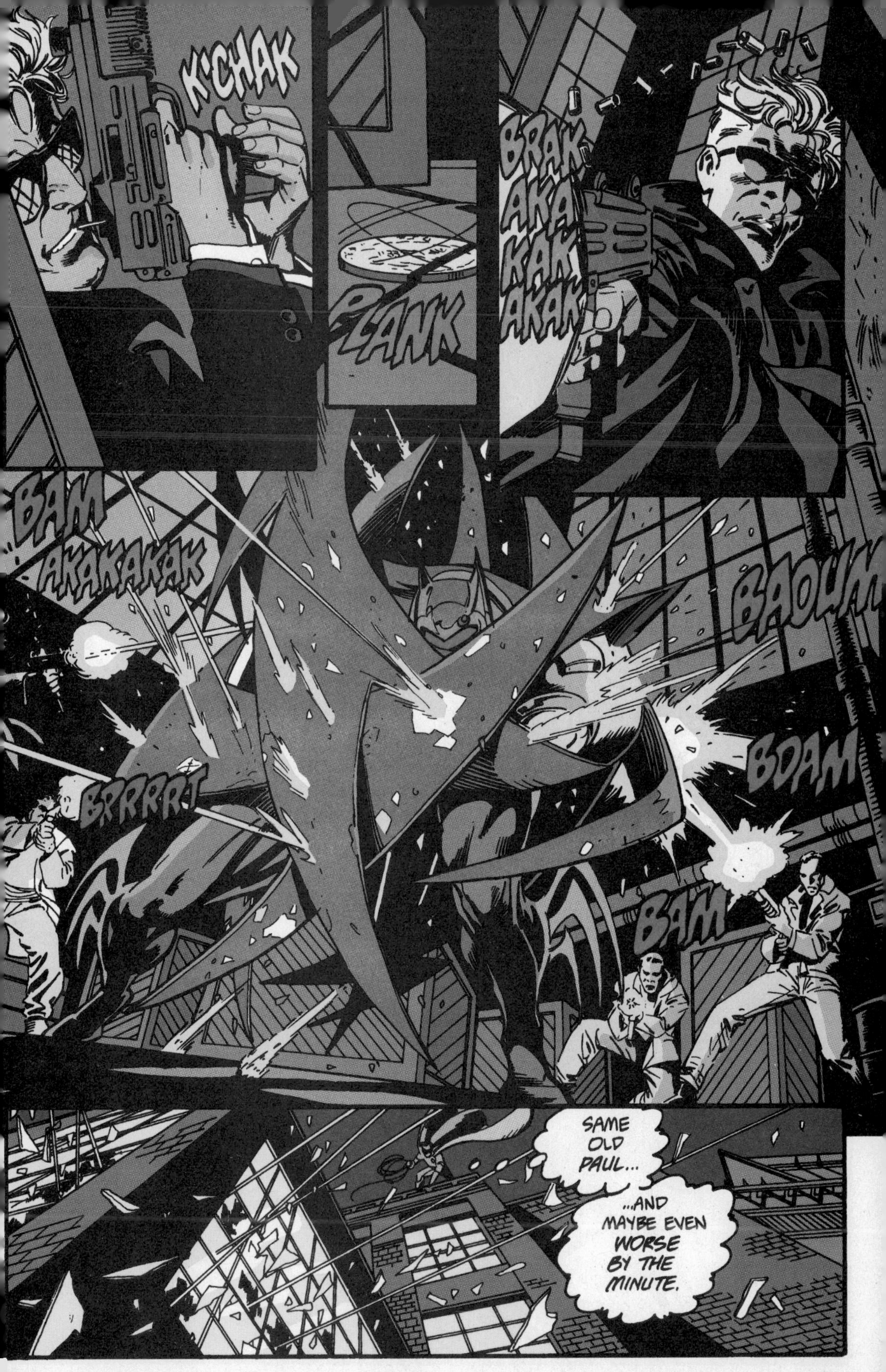
K'CHAK
PLANK
BRAKAKAKAKAKAK
BAM
AKAKAKAKAK
BAOUM
BRRRRT
BDAM
BAM
SAME OLD PAUL...
...AND MAYBE EVEN WORSE BY THE MINUTE.

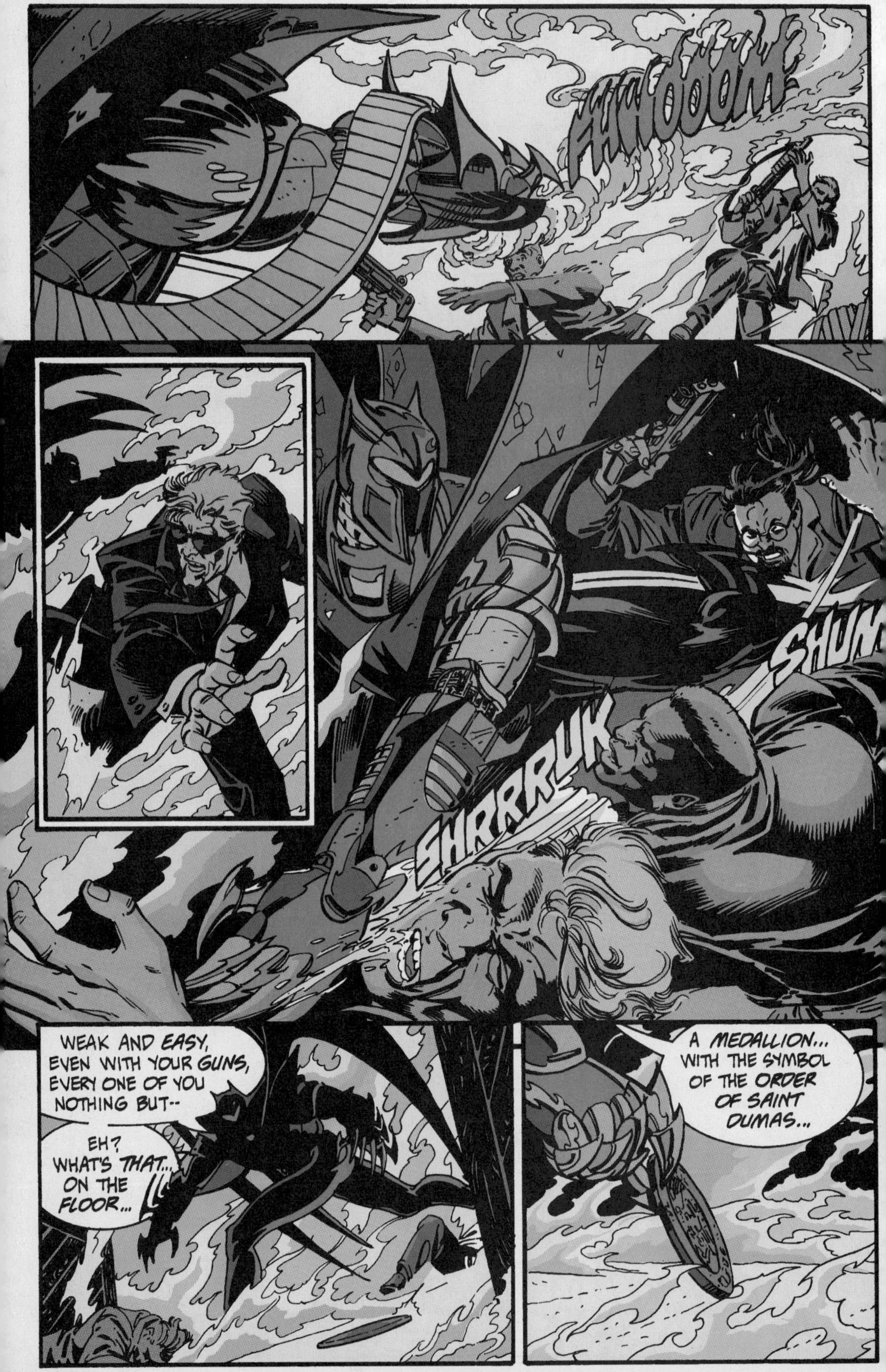
FWOOOM
SHUN
SHRRRUK
WEAK AND EASY, EVEN WITH YOUR GUNS, EVERY ONE OF YOU NOTHING BUT--
EH? WHAT'S THAT... ON THE FLOOR...
A MEDALLION... WITH THE SYMBOL OF THE ORDER OF SAINT DUMAS...

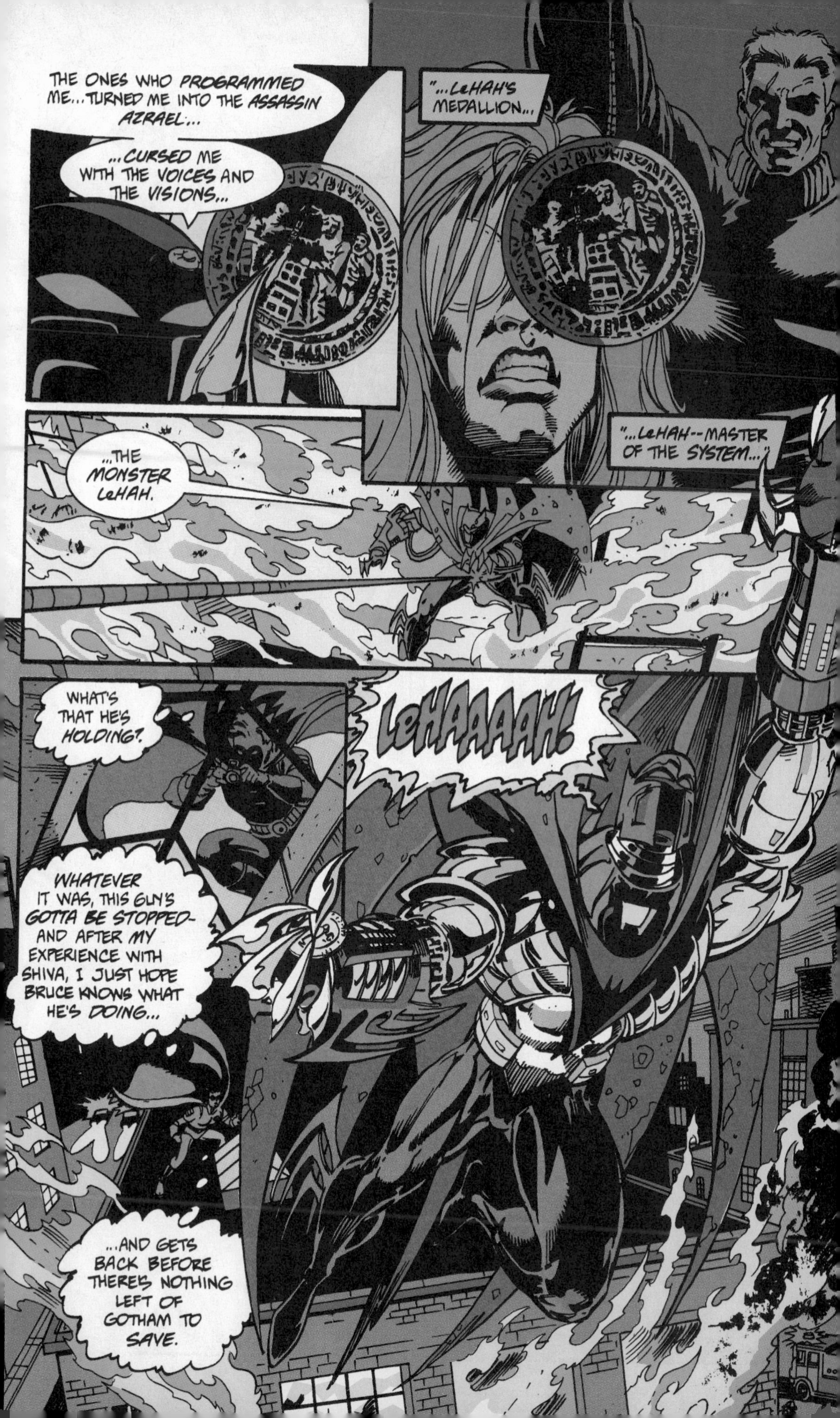
THE ONES WHO PROGRAMMED ME...TURNED ME INTO THE ASSASSIN AZRAEL...
...CURSED ME WITH THE VOICES AND THE VISIONS...
"...LeHAH'S MEDALLION...
...THE MONSTER LeHAH.
"...LeHAH--MASTER OF THE SYSTEM..."
WHAT'S THAT HE'S HOLDING?
LeHAAAAH!
WHATEVER IT WAS, THIS GUY'S GOTTA BE STOPPED-- AND AFTER MY EXPERIENCE WITH SHIVA, I JUST HOPE BRUCE KNOWS WHAT HE'S DOING...
...AND GETS BACK BEFORE THERE'S NOTHING LEFT OF GOTHAM TO SAVE.

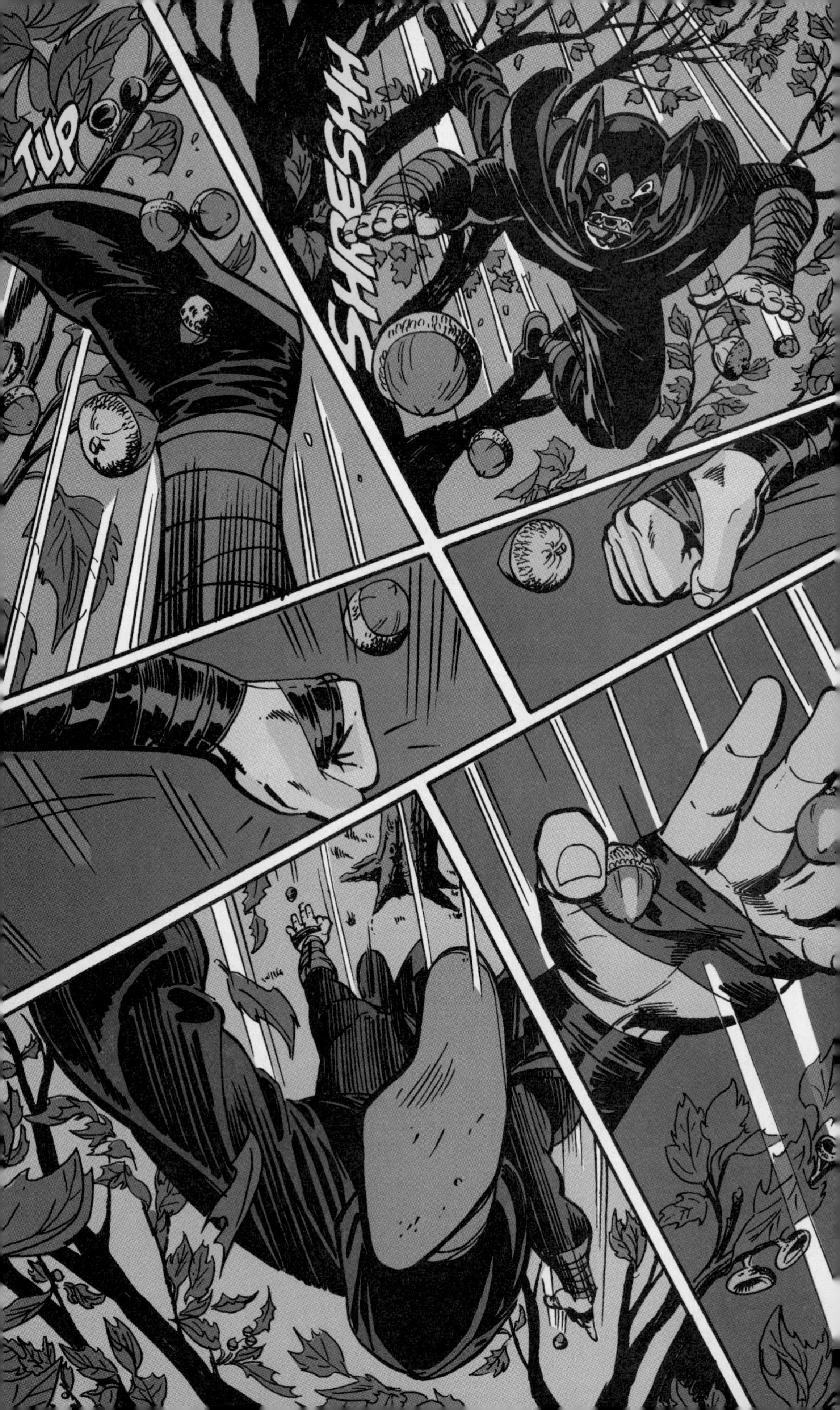
TUP
SHRESH

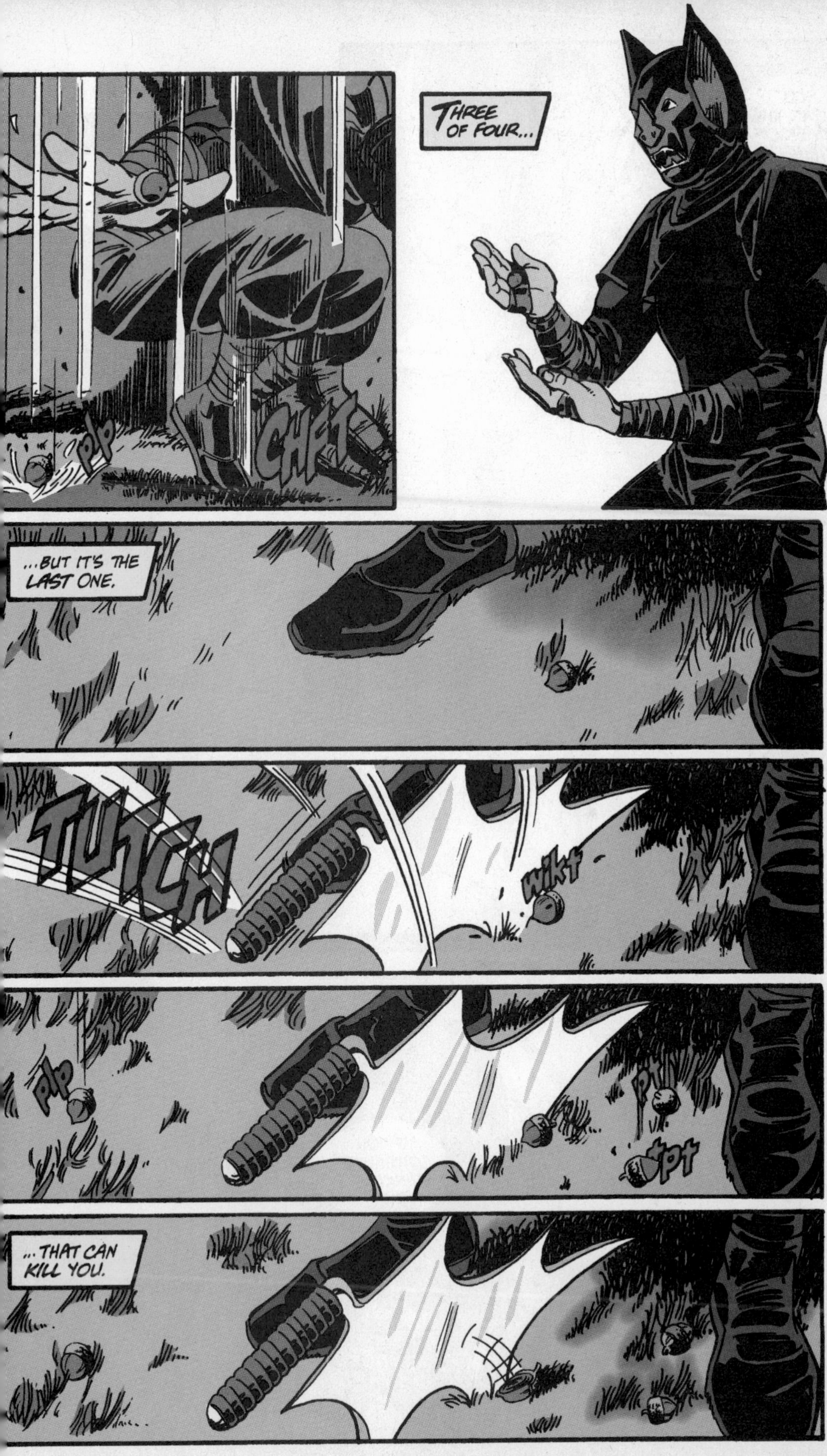
THREE OF FOUR...
plp
CHFT
...BUT IT'S THE LAST ONE.
TUTCH
wikt
plp
pt
tpt
...THAT CAN KILL YOU.

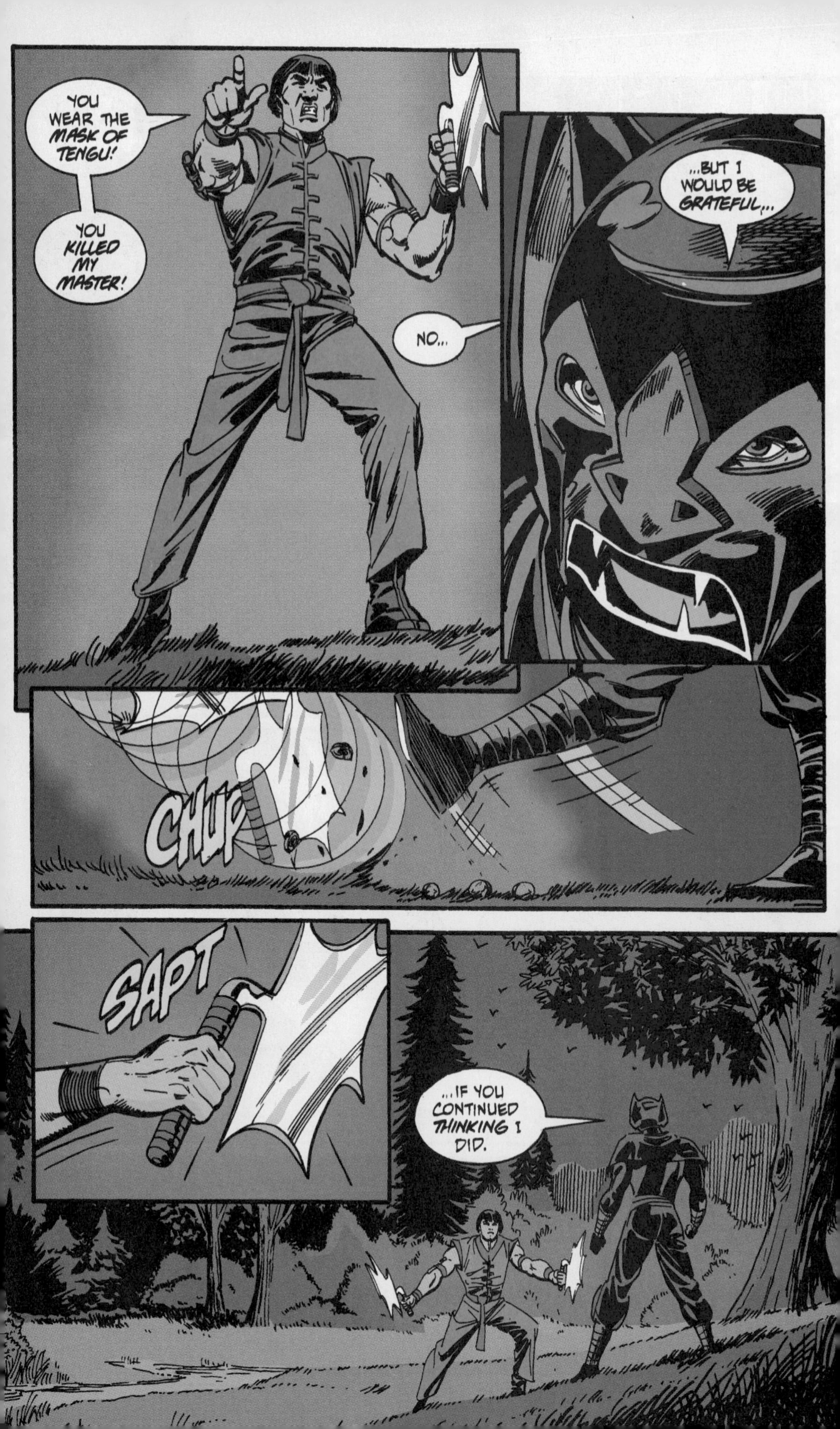
YOU WEAR THE MASK OF TENGU!
YOU KILLED MY MASTER!
NO...
...BUT I WOULD BE GRATEFUL...
CHUP
SAPT
...IF YOU CONTINUED THINKING I DID.

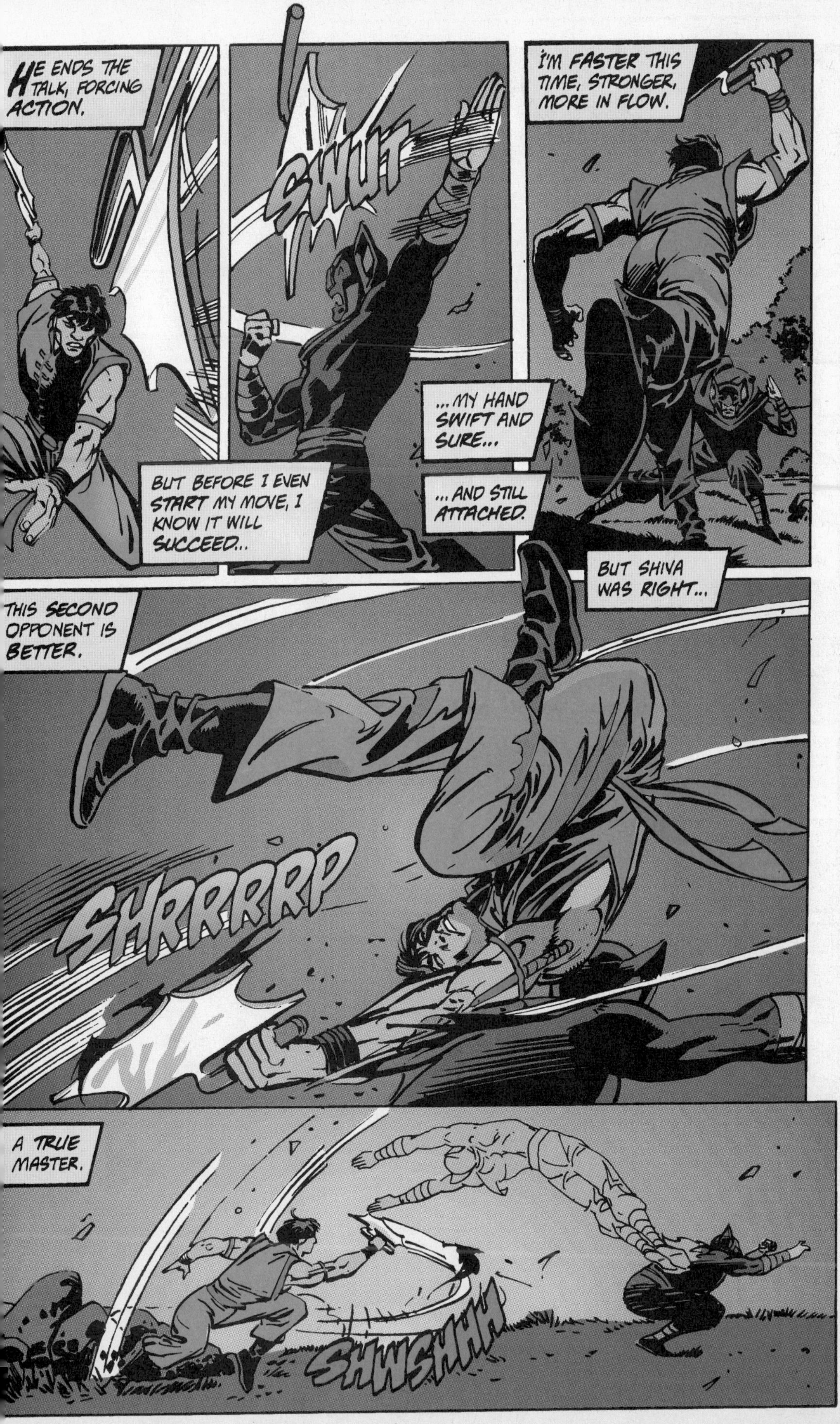
HE ENDS THE TALK, FORCING ACTION.
SWUT
BUT BEFORE I EVEN START MY MOVE, I KNOW IT WILL SUCCEED...
...MY HAND SWIFT AND SURE...
...AND STILL ATTACHED.
I'M FASTER THIS TIME, STRONGER, MORE IN FLOW.
BUT SHIVA WAS RIGHT...
THIS SECOND OPPONENT IS BETTER.
SHRRRRP
A TRUE MASTER.
SHWSHHH

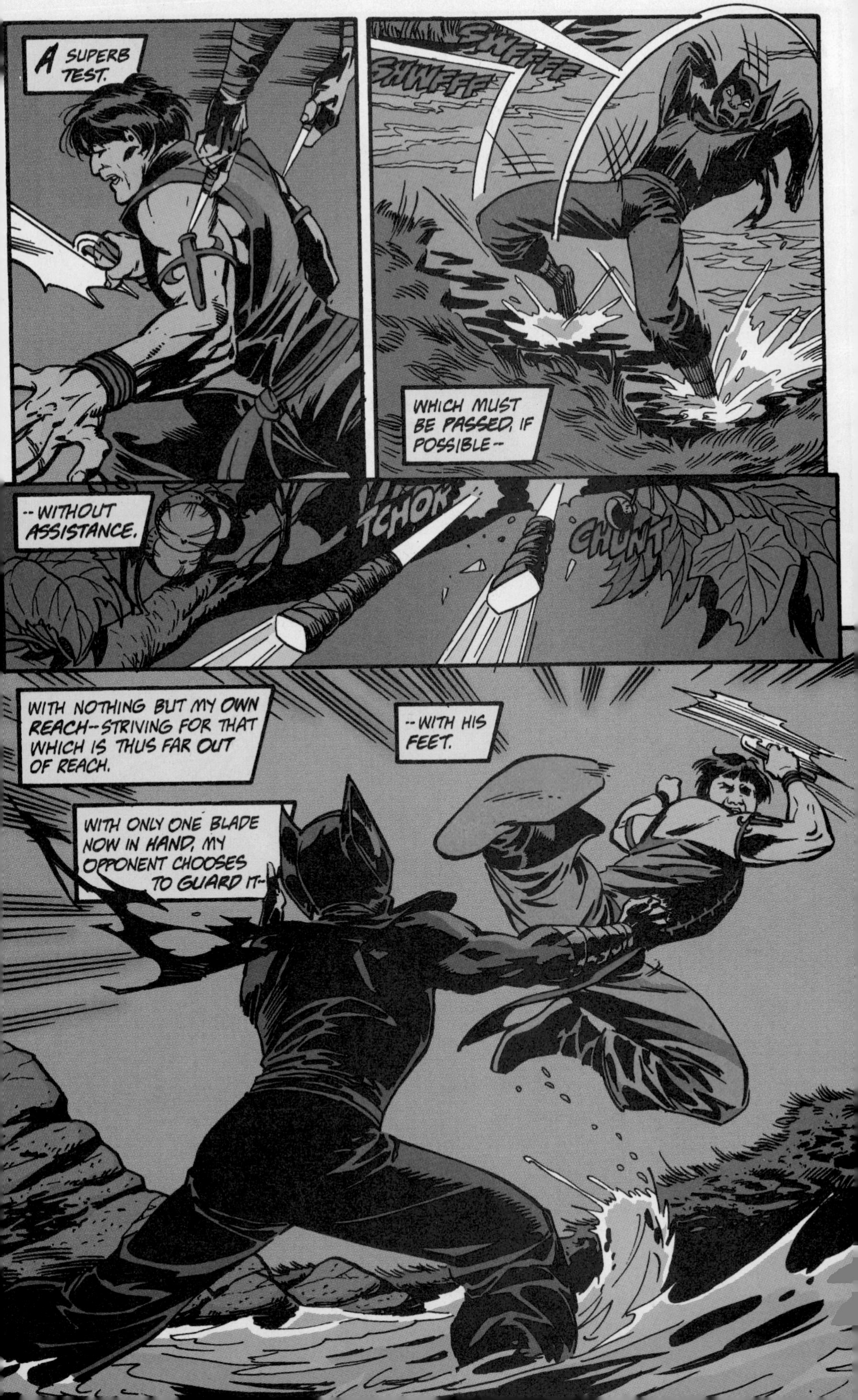
A SUPERB TEST.
SHWFFF
SWFFFF
WHICH MUST BE PASSED, IF POSSIBLE--
--WITHOUT ASSISTANCE.
TCHOK
CHUNT
WITH NOTHING BUT MY OWN REACH--STRIVING FOR THAT WHICH IS THUS FAR OUT OF REACH.
--WITH HIS FEET.
WITH ONLY ONE BLADE NOW IN HAND, MY OPPONENT CHOOSES TO GUARD IT--

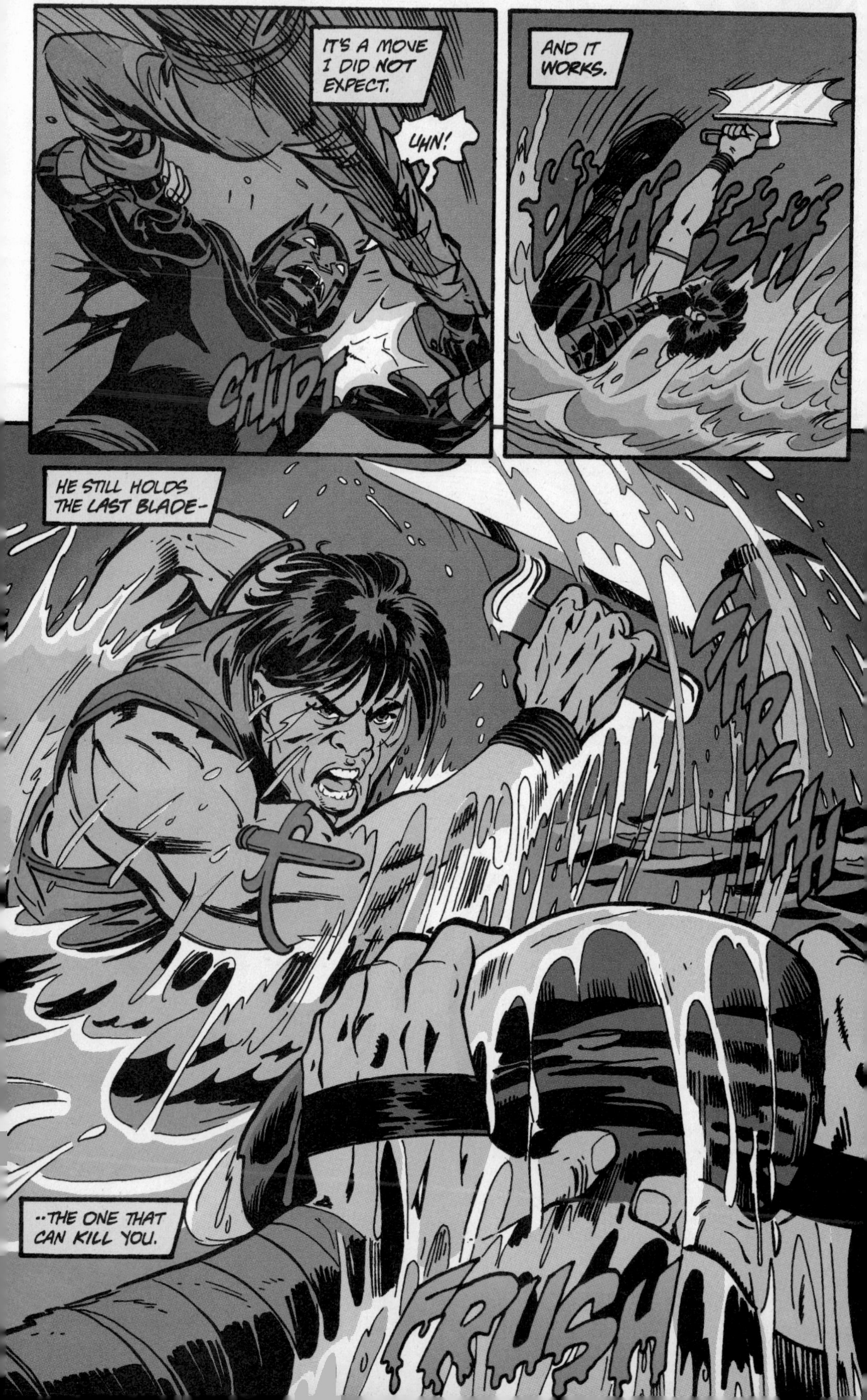
IT'S A MOVE I DID NOT EXPECT.
UHN!
CHUPT
AND IT WORKS.
SPLASSHH
HE STILL HOLDS THE LAST BLADE-
SHRSHH
..THE ONE THAT CAN KILL YOU.
KRUSH

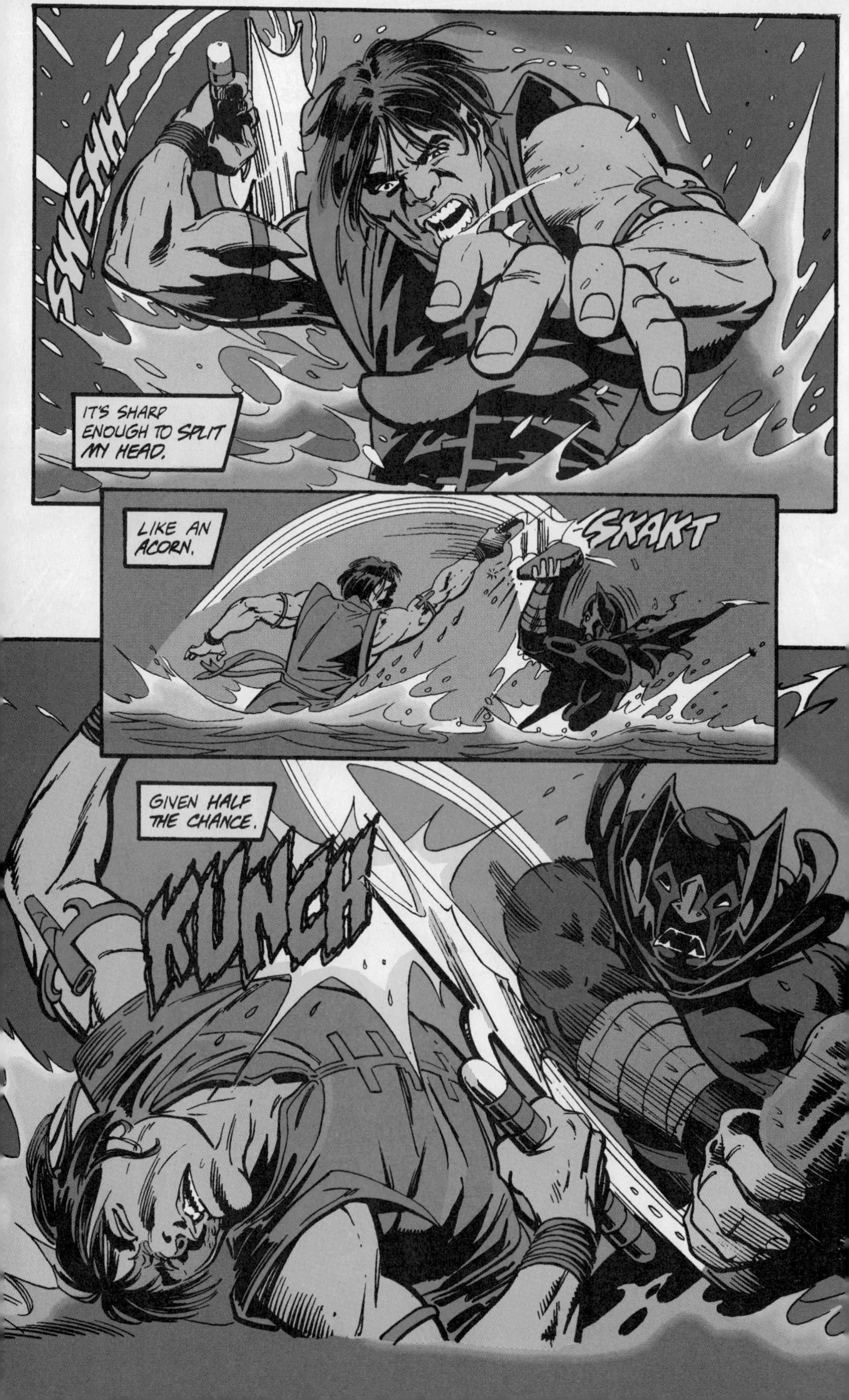
SWSHH
IT'S SHARP ENOUGH TO SPLIT MY HEAD.
LIKE AN ACORN.
SKAKT
GIVEN HALF THE CHANCE.
KUNCH

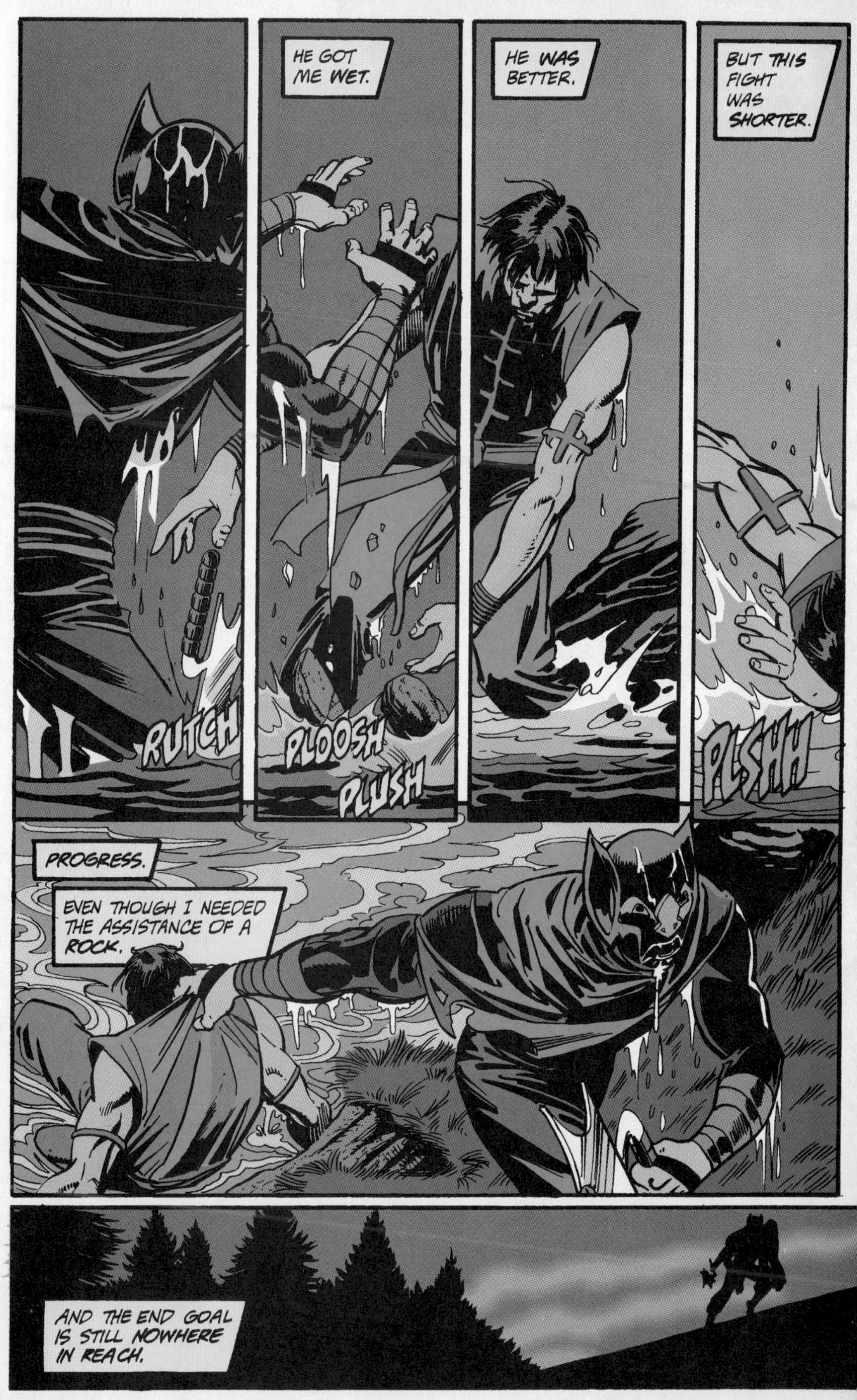
HE GOT ME WET.
HE WAS BETTER.
BUT THIS FIGHT WAS SHORTER.
RUTCH
PLOOSH
PLUSH
PLSHH
PROGRESS.
EVEN THOUGH I NEEDED THE ASSISTANCE OF A ROCK.
AND THE END GOAL IS STILL NOWHERE IN REACH.

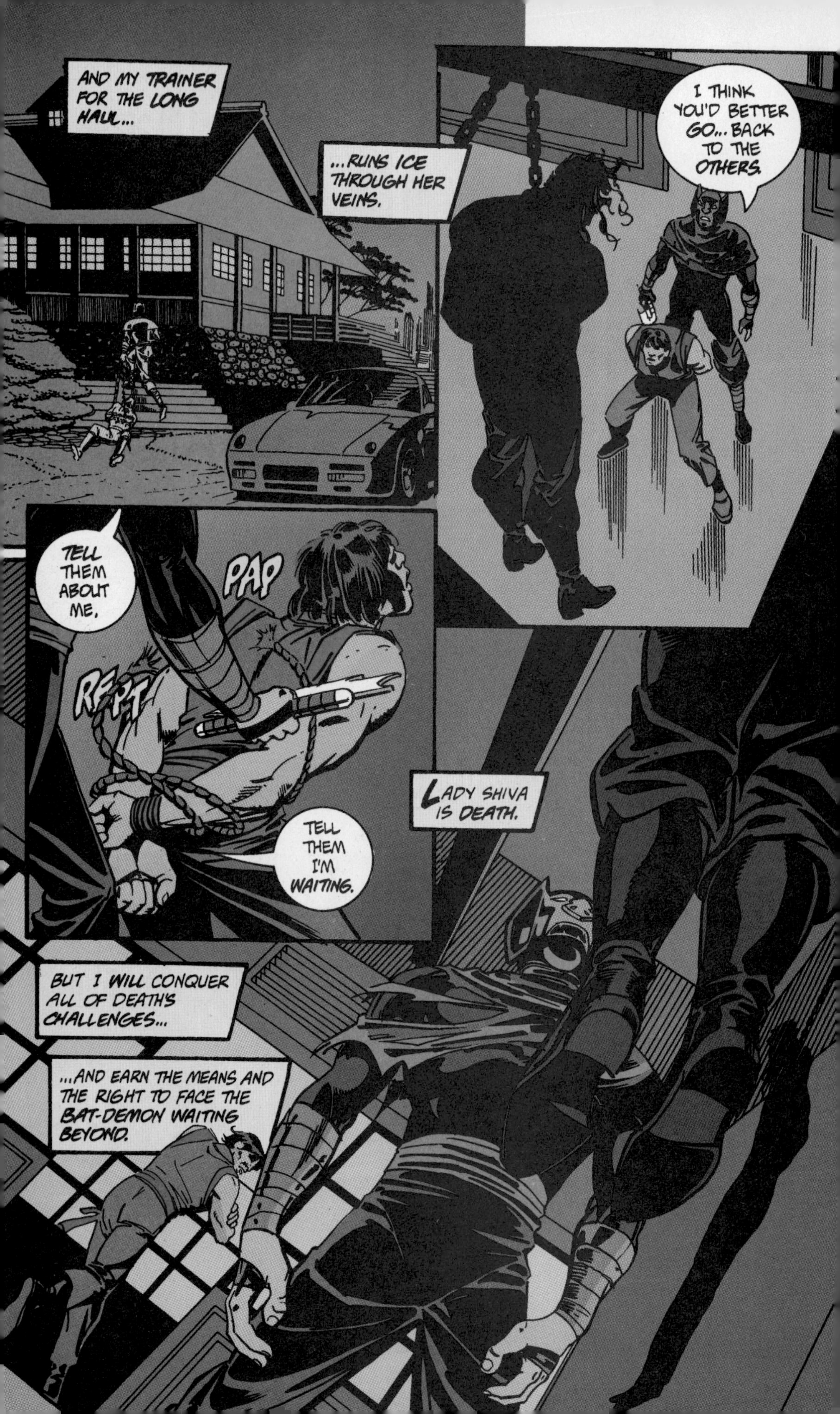
AND MY TRAINER FOR THE LONG HAUL...
...RUNS ICE THROUGH HER VEINS.
I THINK YOU'D BETTER GO... BACK TO THE OTHERS.
TELL THEM ABOUT ME.
PAP
REPT
TELL THEM I'M WAITING.
LADY SHIVA IS DEATH.
BUT I WILL CONQUER ALL OF DEATH'S CHALLENGES...
...AND EARN THE MEANS AND THE RIGHT TO FACE THE BAT-DEMON WAITING BEYOND.

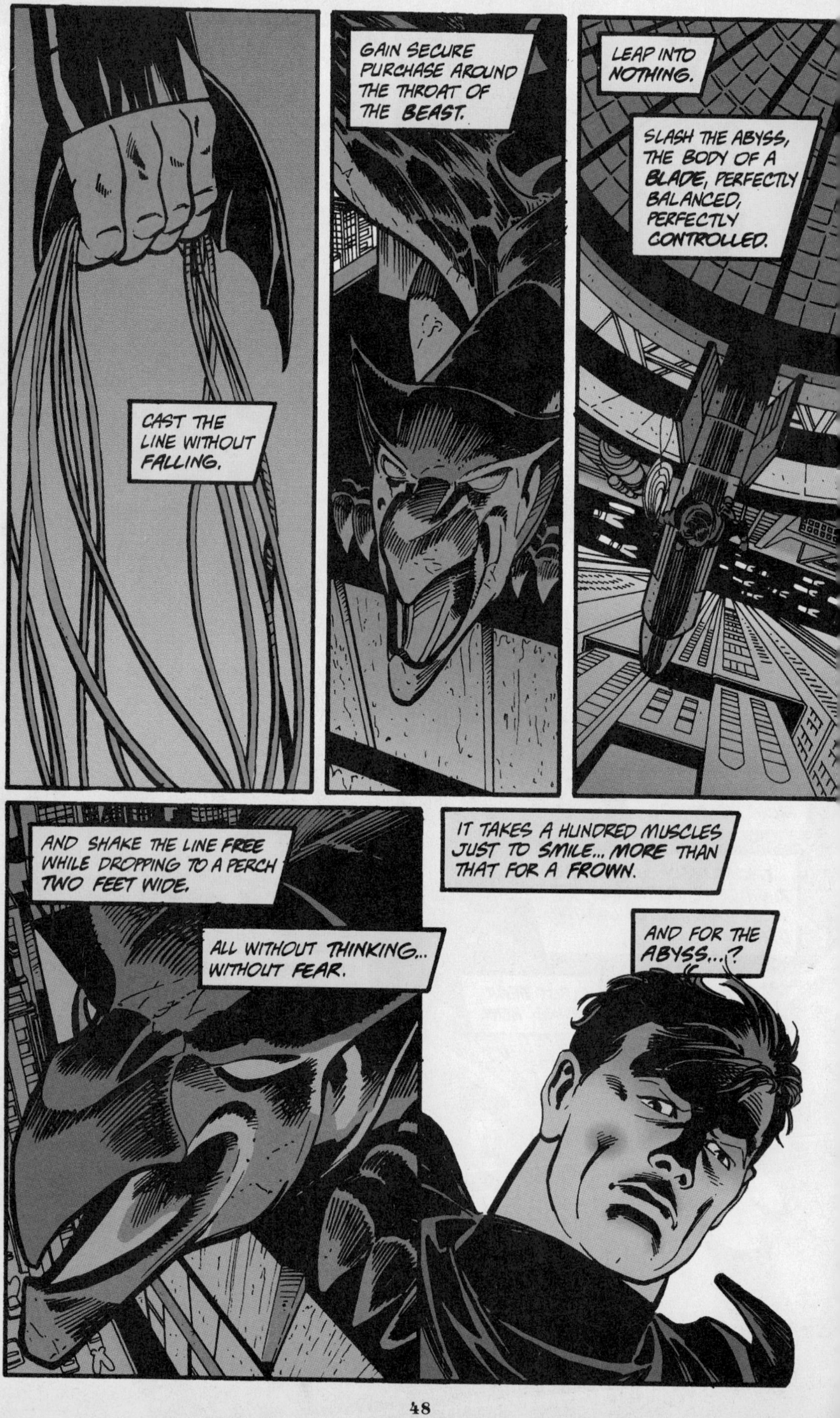
CAST THE LINE WITHOUT FALLING.
GAIN SECURE PURCHASE AROUND THE THROAT OF THE BEAST.
LEAP INTO NOTHING.
SLASH THE ABYSS, THE BODY OF A BLADE, PERFECTLY BALANCED, PERFECTLY CONTROLLED.
AND SHAKE THE LINE FREE WHILE DROPPING TO A PERCH TWO FEET WIDE.
ALL WITHOUT THINKING... WITHOUT FEAR.
IT TAKES A HUNDRED MUSCLES JUST TO SMILE... MORE THAN THAT FOR A FROWN.
AND FOR THE ABYSS...?

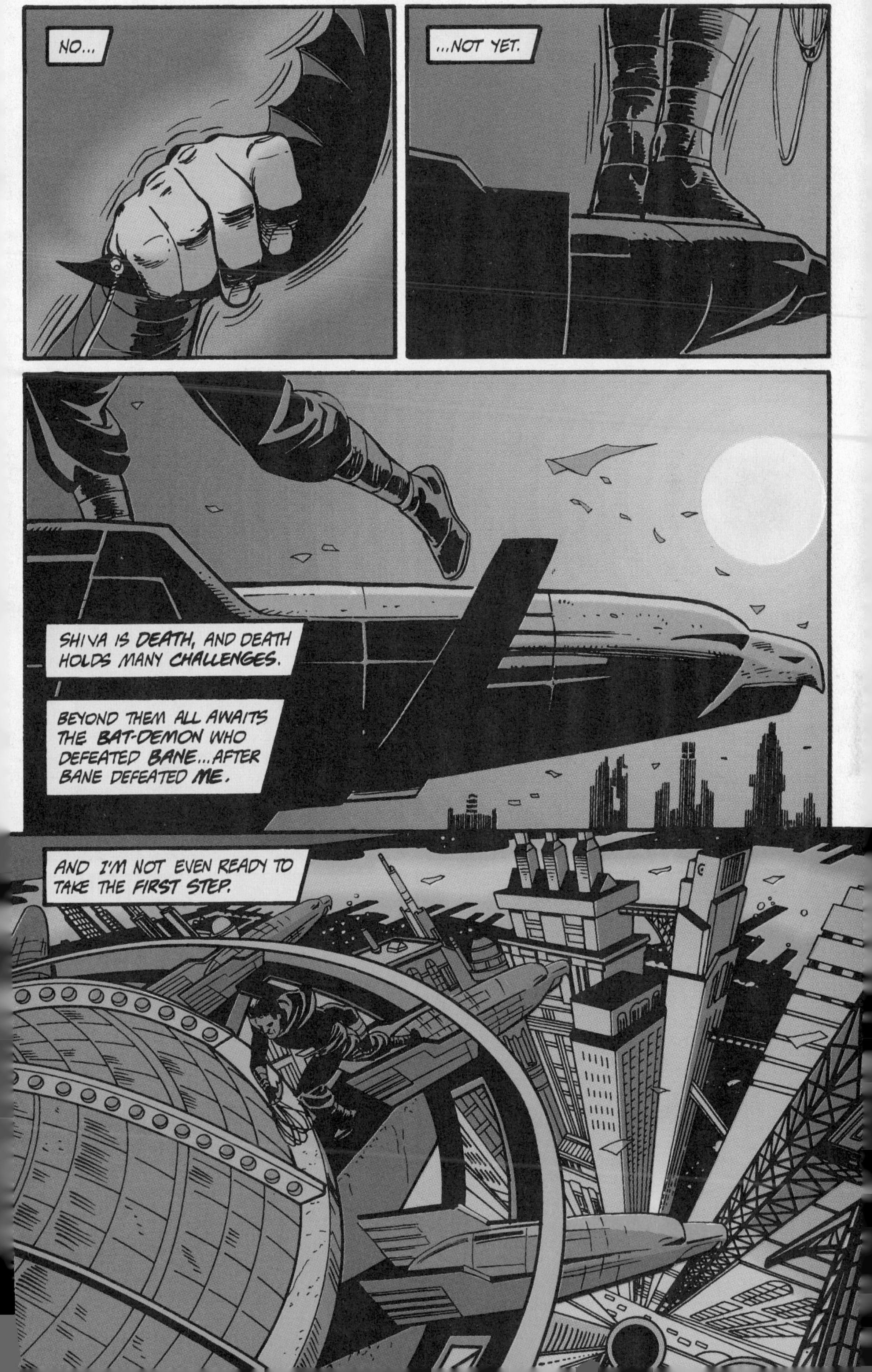
NO...
...NOT YET.
SHIVA IS DEATH, AND DEATH HOLDS MANY CHALLENGES.
BEYOND THEM ALL AWAITS THE BAT-DEMON WHO DEFEATED BANE...AFTER BANE DEFEATED ME.
AND I'M NOT EVEN READY TO TAKE THE FIRST STEP.

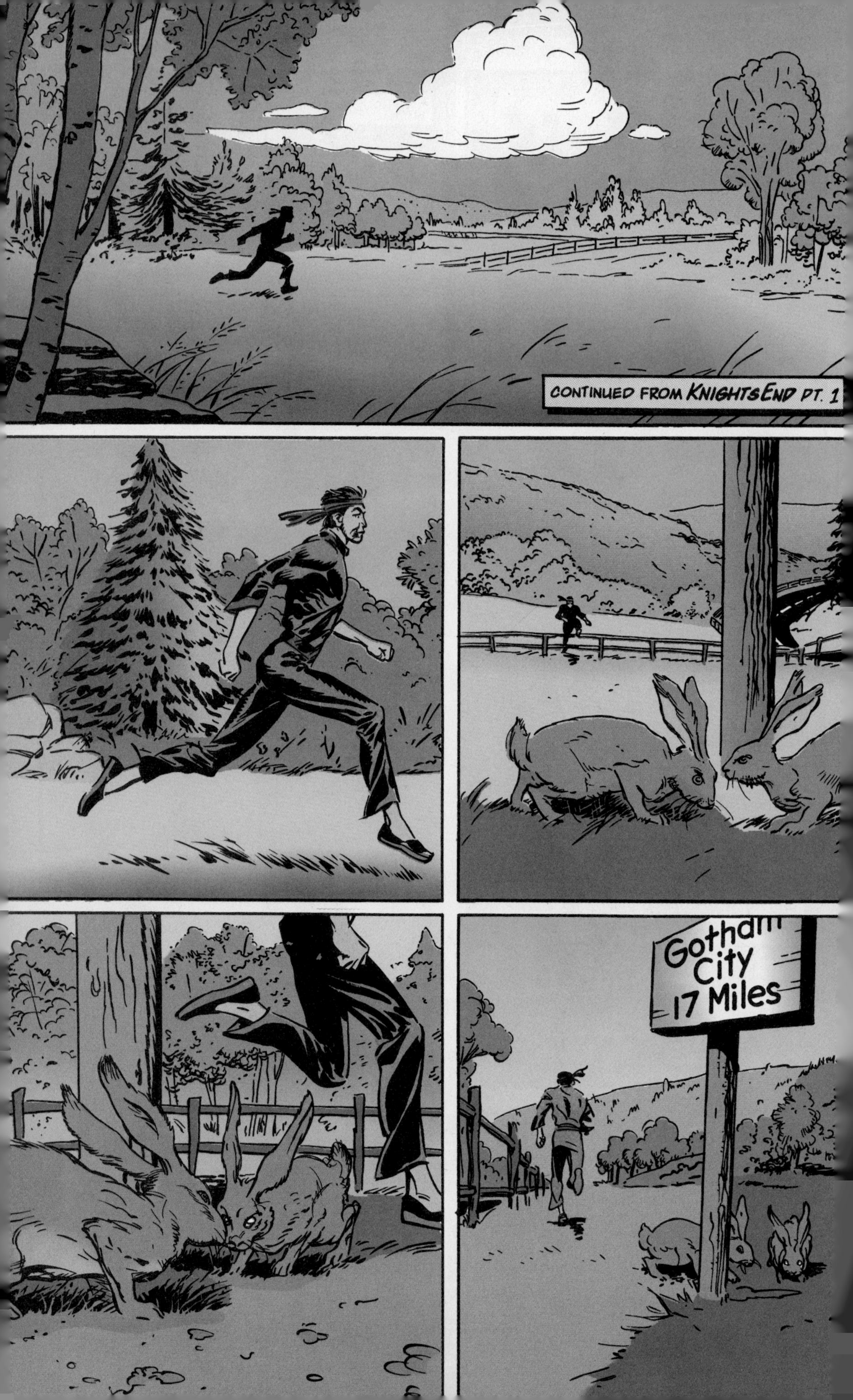
CONTINUED FROM KNIGHTSEND PT. 1
Gotham City 17 Miles

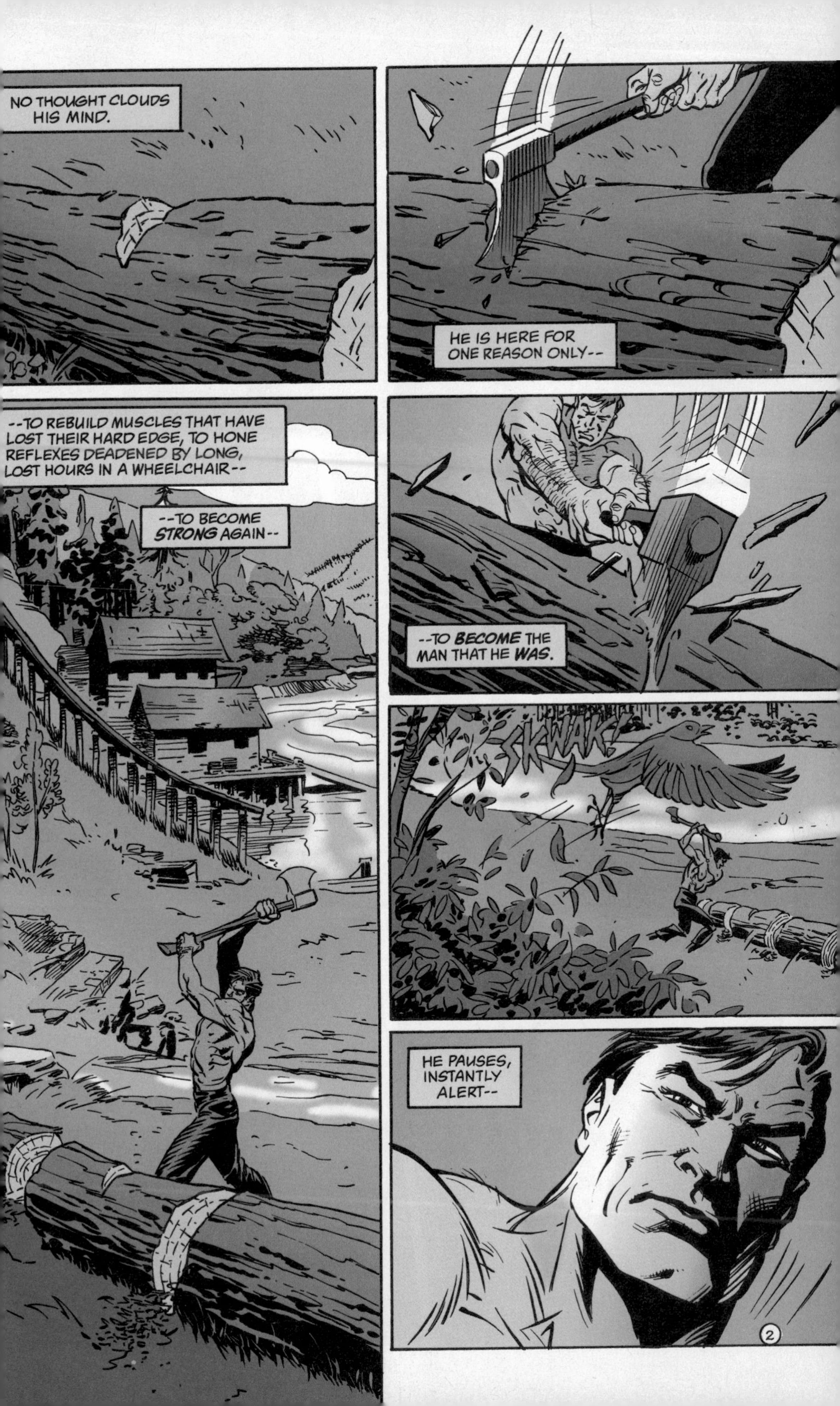
NO THOUGHT CLOUDS HIS MIND.
HE IS HERE FOR ONE REASON ONLY--
--TO REBUILD MUSCLES THAT HAVE LOST THEIR HARD EDGE, TO HONE REFLEXES DEADENED BY LONG, LOST HOURS IN A WHEELCHAIR--
--TO BECOME STRONG AGAIN--
--TO BECOME THE MAN THAT HE WAS.
SKWAK!
HE PAUSES, INSTANTLY ALERT--
2

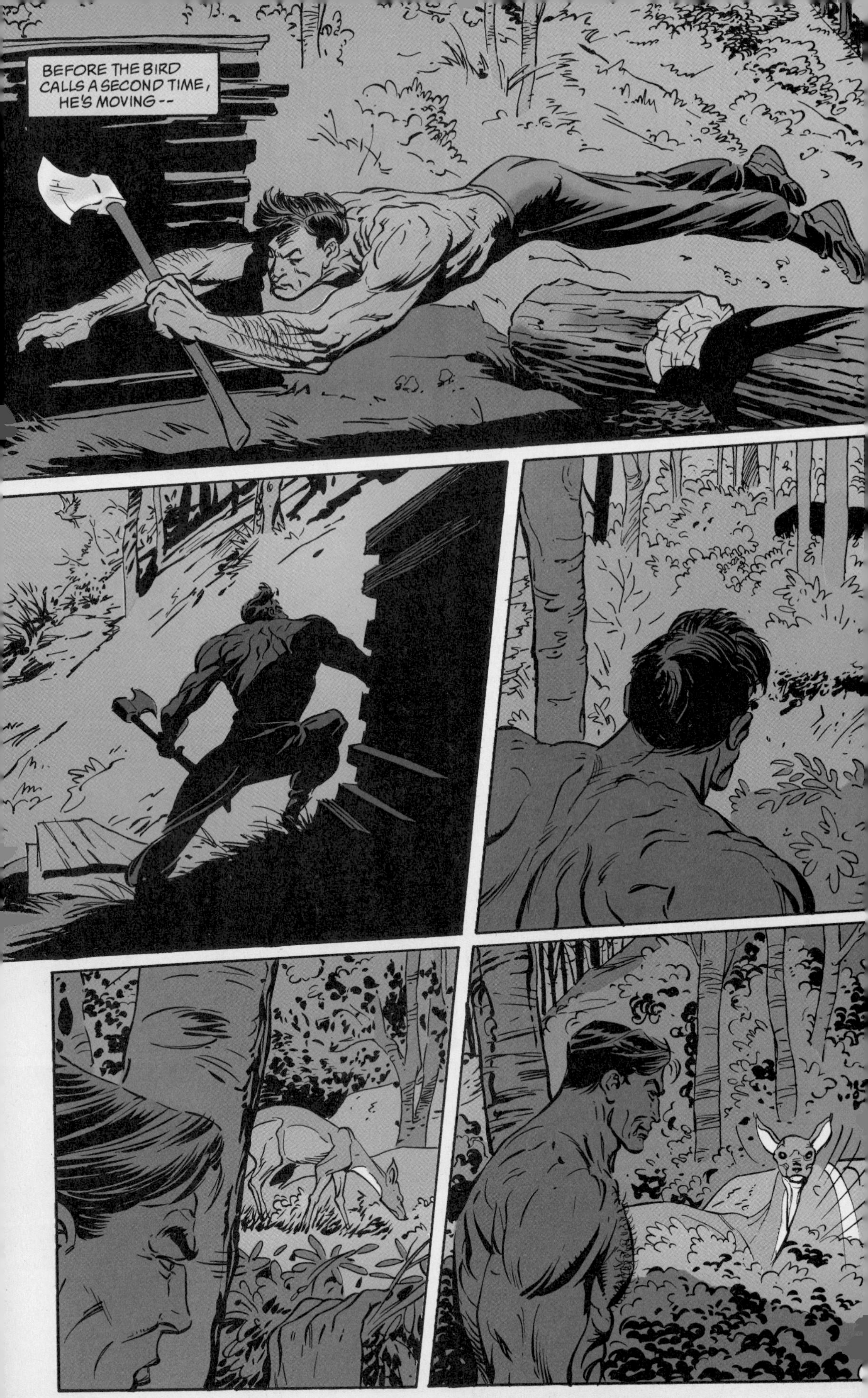
BEFORE THE BIRD CALLS A SECOND TIME, HE'S MOVING --

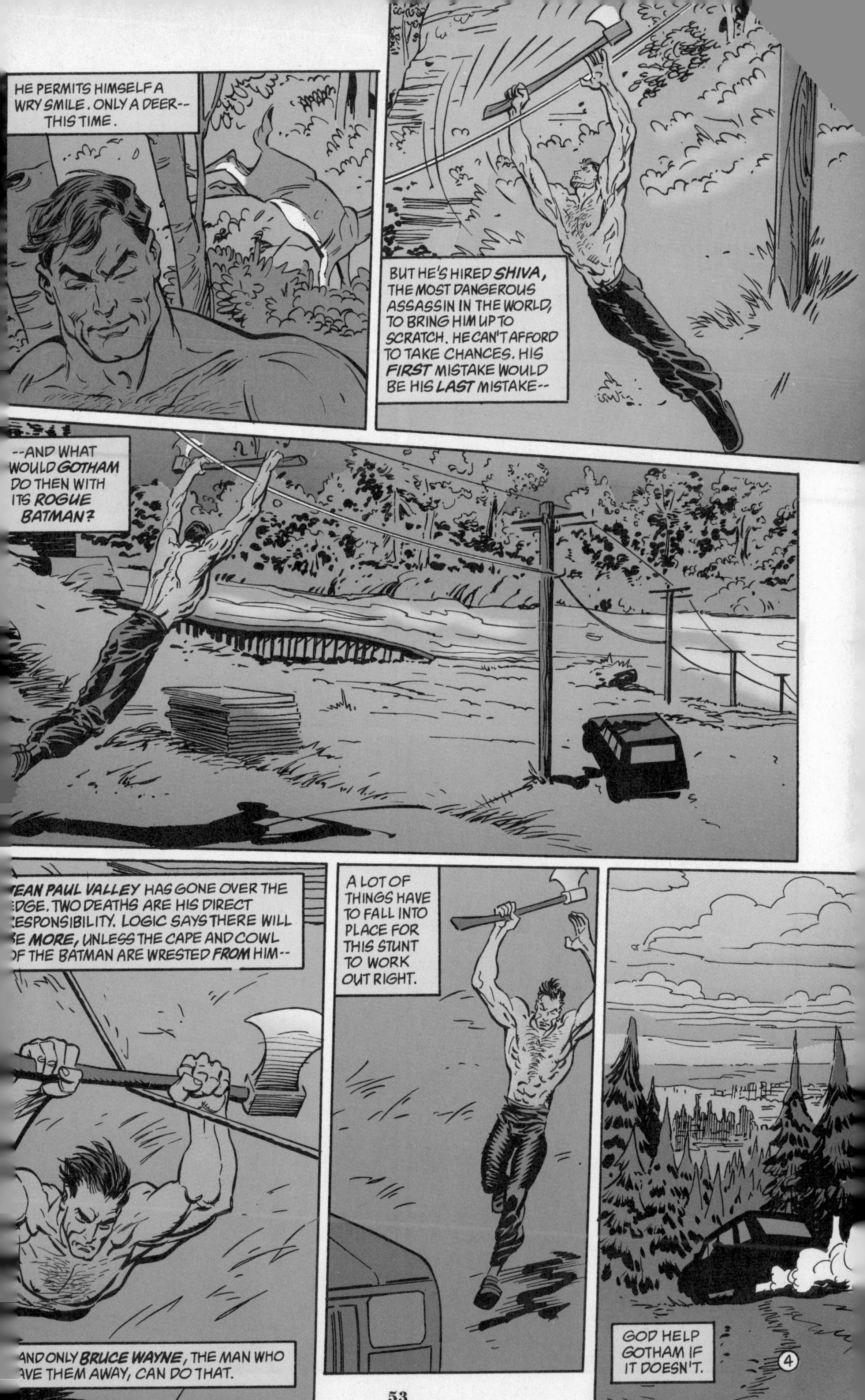
HE PERMITS HIMSELF A WRY SMILE. ONLY A DEER-- THIS TIME.
BUT HE'S HIRED SHIVA, THE MOST DANGEROUS ASSASSIN IN THE WORLD, TO BRING HIM UP TO SCRATCH. HE CAN'T AFFORD TO TAKE CHANCES. HIS FIRST MISTAKE WOULD BE HIS LAST MISTAKE--
--AND WHAT WOULD GOTHAM DO THEN WITH ITS ROGUE BATMAN?
EAN PAUL VALLEY HAS GONE OVER THE EDGE. TWO DEATHS ARE HIS DIRECT ESPONSIBILITY. LOGIC SAYS THERE WILL E MORE, UNLESS THE CAPE AND COWL F THE BATMAN ARE WRESTED FROM HIM--
AND ONLY BRUCE WAYNE, THE MAN WHO AVE THEM AWAY, CAN DO THAT.
A LOT OF THINGS HAVE TO FALL INTO PLACE FOR THIS STUNT TO WORK OUT RIGHT.
GOD HELP GOTHAM IF IT DOESN'T.
4

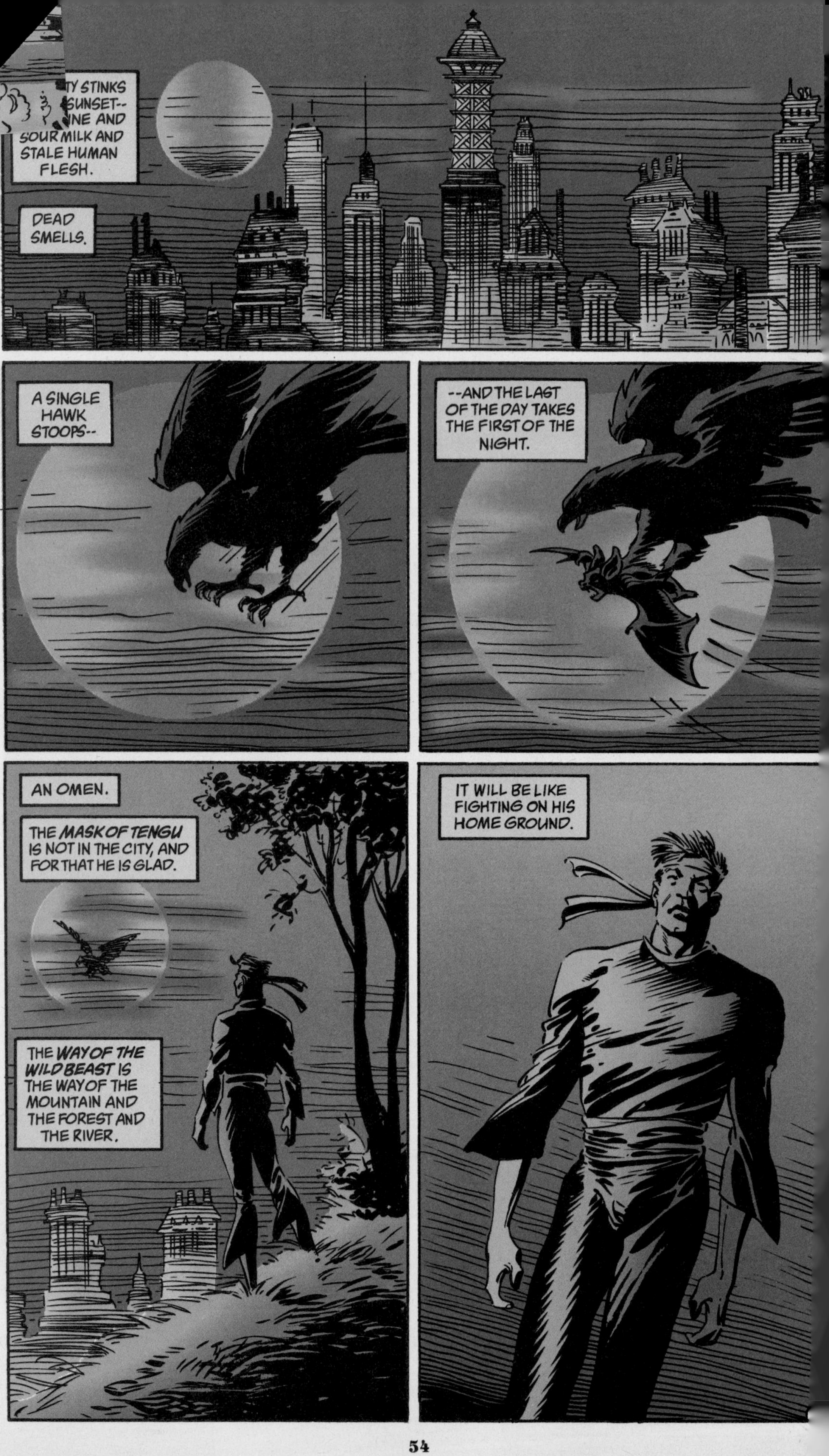
STINKS SUNSET-- AND SOUR MILK AND STALE HUMAN FLESH.
DEAD SMELLS.
A SINGLE HAWK STOOPS--
--AND THE LAST OF THE DAY TAKES THE FIRST OF THE NIGHT.
AN OMEN.
THE *MASK OF TENGU* IS NOT IN THE CITY, AND FOR THAT HE IS GLAD.
THE *WAY OF THE WILD BEAST* IS THE WAY OF THE MOUNTAIN AND THE FOREST AND THE RIVER.
IT WILL BE LIKE FIGHTING ON HIS HOME GROUND.

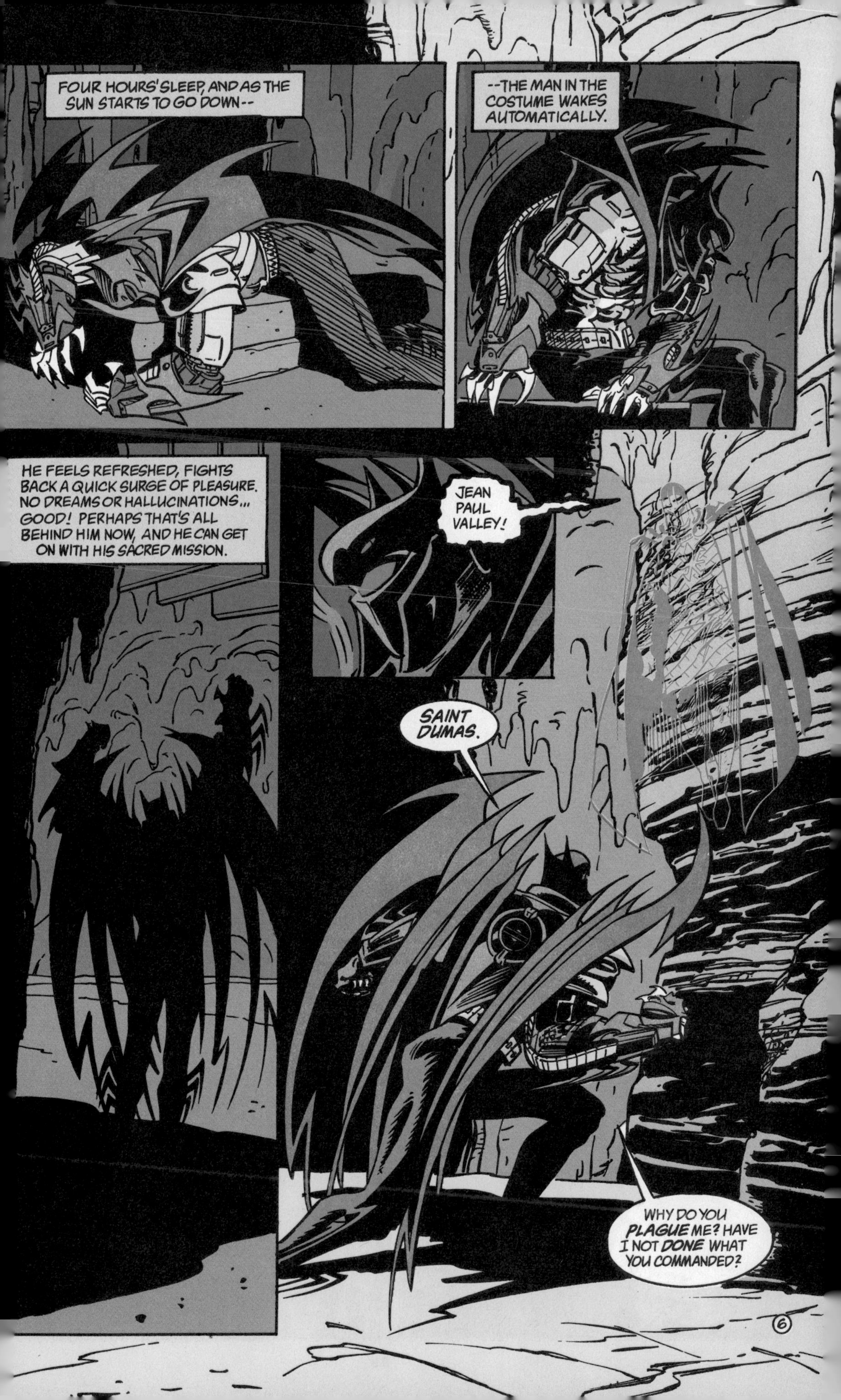

FOUR HOURS' SLEEP, AND AS THE SUN STARTS TO GO DOWN--
--THE MAN IN THE COSTUME WAKES AUTOMATICALLY.
HE FEELS REFRESHED, FIGHTS BACK A QUICK SURGE OF PLEASURE. NO DREAMS OR HALLUCINATIONS... GOOD! PERHAPS THAT'S ALL BEHIND HIM NOW, AND HE CAN GET ON WITH HIS SACRED MISSION.
JEAN PAUL VALLEY!
SAINT DUMAS.
WHY DO YOU PLAGUE ME? HAVE I NOT DONE WHAT YOU COMMANDED?

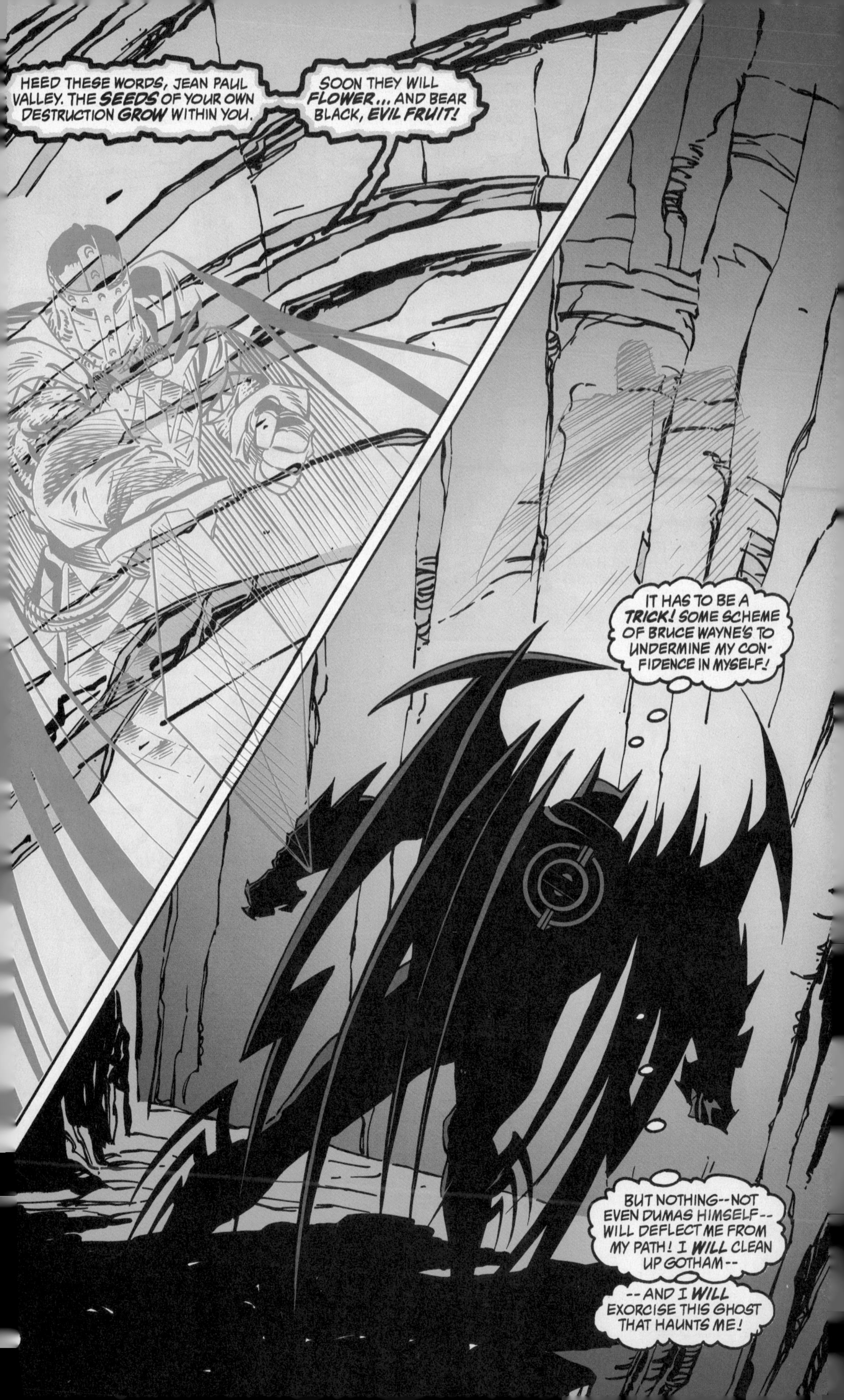
HEED THESE WORDS, JEAN PAUL VALLEY. THE SEEDS OF YOUR OWN DESTRUCTION GROW WITHIN YOU.
SOON THEY WILL FLOWER... AND BEAR BLACK, EVIL FRUIT!
IT HAS TO BE A TRICK! SOME SCHEME OF BRUCE WAYNE'S TO UNDERMINE MY CONFIDENCE IN MYSELF!
BUT NOTHING--NOT EVEN DUMAS HIMSELF--WILL DEFLECT ME FROM MY PATH! I WILL CLEAN UP GOTHAM--
--AND I WILL EXORCISE THIS GHOST THAT HAUNTS ME!

--HAS TO MEAN SOMETHING!

TOLTEC--ANCIENT ROMAN-- MAORI... I'VE DREDGED THE CRAYS' DATA-BANKS FOR EVERY MAJOR CULTURE IN HISTORY--

--BUT DESPITE SOME SUPERFICIAL RESEMBLANCES, THE MEDAL DOESN'T SEEM TO FIT ANY KNOWN CATEGORY!

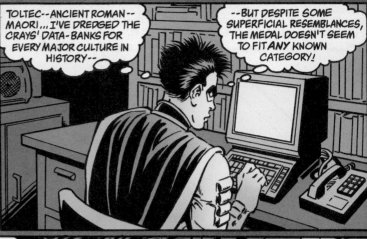

I TOOK THE PHOTO LAST NIGHT, WHEN PAUL FOUND THE MEDAL DURING THAT ARMS DEAL BUST. HE SEEMED TO KNOW WHAT IT WAS ALL ABOUT-- WHICH SUGGESTS I SHOULD FIND OUT FAST!

I'LL FAX IT TO BRUCE'S APARTMENT-- GIVE HIM A HEAD START AT FIGURING IT OUT.

PAUL SEEMS TO BE GOING CRAZY, SPINNING OUT OF ALL CONTROL.

HOW MANY MORE CORPSES WILL WE HAVE TO PICK OFF GOTHAM'S STREETS, COURTESY OF ITS ONE-TIME PROTECTOR-- THE BATMAN?

I'VE GOT A GUT FEELING THAT THE QUICKER WE SOLVE THIS ONE, THE BETTER! BUT I'M GETTING NO-WHERE FAST.

MAYBE A *WISER* HEAD THAN MINE'LL KNOW...!

... ONE NINETY-THREE...

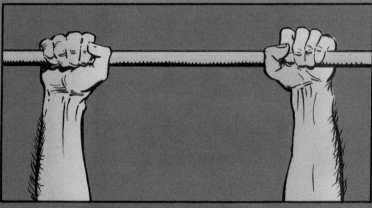

... ONE NINETY-FOUR...

RAP RAP!

⑩

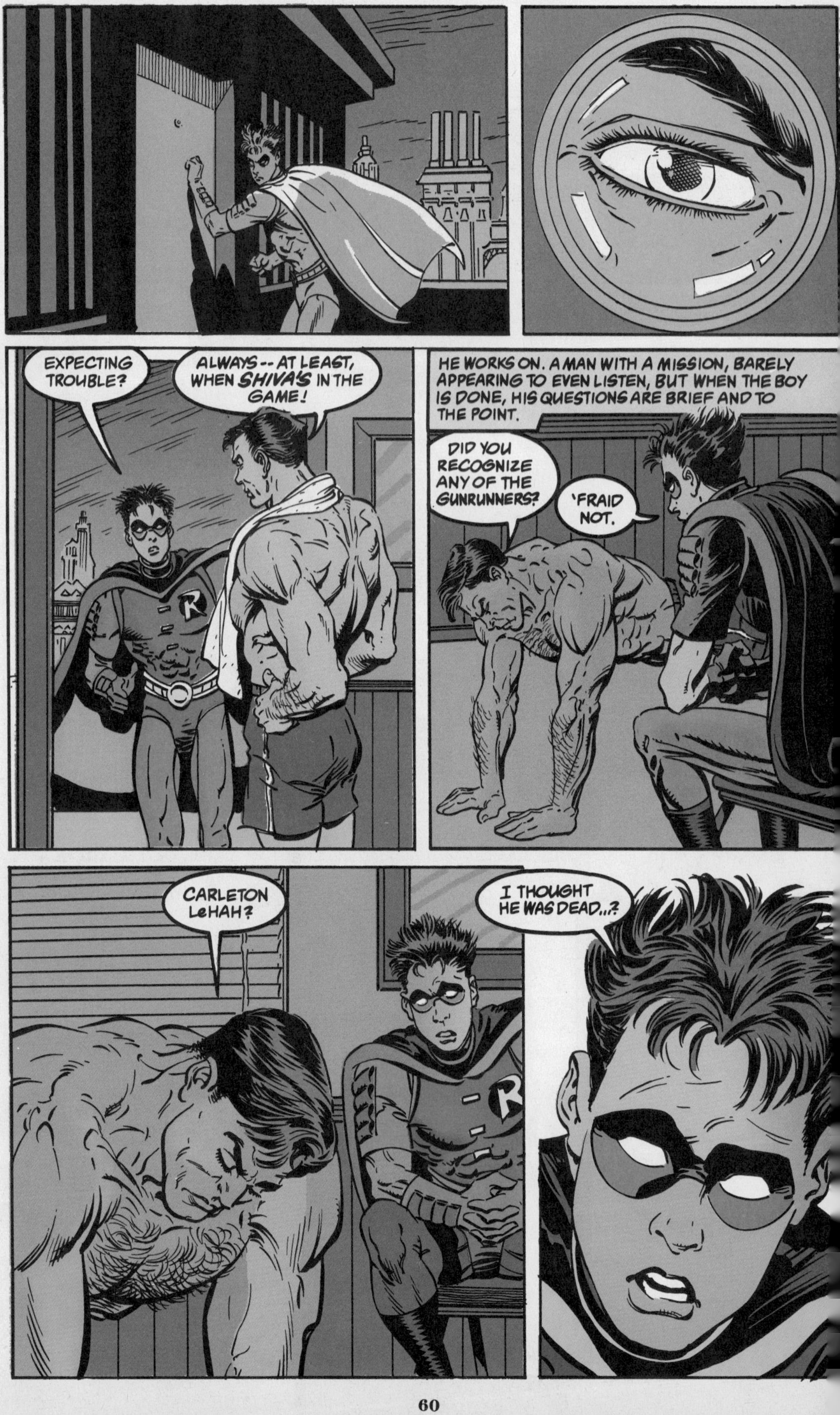
EXPECTING TROUBLE?
ALWAYS -- AT LEAST, WHEN SHIVA'S IN THE GAME!
HE WORKS ON. A MAN WITH A MISSION, BARELY APPEARING TO EVEN LISTEN, BUT WHEN THE BOY IS DONE, HIS QUESTIONS ARE BRIEF AND TO THE POINT.
DID YOU RECOGNIZE ANY OF THE GUNRUNNERS?
'FRAID NOT.
CARLETON LeHAH?
I THOUGHT HE WAS DEAD...?

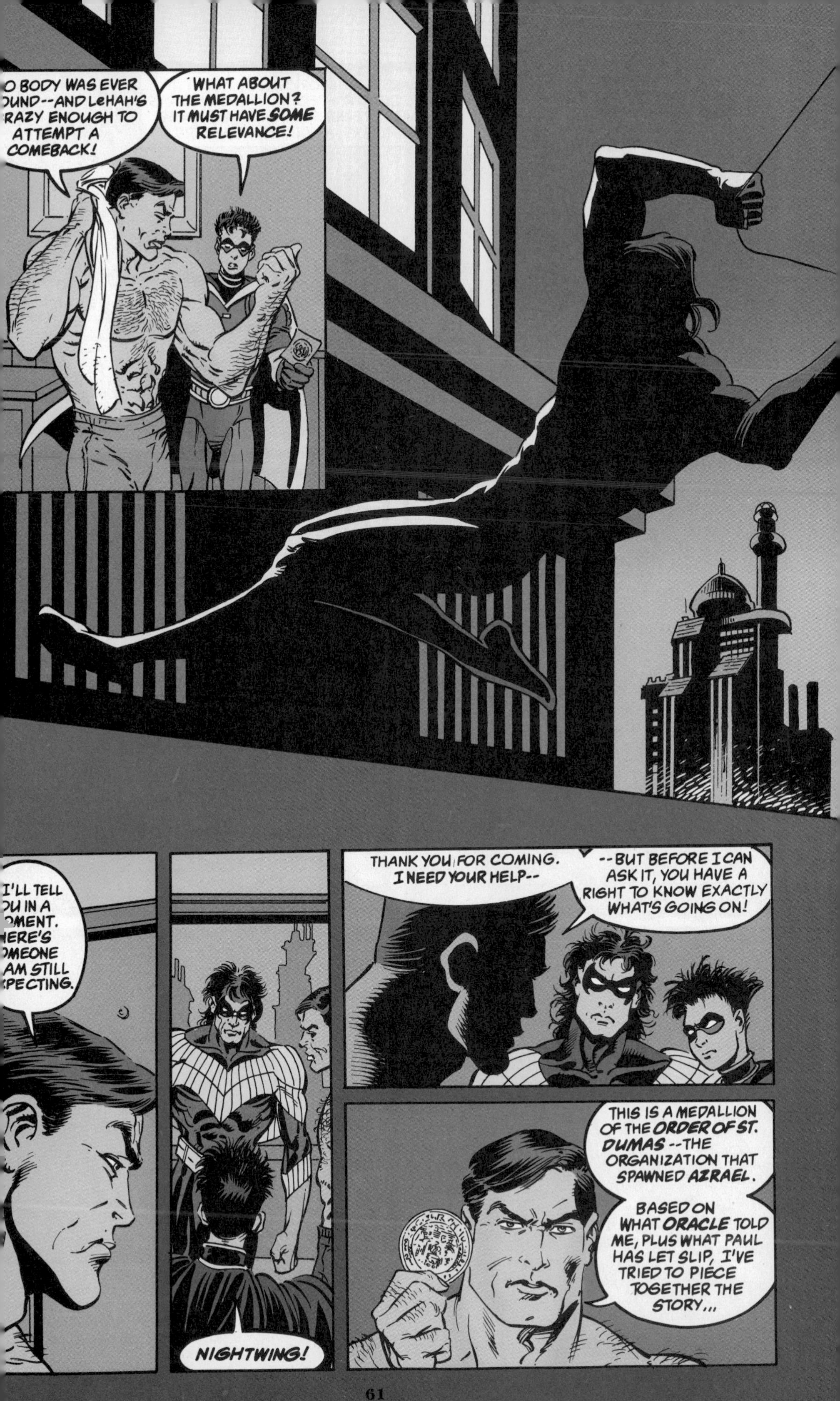
O BODY WAS EVER OUND--AND LeHAH'S RAZY ENOUGH TO ATTEMPT A COMEBACK!
WHAT ABOUT THE MEDALLION? IT MUST HAVE SOME RELEVANCE!
I'LL TELL OU IN A OMENT. HERE'S OMEONE AM STILL PECTING.
NIGHTWING!
THANK YOU FOR COMING. I NEED YOUR HELP--
--BUT BEFORE I CAN ASK IT, YOU HAVE A RIGHT TO KNOW EXACTLY WHAT'S GOING ON!
THIS IS A MEDALLION OF THE ORDER OF ST. DUMAS --THE ORGANIZATION THAT SPAWNED AZRAEL.
BASED ON WHAT ORACLE TOLD ME, PLUS WHAT PAUL HAS LET SLIP, I'VE TRIED TO PIECE TOGETHER THE STORY...

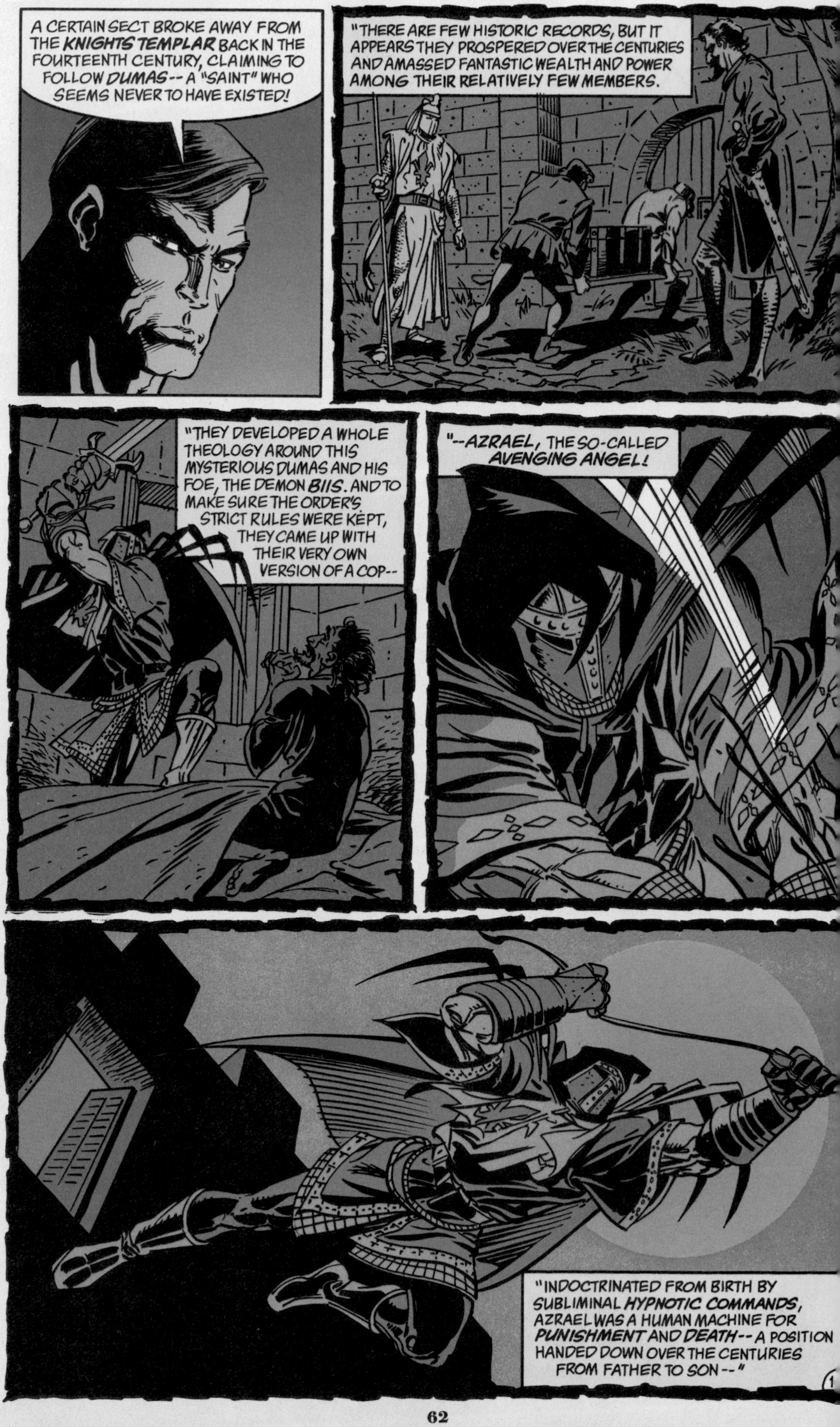
A CERTAIN SECT BROKE AWAY FROM THE KNIGHTS TEMPLAR BACK IN THE FOURTEENTH CENTURY, CLAIMING TO FOLLOW DUMAS-- A "SAINT" WHO SEEMS NEVER TO HAVE EXISTED!
"THERE ARE FEW HISTORIC RECORDS, BUT IT APPEARS THEY PROSPERED OVER THE CENTURIES AND AMASSED FANTASTIC WEALTH AND POWER AMONG THEIR RELATIVELY FEW MEMBERS.
"THEY DEVELOPED A WHOLE THEOLOGY AROUND THIS MYSTERIOUS DUMAS AND HIS FOE, THE DEMON BIIS. AND TO MAKE SURE THE ORDER'S STRICT RULES WERE KEPT, THEY CAME UP WITH THEIR VERY OWN VERSION OF A COP--
"--AZRAEL, THE SO-CALLED AVENGING ANGEL!
"INDOCTRINATED FROM BIRTH BY SUBLIMINAL HYPNOTIC COMMANDS, AZRAEL WAS A HUMAN MACHINE FOR PUNISHMENT AND DEATH-- A POSITION HANDED DOWN OVER THE CENTURIES FROM FATHER TO SON--"

--FINALLY ENDING UP WITH *JEAN PAUL VALLEY!*

AND YOU CHOSE *HIM* OVER *ME* TO CARRY THE MANTLE OF THE BAT? A PROGRAMMED *MURDERER?*

IF I'D KNOWN, MY FEELINGS WOULD HAVE BEEN EVEN *MORE* HURT THAN THEY WERE!

IF *I* HAD KNOWN, DO YOU THINK I'D HAVE *DONE* IT?

NOW I'M ASKING... CAN I COUNT ON YOUR HELP?

YOU KNOW IT.

YEAH!

ONE FOR ALL...!

[MO]RE THAN ANYTHING, PAUL-- [A]ZRAEL--WANTS *REVENGE* [O]N THE MAN WHO SLEW HIS [FA]THER. IF HE GETS TO THAT [M]AN, MURDER MAY BE THE *LEAST* OF WHAT HAPPENS!

IF I'M GOING TO [S]TOP HIM, I NEED TO [K]NOW HIS EVERY MOVE. [I] WANT YOU TWO TO FIND [H]IM--FOLLOW HIM-- [A]ND REPORT BACK TO ME!

"AND IF THINGS DON'T WORK OUT, I CAN PROBABLY MAKE A *SHREWD* GUESS AT WHERE THIS IS ALL GOING TO END UP...!"

⑭

GOTHAM
CITY
LIMITS

SO HE HAD A
VISION. SO WHAT?

WHO CARES IF IT WAS REAL OR
A HALLUCINATION, OR ANOTHER
OF *THE SYSTEM'S* INEXHAUSTIBLE
TRICKS? WHAT DOES IT MATTER,
WHEN THE CITY LIGHTS BECKON
AND HE THRILLS TO THE SEDUCTION
OF THE NIGHT?

HE FEELS AS IF HE'S WALKING A
RAZOR'S EDGE.

AND HE *LIKES* IT.

YEAH?

RUDY ELZEN?
I HAVE A DEAL
TO OFFER YOU.

WHO *IS* THIS?
HOW THE HELL DO
YOU KNOW MY
PRIVATE NUMBER?

I KNOW A LOT ABOUT YOU, RUDY. I
KNOW YOU'D LIKE TO GET YOUR
HANDS ON A DOZEN CRATES OF
SEMI-AUTOMATICS -- AND I
KNOW YOU'LL JUST *LOVE*
MY PRICE.

MOHAWK
PLAZA -- THIRTY
MINUTES.
ALONE!

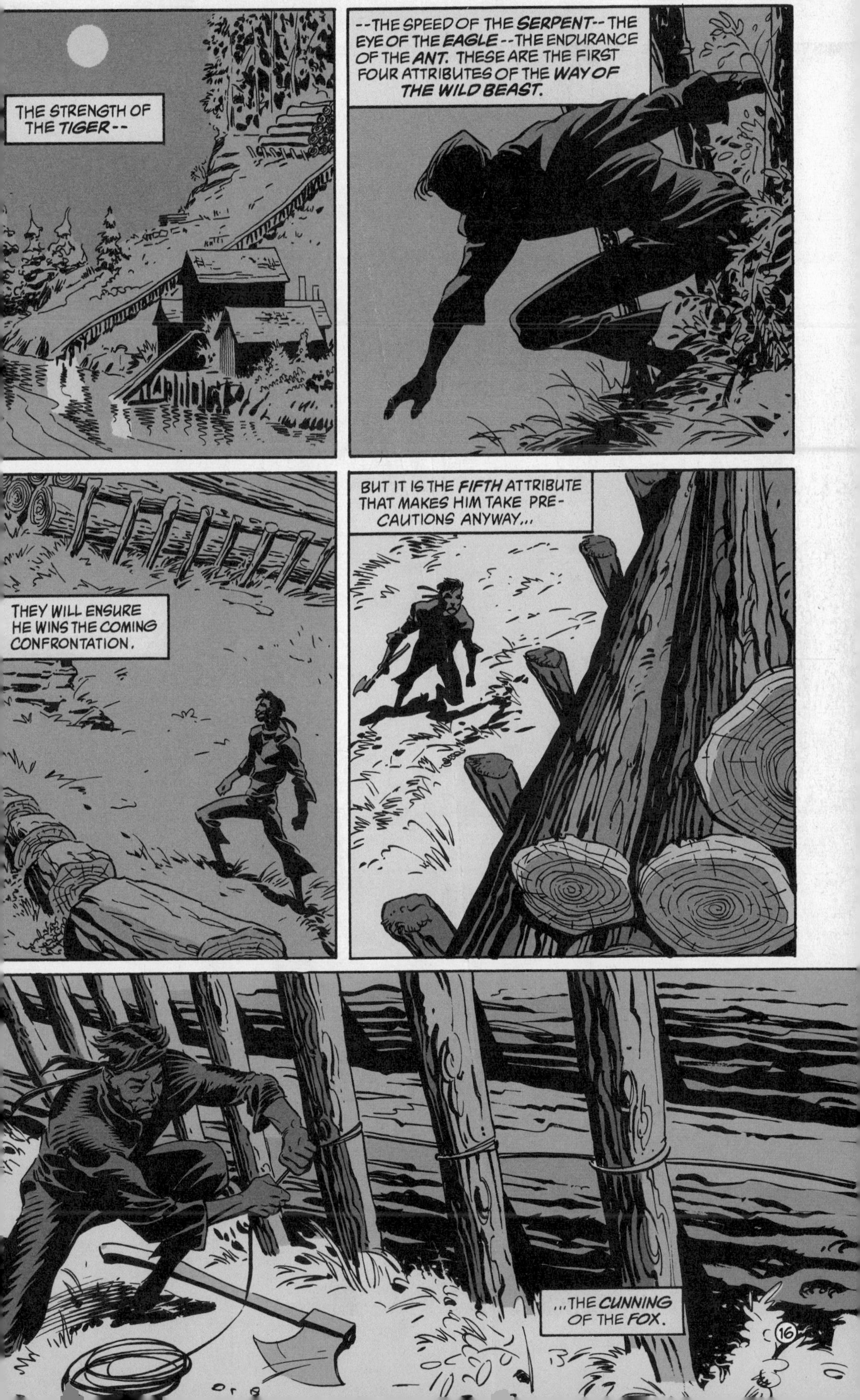
THE STRENGTH OF THE TIGER--
--THE SPEED OF THE SERPENT--THE EYE OF THE EAGLE--THE ENDURANCE OF THE ANT. THESE ARE THE FIRST FOUR ATTRIBUTES OF THE WAY OF THE WILD BEAST.
THEY WILL ENSURE HE WINS THE COMING CONFRONTATION.
BUT IT IS THE FIFTH ATTRIBUTE THAT MAKES HIM TAKE PRE-CAUTIONS ANYWAY...
...THE CUNNING OF THE FOX.
16

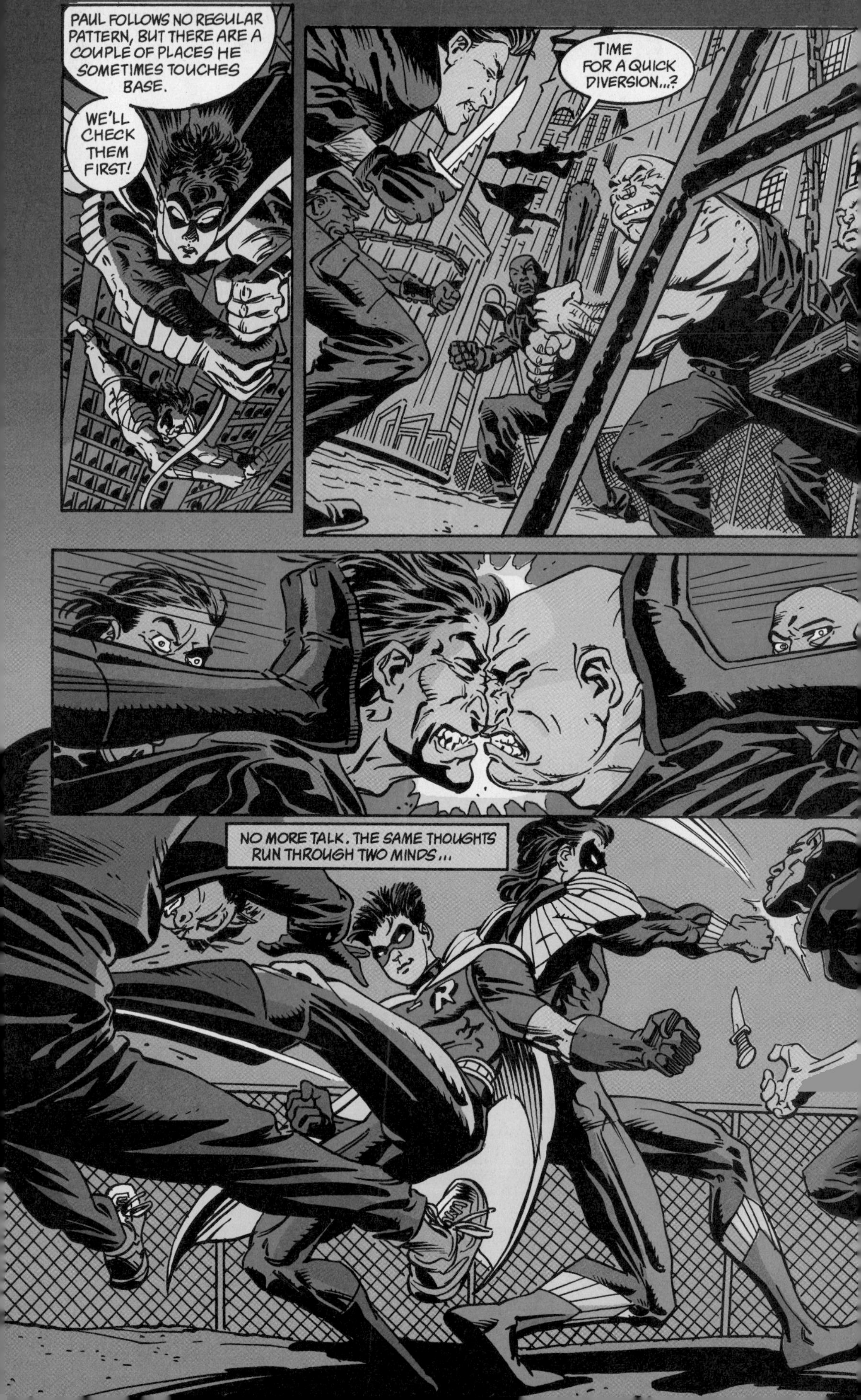
PAUL FOLLOWS NO REGULAR PATTERN, BUT THERE ARE A COUPLE OF PLACES HE SOMETIMES TOUCHES BASE.
WE'LL CHECK THEM FIRST!
TIME FOR A QUICK DIVERSION...?
NO MORE TALK. THE SAME THOUGHTS RUN THROUGH TWO MINDS...

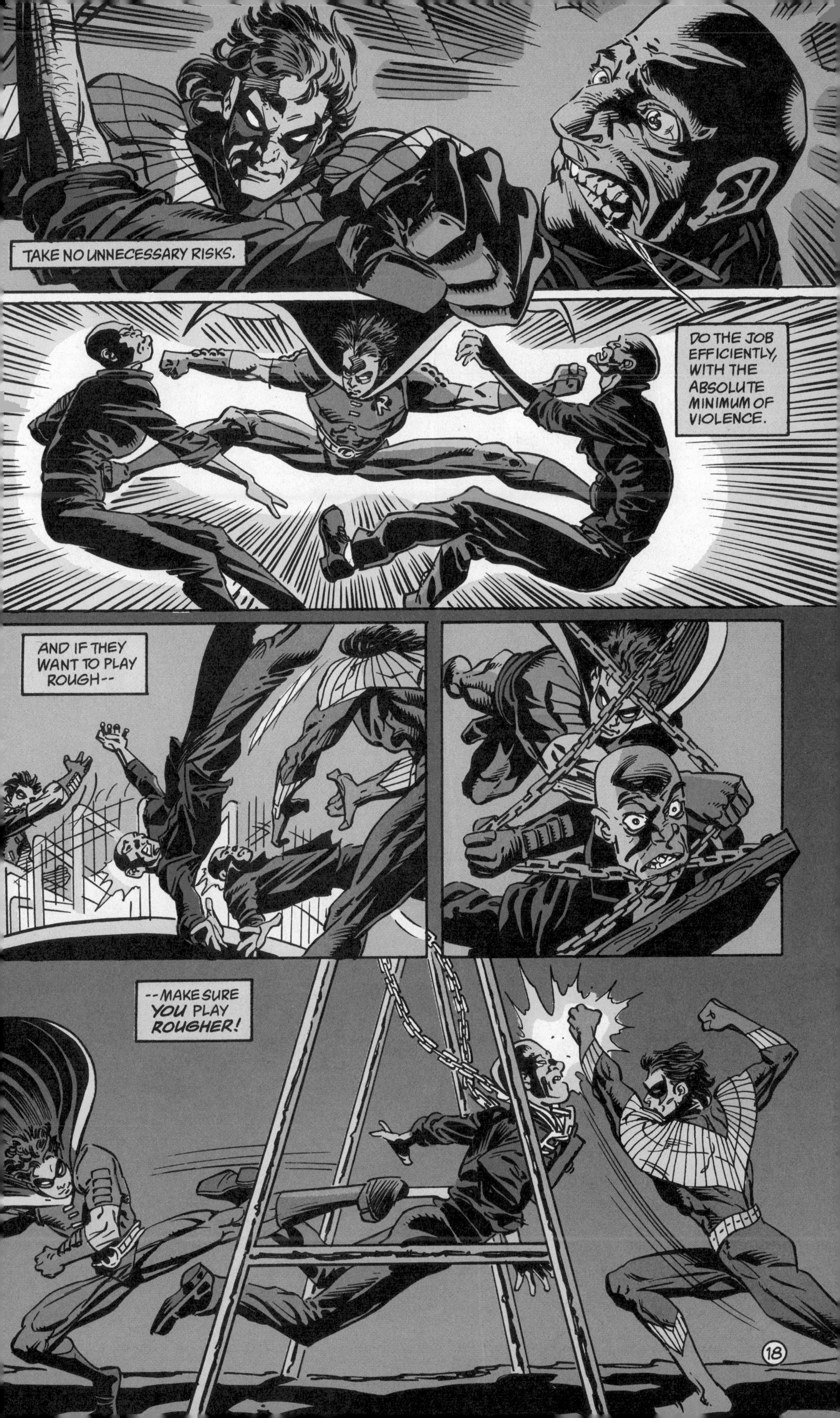
TAKE NO UNNECESSARY RISKS.
DO THE JOB EFFICIENTLY, WITH THE ABSOLUTE MINIMUM OF VIOLENCE.
AND IF THEY WANT TO PLAY ROUGH--
--MAKE SURE YOU PLAY ROUGHER!
18

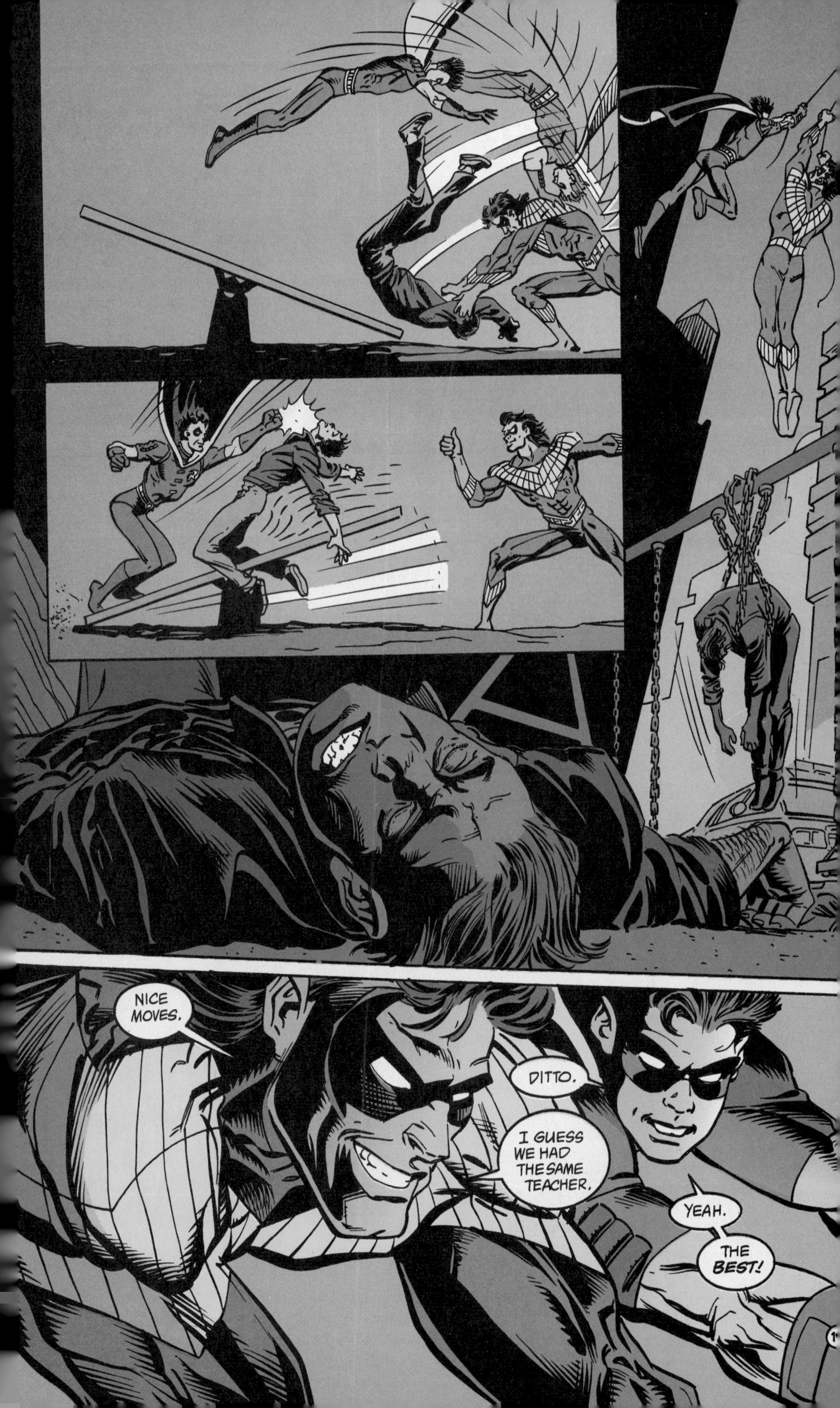
NICE MOVES.
DITTO.
I GUESS WE HAD THE SAME TEACHER.
YEAH.
THE BEST!

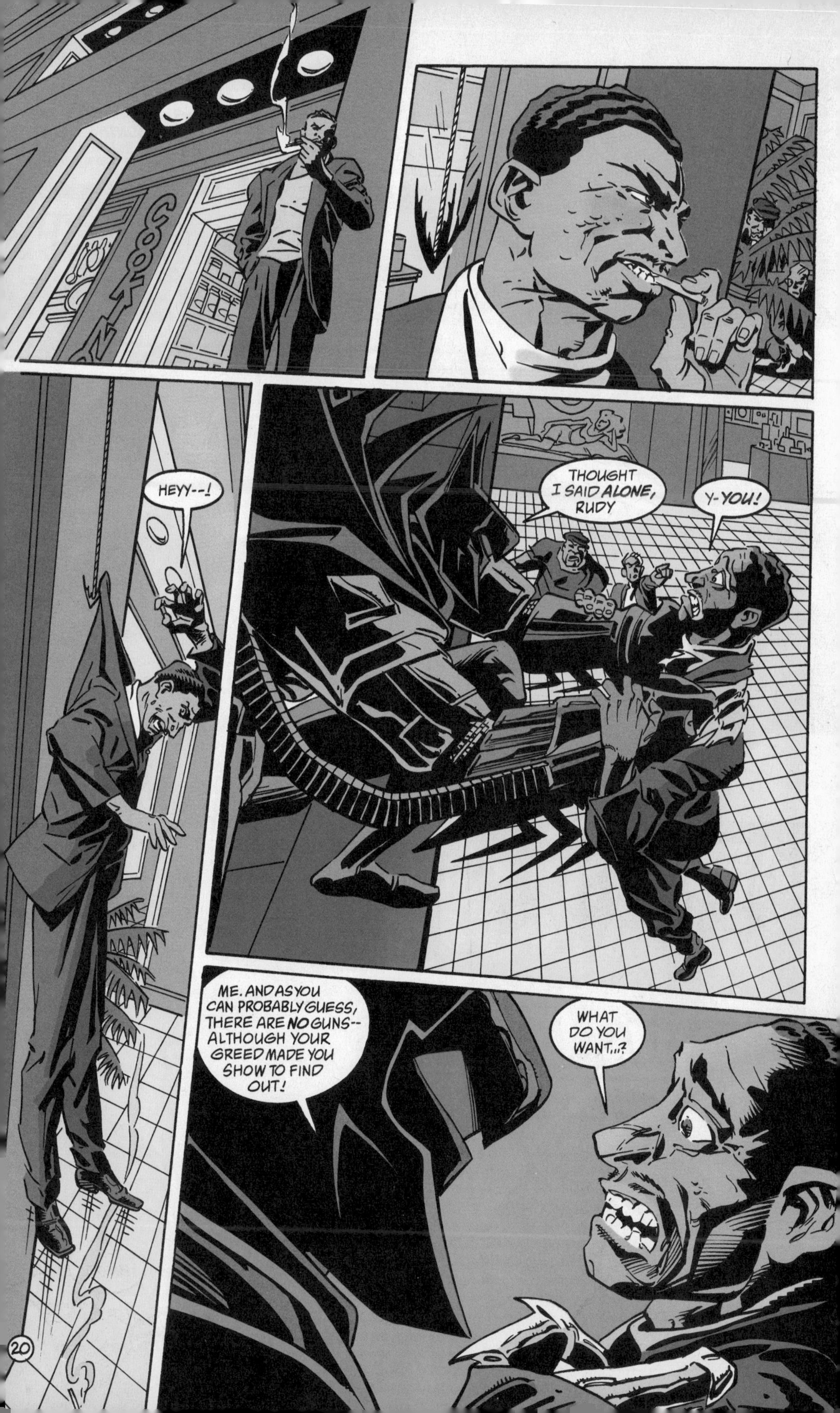

HEYY--!
THOUGHT I SAID ALONE, RUDY
Y-YOU!
ME. AND AS YOU CAN PROBABLY GUESS, THERE ARE NO GUNS-- ALTHOUGH YOUR GREED MADE YOU SHOW TO FIND OUT!
WHAT DO YOU WANT...?

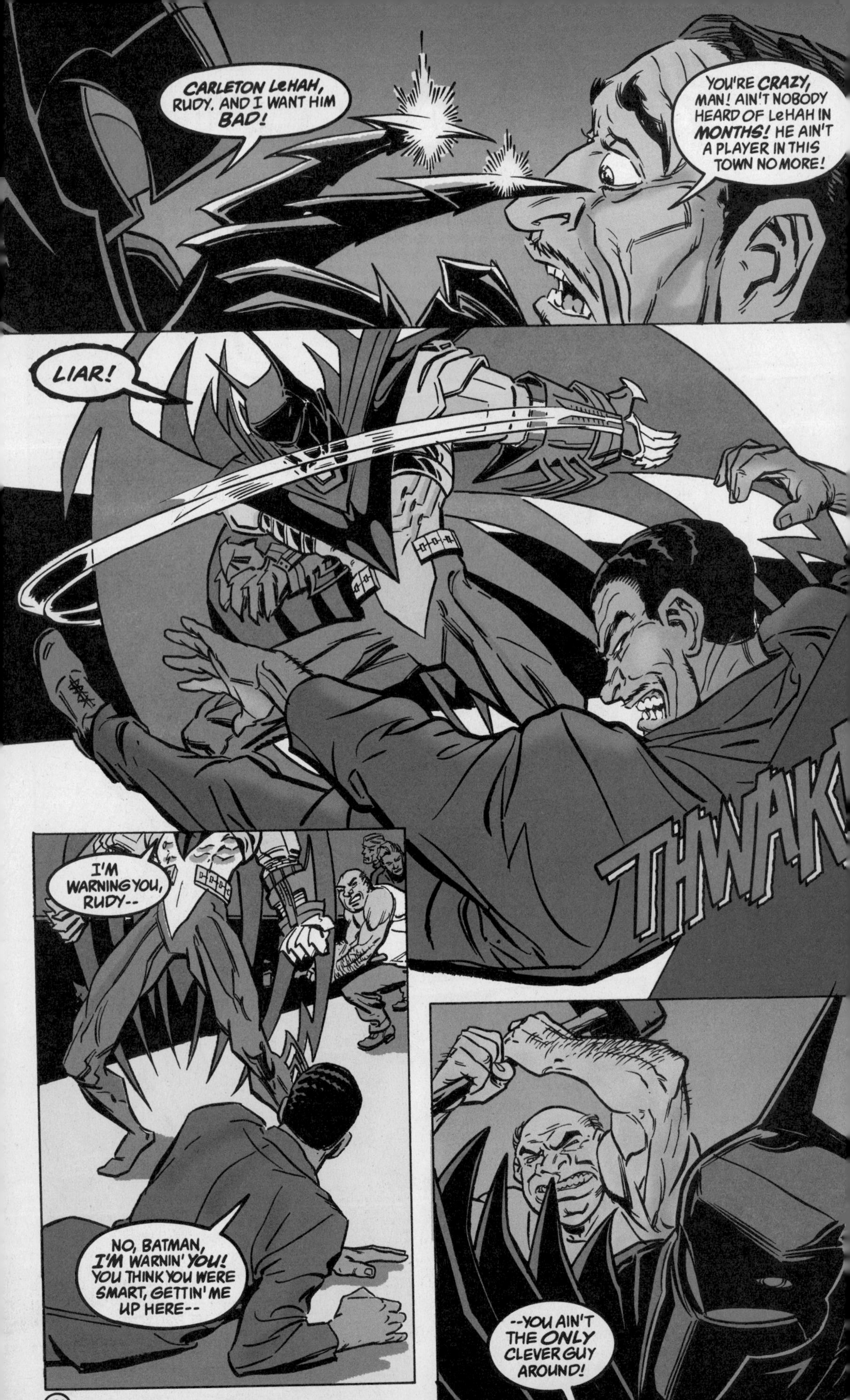
CARLETON LeHAH, RUDY. AND I WANT HIM BAD!
YOU'RE CRAZY, MAN! AIN'T NOBODY HEARD OF LeHAH IN MONTHS! HE AIN'T A PLAYER IN THIS TOWN NO MORE!
LIAR!
THWAK!
I'M WARNING YOU, RUDY--
NO, BATMAN, I'M WARNIN' YOU! YOU THINK YOU WERE SMART, GETTIN' ME UP HERE--
--YOU AIN'T THE ONLY CLEVER GUY AROUND!

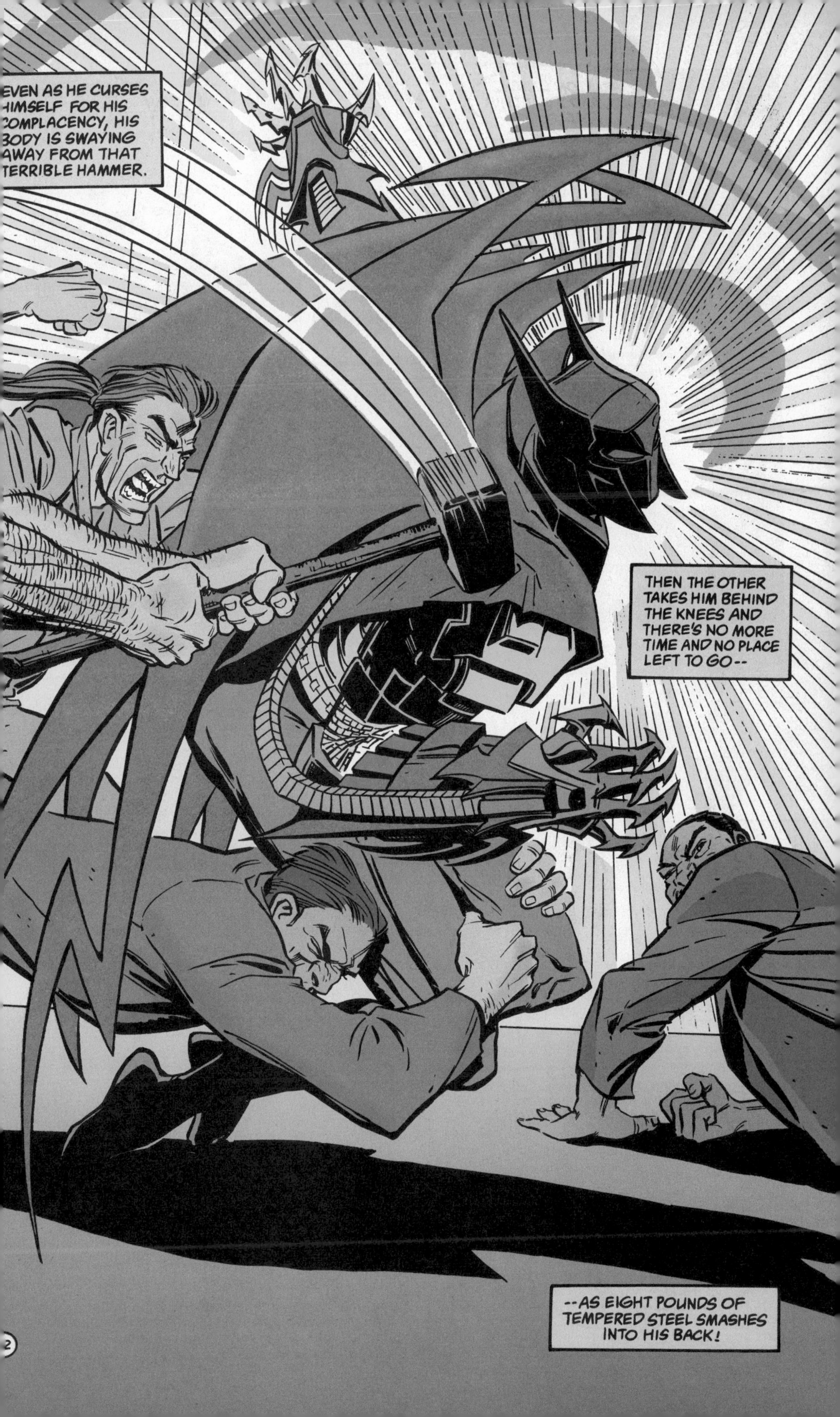
EVEN AS HE CURSES HIMSELF FOR HIS COMPLACENCY, HIS BODY IS SWAYING AWAY FROM THAT TERRIBLE HAMMER.
THEN THE OTHER TAKES HIM BEHIND THE KNEES AND THERE'S NO MORE TIME AND NO PLACE LEFT TO GO--
--AS EIGHT POUNDS OF TEMPERED STEEL SMASHES INTO HIS BACK!

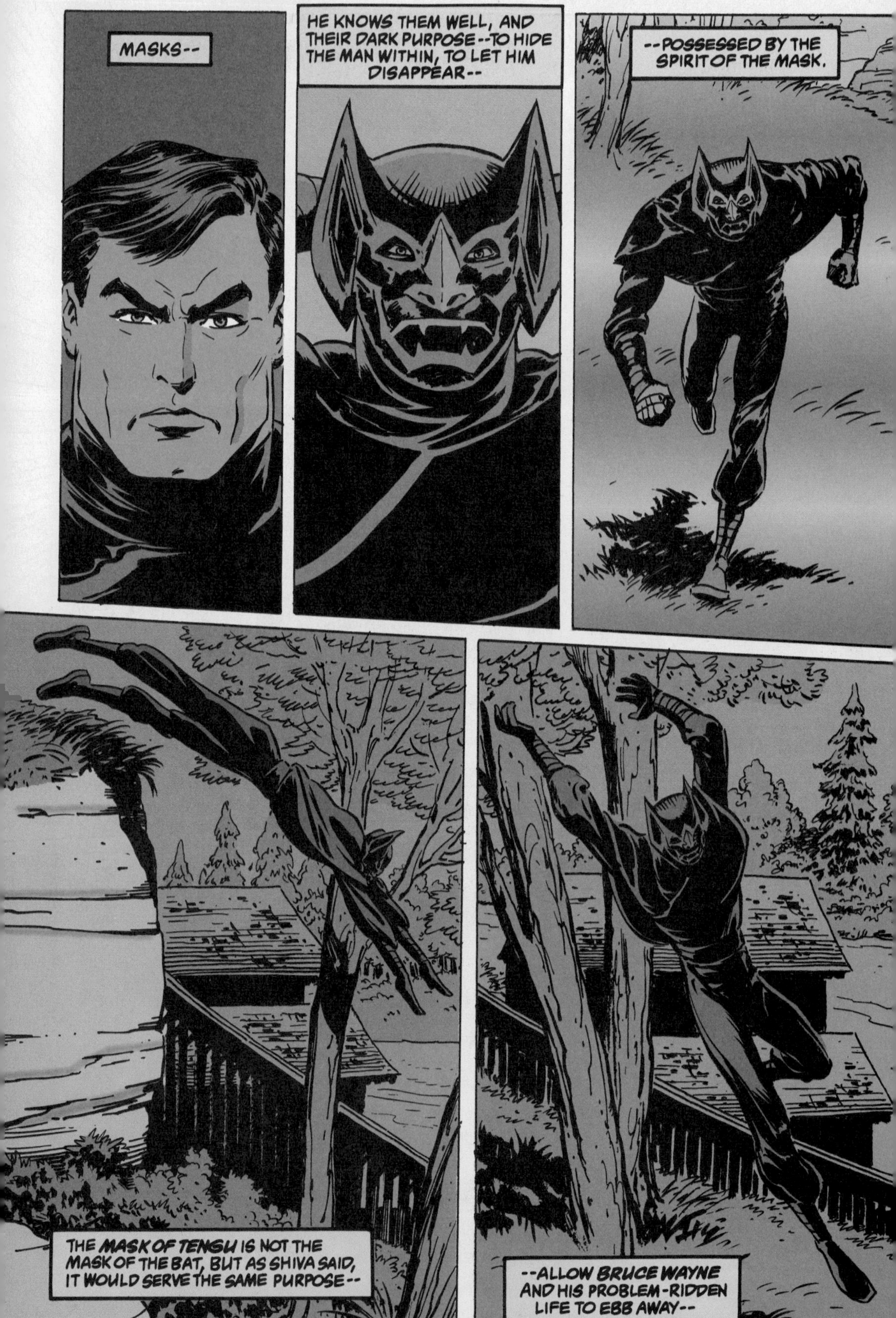
MASKS--
HE KNOWS THEM WELL, AND THEIR DARK PURPOSE--TO HIDE THE MAN WITHIN, TO LET HIM DISAPPEAR--
--POSSESSED BY THE SPIRIT OF THE MASK.
THE MASK OF TENGU IS NOT THE MASK OF THE BAT, BUT AS SHIVA SAID, IT WOULD SERVE THE SAME PURPOSE--
--ALLOW BRUCE WAYNE AND HIS PROBLEM-RIDDEN LIFE TO EBB AWAY--
23

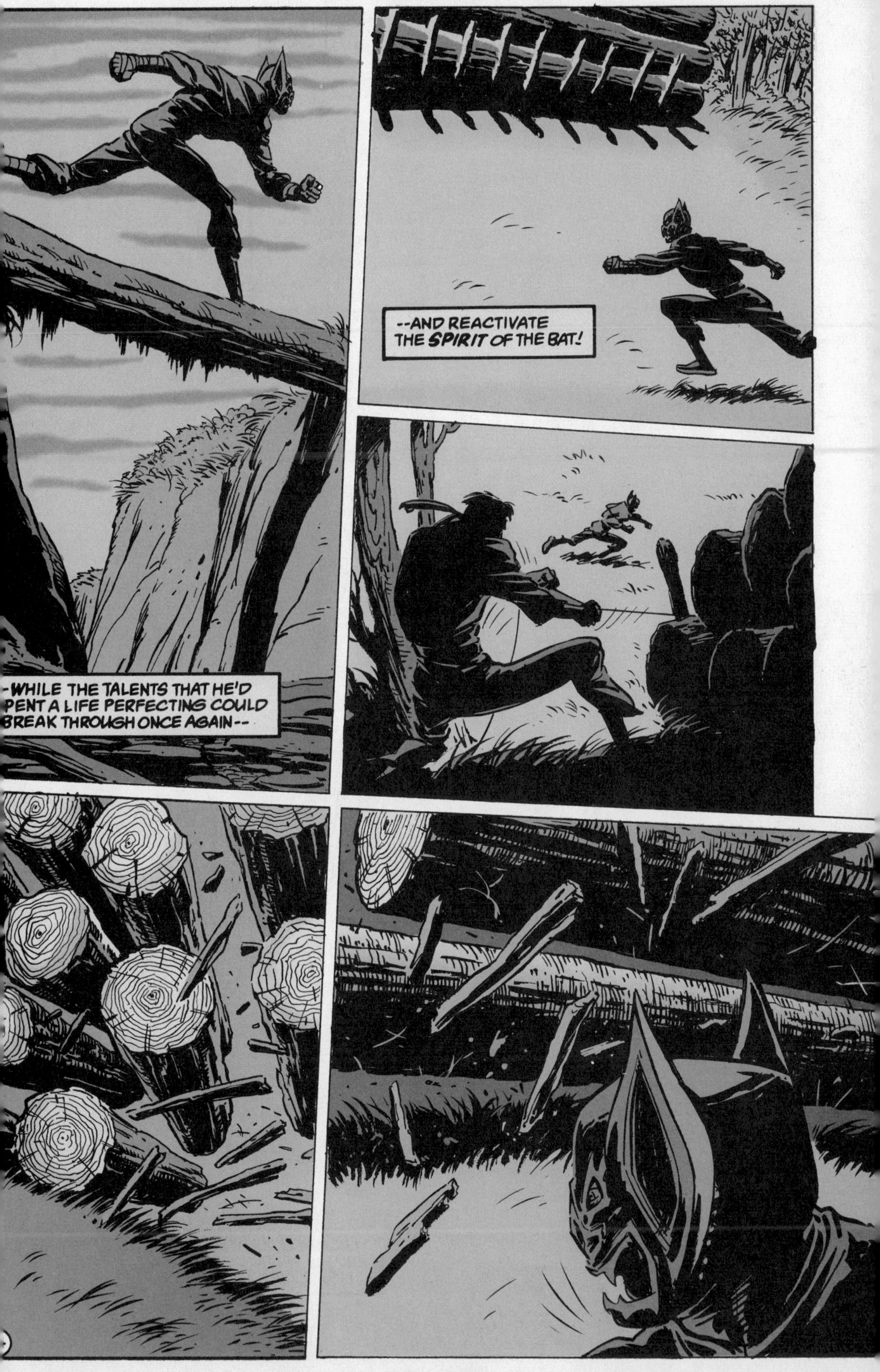
-WHILE THE TALENTS THAT HE'D
PENT A LIFE PERFECTING COULD
BREAK THROUGH ONCE AGAIN--
--AND REACTIVATE
THE SPIRIT OF THE BAT!

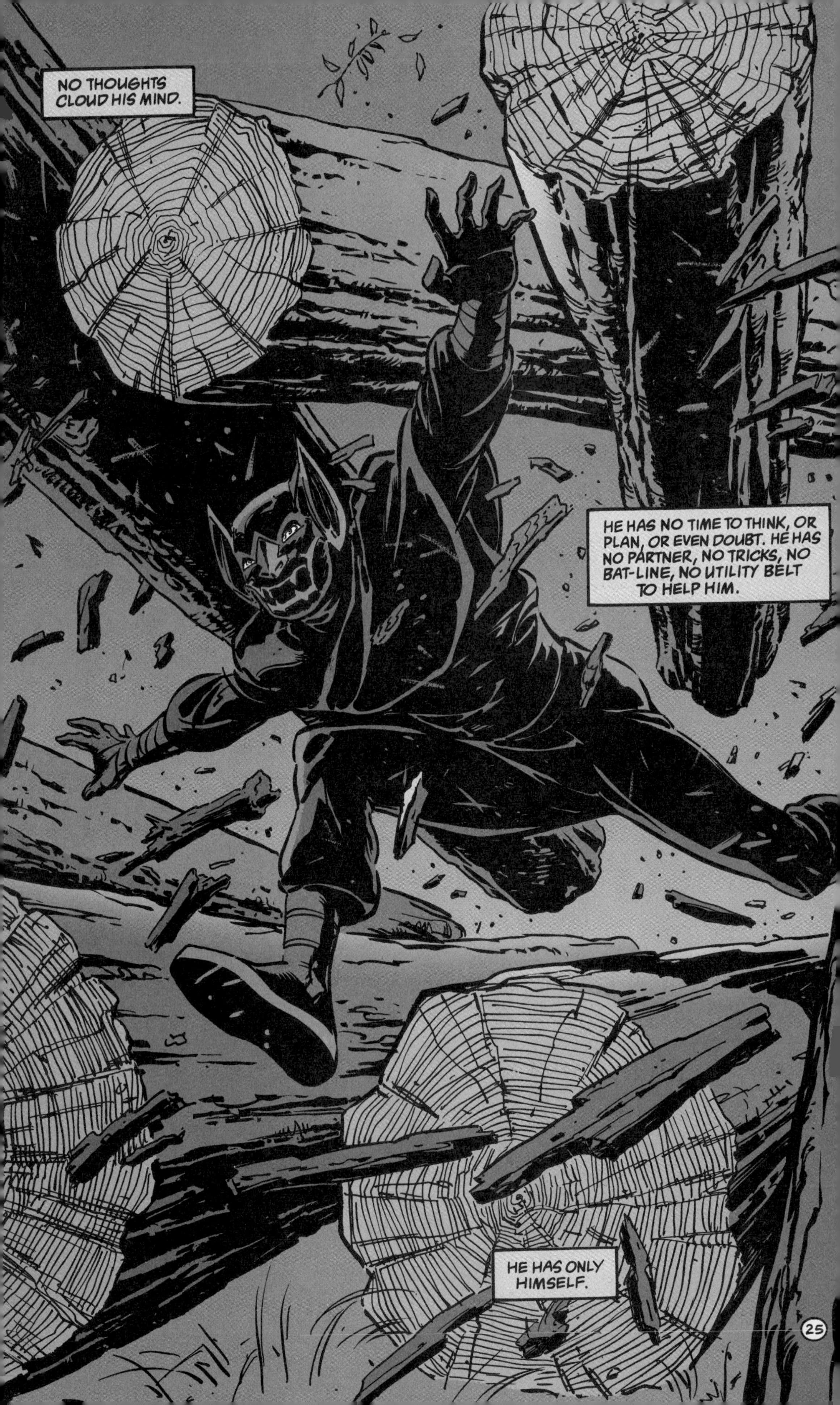
NO THOUGHTS CLOUD HIS MIND.
HE HAS NO TIME TO THINK, OR PLAN, OR EVEN DOUBT. HE HAS NO PARTNER, NO TRICKS, NO BAT-LINE, NO UTILITY BELT TO HELP HIM.
HE HAS ONLY HIMSELF.

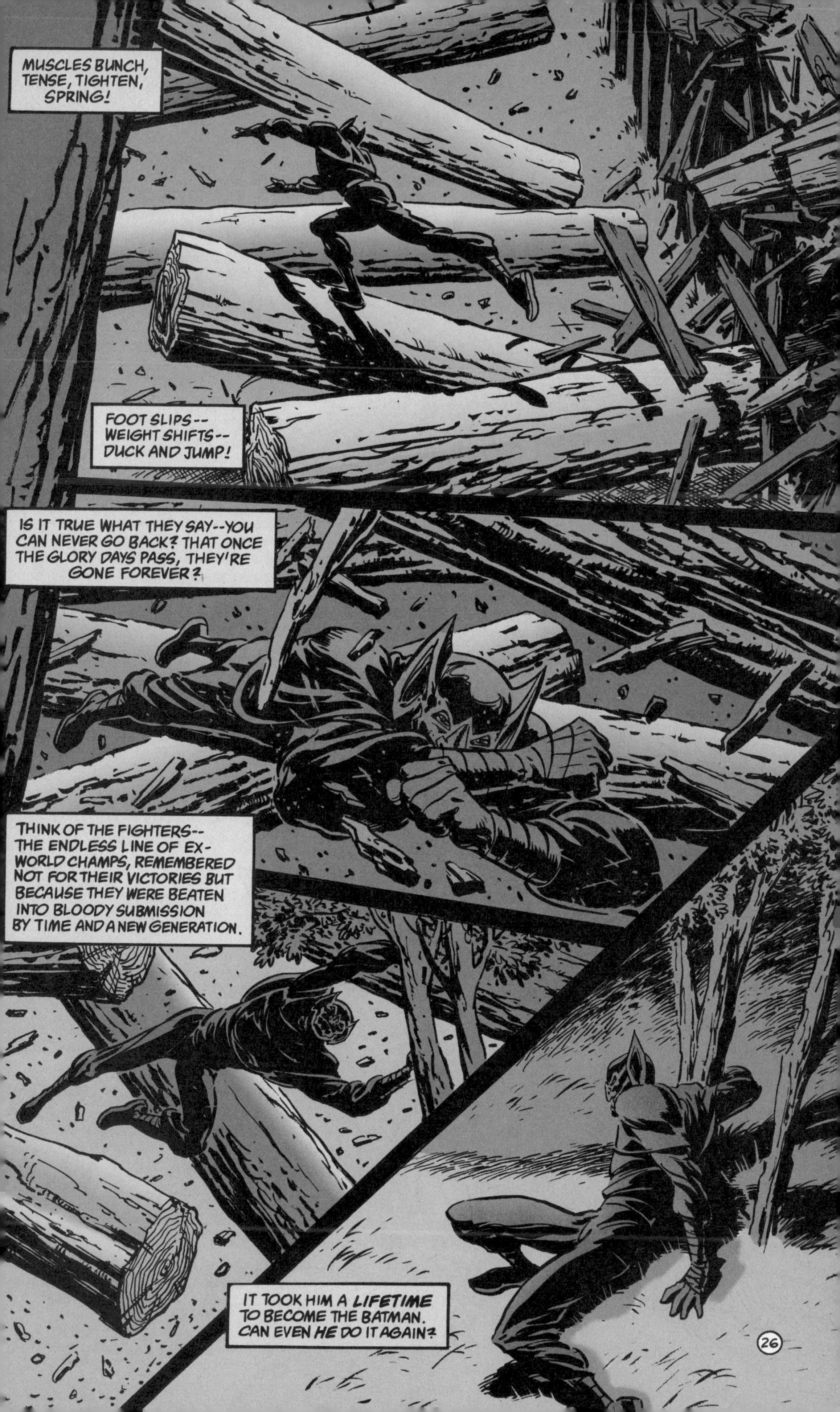
MUSCLES BUNCH, TENSE, TIGHTEN, SPRING!
FOOT SLIPS-- WEIGHT SHIFTS-- DUCK AND JUMP!
IS IT TRUE WHAT THEY SAY--YOU CAN NEVER GO BACK? THAT ONCE THE GLORY DAYS PASS, THEY'RE GONE FOREVER?
THINK OF THE FIGHTERS-- THE ENDLESS LINE OF EX-WORLD CHAMPS, REMEMBERED NOT FOR THEIR VICTORIES BUT BECAUSE THEY WERE BEATEN INTO BLOODY SUBMISSION BY TIME AND A NEW GENERATION.
IT TOOK HIM A LIFETIME TO BECOME THE BATMAN. CAN EVEN HE DO IT AGAIN?
26

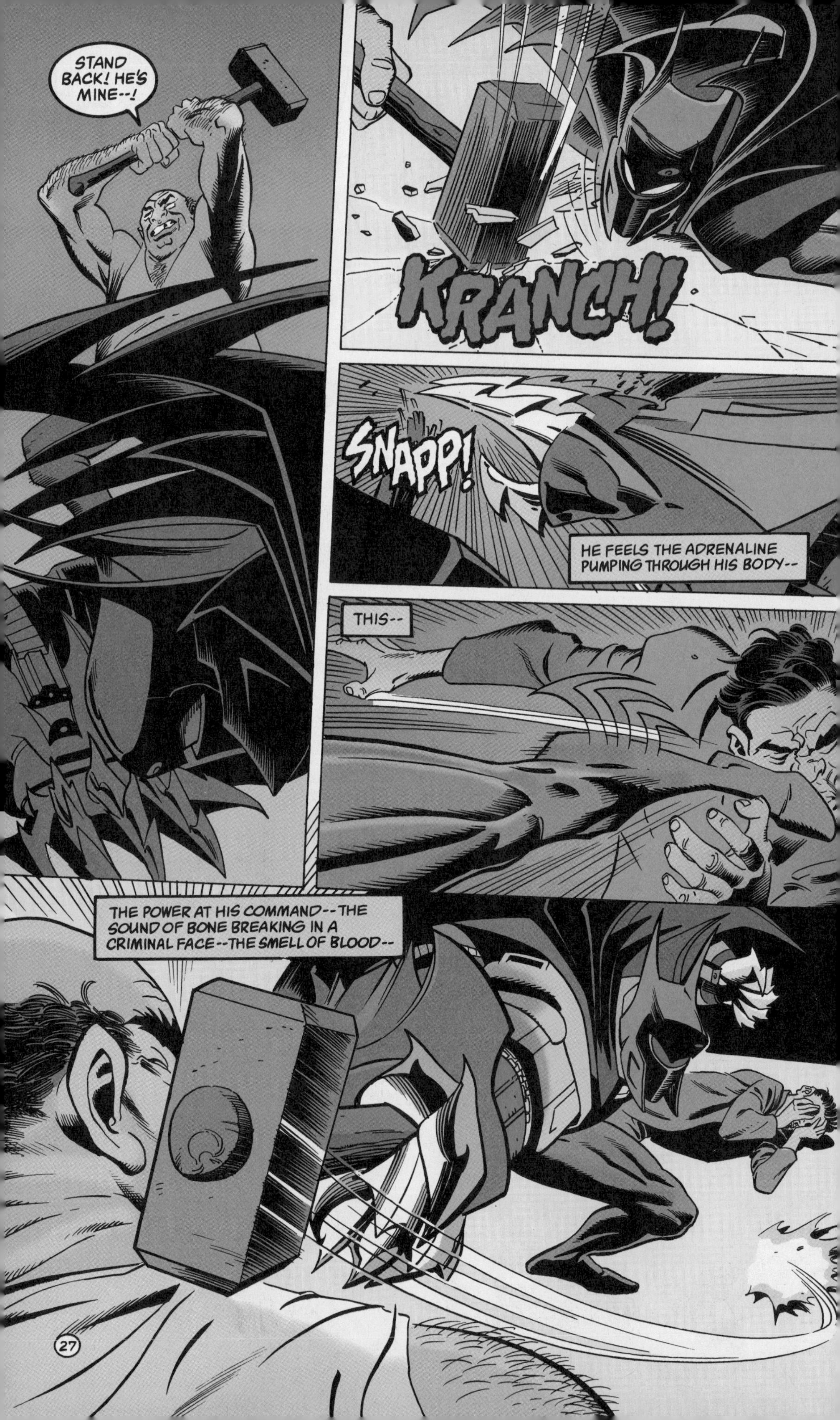

STAND BACK! HE'S MINE--!
KRANCH!
SNAPP!
HE FEELS THE ADRENALINE PUMPING THROUGH HIS BODY--
THIS--
THE POWER AT HIS COMMAND--THE SOUND OF BONE BREAKING IN A CRIMINAL FACE--THE SMELL OF BLOOD--

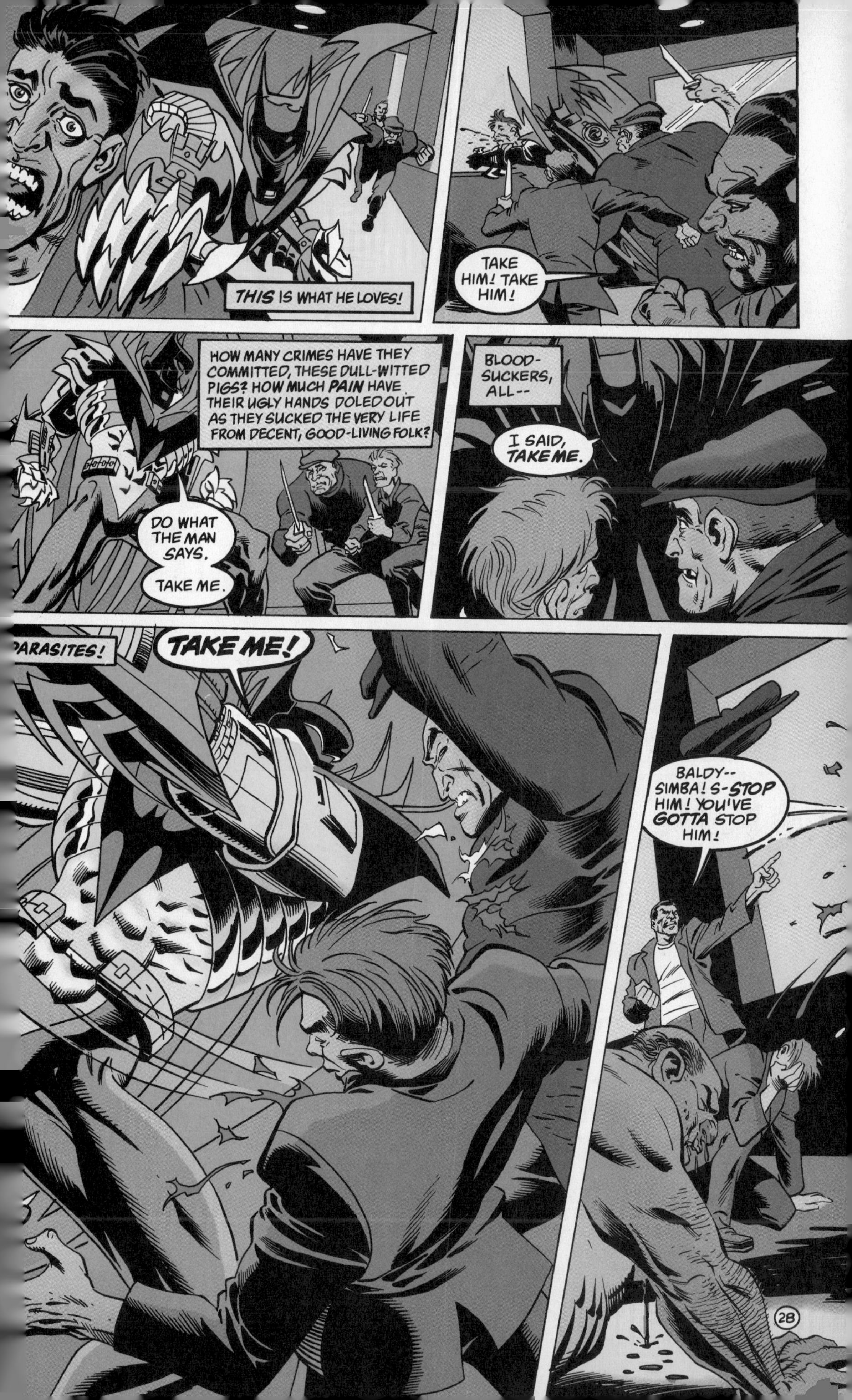
THIS IS WHAT HE LOVES!
TAKE HIM! TAKE HIM!
HOW MANY CRIMES HAVE THEY COMMITTED, THESE DULL-WITTED PIGS? HOW MUCH PAIN HAVE THEIR UGLY HANDS DOLED OUT AS THEY SUCKED THE VERY LIFE FROM DECENT, GOOD-LIVING FOLK?
DO WHAT THE MAN SAYS.
TAKE ME.
BLOOD-SUCKERS, ALL--
I SAID, TAKE ME.
PARASITES!
TAKE ME!
BALDY-- SIMBA! S-STOP HIM! YOU'VE GOTTA STOP HIM!
28

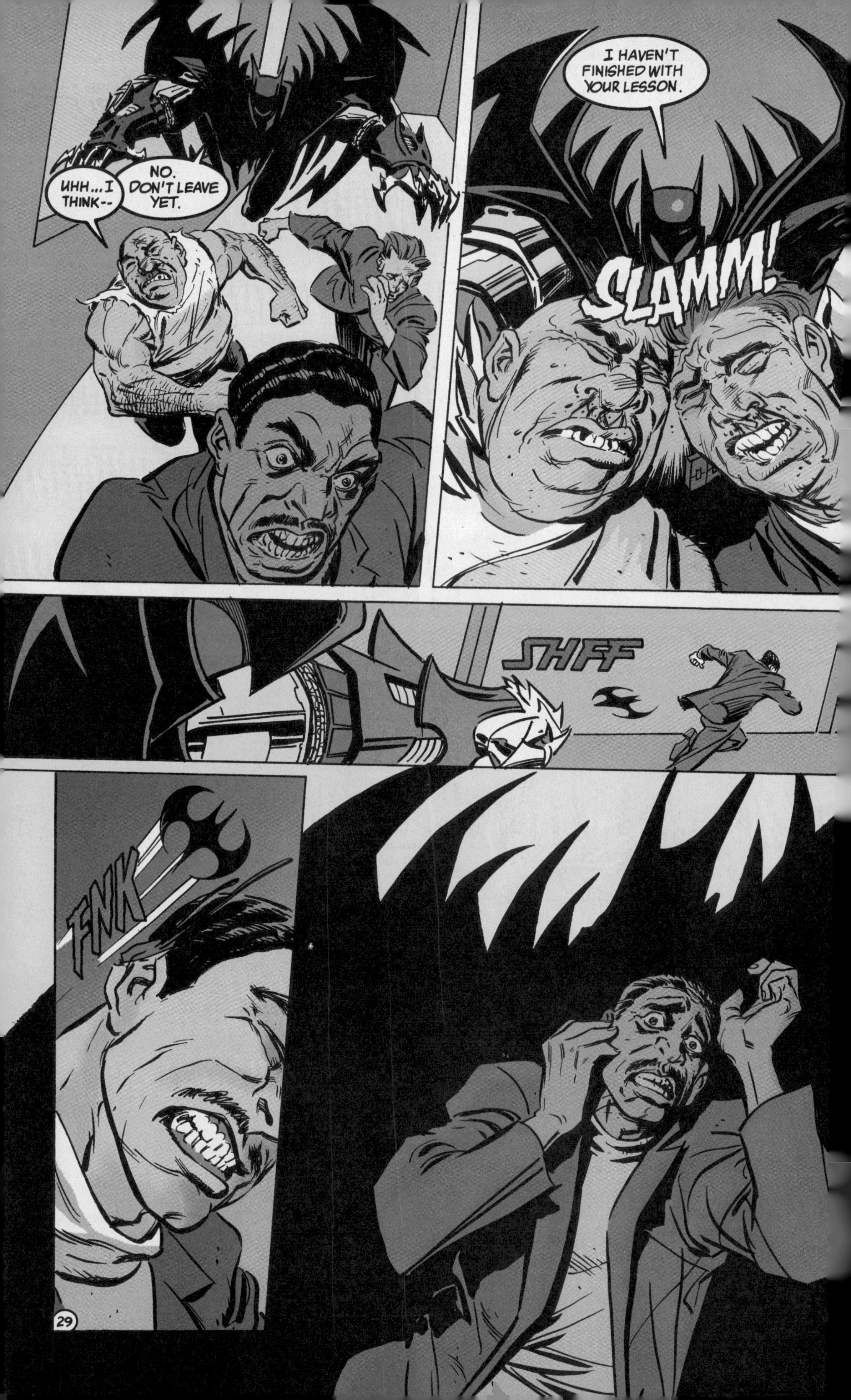
UHH... I THINK--
NO. DON'T LEAVE YET.
I HAVEN'T FINISHED WITH YOUR LESSON.
SLAMM!
SHFF
FNK
29

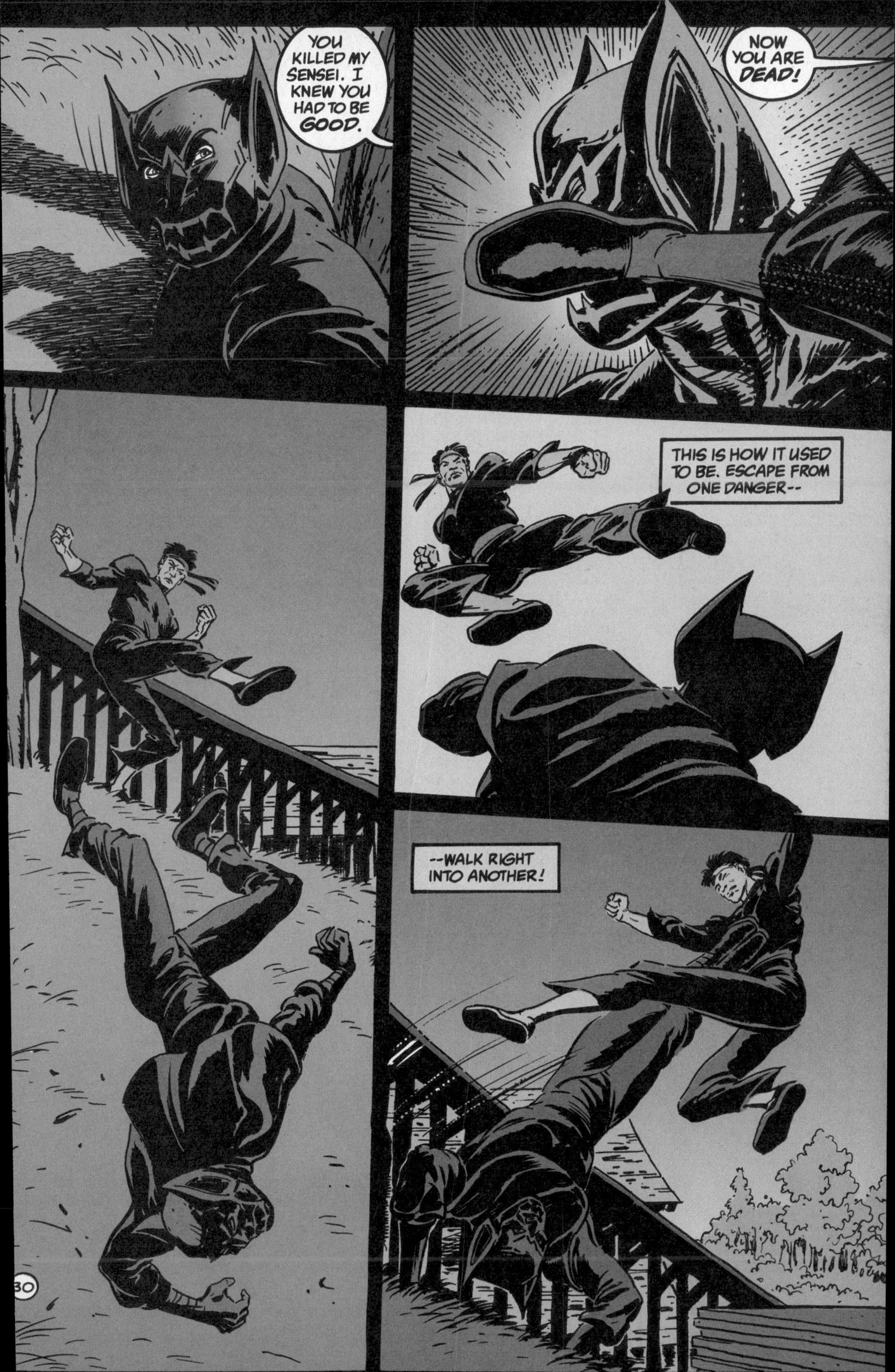
YOU KILLED MY SENSEI. I KNEW YOU HAD TO BE GOOD.
NOW YOU ARE DEAD!
THIS IS HOW IT USED TO BE. ESCAPE FROM ONE DANGER--
--WALK RIGHT INTO ANOTHER!

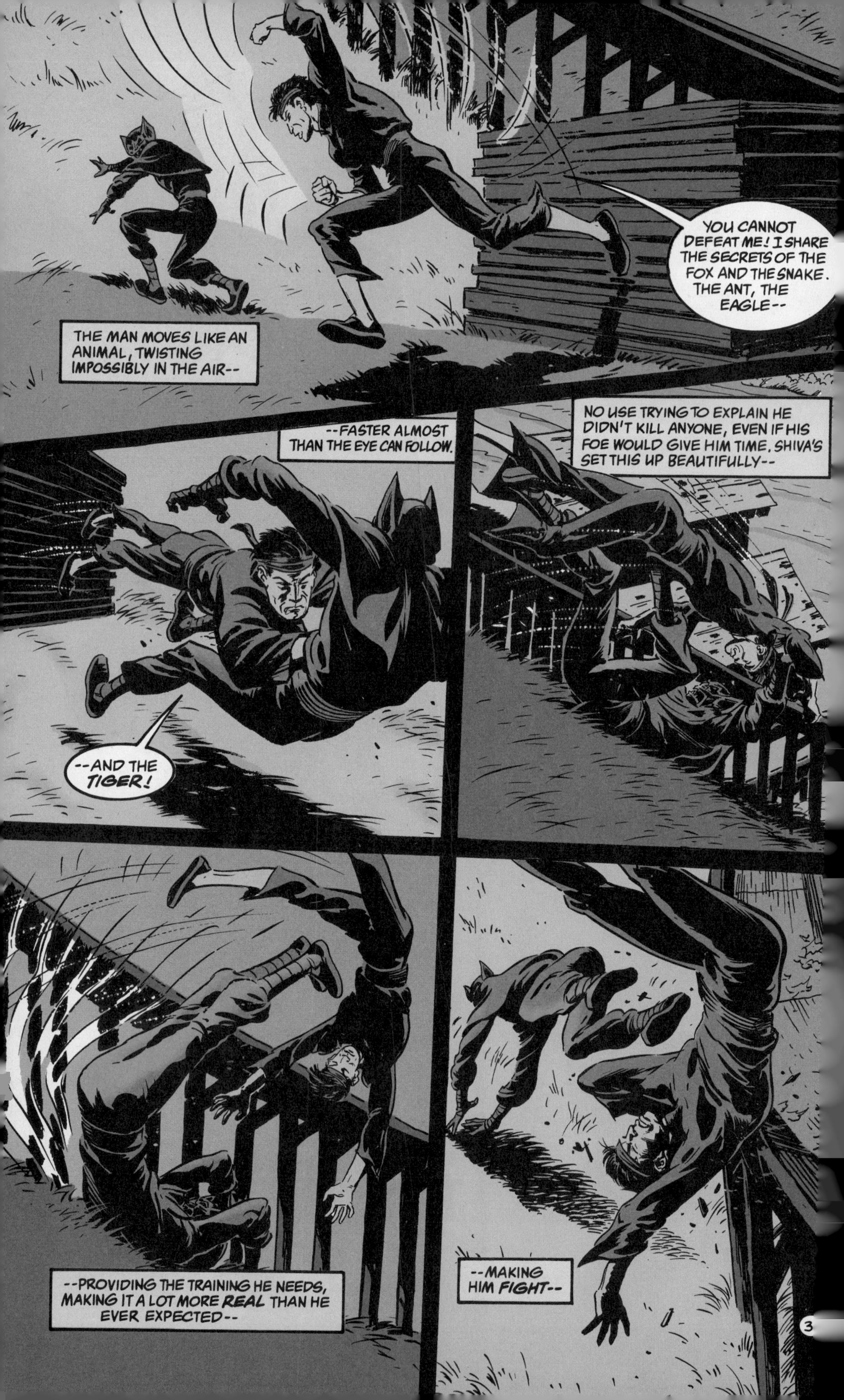
THE MAN MOVES LIKE AN ANIMAL, TWISTING IMPOSSIBLY IN THE AIR--
YOU CANNOT DEFEAT ME! I SHARE THE SECRETS OF THE FOX AND THE SNAKE. THE ANT, THE EAGLE--
--FASTER ALMOST THAN THE EYE CAN FOLLOW.
--AND THE TIGER!
NO USE TRYING TO EXPLAIN HE DIDN'T KILL ANYONE, EVEN IF HIS FOE WOULD GIVE HIM TIME. SHIVA'S SET THIS UP BEAUTIFULLY--
--PROVIDING THE TRAINING HE NEEDS, MAKING IT A LOT MORE REAL THAN HE EVER EXPECTED--
--MAKING HIM FIGHT--

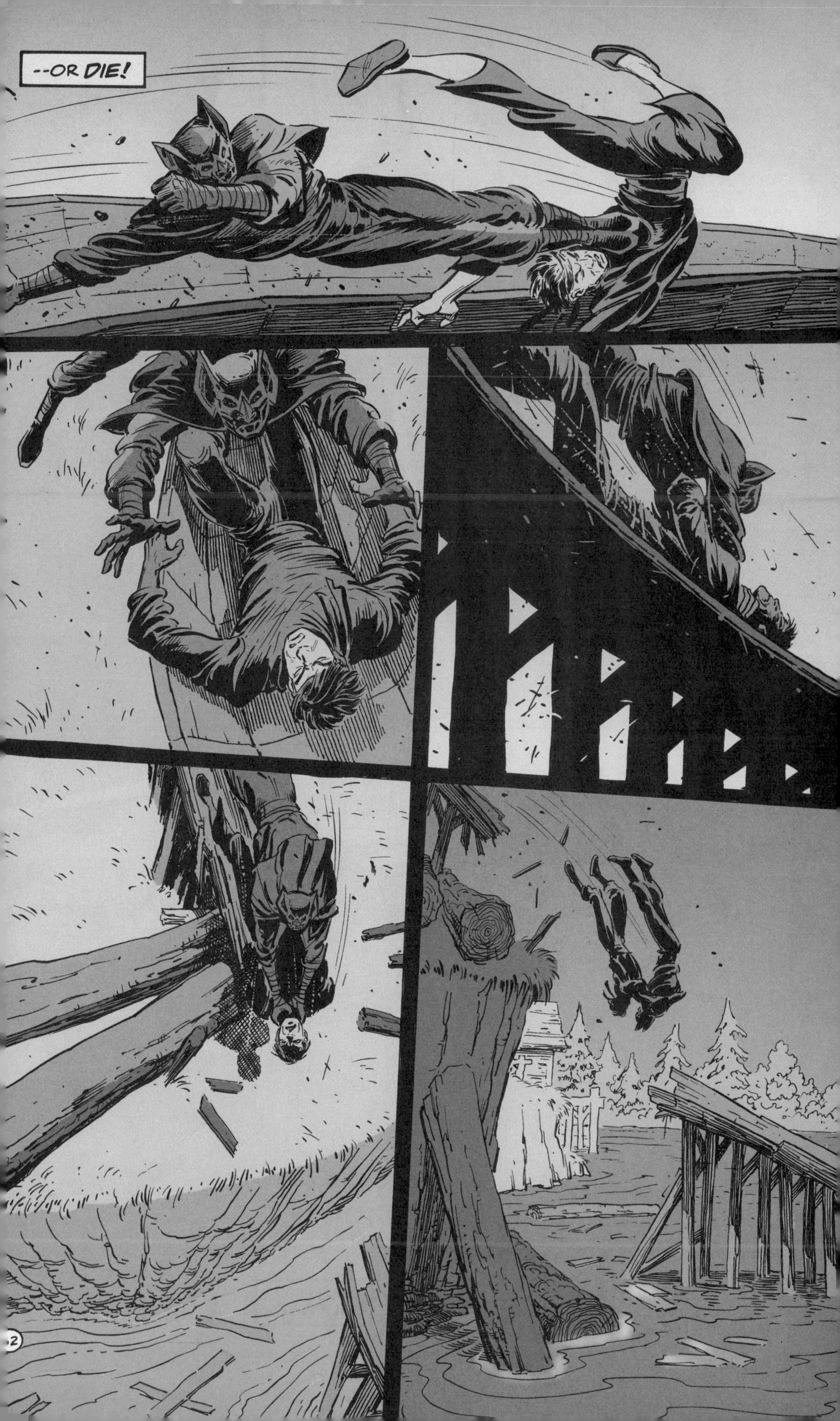
--OR DIE!

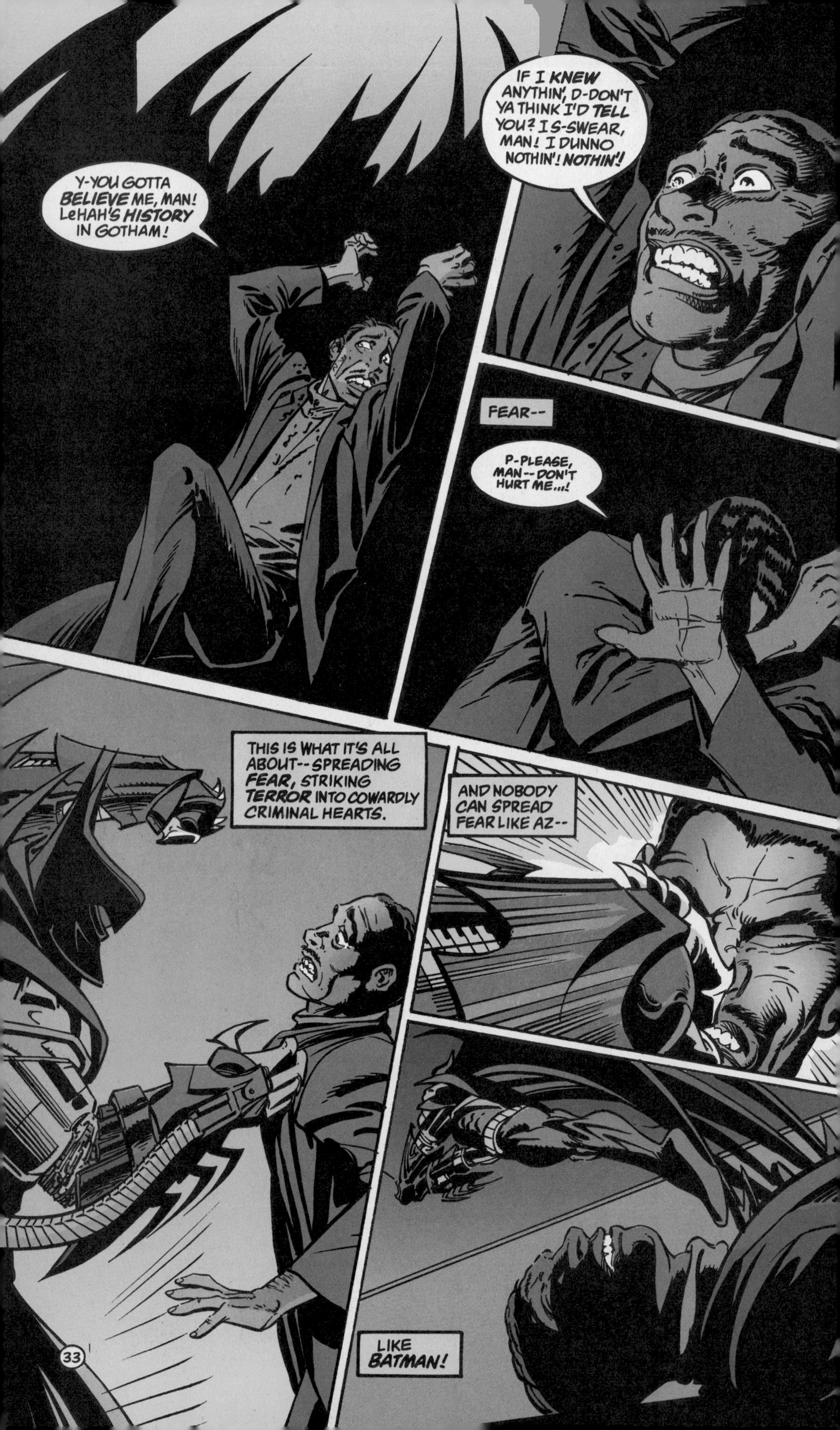

Y-YOU GOTTA BELIEVE ME, MAN! LeHAH'S HISTORY IN GOTHAM!
IF I KNEW ANYTHIN', D-DON'T YA THINK I'D TELL YOU? I-S-SWEAR, MAN! I DUNNO NOTHIN'! NOTHIN'!
FEAR--
P-PLEASE, MAN--DON'T HURT ME...!
THIS IS WHAT IT'S ALL ABOUT--SPREADING FEAR, STRIKING TERROR INTO COWARDLY CRIMINAL HEARTS.
AND NOBODY CAN SPREAD FEAR LIKE AZ--
LIKE BATMAN!

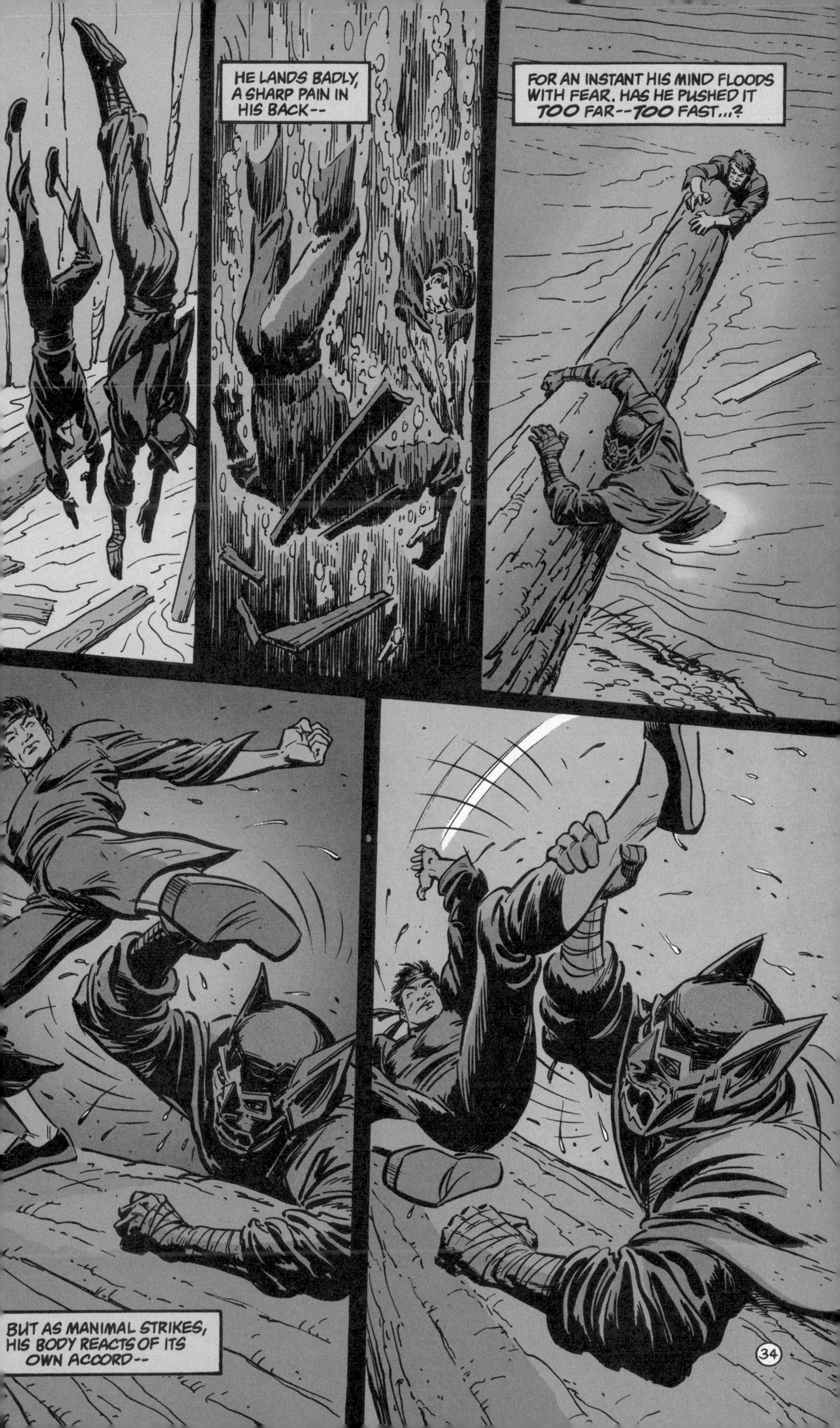
HE LANDS BADLY, A SHARP PAIN IN HIS BACK--
FOR AN INSTANT HIS MIND FLOODS WITH FEAR. HAS HE PUSHED IT TOO FAR--TOO FAST...?
BUT AS MANIMAL STRIKES, HIS BODY REACTS OF ITS OWN ACCORD--

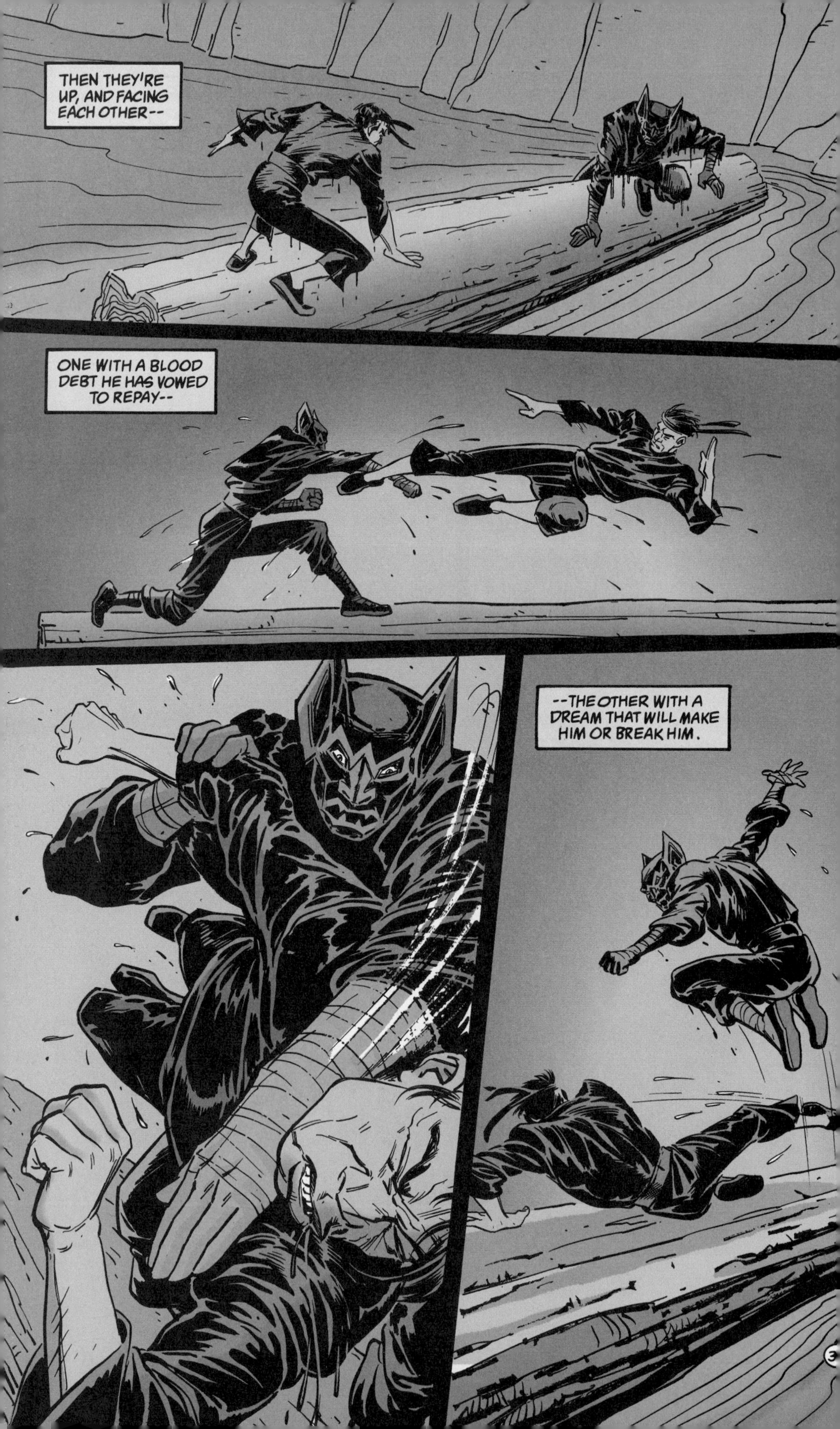
THEN THEY'RE UP, AND FACING EACH OTHER--
ONE WITH A BLOOD DEBT HE HAS VOWED TO REPAY--
--THE OTHER WITH A DREAM THAT WILL MAKE HIM OR BREAK HIM.

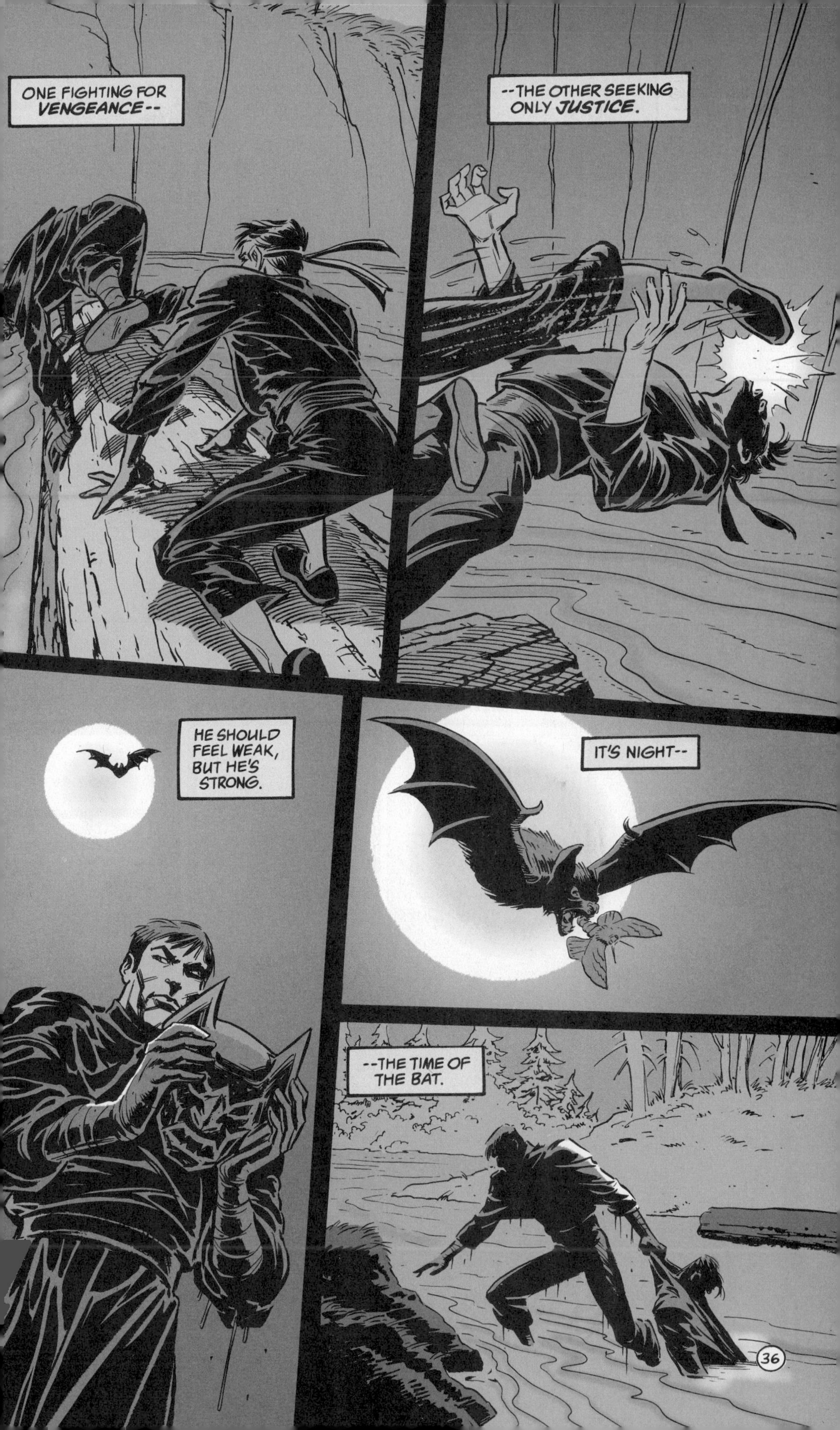
ONE FIGHTING FOR VENGEANCE--
--THE OTHER SEEKING ONLY JUSTICE.
HE SHOULD FEEL WEAK, BUT HE'S STRONG.
IT'S NIGHT--
--THE TIME OF THE BAT.
36

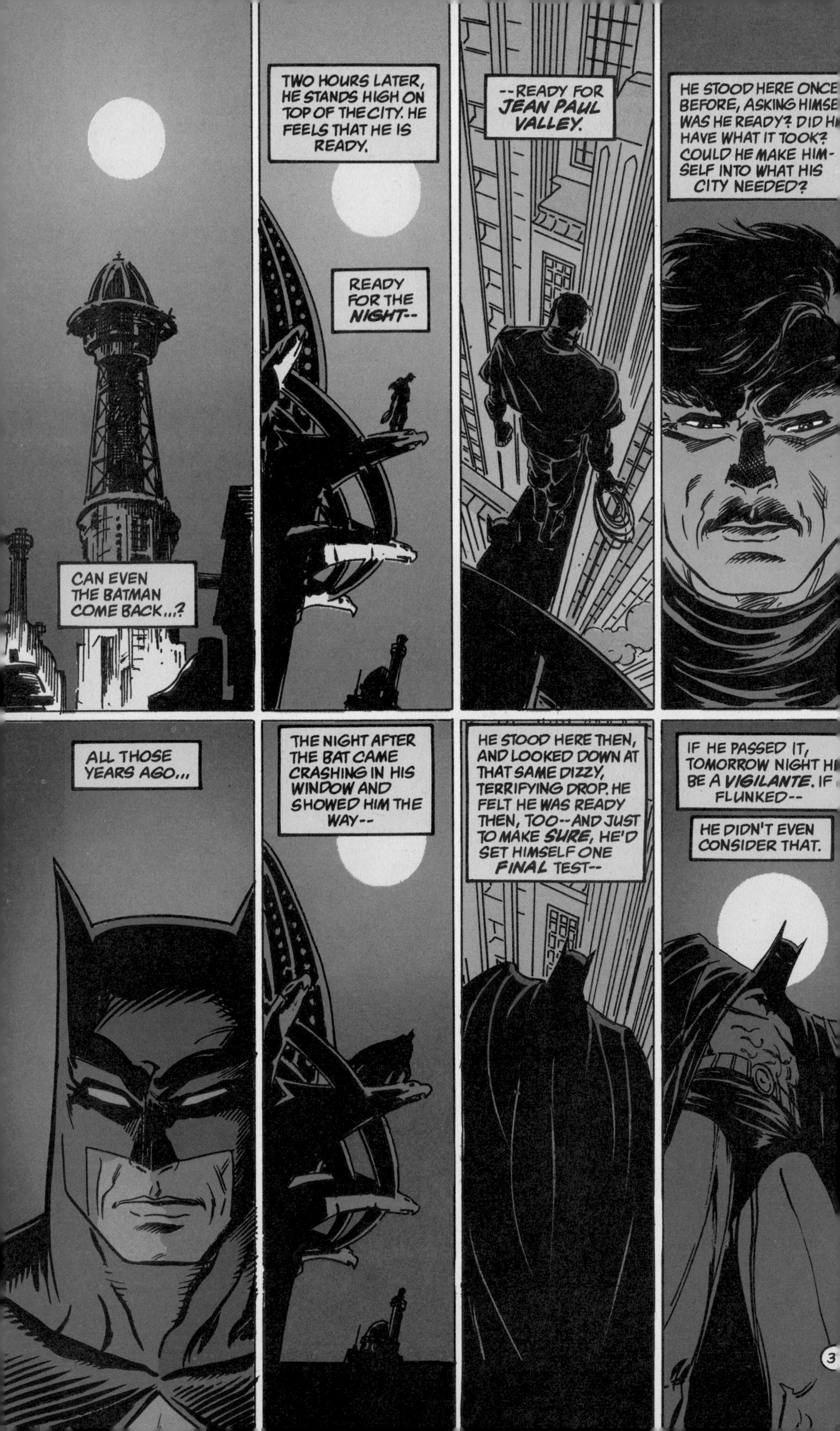

CAN EVEN THE BATMAN COME BACK...?
TWO HOURS LATER, HE STANDS HIGH ON TOP OF THE CITY. HE FEELS THAT HE IS READY.
READY FOR THE *NIGHT*--
--READY FOR *JEAN PAUL VALLEY.*
HE STOOD HERE ONCE BEFORE, ASKING HIMSE WAS HE READY? DID H HAVE WHAT IT TOOK? COULD HE MAKE HIM-SELF INTO WHAT HIS CITY NEEDED?
ALL THOSE YEARS AGO...
THE NIGHT AFTER THE BAT CAME CRASHING IN HIS WINDOW AND SHOWED HIM THE WAY--
HE STOOD HERE THEN, AND LOOKED DOWN AT THAT SAME DIZZY, TERRIFYING DROP. HE FELT HE WAS READY THEN, TOO--AND JUST TO MAKE *SURE*, HE'D SET HIMSELF ONE *FINAL* TEST--
IF HE PASSED IT, TOMORROW NIGHT H BE A *VIGILANTE*. IF FLUNKED--
HE DIDN'T EVEN CONSIDER THAT.

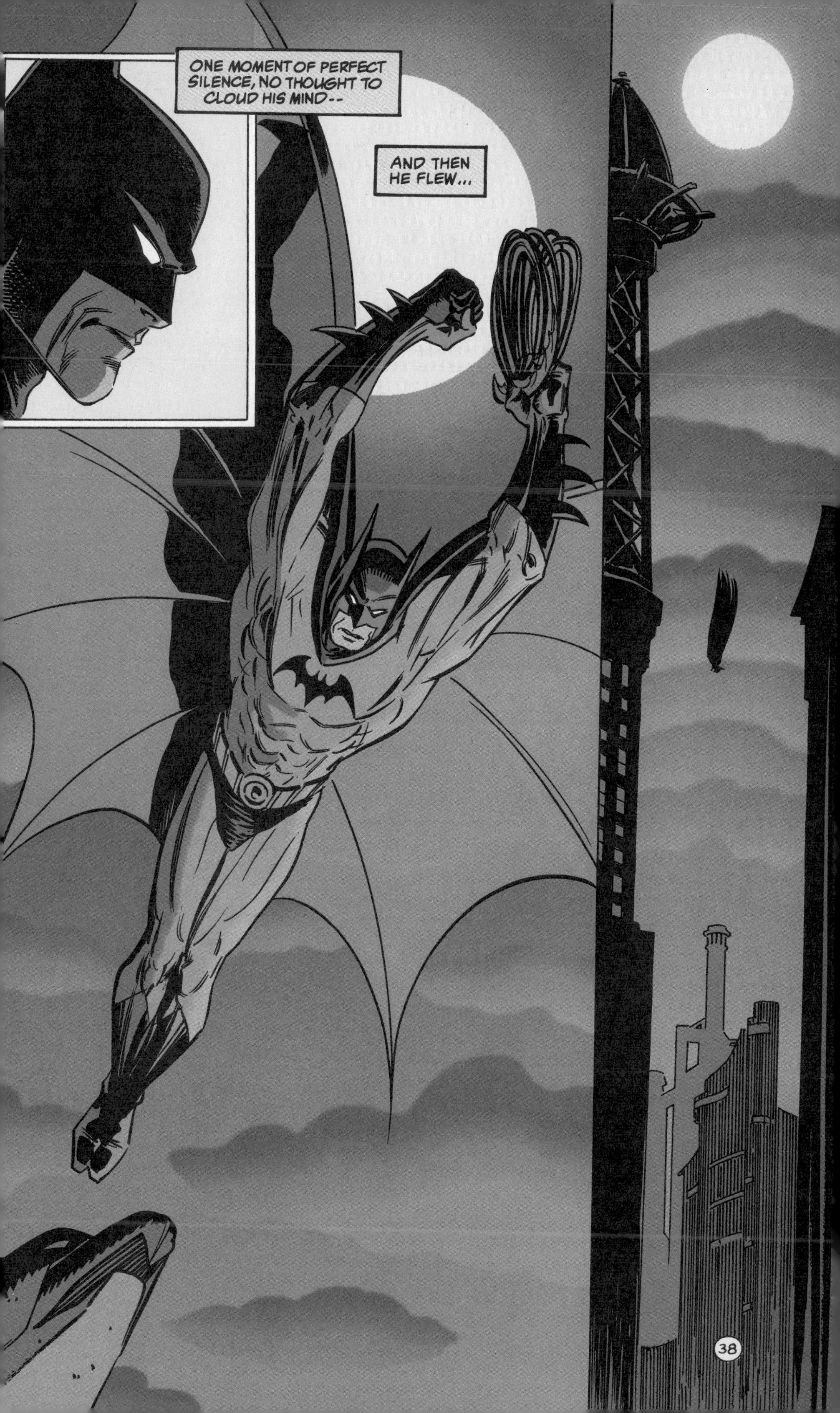
ONE MOMENT OF PERFECT SILENCE, NO THOUGHT TO CLOUD HIS MIND--
AND THEN HE FLEW...

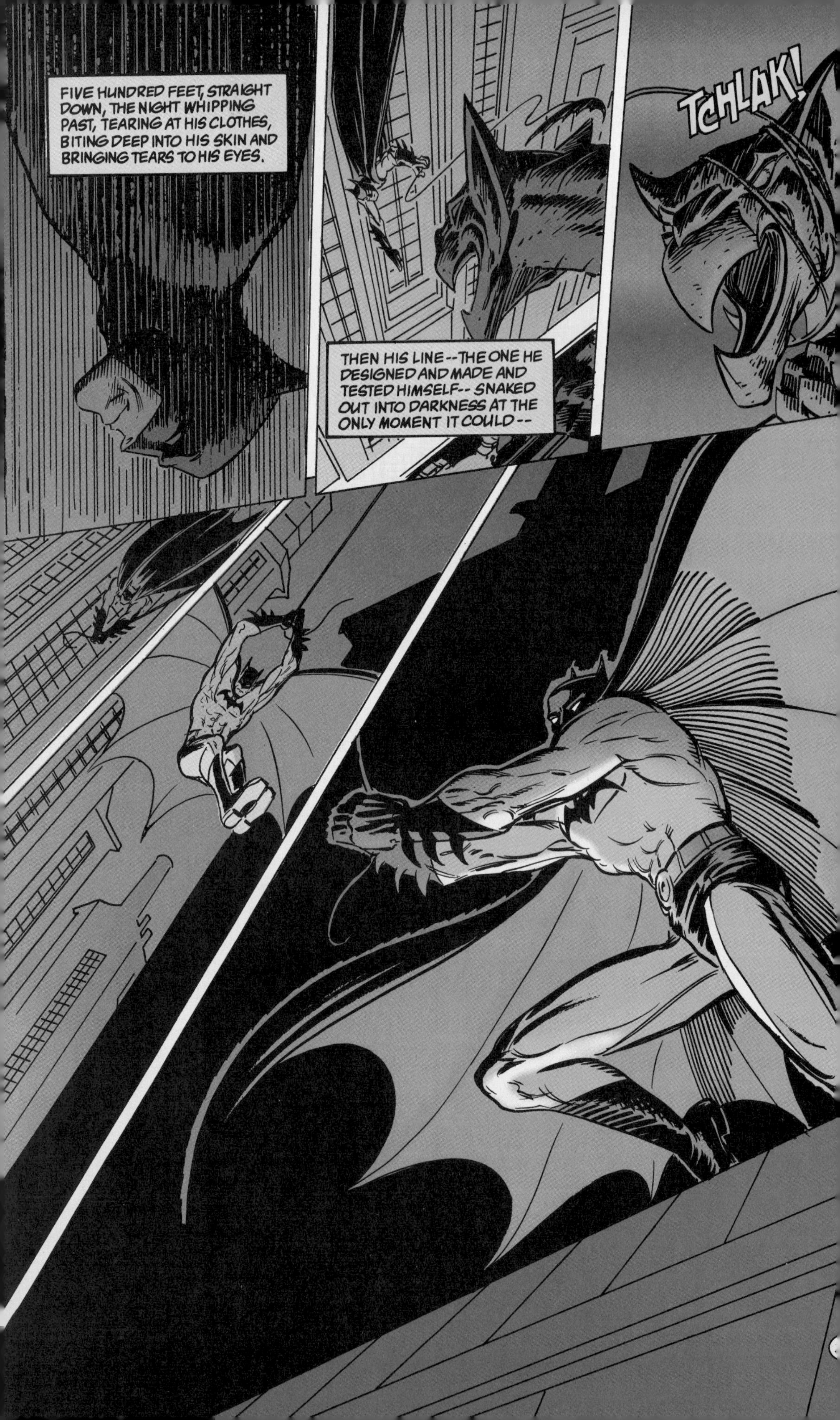
FIVE HUNDRED FEET, STRAIGHT DOWN, THE NIGHT WHIPPING PAST, TEARING AT HIS CLOTHES, BITING DEEP INTO HIS SKIN AND BRINGING TEARS TO HIS EYES.
THEN HIS LINE--THE ONE HE DESIGNED AND MADE AND TESTED HIMSELF-- SNAKED OUT INTO DARKNESS AT THE ONLY MOMENT IT COULD--
TCHLAK!

TILL THEN, IT HAD ALL BEEN A GAME.

FROM TONIGHT, THE GAME GOT SERIOUS!

ALL THOSE YEARS AGO...

AND HE STANDS HERE NOW, FACING THAT SAME FINAL TEST. HE REMEMBERS EXACTLY WHAT IT NEEDS, BUT EVEN THOUGH HE THINKS HE'S READY--

--SOMETHING IN HIM, OLDER AND WISER, TELLS HIM NO.

NOT YET.

CONTINUED IN KNIGHTS END PART 3
TOO MANY NINJAS

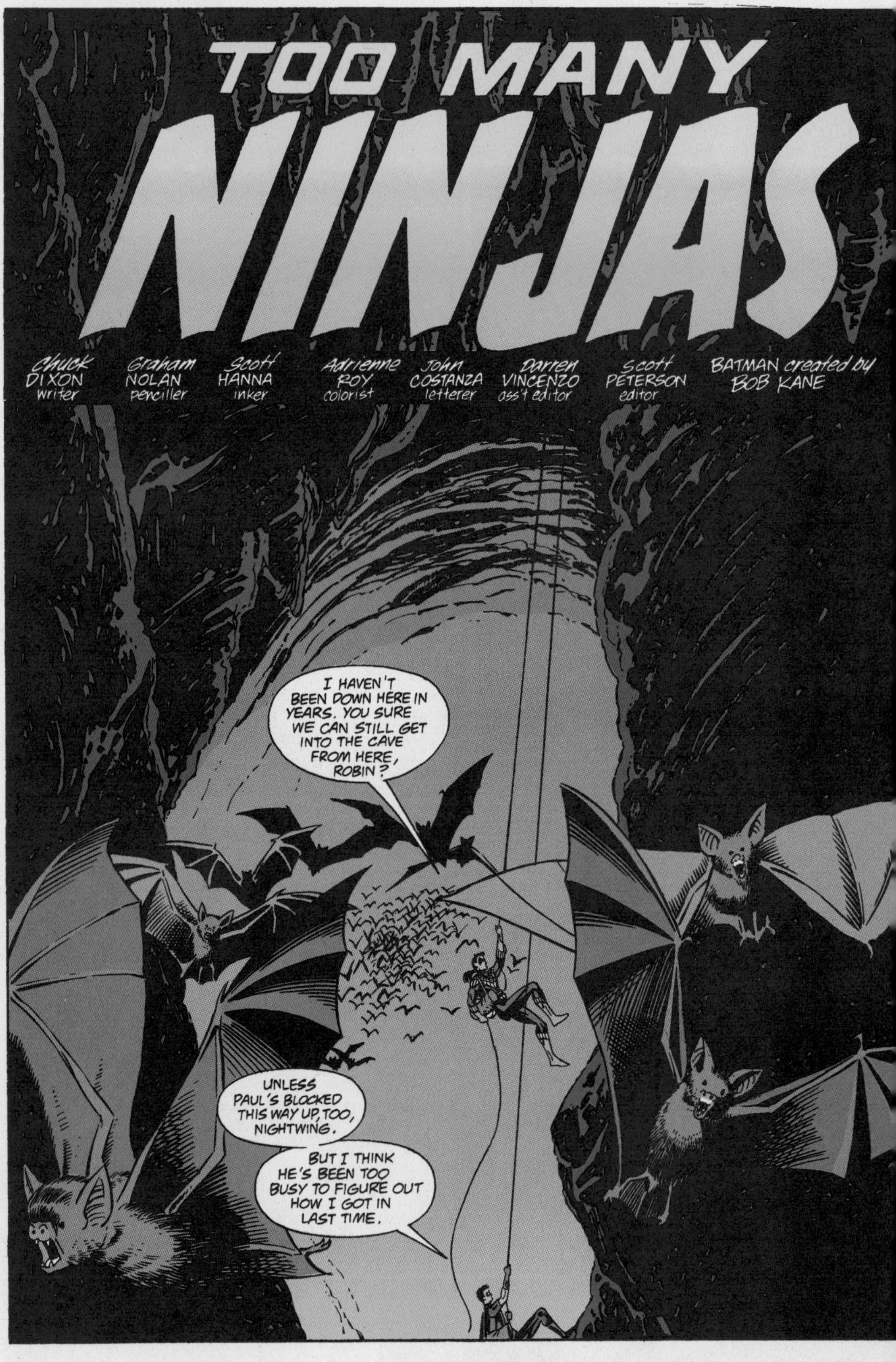
TOO MANY NINJAS
Chuck DIXON writer
Graham NOLAN penciller
Scott HANNA inker
Adrienne ROY colorist
John COSTANZA letterer
Darren VINCENZO ass't editor
Scott PETERSON editor
BATMAN created by BOB KANE
I HAVEN'T BEEN DOWN HERE IN YEARS. YOU SURE WE CAN STILL GET INTO THE CAVE FROM HERE, ROBIN?
UNLESS PAUL'S BLOCKED THIS WAY UP, TOO, NIGHTWING.
BUT I THINK HE'S BEEN TOO BUSY TO FIGURE OUT HOW I GOT IN LAST TIME.

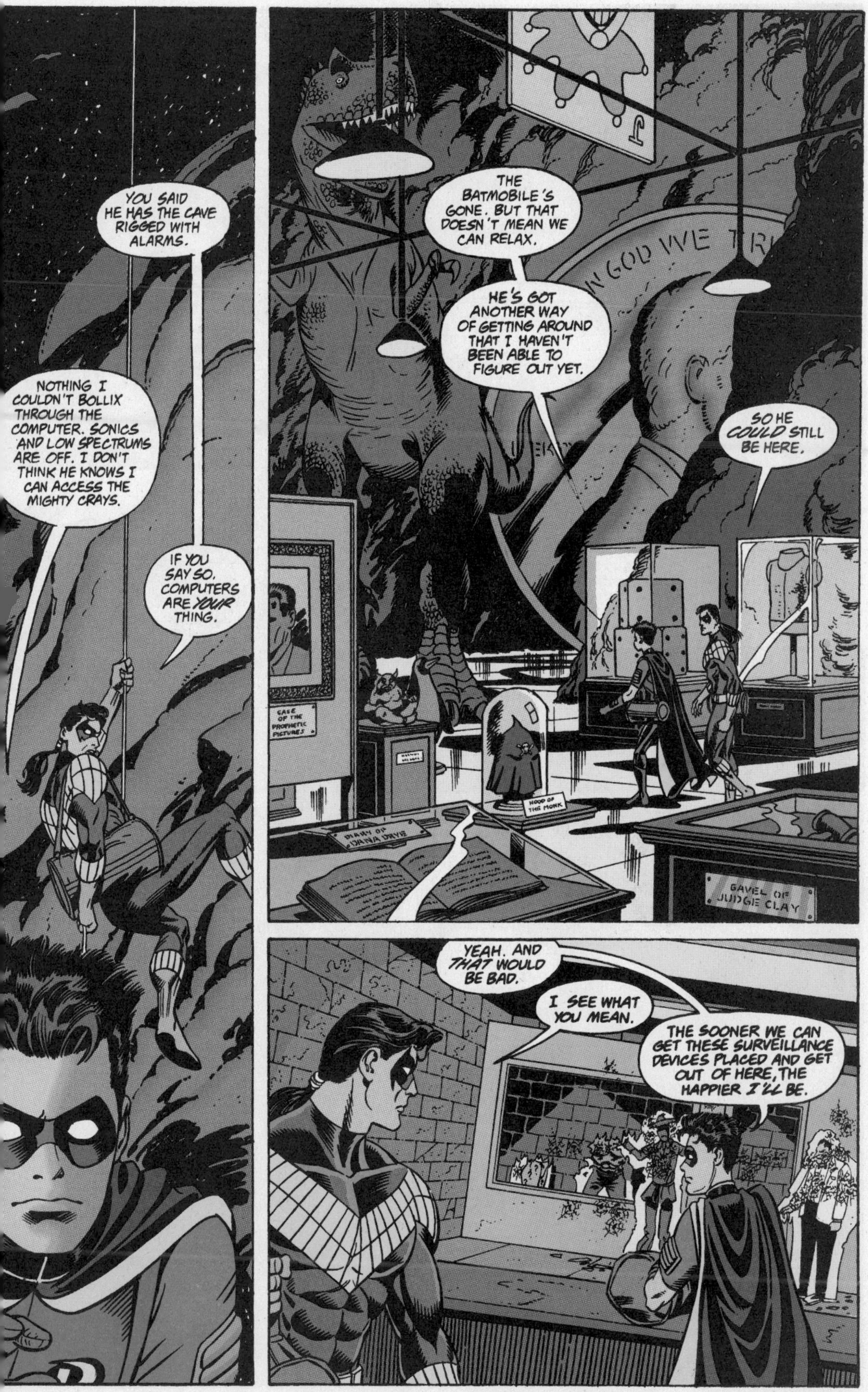
YOU SAID HE HAS THE CAVE RIGGED WITH ALARMS.
NOTHING I COULDN'T BOLLIX THROUGH THE COMPUTER. SONICS AND LOW SPECTRUMS ARE OFF. I DON'T THINK HE KNOWS I CAN ACCESS THE MIGHTY CRAYS.
IF YOU SAY SO. COMPUTERS ARE *YOUR* THING.
THE BATMOBILE'S GONE. BUT THAT DOESN'T MEAN WE CAN RELAX.
HE'S GOT ANOTHER WAY OF GETTING AROUND THAT I HAVEN'T BEEN ABLE TO FIGURE OUT YET.
SO HE *COULD* STILL BE HERE.
CASE OF THE PROPHETIC PICTURES
DIARY OF DANA DRYE
HOOD OF THE MONK
GAVEL OF JUDGE CLAY
YEAH. AND *THAT* WOULD BE BAD.
I SEE WHAT YOU MEAN.
THE SOONER WE CAN GET THESE SURVEILLANCE DEVICES PLACED AND GET OUT OF HERE, THE HAPPIER I'LL BE.

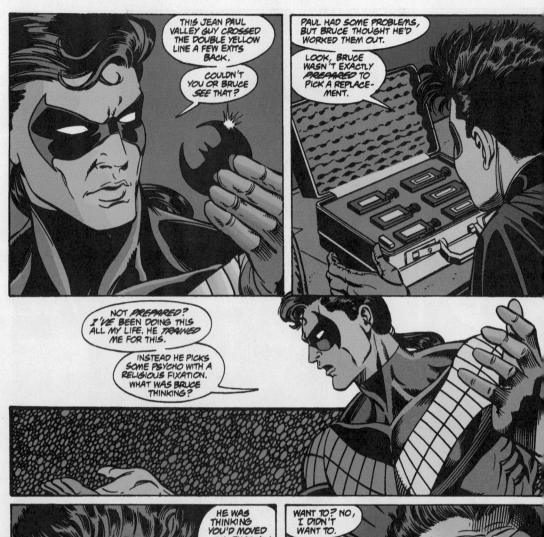

THIS JEAN PAUL VALLEY GUY CROSSED THE DOUBLE YELLOW LINE A FEW EXITS BACK.

COULDN'T YOU OR BRUCE SEE THAT?

PAUL HAD SOME PROBLEMS, BUT BRUCE THOUGHT HE'D WORKED THEM OUT.

LOOK, BRUCE WASN'T EXACTLY *PREPARED* TO PICK A REPLACEMENT.

NOT *PREPARED*? *I'VE* BEEN DOING THIS ALL MY LIFE. HE *TRAINED* ME FOR THIS.

INSTEAD HE PICKS SOME PSYCHO WITH A RELIGIOUS FIXATION. WHAT WAS BRUCE THINKING?

HE WAS THINKING YOU'D MOVED ON. THAT YOU WERE YOUR OWN MAN NOW.

HE DIDN'T THINK YOU'D WANT TO COME BACK.

WANT TO? NO, I DIDN'T WANT TO.

BUT I'D DO ANYTHING FOR BRUCE. I THOUGHT HE KNEW THAT. I --

HOLD ON. DID YOU HEAR THAT?

FOOTSTEPS.

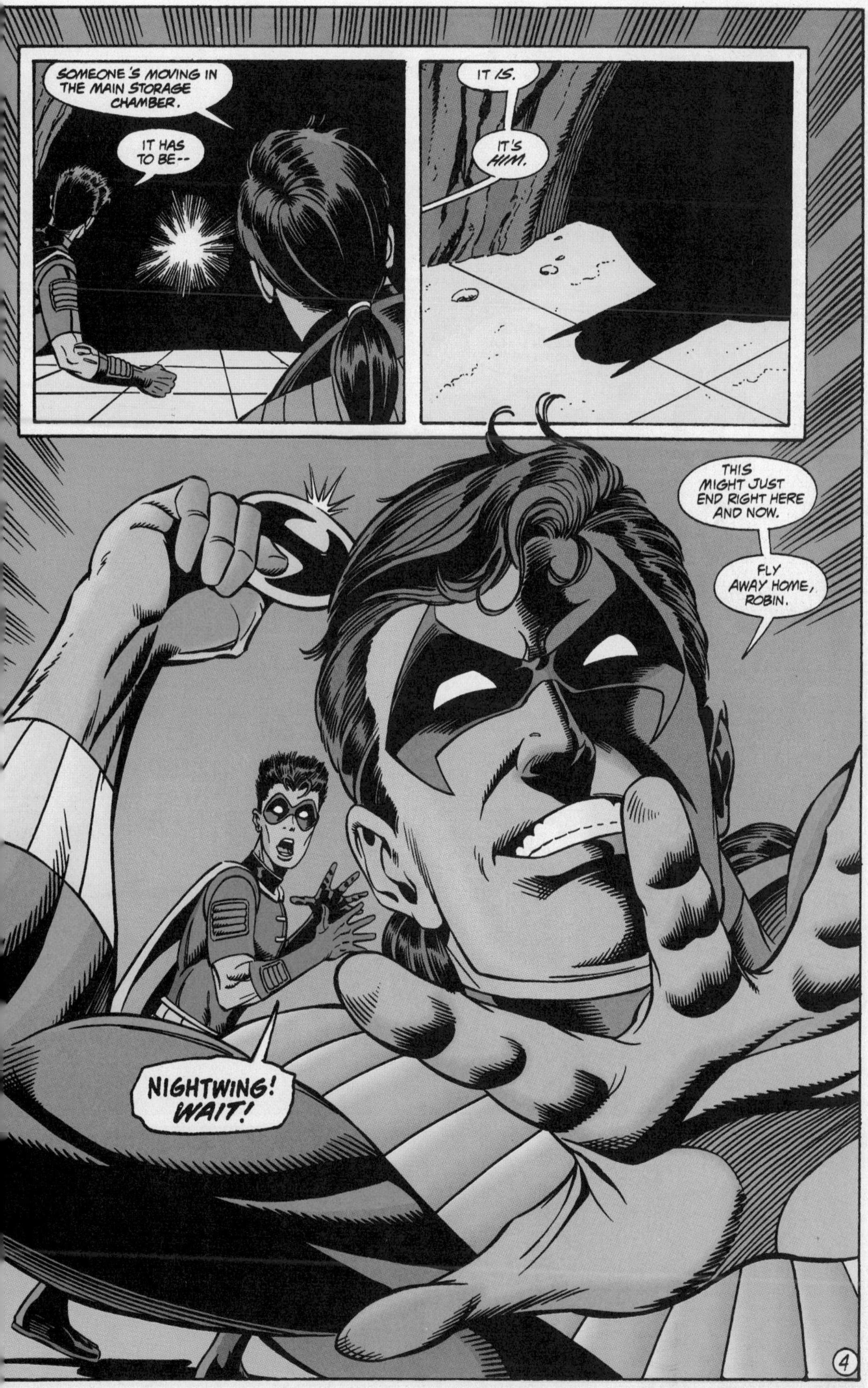
SOMEONE'S MOVING IN THE MAIN STORAGE CHAMBER.
IT HAS TO BE--
IT IS.
IT'S HIM.
THIS MIGHT JUST END RIGHT HERE AND NOW.
FLY AWAY HOME, ROBIN.
NIGHTWING! WAIT!
4

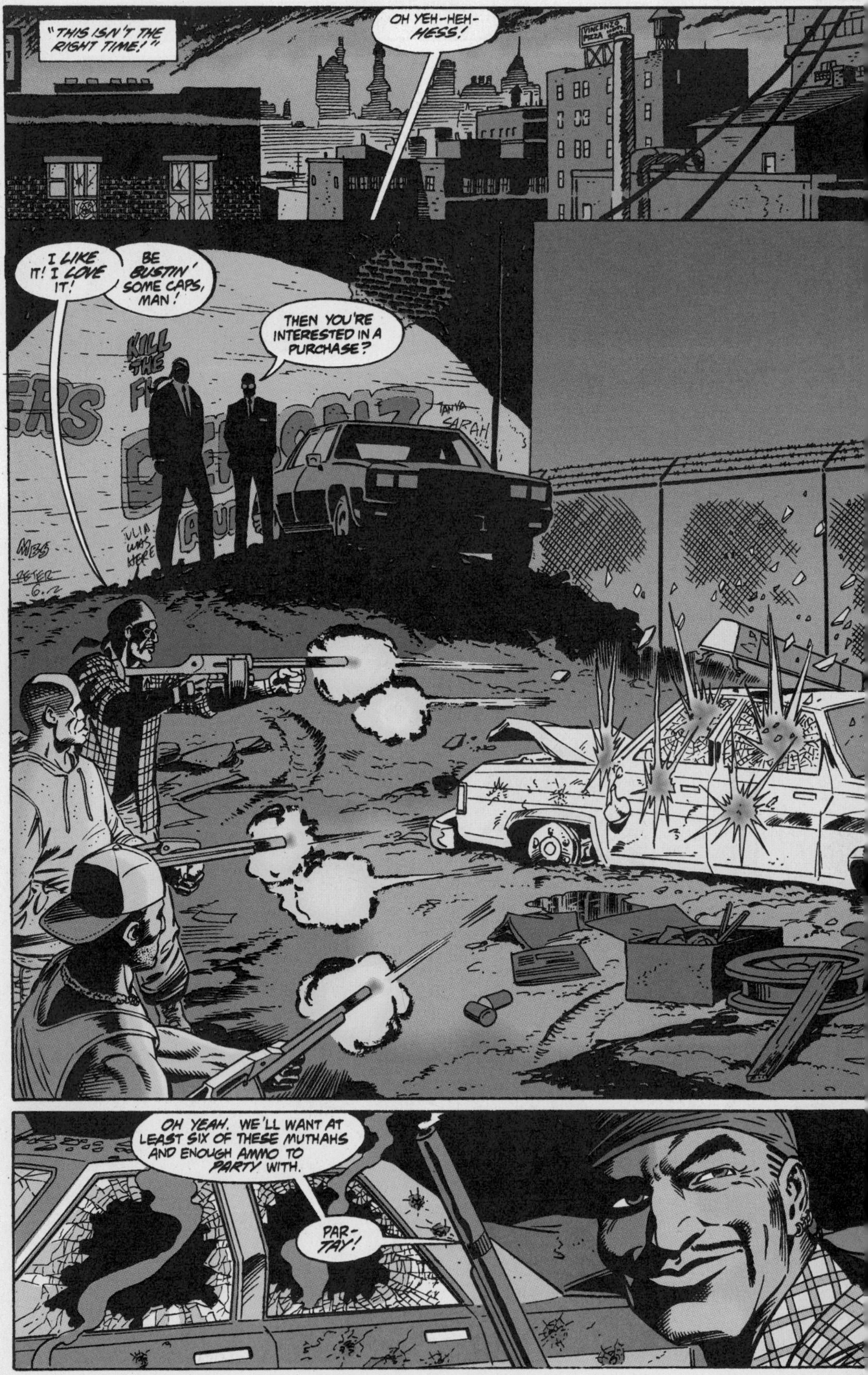
"THIS ISN'T THE RIGHT TIME!"
OH YEH-HEH-HESS!
VINCENZO PIZZA
I LIKE IT! I LOVE IT!
BE BUSTIN' SOME CAPS, MAN!
THEN YOU'RE INTERESTED IN A PURCHASE?
KILL THE
SARAH
OH YEAH. WE'LL WANT AT LEAST SIX OF THESE MUTHAHS AND ENOUGH AMMO TO PARTY WITH.
PAR-TAY!

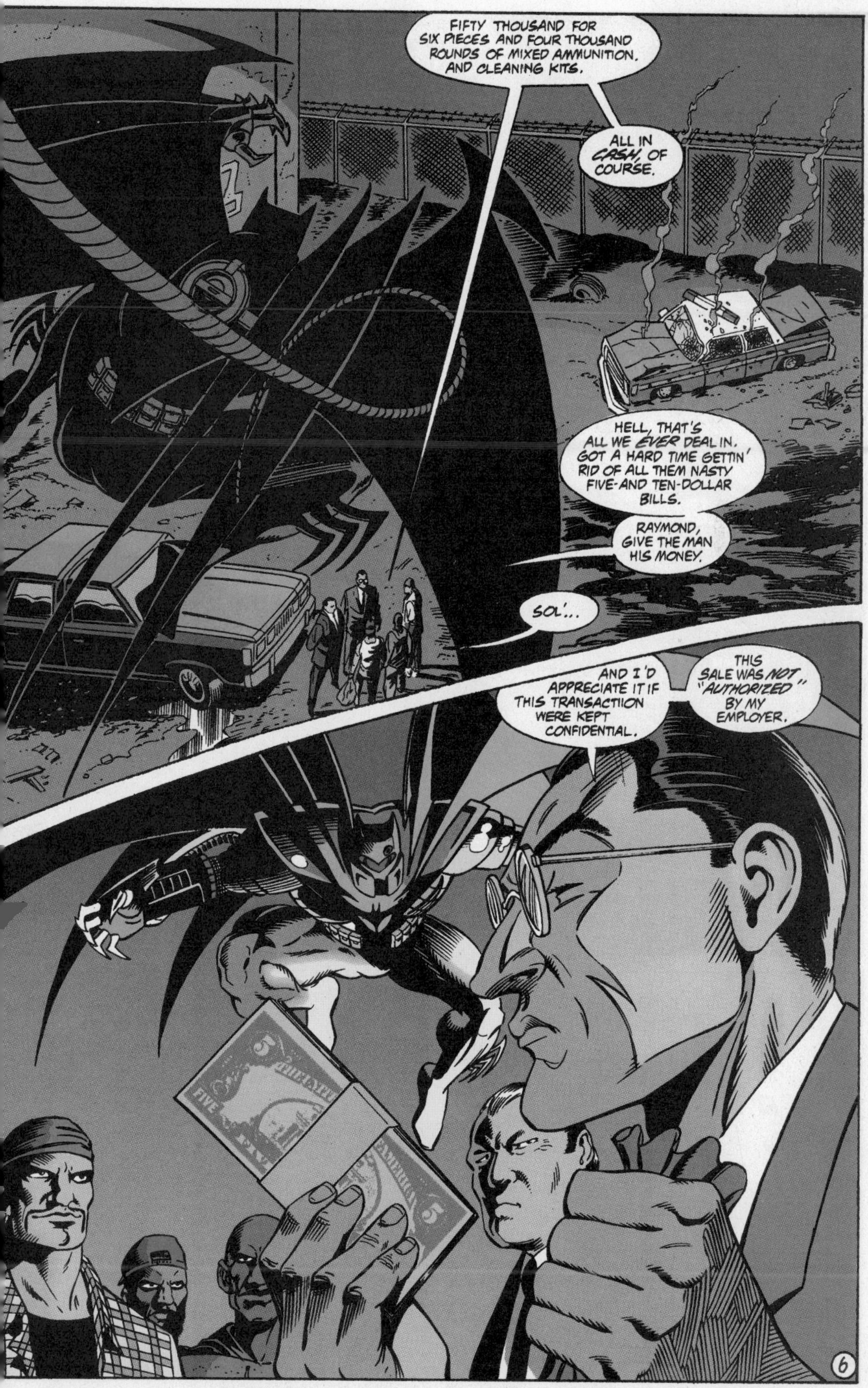

FIFTY THOUSAND FOR SIX PIECES AND FOUR THOUSAND ROUNDS OF MIXED AMMUNITION. AND CLEANING KITS.
ALL IN CASH, OF COURSE.
HELL, THAT'S ALL WE EVER DEAL IN. GOT A HARD TIME GETTIN' RID OF ALL THEM NASTY FIVE-AND TEN-DOLLAR BILLS.
RAYMOND, GIVE THE MAN HIS MONEY.
SOL'...
AND I'D APPRECIATE IT IF THIS TRANSACTIION WERE KEPT CONFIDENTIAL.
THIS SALE WAS NOT "AUTHORIZED" BY MY EMPLOYER.
6

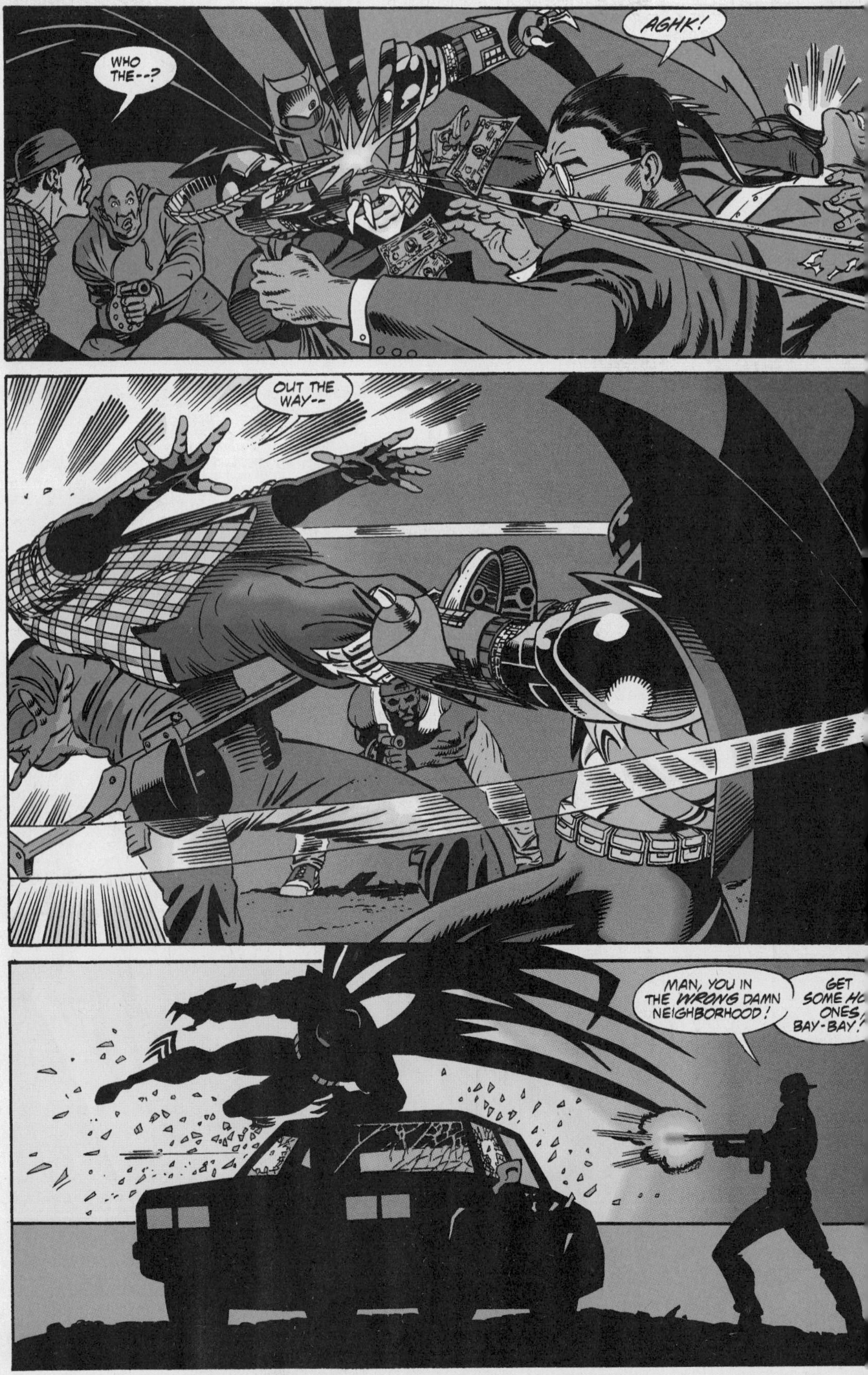
WHO THE--?
AGHK!
OUT THE WAY--
MAN, YOU IN THE WRONG DAMN NEIGHBORHOOD!
GET SOME HO ONES, BAY-BAY!

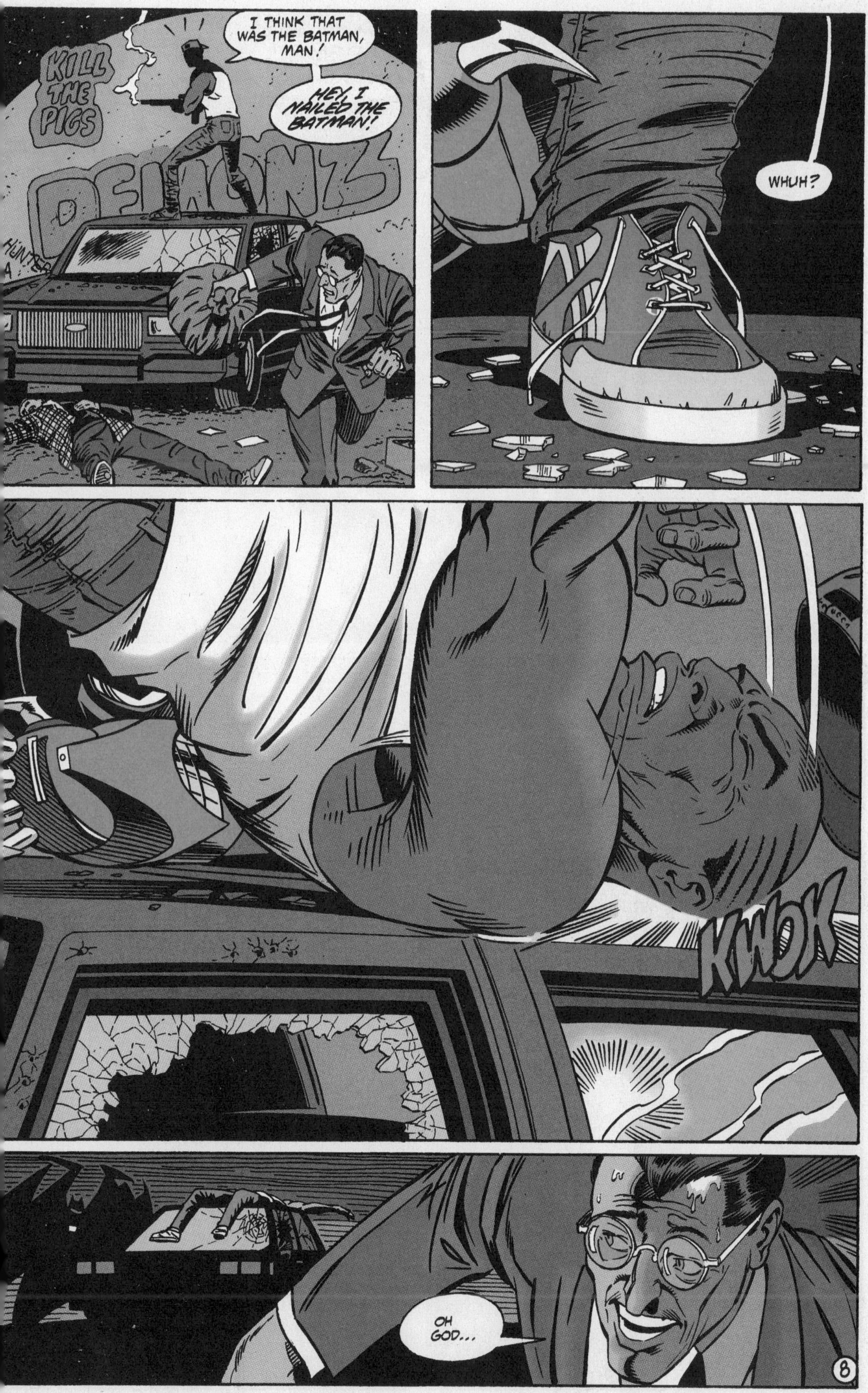
KILL THE PIGS
DEMONZ
I THINK THAT WAS THE BATMAN, MAN!
HEY, I NAILED THE BATMAN!
WHUH?
KWOK
OH GOD...
8

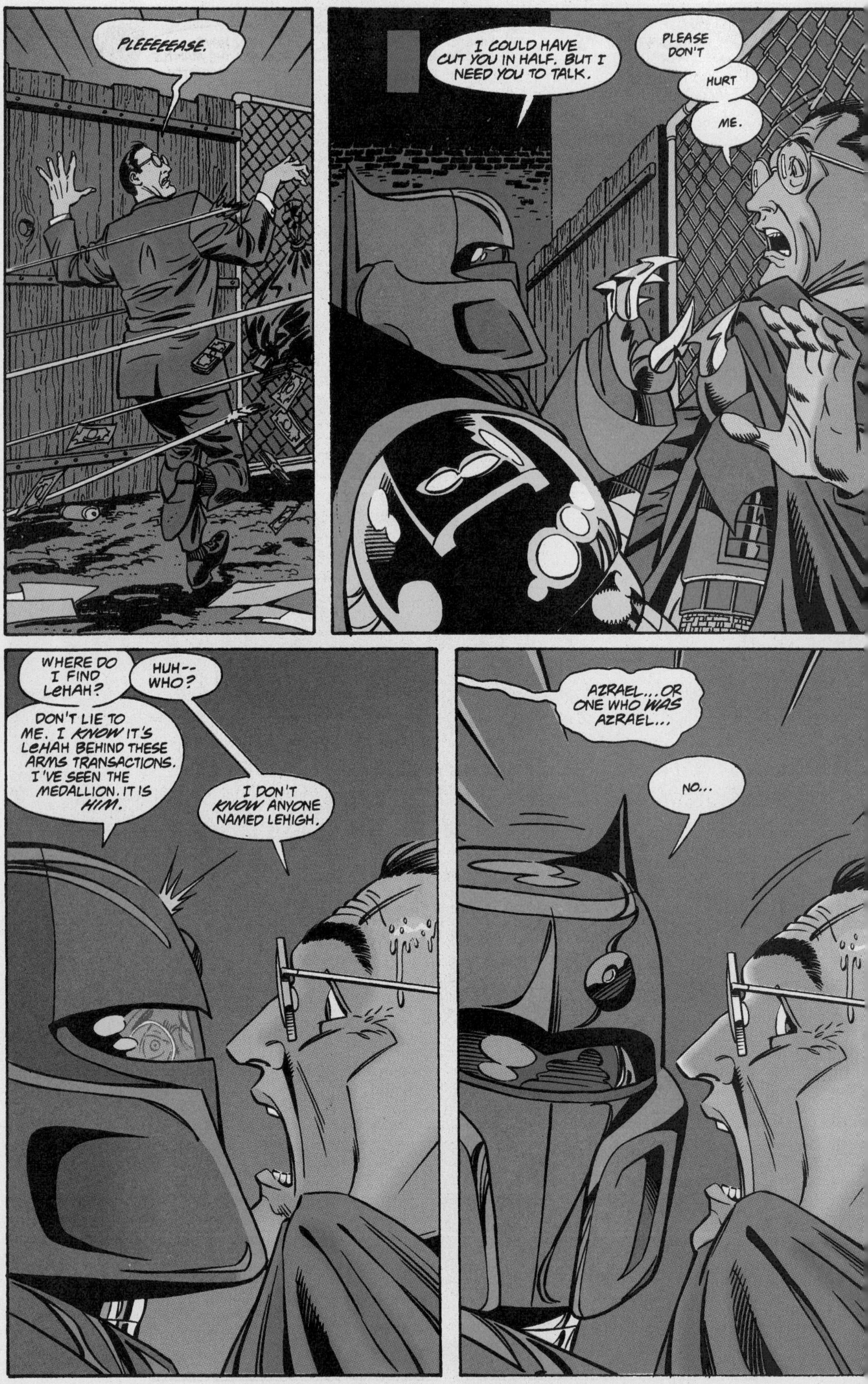
PLEEEEEASE.
I COULD HAVE CUT YOU IN HALF. BUT I NEED YOU TO TALK.
PLEASE DON'T
HURT
ME.
WHERE DO I FIND LEHAH?
HUH-- WHO?
DON'T LIE TO ME. I KNOW IT'S LEHAH BEHIND THESE ARMS TRANSACTIONS. I'VE SEEN THE MEDALLION. IT IS HIM.
I DON'T KNOW ANYONE NAMED LEHIGH.
AZRAEL... OR ONE WHO WAS AZRAEL...
NO...

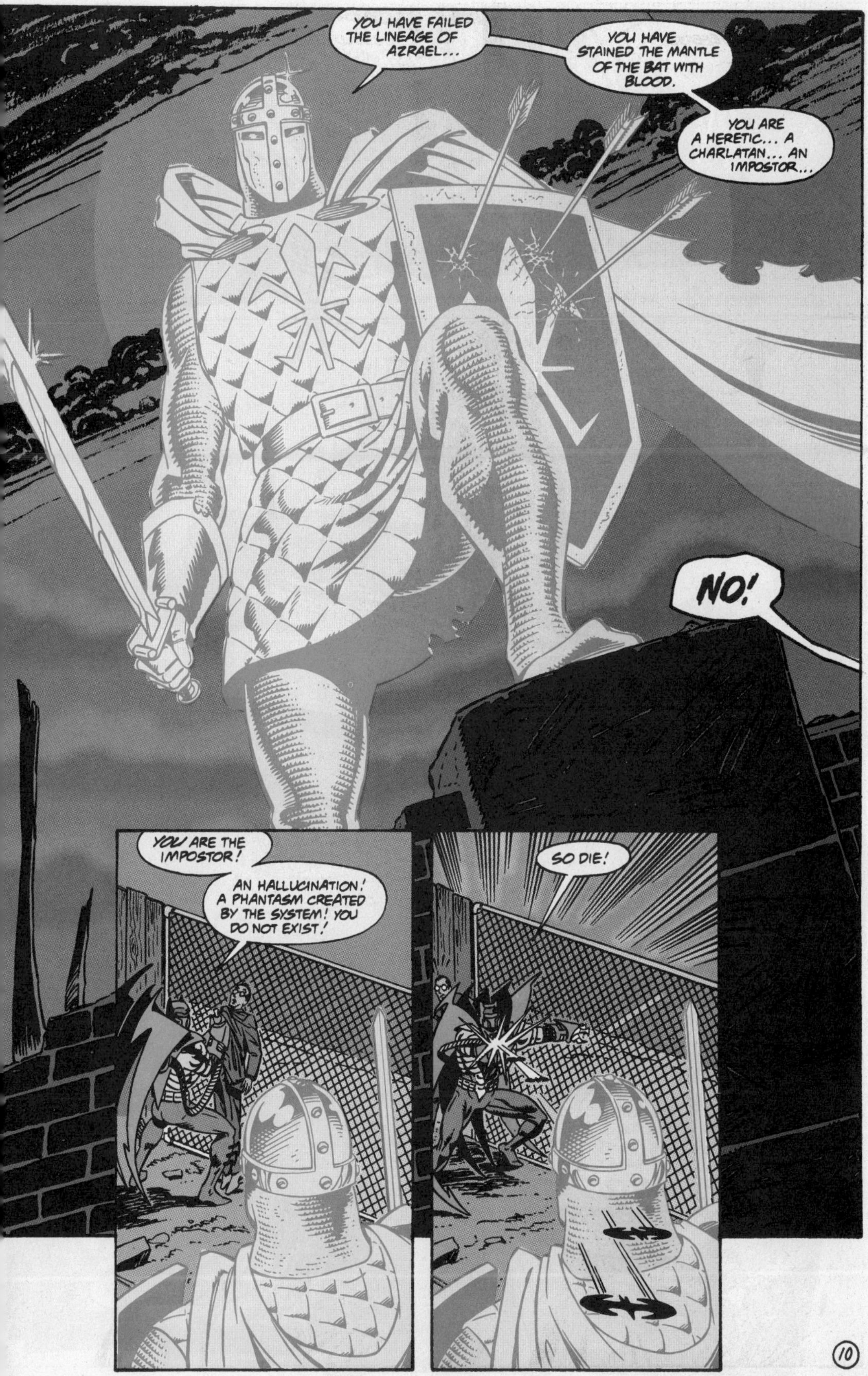
YOU HAVE FAILED THE LINEAGE OF AZRAEL...
YOU HAVE STAINED THE MANTLE OF THE BAT WITH BLOOD.
YOU ARE A HERETIC... A CHARLATAN... AN IMPOSTOR...
NO!
YOU ARE THE IMPOSTOR!
AN HALLUCINATION! A PHANTASM CREATED BY THE SYSTEM! YOU DO NOT EXIST!
SO DIE!
10

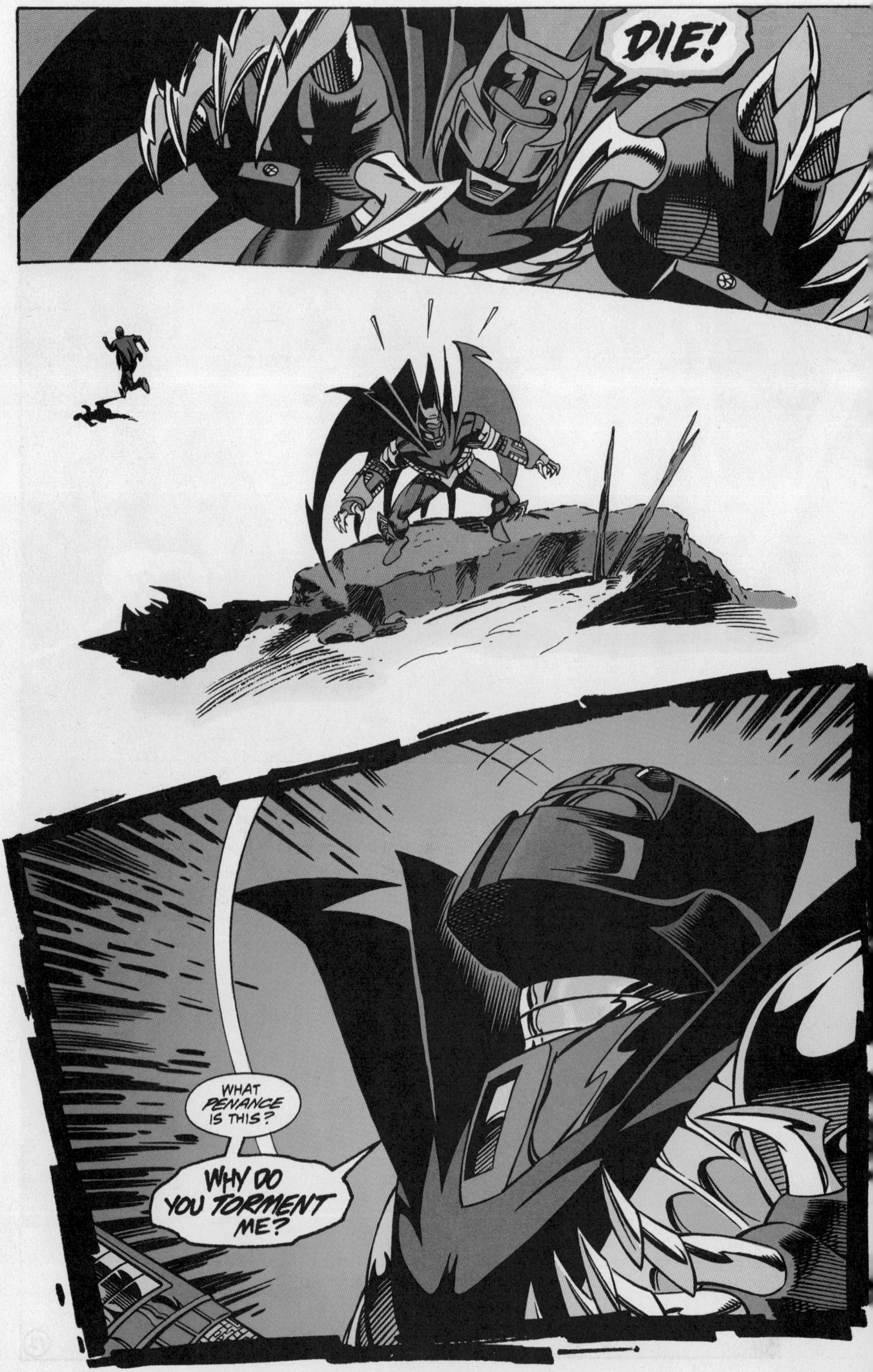
DIE!
WHAT PENANCE IS THIS?
WHY DO YOU TORMENT ME?

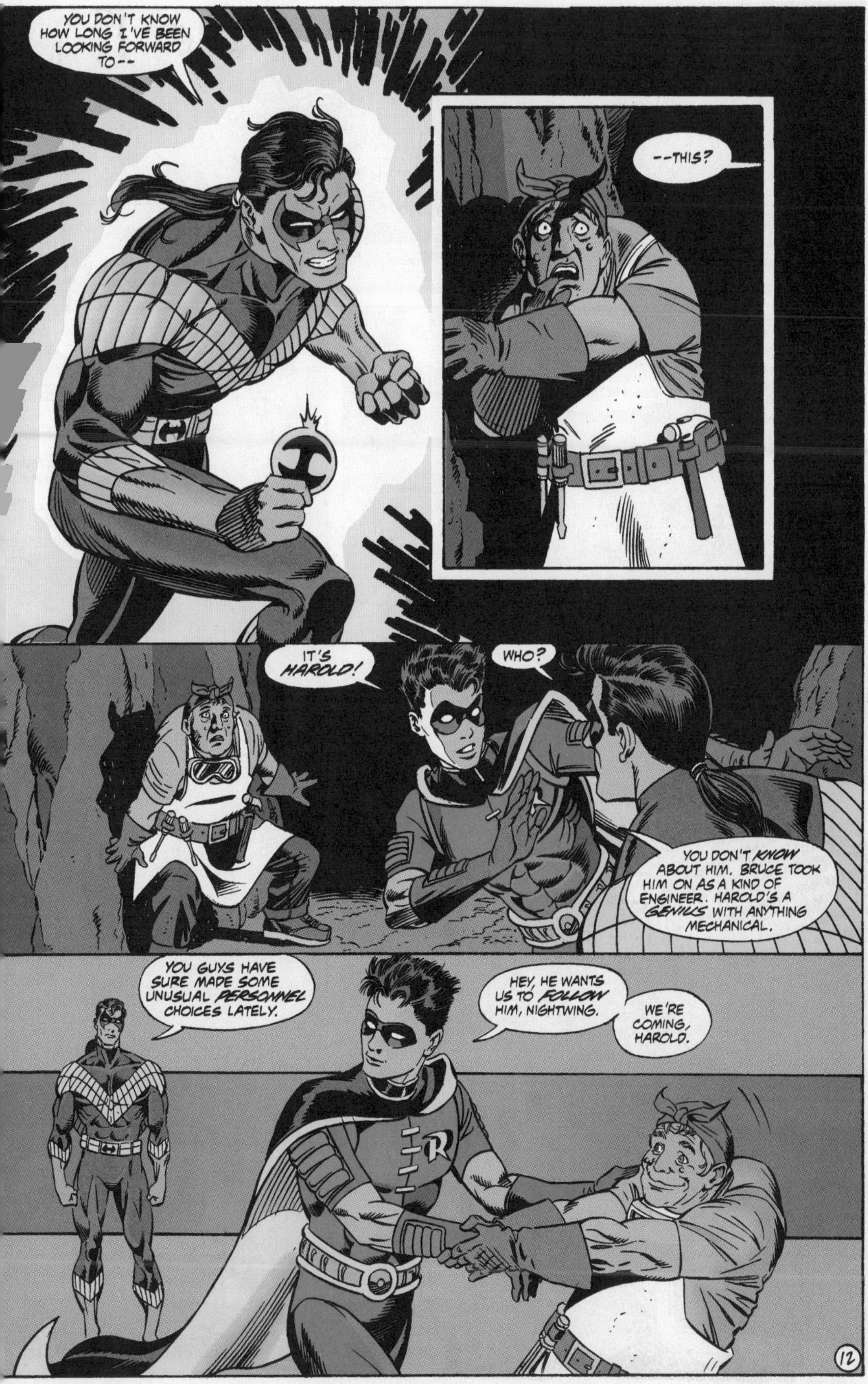
YOU DON'T KNOW HOW LONG I'VE BEEN LOOKING FORWARD TO--
--THIS?
IT'S HAROLD!
WHO?
YOU DON'T KNOW ABOUT HIM. BRUCE TOOK HIM ON AS A KIND OF ENGINEER. HAROLD'S A GENIUS WITH ANYTHING MECHANICAL.
YOU GUYS HAVE SURE MADE SOME UNUSUAL PERSONNEL CHOICES LATELY.
HEY, HE WANTS US TO FOLLOW HIM, NIGHTWING.
WE'RE COMING, HAROLD.
12

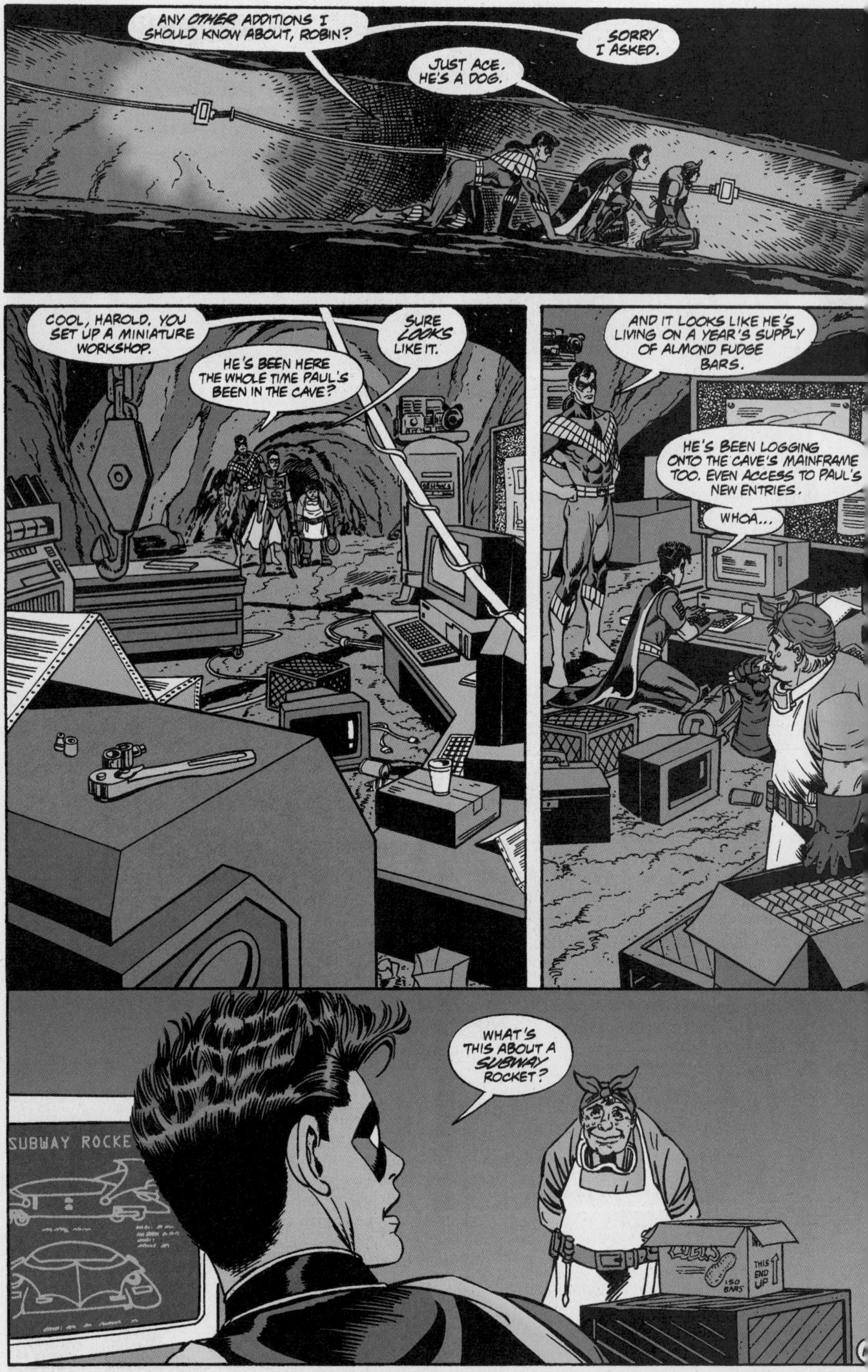
ANY OTHER ADDITIONS I SHOULD KNOW ABOUT, ROBIN?
JUST ACE. HE'S A DOG.
SORRY I ASKED.
COOL, HAROLD. YOU SET UP A MINIATURE WORKSHOP.
HE'S BEEN HERE THE WHOLE TIME PAUL'S BEEN IN THE CAVE?
SURE LOOKS LIKE IT.
AND IT LOOKS LIKE HE'S LIVING ON A YEAR'S SUPPLY OF ALMOND FUDGE BARS.
HE'S BEEN LOGGING ONTO THE CAVE'S MAINFRAME TOO. EVEN ACCESS TO PAUL'S NEW ENTRIES.
WHOA...
WHAT'S THIS ABOUT A SUBWAY ROCKET?
SUBWAY ROCKE
THIS END UP

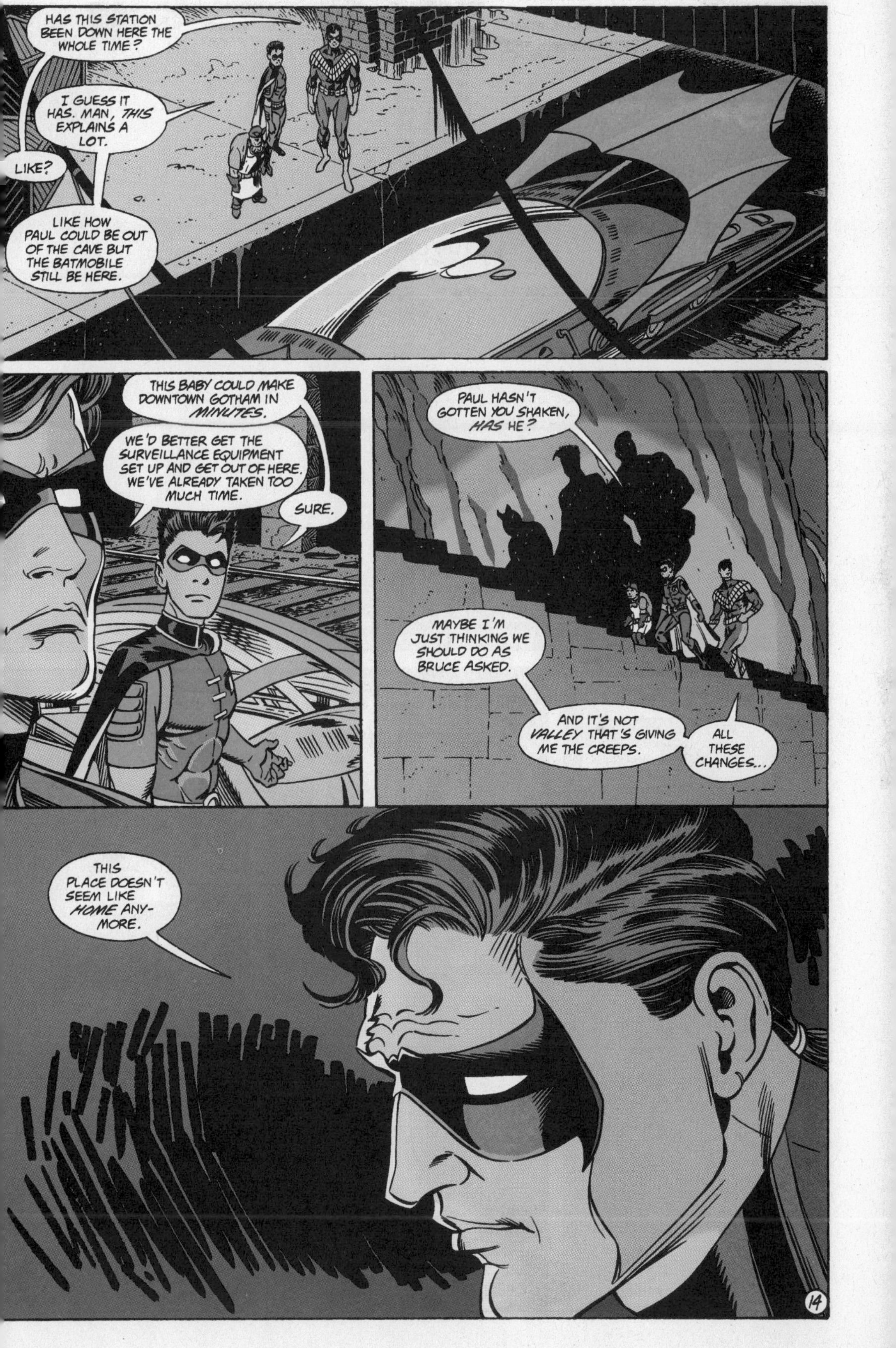
HAS THIS STATION BEEN DOWN HERE THE WHOLE TIME?
I GUESS IT HAS. MAN, THIS EXPLAINS A LOT.
LIKE?
LIKE HOW PAUL COULD BE OUT OF THE CAVE BUT THE BATMOBILE STILL BE HERE.
THIS BABY COULD MAKE DOWNTOWN GOTHAM IN MINUTES.
WE'D BETTER GET THE SURVEILLANCE EQUIPMENT SET UP AND GET OUT OF HERE. WE'VE ALREADY TAKEN TOO MUCH TIME.
SURE.
PAUL HASN'T GOTTEN YOU SHAKEN, HAS HE?
MAYBE I'M JUST THINKING WE SHOULD DO AS BRUCE ASKED.
AND IT'S NOT VALLEY THAT'S GIVING ME THE CREEPS.
ALL THESE CHANGES...
THIS PLACE DOESN'T SEEM LIKE HOME ANY-MORE.
14

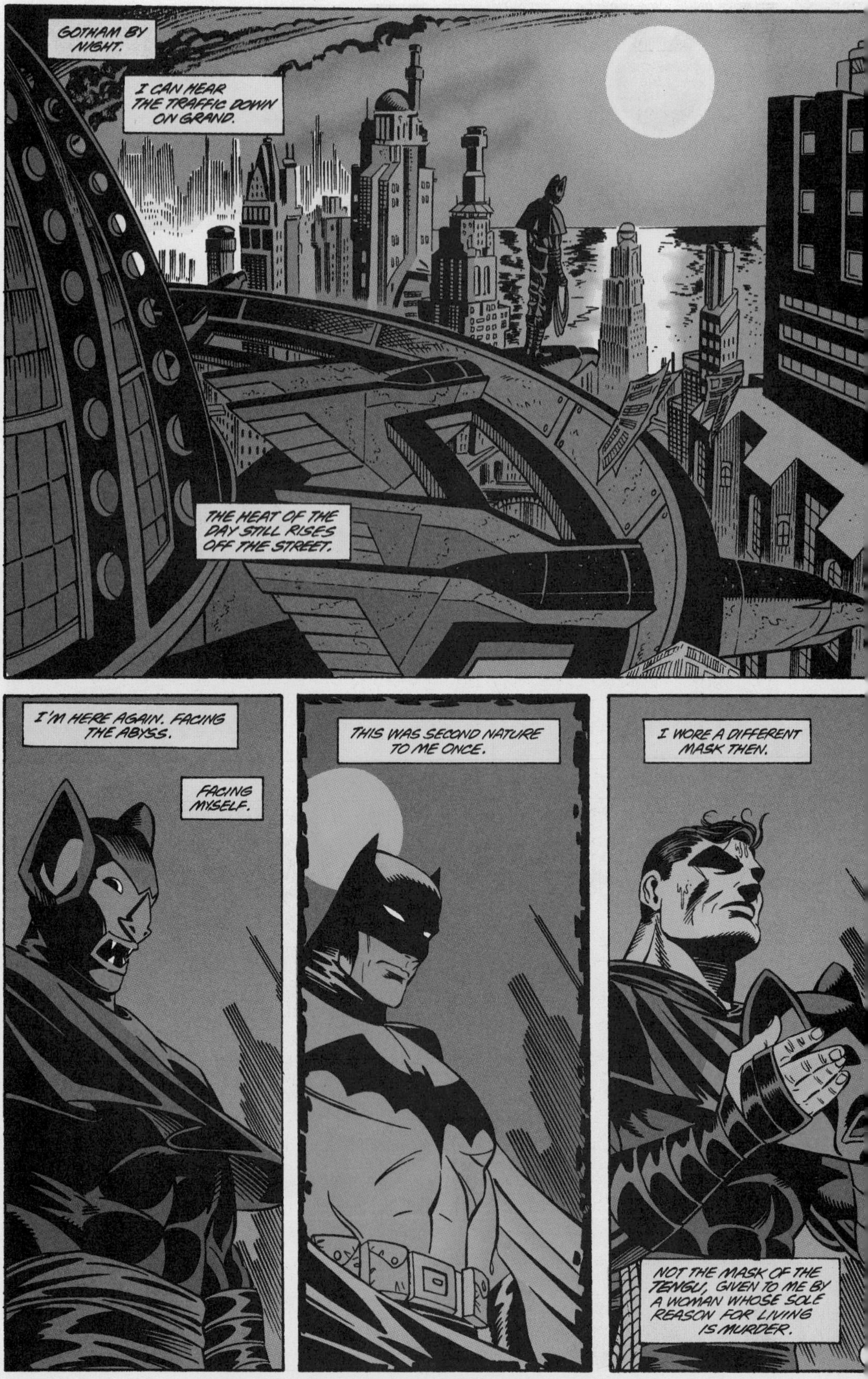
GOTHAM BY NIGHT.
I CAN HEAR THE TRAFFIC DOWN ON GRAND.
THE HEAT OF THE DAY STILL RISES OFF THE STREET.
I'M HERE AGAIN. FACING THE ABYSS.
FACING MYSELF.
THIS WAS SECOND NATURE TO ME ONCE.
I WORE A DIFFERENT MASK THEN.
NOT THE MASK OF THE TENGU, GIVEN TO ME BY A WOMAN WHOSE SOLE REASON FOR LIVING IS MURDER.

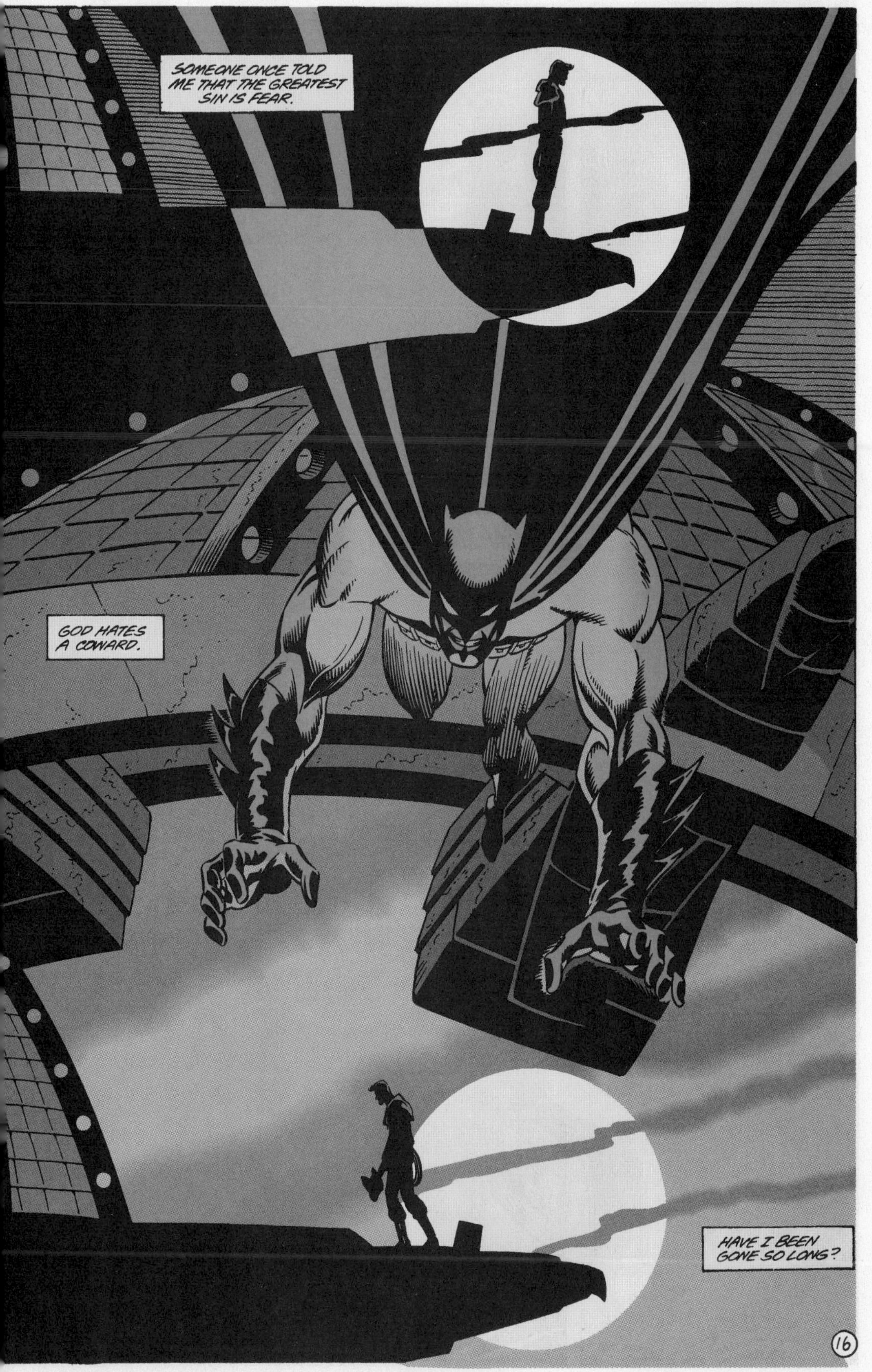
SOMEONE ONCE TOLD ME THAT THE GREATEST SIN IS FEAR.
GOD HATES A COWARD.
HAVE I BEEN GONE SO LONG?
16

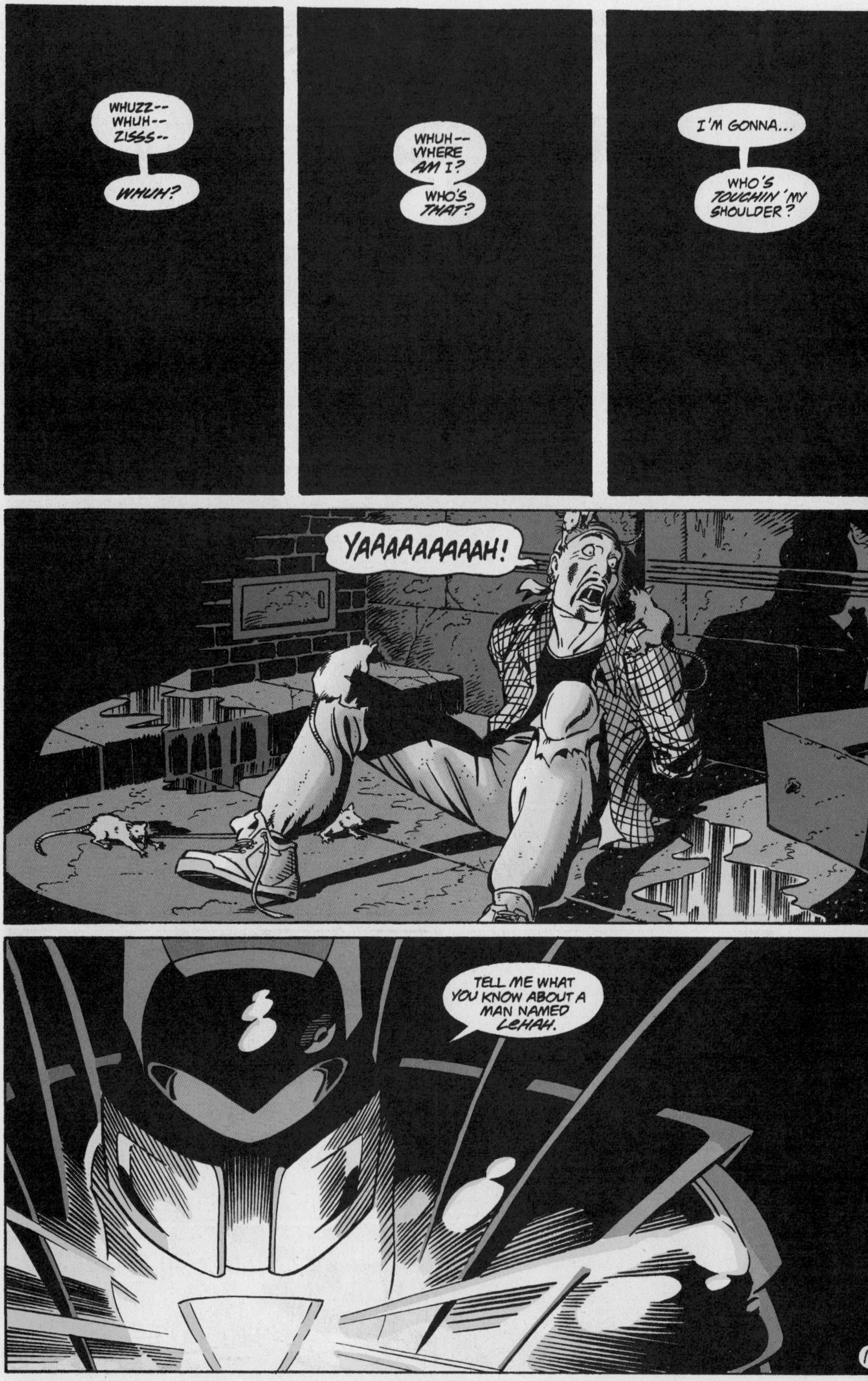
WHUZZ--
WHUH--
ZISSS--
WHUH?
WHUH--
WHERE AM I?
WHO'S THAT?
I'M GONNA...
WHO'S TOUCHIN' MY SHOULDER?
YAAAAAAAAAH!
TELL ME WHAT YOU KNOW ABOUT A MAN NAMED LEHAH.

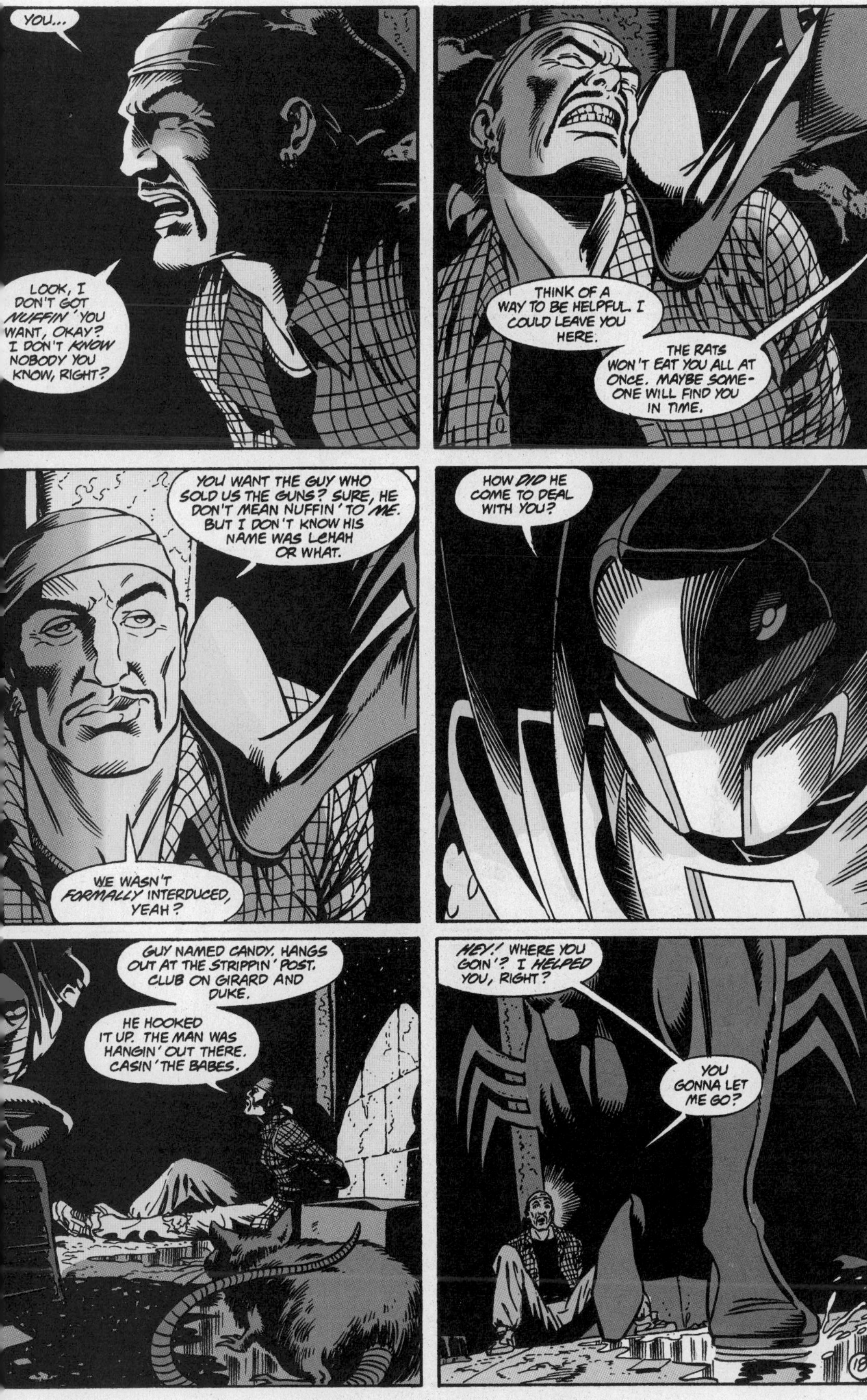

YOU...
LOOK, I DON'T GOT NUFFIN' YOU WANT, OKAY? I DON'T KNOW NOBODY YOU KNOW, RIGHT?
THINK OF A WAY TO BE HELPFUL. I COULD LEAVE YOU HERE.
THE RATS WON'T EAT YOU ALL AT ONCE. MAYBE SOME-ONE WILL FIND YOU IN TIME.
YOU WANT THE GUY WHO SOLD US THE GUNS? SURE, HE DON'T MEAN NUFFIN' TO ME. BUT I DON'T KNOW HIS NAME WAS LEHAH OR WHAT.
WE WASN'T FORMALLY INTERDUCED, YEAH?
HOW DID HE COME TO DEAL WITH YOU?
GUY NAMED CANDY. HANGS OUT AT THE STRIPPIN' POST. CLUB ON GIRARD AND DUKE.
HE HOOKED IT UP. THE MAN WAS HANGIN' OUT THERE. CASIN' THE BABES.
HEY! WHERE YOU GOIN'? I HELPED YOU, RIGHT?
YOU GONNA LET ME GO?
18

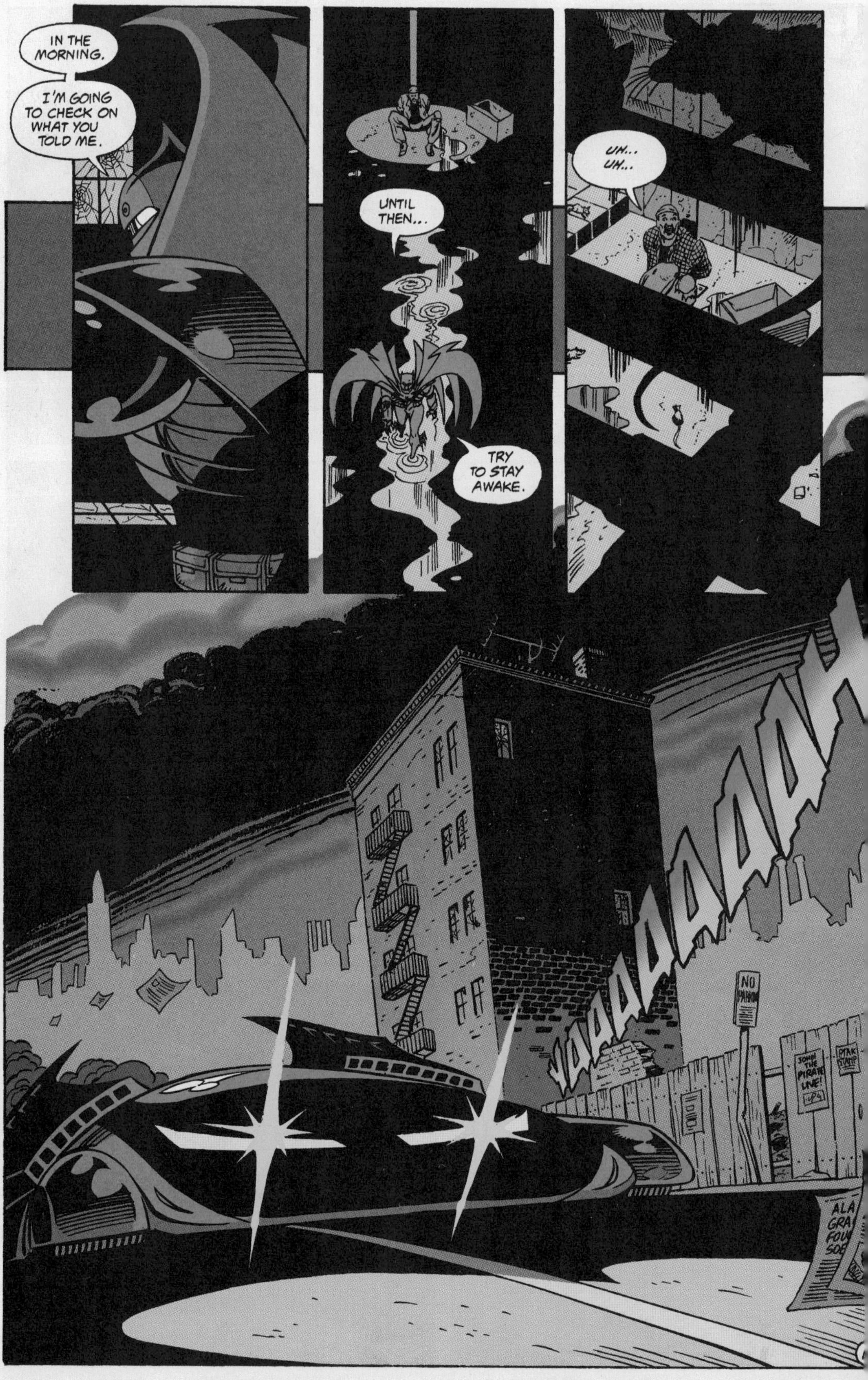
IN THE MORNING.
I'M GOING TO CHECK ON WHAT YOU TOLD ME.
UNTIL THEN...
TRY TO STAY AWAKE.
UH... UH...

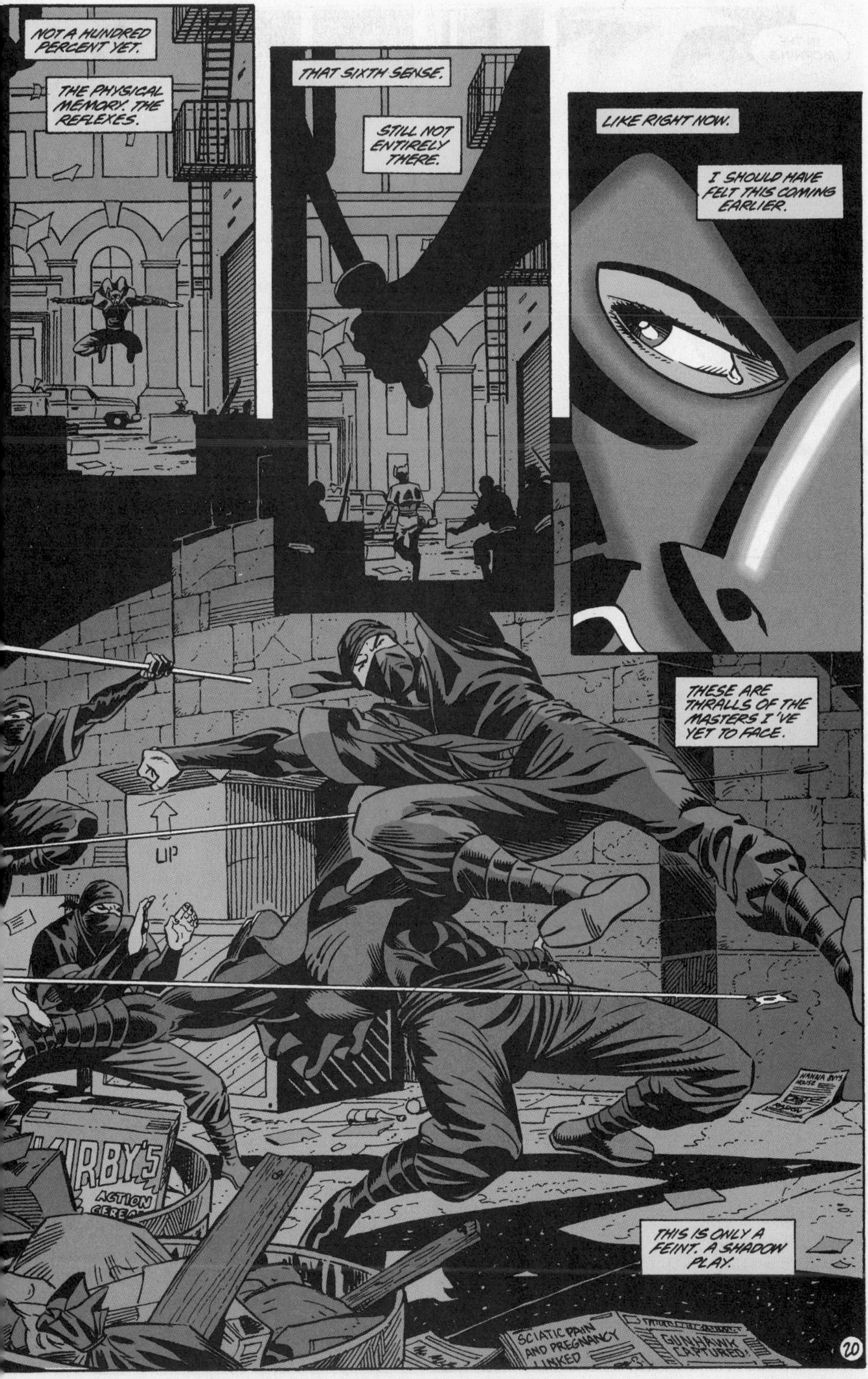
NOT A HUNDRED PERCENT YET.
THE PHYSICAL MEMORY. THE REFLEXES.
THAT SIXTH SENSE.
STILL NOT ENTIRELY THERE.
LIKE RIGHT NOW.
I SHOULD HAVE FELT THIS COMING EARLIER.
THESE ARE THRALLS OF THE MASTERS I'VE YET TO FACE.
UP
THIS IS ONLY A FEINT. A SHADOW PLAY.
SCIATIC PAIN AND PREGNANCY LINKED
GUNHAWK CAPTURED!
20

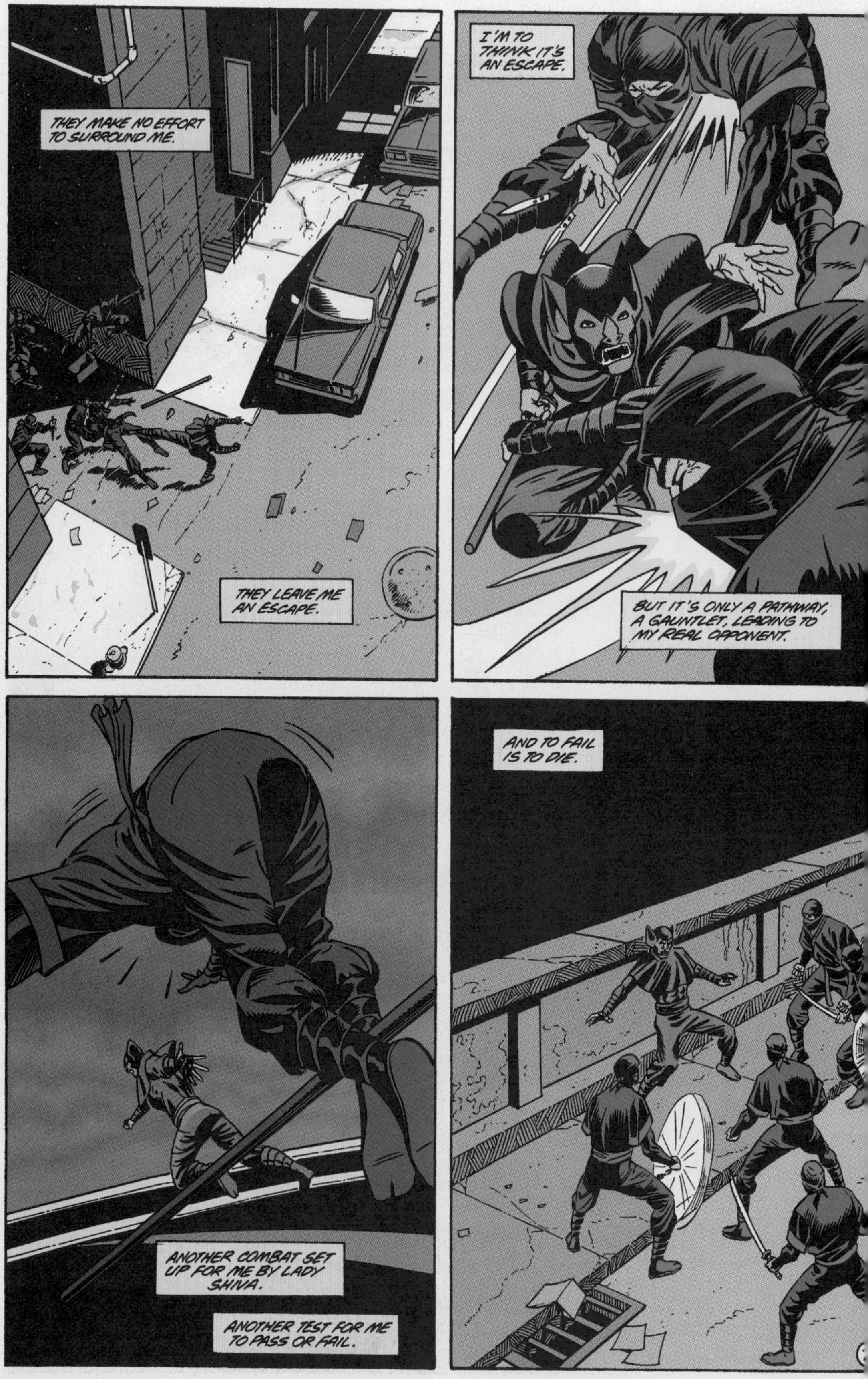
THEY MAKE NO EFFORT TO SURROUND ME.
THEY LEAVE ME AN ESCAPE.
I'M TO THINK IT'S AN ESCAPE.
BUT IT'S ONLY A PATHWAY, A GAUNTLET, LEADING TO MY REAL OPPONENT.
ANOTHER COMBAT SET UP FOR ME BY LADY SHIVA.
ANOTHER TEST FOR ME TO PASS OR FAIL.
AND TO FAIL IS TO DIE.

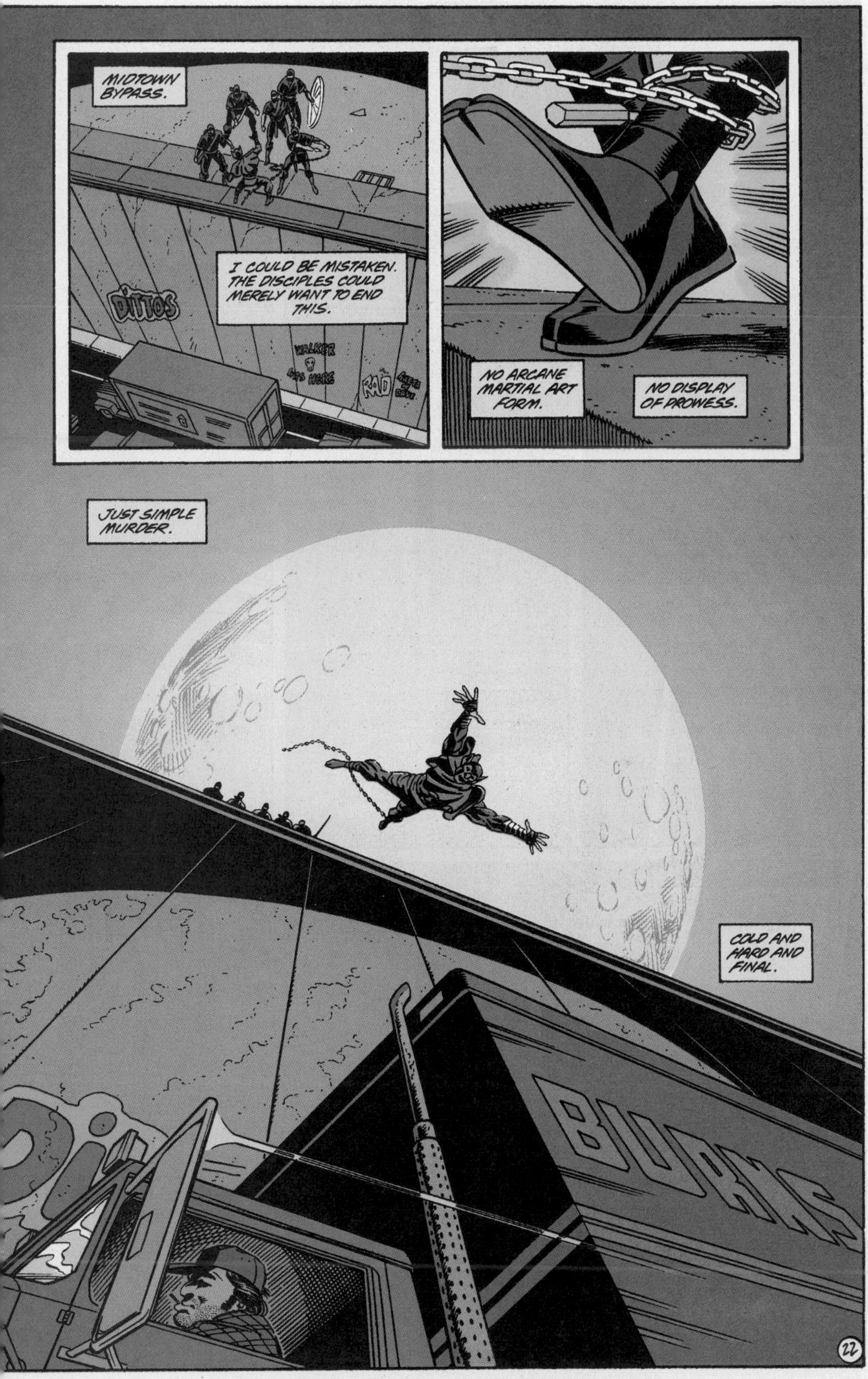
MIDTOWN BYPASS.
I COULD BE MISTAKEN. THE DISCIPLES COULD MERELY WANT TO END THIS.
DITTOS
WALKER WAS HERE
RAD
NO ARCANE MARTIAL ART FORM.
NO DISPLAY OF PROWESS.
JUST SIMPLE MURDER.
COLD AND HARD AND FINAL.
22

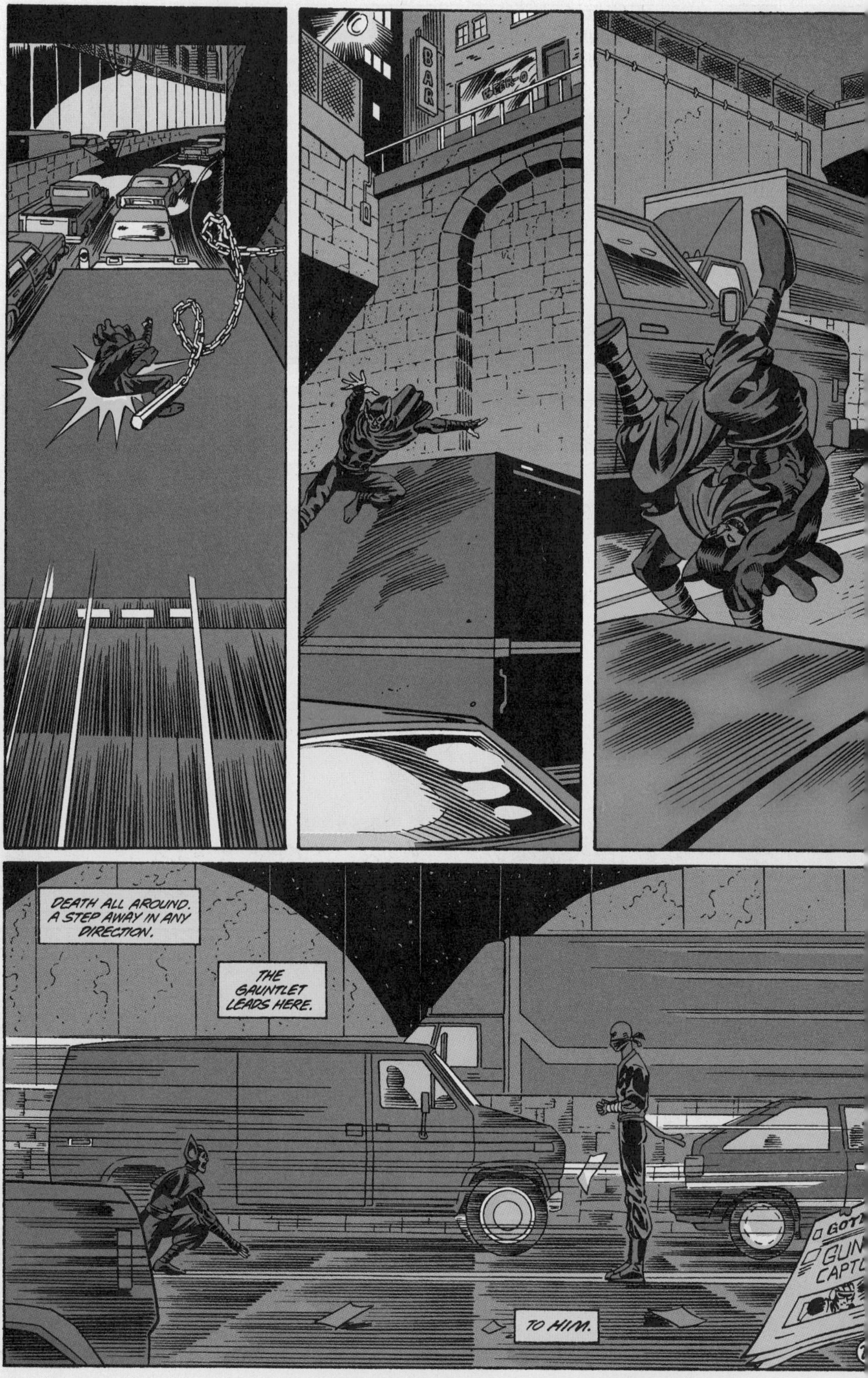
BAR
DEATH ALL AROUND. A STEP AWAY IN ANY DIRECTION.
THE GAUNTLET LEADS HERE.
TO HIM.

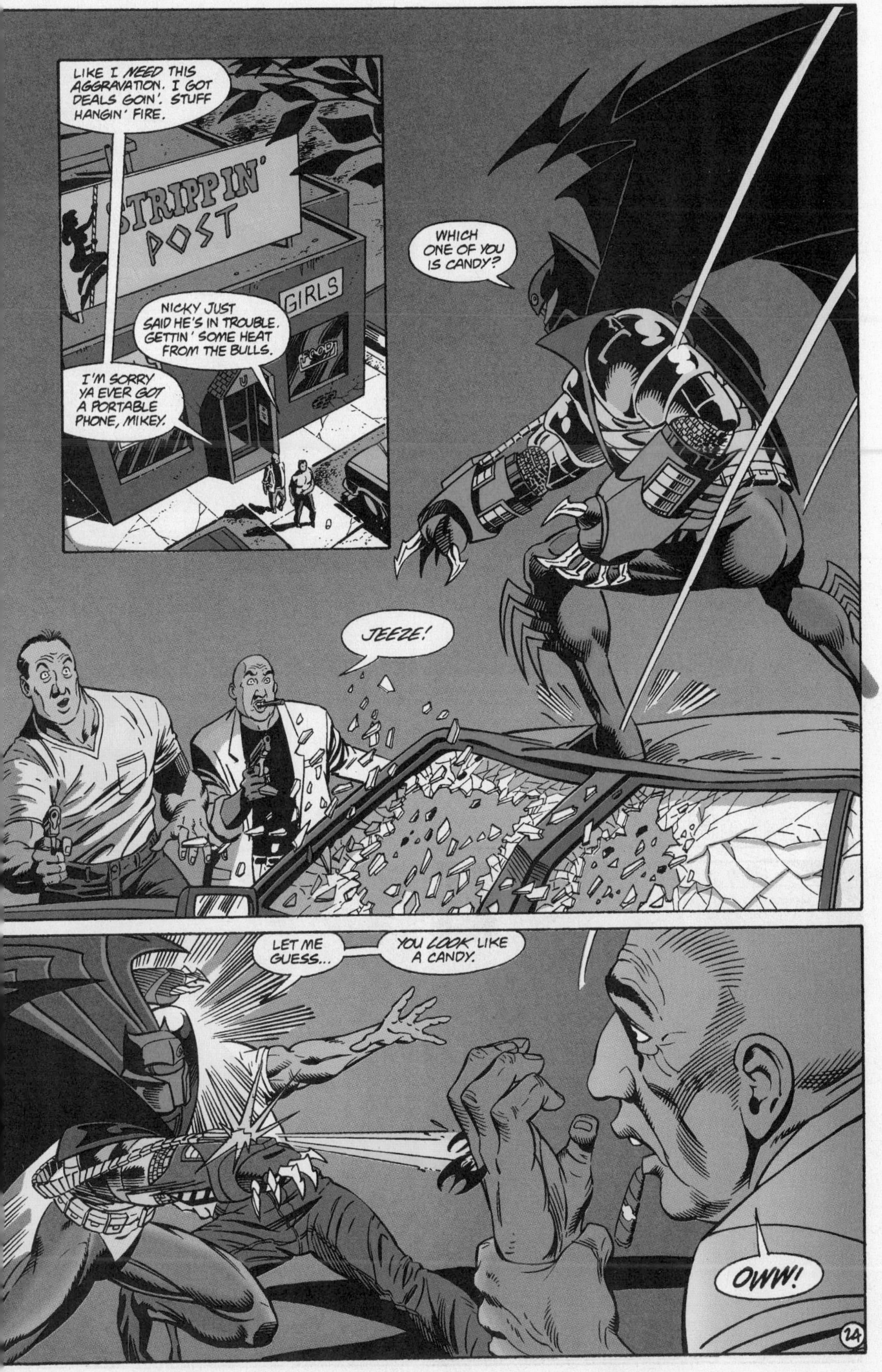
LIKE I NEED THIS AGGRAVATION. I GOT DEALS GOIN'. STUFF HANGIN' FIRE.
STRIPPIN' POST
GIRLS
NICKY JUST SAID HE'S IN TROUBLE. GETTIN' SOME HEAT FROM THE BULLS.
I'M SORRY YA EVER GOT A PORTABLE PHONE, MIKEY.
WHICH ONE OF YOU IS CANDY?
JEEZE!
LET ME GUESS...
YOU LOOK LIKE A CANDY.
OWW!
24

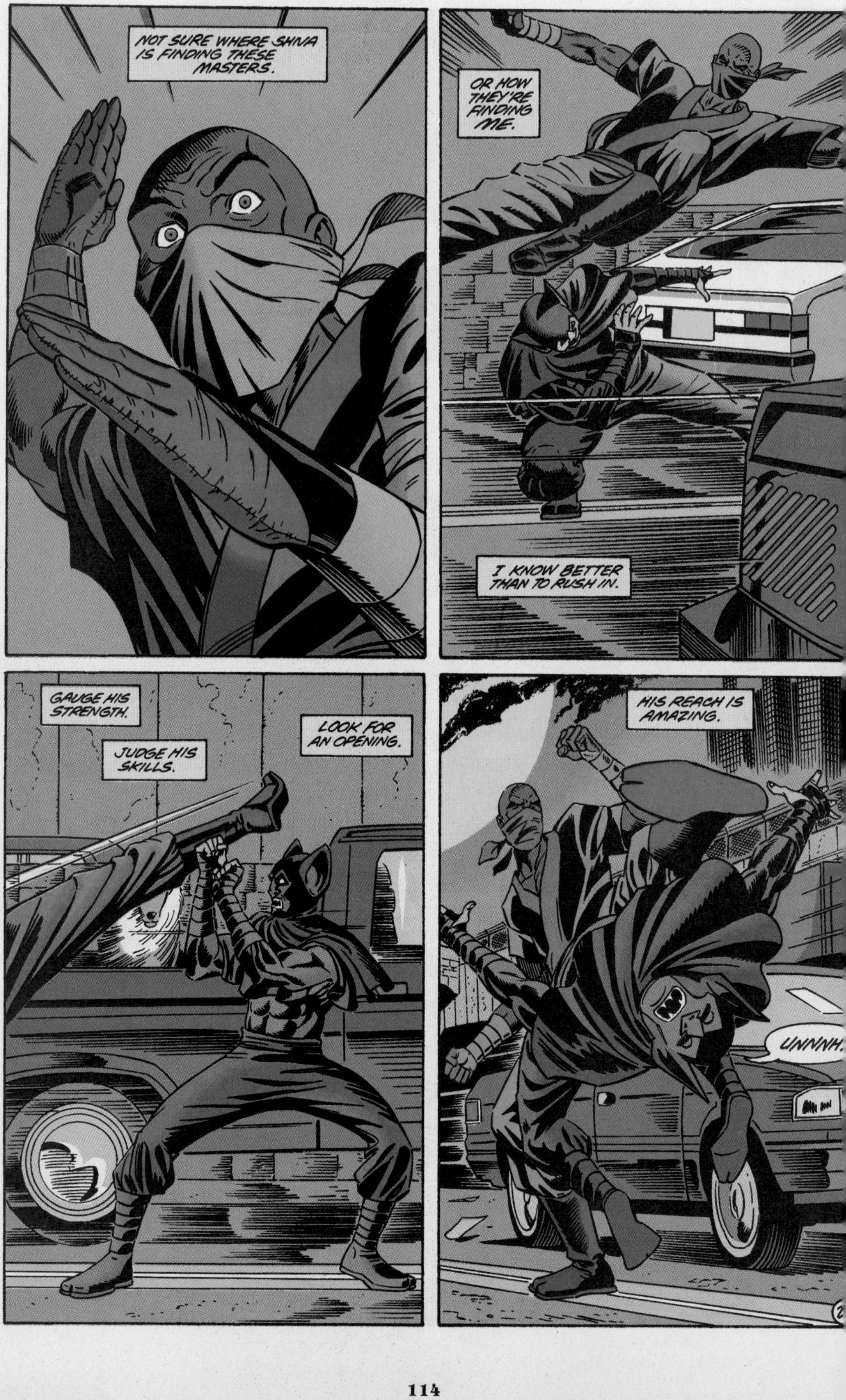
NOT SURE WHERE SHIVA IS FINDING THESE MASTERS.
OR HOW THEY'RE FINDING ME.
I KNOW BETTER THAN TO RUSH IN.
GAUGE HIS STRENGTH.
JUDGE HIS SKILLS.
LOOK FOR AN OPENING.
HIS REACH IS AMAZING.
UNNNH.

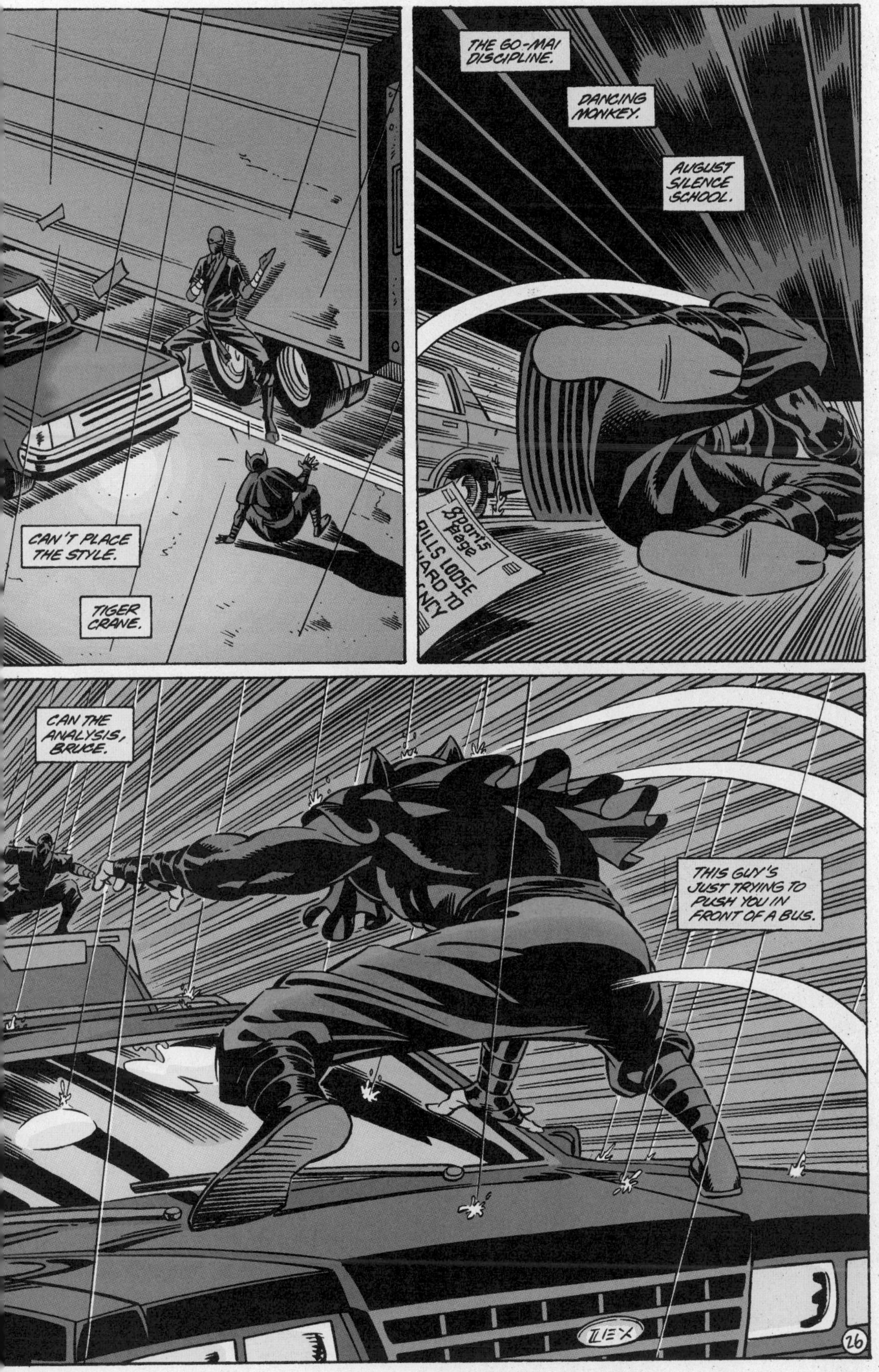
CAN'T PLACE THE STYLE.
TIGER CRANE.
THE GO-MAI DISCIPLINE.
DANCING MONKEY.
AUGUST SILENCE SCHOOL.
CAN THE ANALYSIS, BRUCE.
THIS GUY'S JUST TRYING TO PUSH YOU IN FRONT OF A BUS.
26

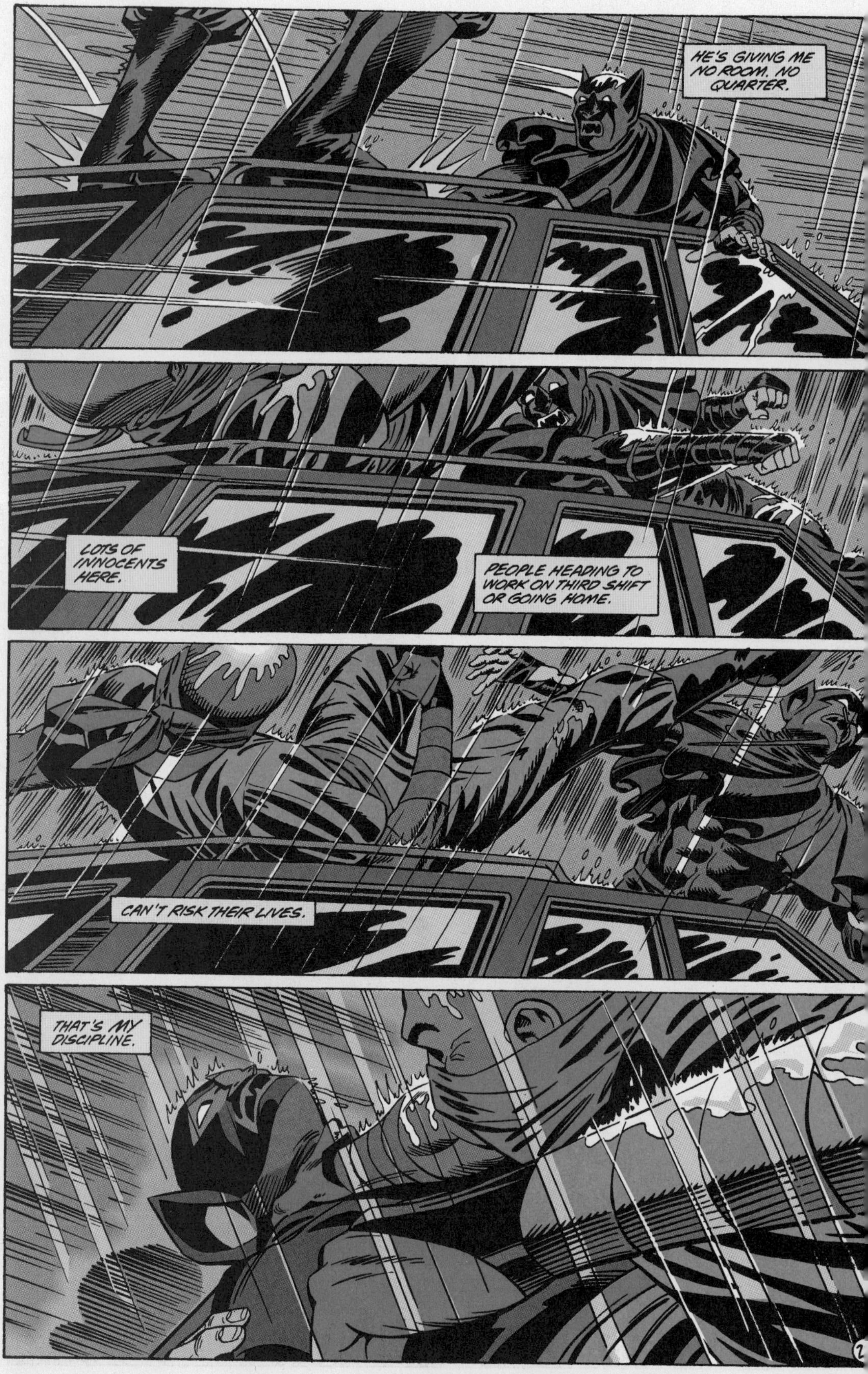
HE'S GIVING ME NO ROOM. NO QUARTER.
LOTS OF INNOCENTS HERE.
PEOPLE HEADING TO WORK ON THIRD SHIFT OR GOING HOME.
CAN'T RISK THEIR LIVES.
THAT'S MY DISCIPLINE.

I--I-- DON'T KNOW WHY YA NEED *ME* HERE.

THINK ABOUT IT, CANDY.

VELCOME Track Tower

IF YOU'RE LYING, THEN I'LL JUST HAVE TO GO LOOKING FOR YOU AGAIN. AND YOU'D MAKE IT *HARDER* NEXT TIME, WOULDN'T YOU?

PLOK

YA GOT *THAT* RIGHT.

YOU SAY YOU MET THIS GUN DEALER ON THE FIFTH FLOOR?

YUH-YEAH!

HOLEEE...

THUH-THUH-- THAT'S HIM...

SOMEONE WENT TO A LOT OF TROUBLE. THIS IS MORE THAN JUST MURDER.

28

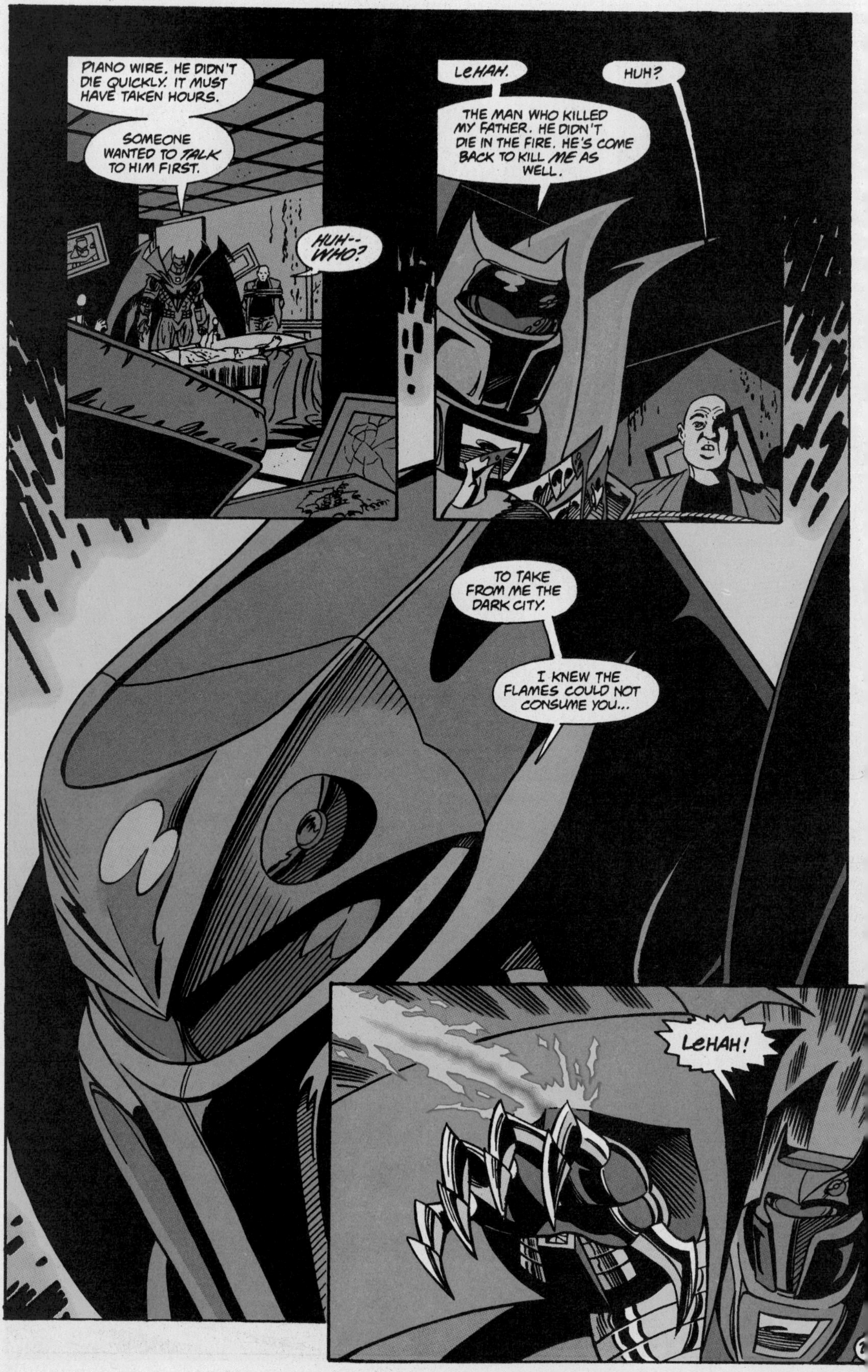
PIANO WIRE. HE DIDN'T DIE QUICKLY. IT MUST HAVE TAKEN HOURS.
SOMEONE WANTED TO TALK TO HIM FIRST.
HUH-- WHO?
LeHAH.
HUH?
THE MAN WHO KILLED MY FATHER. HE DIDN'T DIE IN THE FIRE. HE'S COME BACK TO KILL ME AS WELL.
TO TAKE FROM ME THE DARK CITY.
I KNEW THE FLAMES COULD NOT CONSUME YOU...
LeHAH!

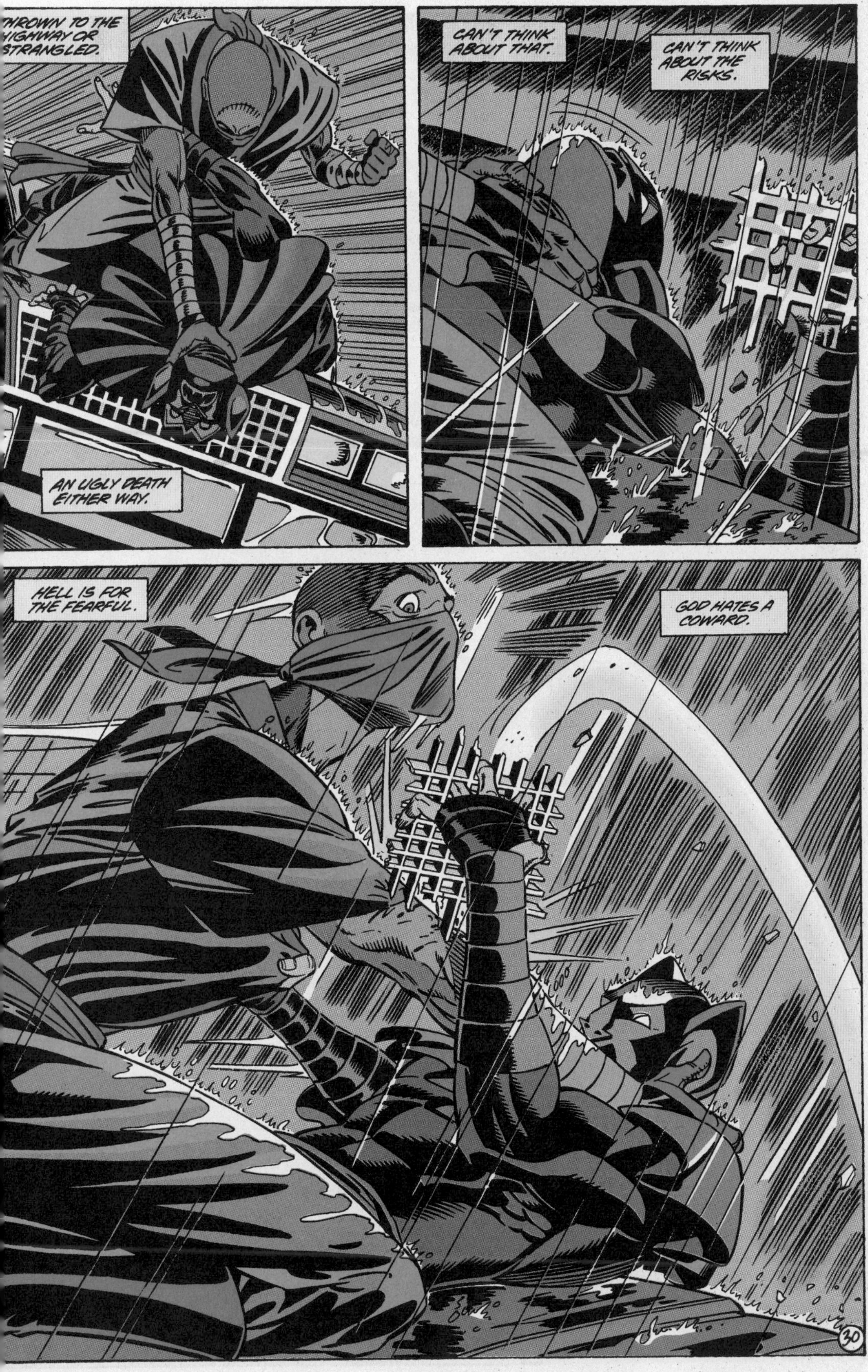
THROWN TO THE HIGHWAY OR STRANGLED.
AN UGLY DEATH EITHER WAY.
CAN'T THINK ABOUT THAT.
CAN'T THINK ABOUT THE RISKS.
HELL IS FOR THE FEARFUL.
GOD HATES A COWARD.
30

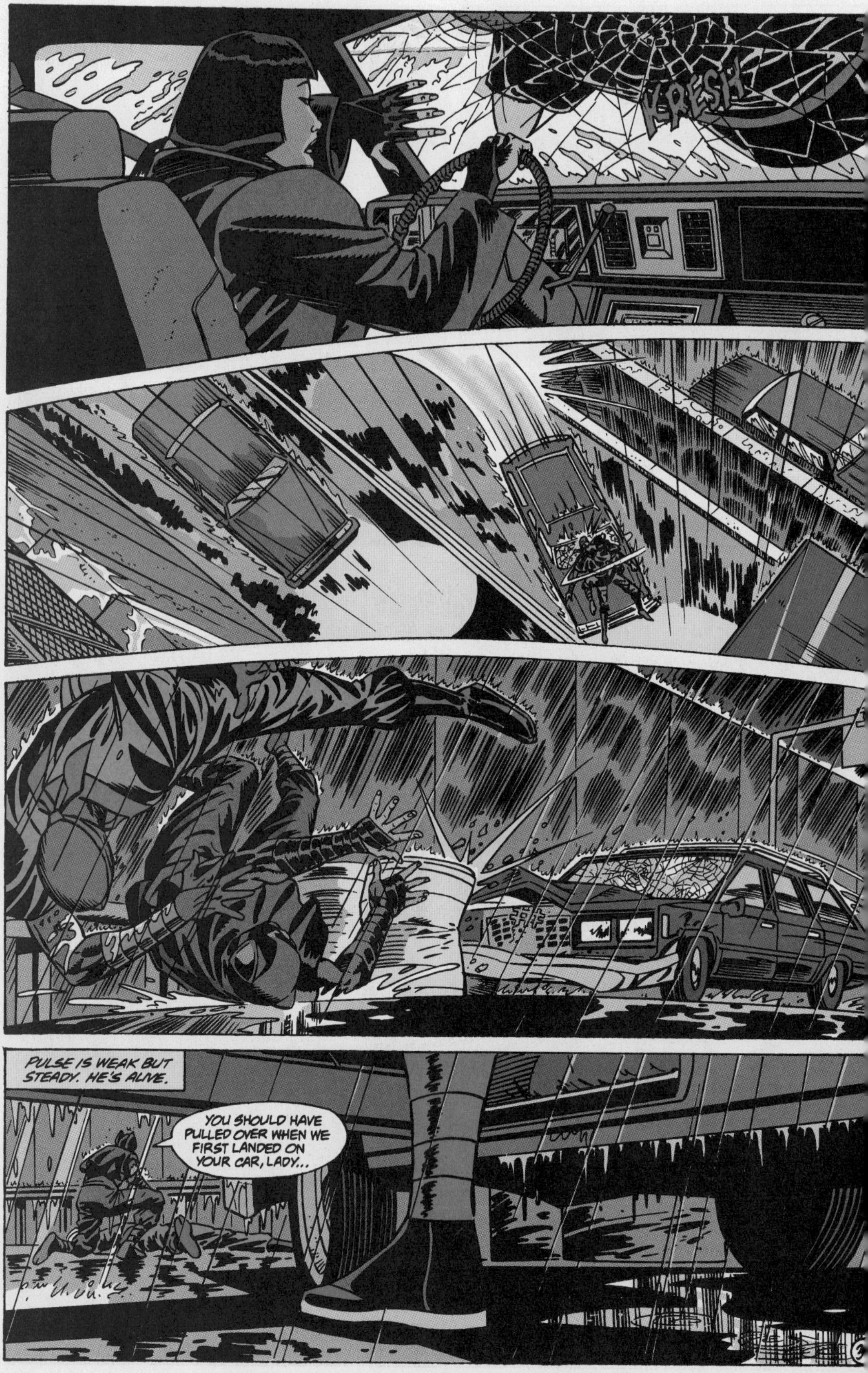
KRESH
PULSE IS WEAK BUT STEADY. HE'S ALIVE.
YOU SHOULD HAVE PULLED OVER WHEN WE FIRST LANDED ON YOUR CAR, LADY...

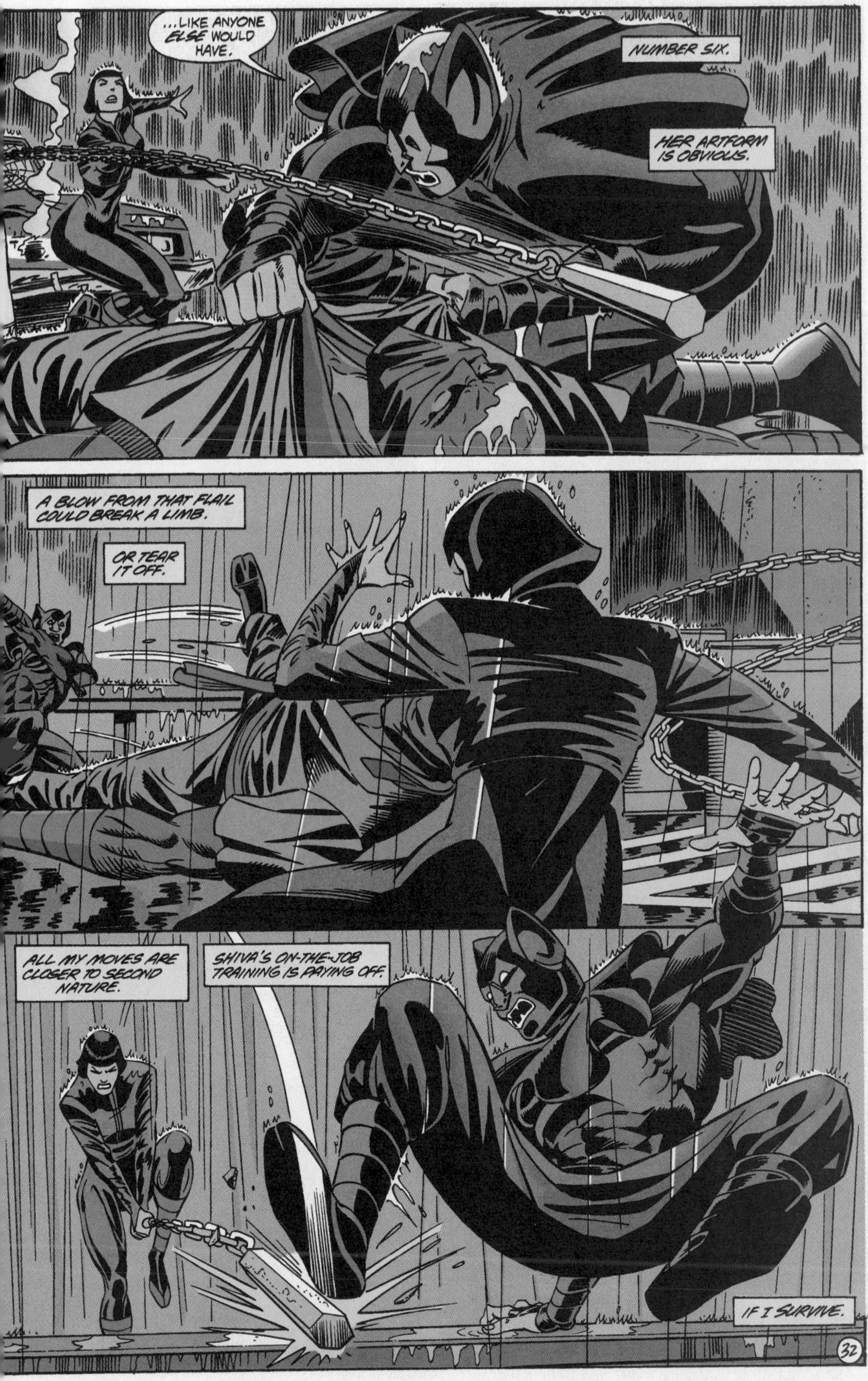
...LIKE ANYONE ELSE WOULD HAVE.
NUMBER SIX.
HER ARTFORM IS OBVIOUS.
A BLOW FROM THAT FLAIL COULD BREAK A LIMB.
OR TEAR IT OFF.
ALL MY MOVES ARE CLOSER TO SECOND NATURE.
SHIVA'S ON-THE-JOB TRAINING IS PAYING OFF.
IF I SURVIVE.
32

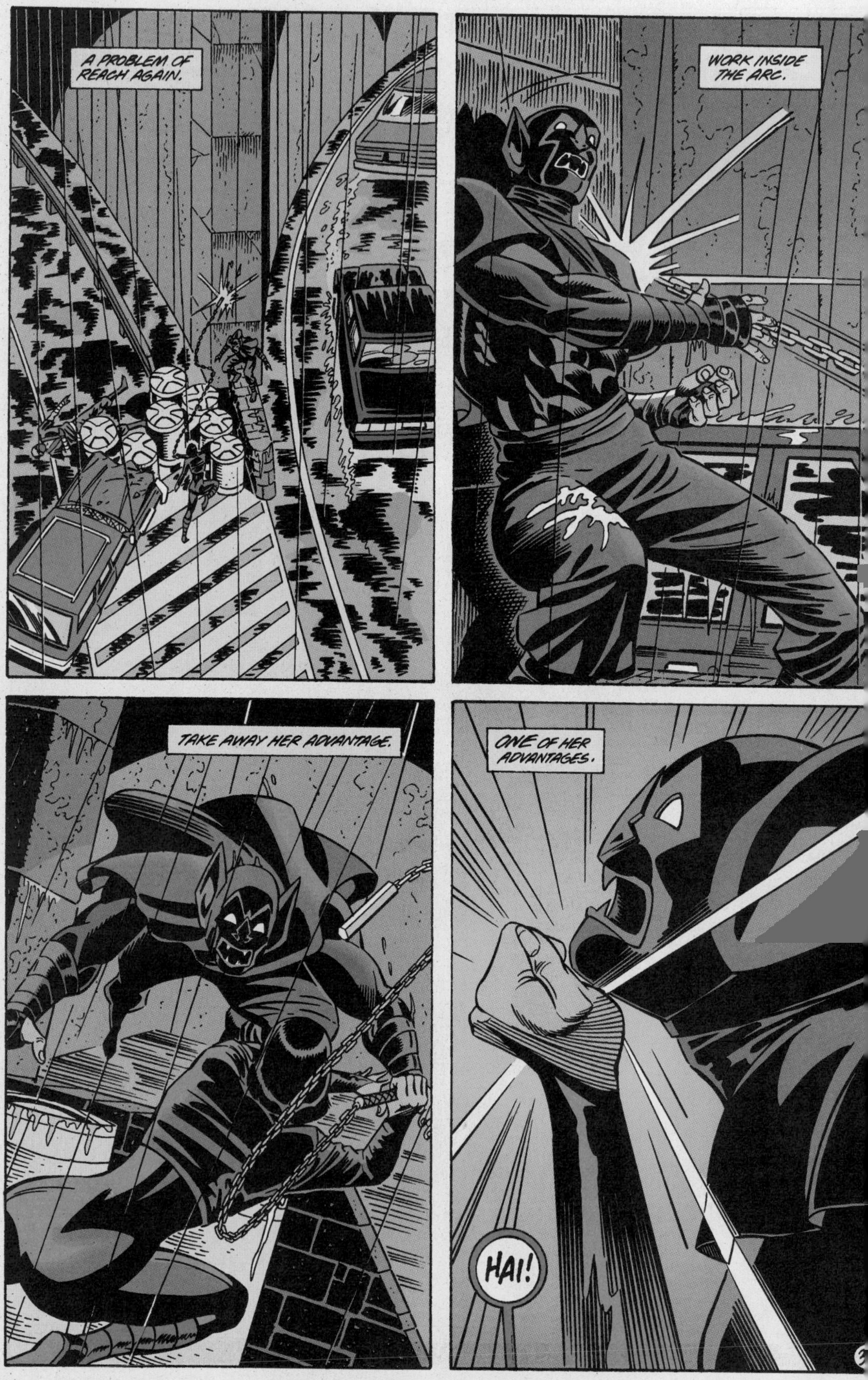
A PROBLEM OF REACH AGAIN.
WORK INSIDE THE ARC.
TAKE AWAY HER ADVANTAGE.
ONE OF HER ADVANTAGES.
HAI!

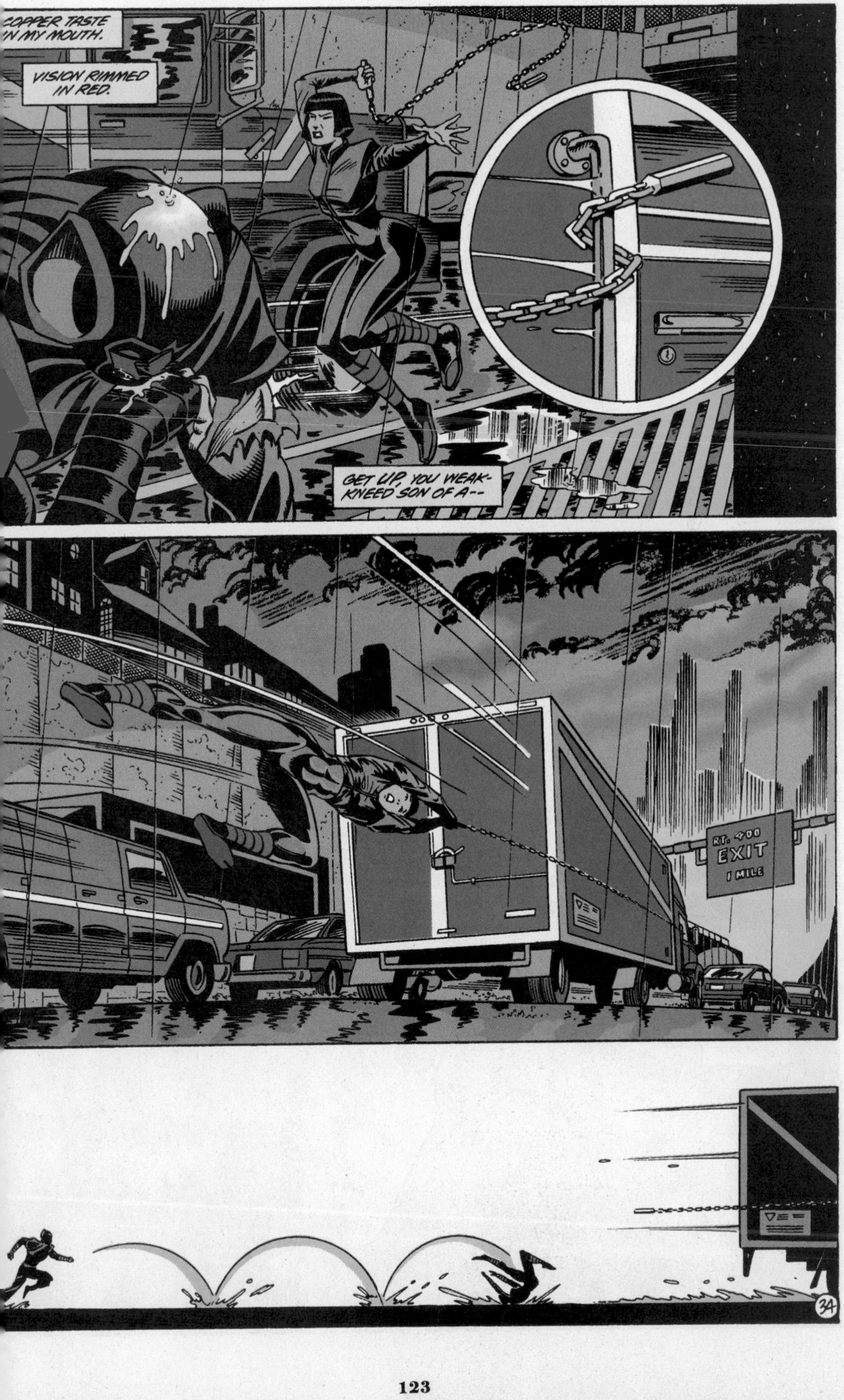
COPPER TASTE IN MY MOUTH.
VISION RIMMED IN RED.
GET UP, YOU WEAK-KNEED SON OF A--
RT. 400
EXIT
1 MILE
34

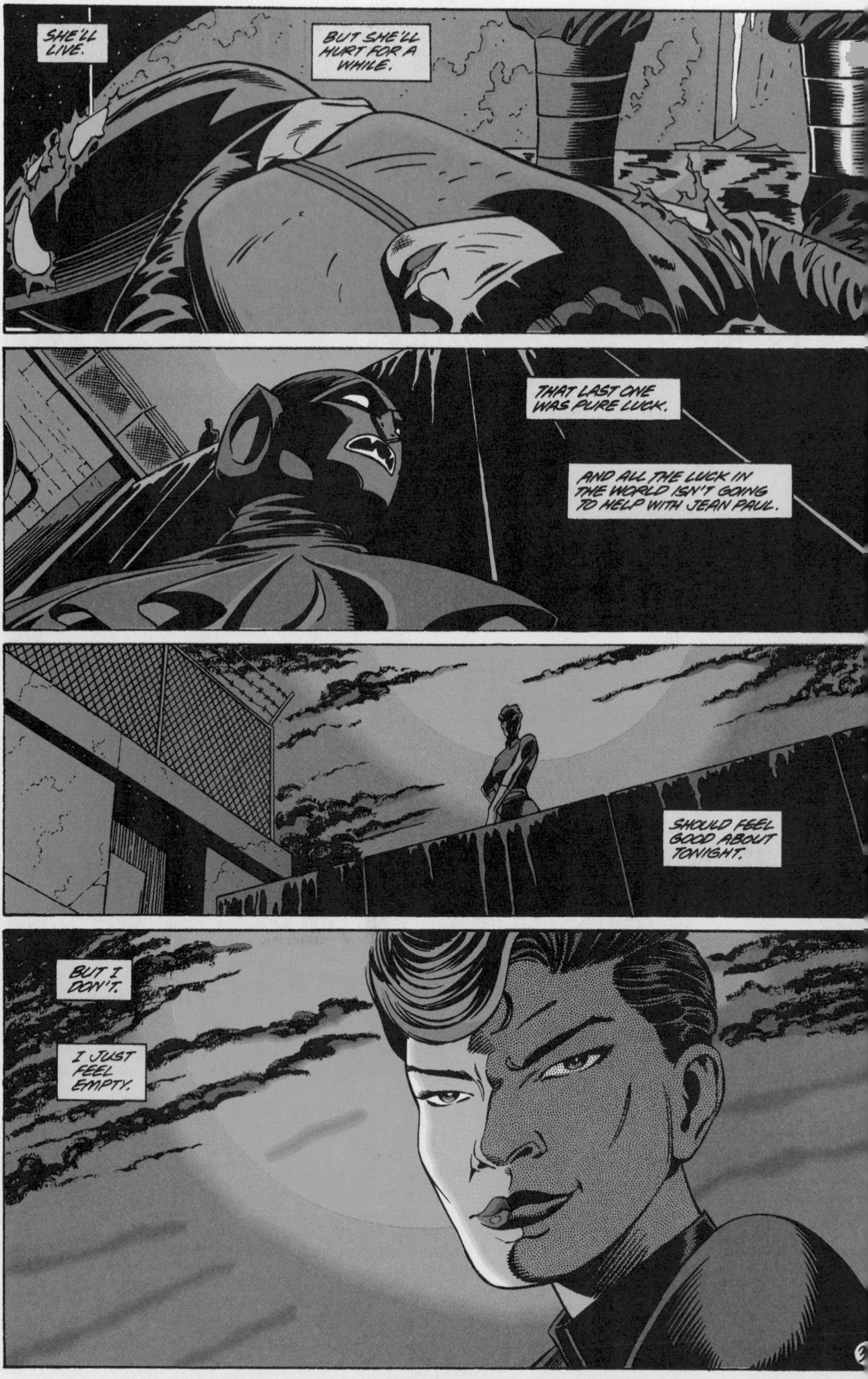
SHE'LL LIVE.
BUT SHE'LL HURT FOR A WHILE.
THAT LAST ONE WAS PURE LUCK.
AND ALL THE LUCK IN THE WORLD ISN'T GOING TO HELP WITH JEAN PAUL.
SHOULD FEEL GOOD ABOUT TONIGHT.
BUT I DON'T.
I JUST FEEL EMPTY.

IT CAME FROM DOWN HERE? SOMEONE SCREAMING?

YOU SWEAT THE *DETAILS* TOO MUCH, NEAL.

AND YOU *DON'T*, DANNY? WHO ALWAYS ASKS WHERE THE EMPTY HORSES RUN OFF TO IN THE COWBOY MOVIES?

SHUT UP, NEAL. I SEE SOMETHING...

EMPTY HORSES?

YOU KNOW, LIKE WHEN THE INDIANS GET SHOT OFFA THEM.

WHERE?

WHO YOU THINK CALLED IN A GUY SCREAMING IN *THIS* NEIGHBORHOOD AT *THIS* HOUR?

STAY AWAKE... STAY AWAKE...

RUH...RUH... RATS...BUH...BUH... BATS...

36

125

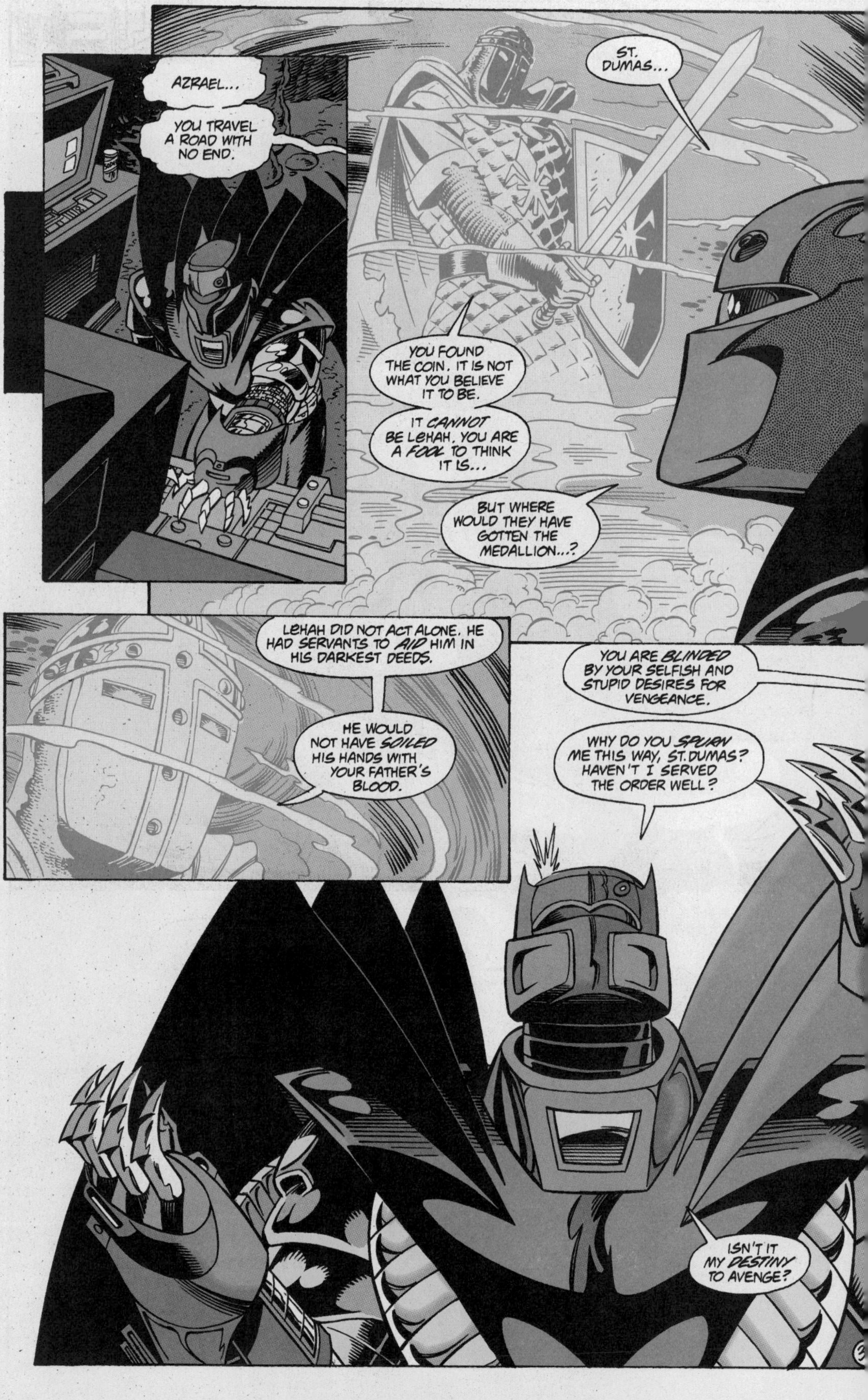
AZRAEL...
YOU TRAVEL A ROAD WITH NO END.
ST. DUMAS...
YOU FOUND THE COIN. IT IS NOT WHAT YOU BELIEVE IT TO BE.
IT CANNOT BE LEHAH. YOU ARE A FOOL TO THINK IT IS...
BUT WHERE WOULD THEY HAVE GOTTEN THE MEDALLION...?
LEHAH DID NOT ACT ALONE. HE HAD SERVANTS TO AID HIM IN HIS DARKEST DEEDS.
HE WOULD NOT HAVE SOILED HIS HANDS WITH YOUR FATHER'S BLOOD.
YOU ARE BLINDED BY YOUR SELFISH AND STUPID DESIRES FOR VENGEANCE.
WHY DO YOU SPURN ME THIS WAY, ST. DUMAS? HAVEN'T I SERVED THE ORDER WELL?
ISN'T IT MY DESTINY TO AVENGE?

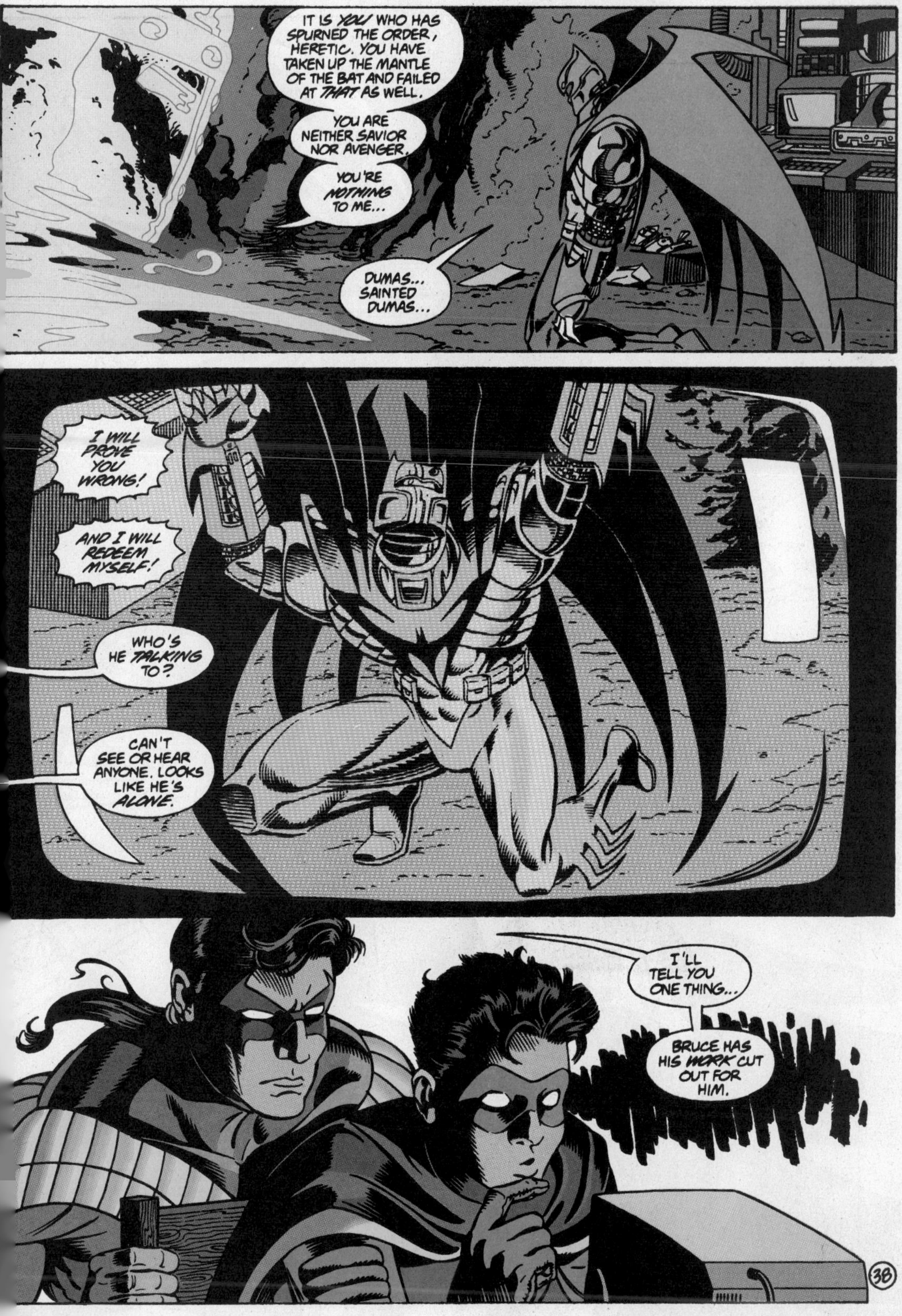
IT IS YOU WHO HAS SPURNED THE ORDER, HERETIC. YOU HAVE TAKEN UP THE MANTLE OF THE BAT AND FAILED AT THAT AS WELL.
YOU ARE NEITHER SAVIOR NOR AVENGER.
YOU'RE NOTHING TO ME...
DUMAS... SAINTED DUMAS...
I WILL PROVE YOU WRONG!
AND I WILL REDEEM MYSELF!
WHO'S HE TALKING TO?
CAN'T SEE OR HEAR ANYONE. LOOKS LIKE HE'S ALONE.
I'LL TELL YOU ONE THING...
BRUCE HAS HIS WORK CUT OUT FOR HIM.
38

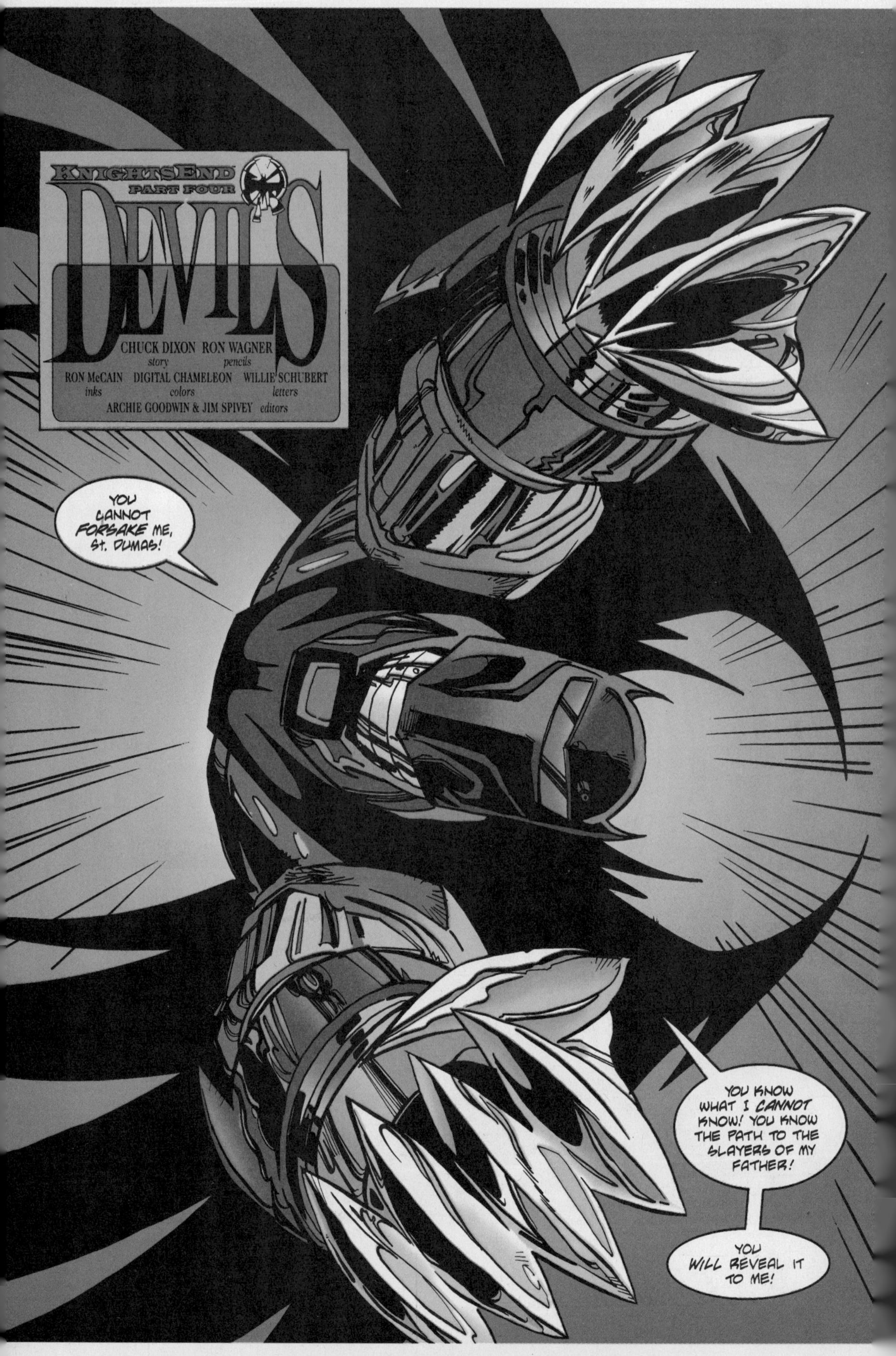

KNIGHTSEND PART FOUR
DEVILS
CHUCK DIXON story RON WAGNER pencils
RON McCAIN inks DIGITAL CHAMELEON colors WILLIE SCHUBERT letters
ARCHIE GOODWIN & JIM SPIVEY editors
YOU CANNOT FORSAKE ME, St. DUMAS!
YOU KNOW WHAT I CANNOT KNOW! YOU KNOW THE PATH TO THE SLAYERS OF MY FATHER!
YOU WILL REVEAL IT TO ME!

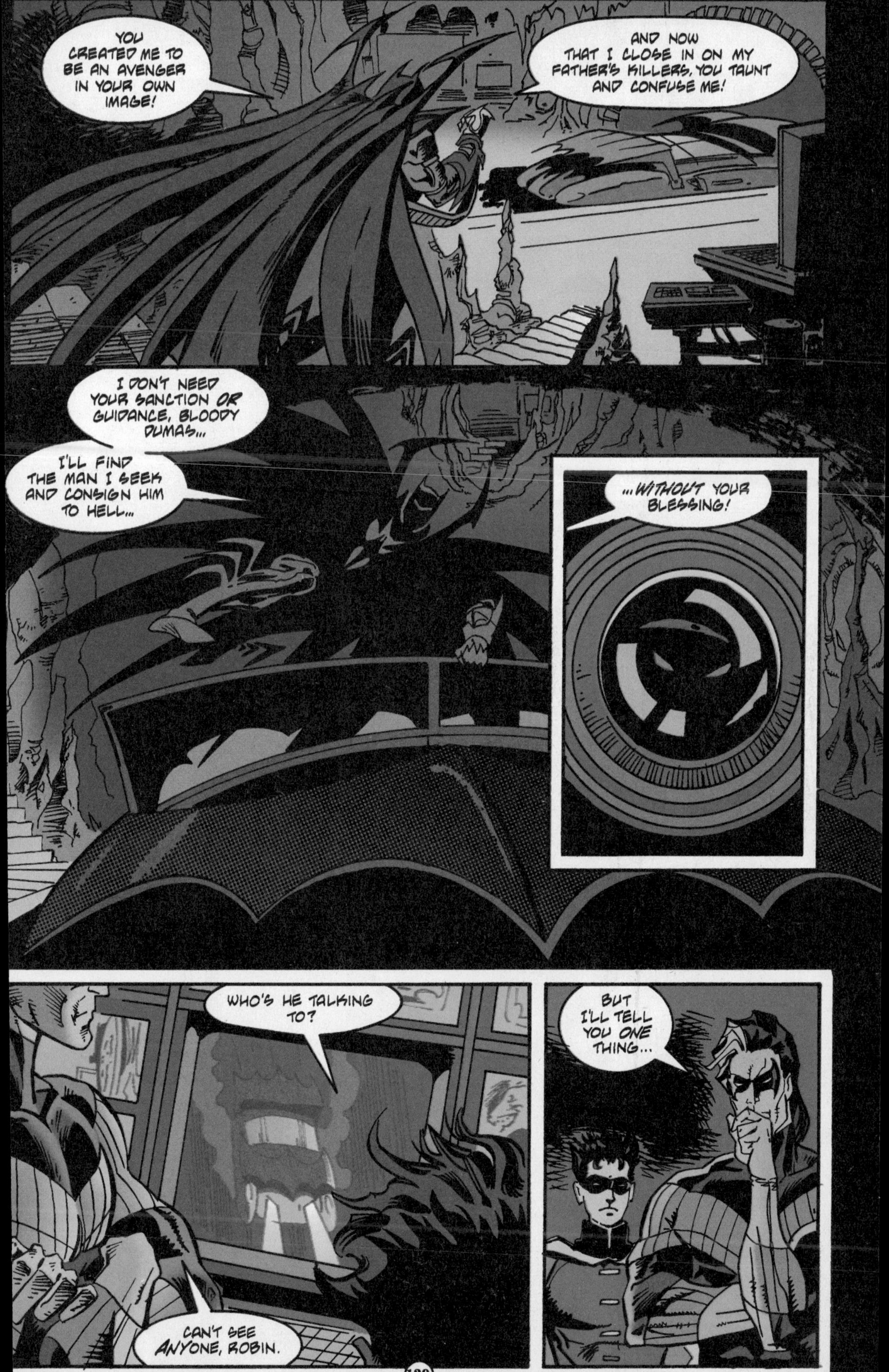

YOU CREATED ME TO BE AN AVENGER IN YOUR OWN IMAGE!
AND NOW THAT I CLOSE IN ON MY FATHER'S KILLERS, YOU TAUNT AND CONFUSE ME!
I DON'T NEED YOUR SANCTION OR GUIDANCE, BLOODY DUMAS...
I'LL FIND THE MAN I SEEK AND CONSIGN HIM TO HELL...
...WITHOUT YOUR BLESSING!
WHO'S HE TALKING TO?
CAN'T SEE ANYONE, ROBIN.
BUT I'LL TELL YOU ONE THING...

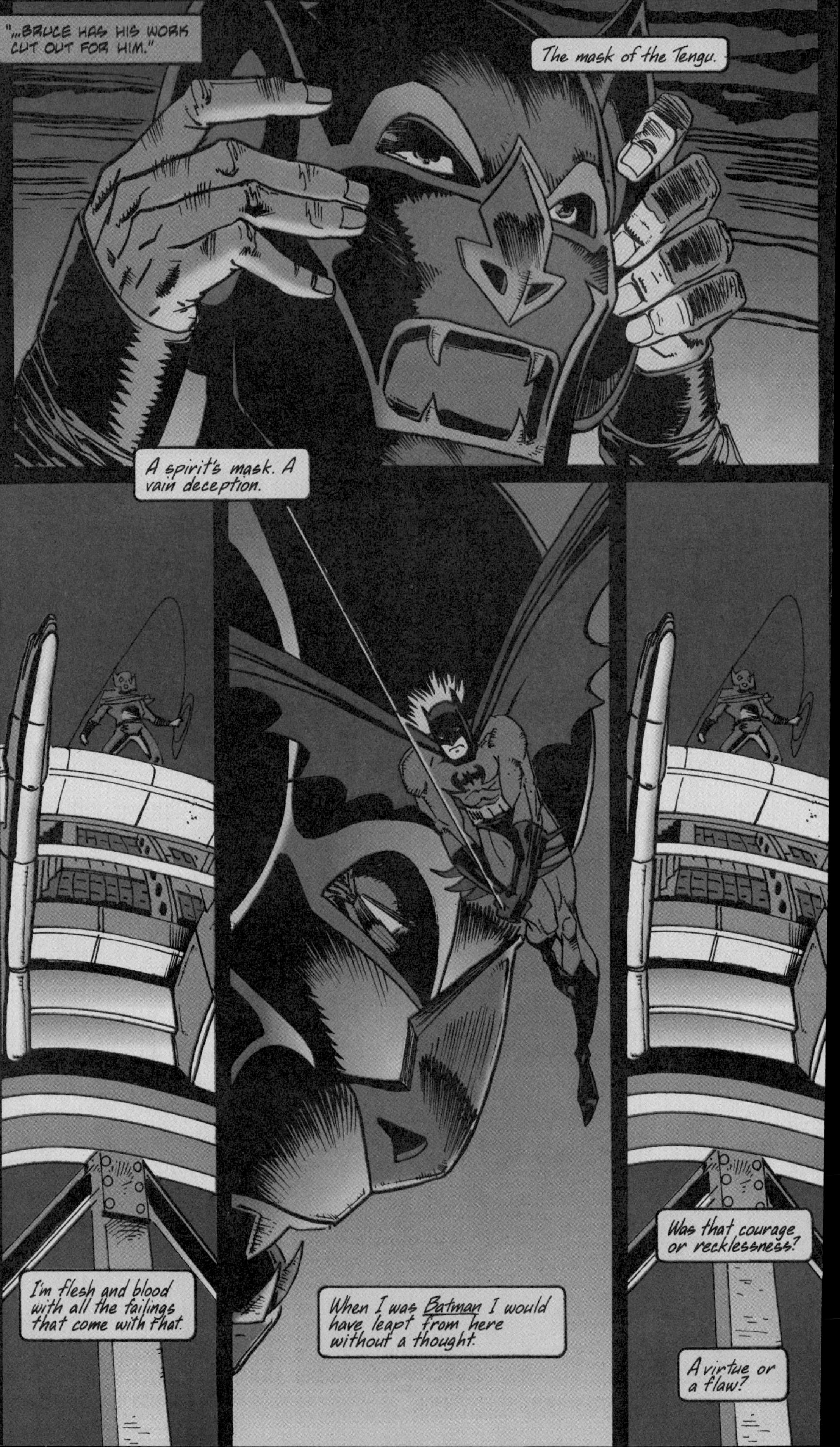
"...BRUCE HAS HIS WORK CUT OUT FOR HIM."
The mask of the Tengu.
A spirit's mask. A vain deception.
I'm flesh and blood with all the failings that come with that.
When I was Batman I would have leapt from here without a thought.
Was that courage or recklessness?
A virtue or a flaw?

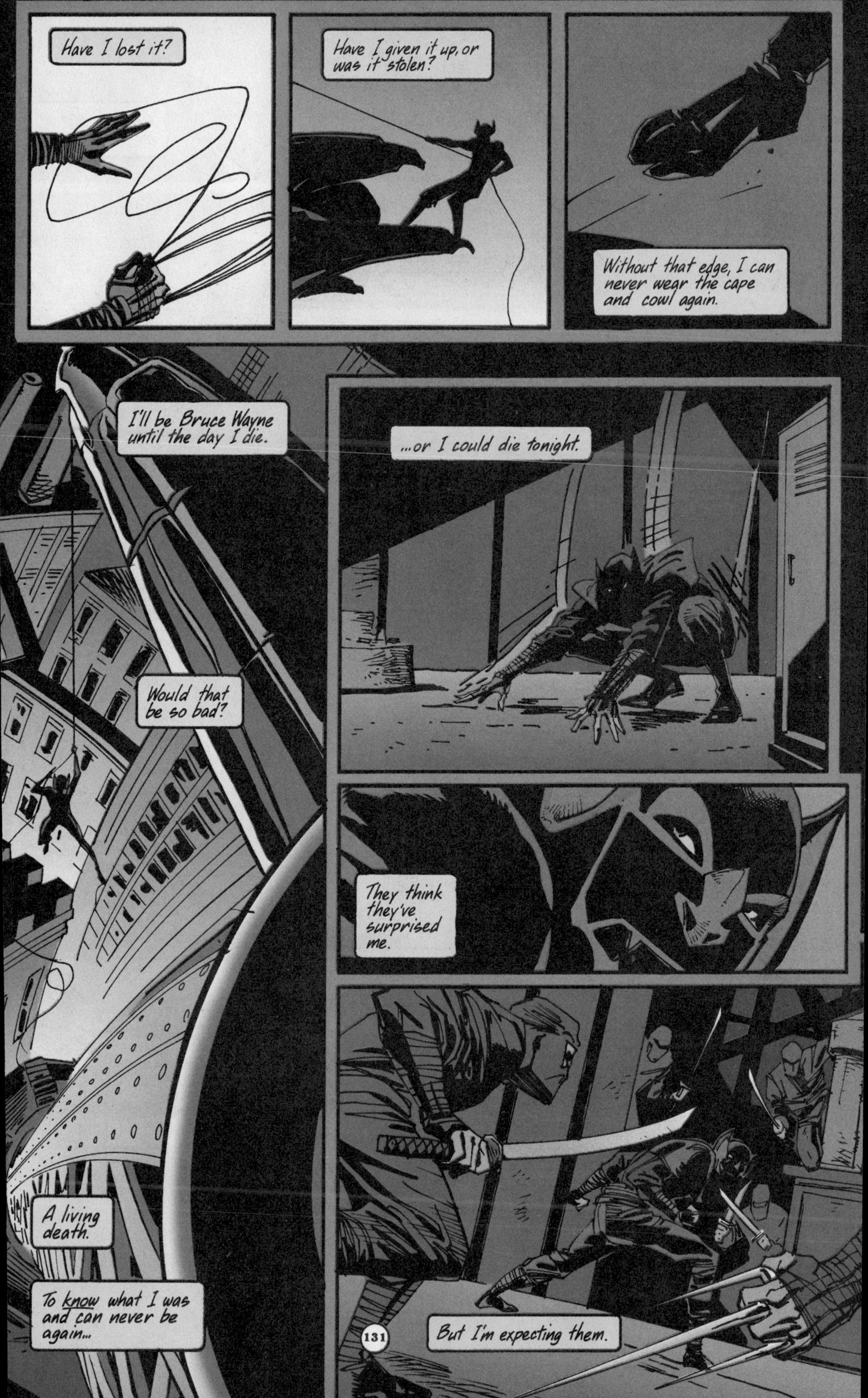

Have I lost it?
Have I given it up, or was it stolen?
Without that edge, I can never wear the cape and cowl again.
I'll be Bruce Wayne until the day I die.
Would that be so bad?
A living death.
To know what I was and can never be again...
...or I could die tonight.
They think they've surprised me.
But I'm expecting them.

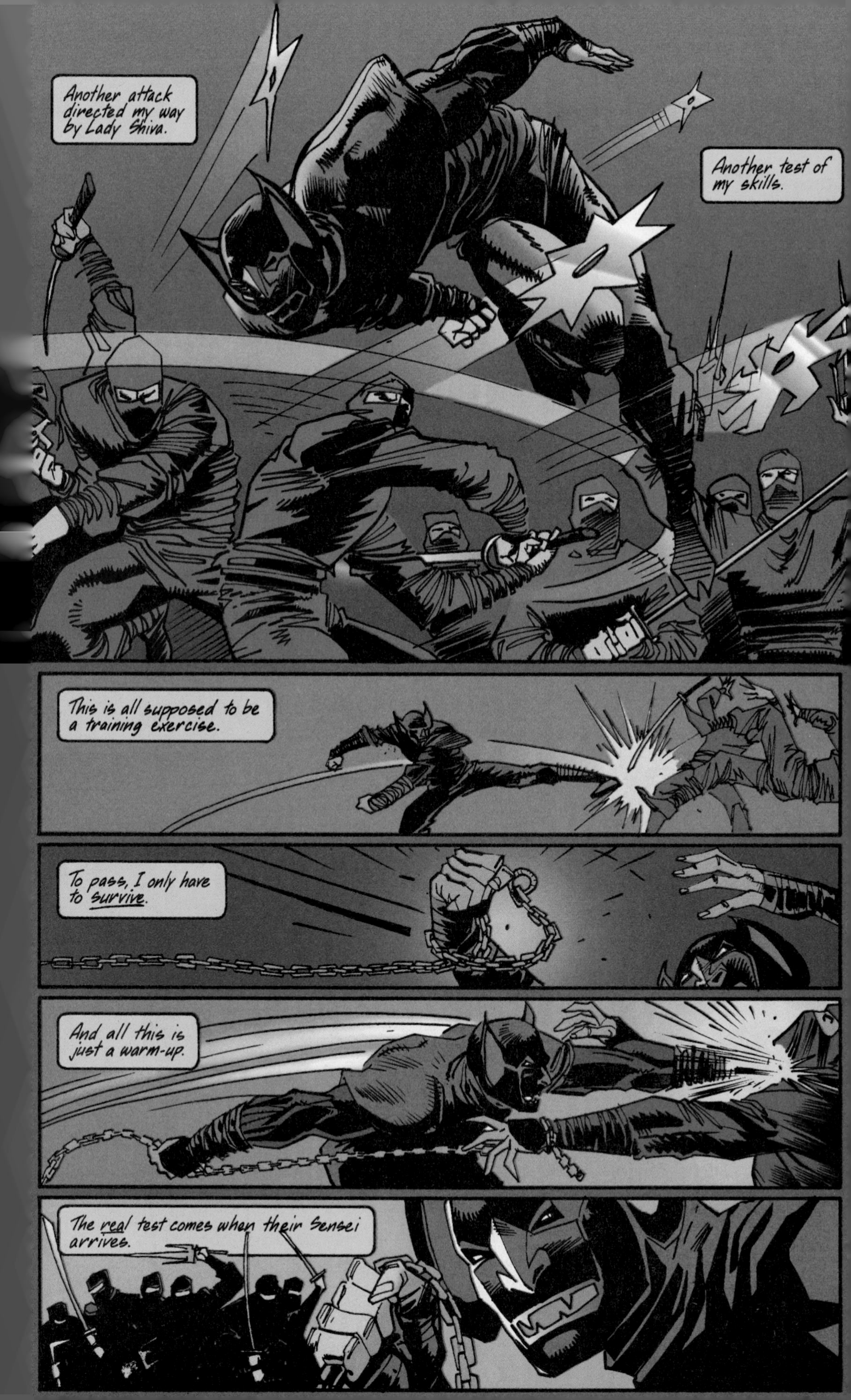
Another attack directed my way by Lady Shiva.
Another test of my skills.
This is all supposed to be a training exercise.
To pass, I only have to survive.
And all this is just a warm-up.
The real test comes when their Sensei arrives.

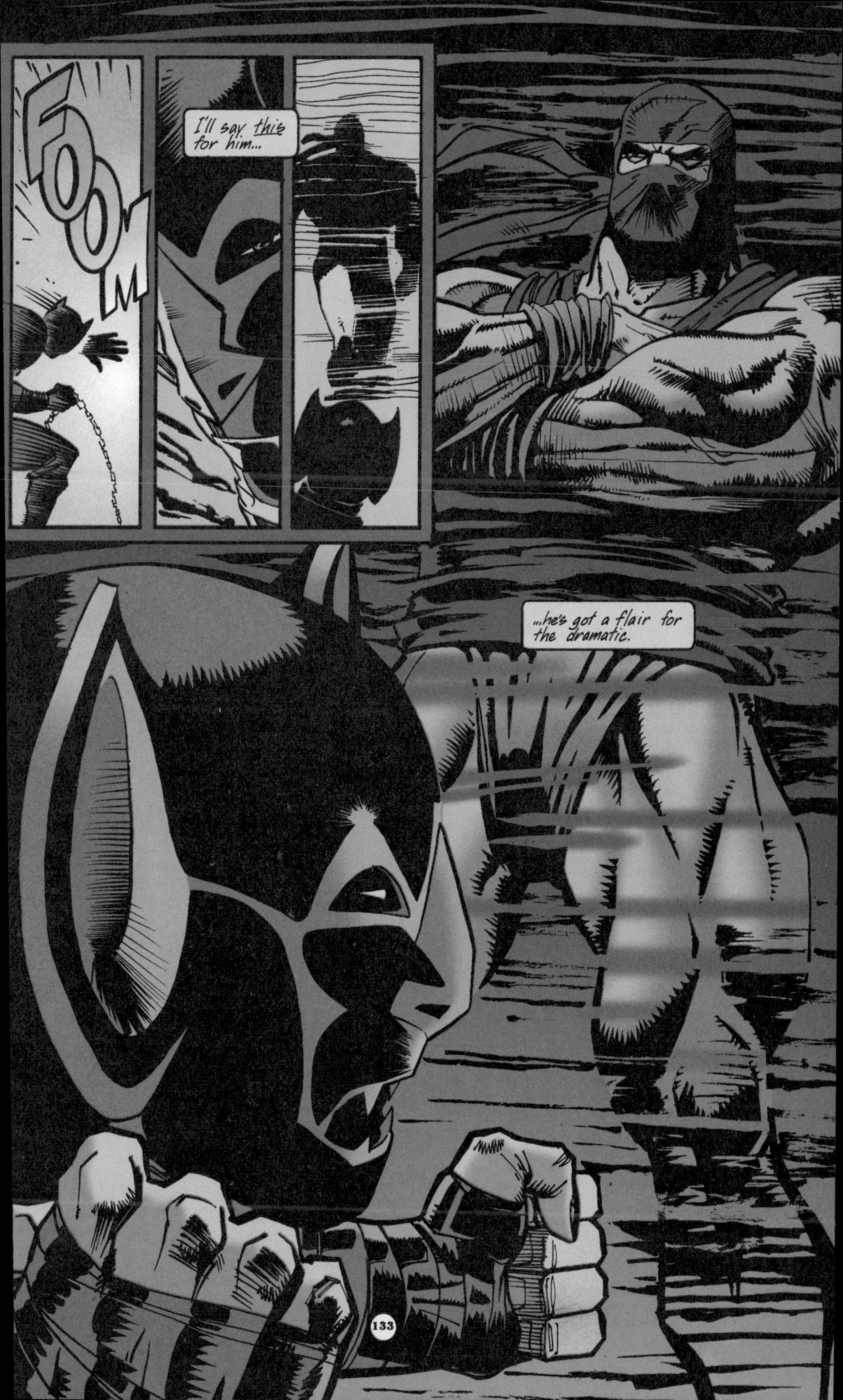

FOOOM
I'll say this for him...
...he's got a flair for the dramatic.

WHUH?

AW NO...

YOU SHOULDN'T TELL SO MANY OF YOUR FRIENDS WHERE YOU GO TO LIE LOW, CANDY.

TELL ME EVERYTHING YOU DIDN'T TELL ME BEFORE ABOUT THE GUNRUNNER...

HE DRANK SOME KINDA FRUITY WINE...

...HE BET THE HORSES HEAVY...

...SMOKED IMPORTS...

NOTHING HELPFUL, CANDY. THINK HARDER.

uh... uh... uh...

SOMETHIN' ABOUT... THE NAVY YARD...

134

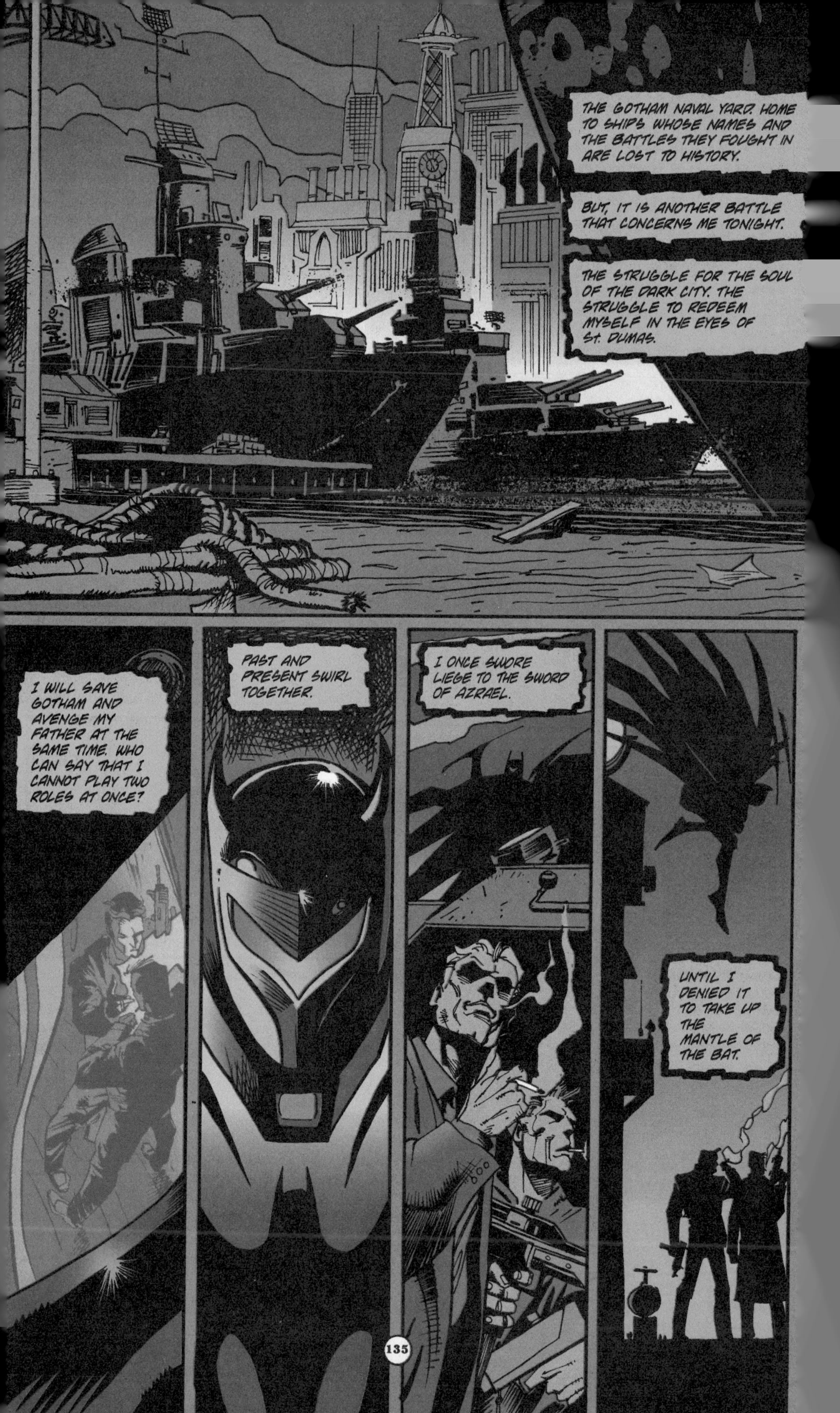
THE GOTHAM NAVAL YARD. HOME TO SHIPS WHOSE NAMES AND THE BATTLES THEY FOUGHT IN ARE LOST TO HISTORY.
BUT, IT IS ANOTHER BATTLE THAT CONCERNS ME TONIGHT.
THE STRUGGLE FOR THE SOUL OF THE DARK CITY. THE STRUGGLE TO REDEEM MYSELF IN THE EYES OF St. DUMAS.
I WILL SAVE GOTHAM AND AVENGE MY FATHER AT THE SAME TIME. WHO CAN SAY THAT I CANNOT PLAY TWO ROLES AT ONCE?
PAST AND PRESENT SWIRL TOGETHER.
I ONCE SWORE LIEGE TO THE SWORD OF AZRAEL.
UNTIL I DENIED IT TO TAKE UP THE MANTLE OF THE BAT.

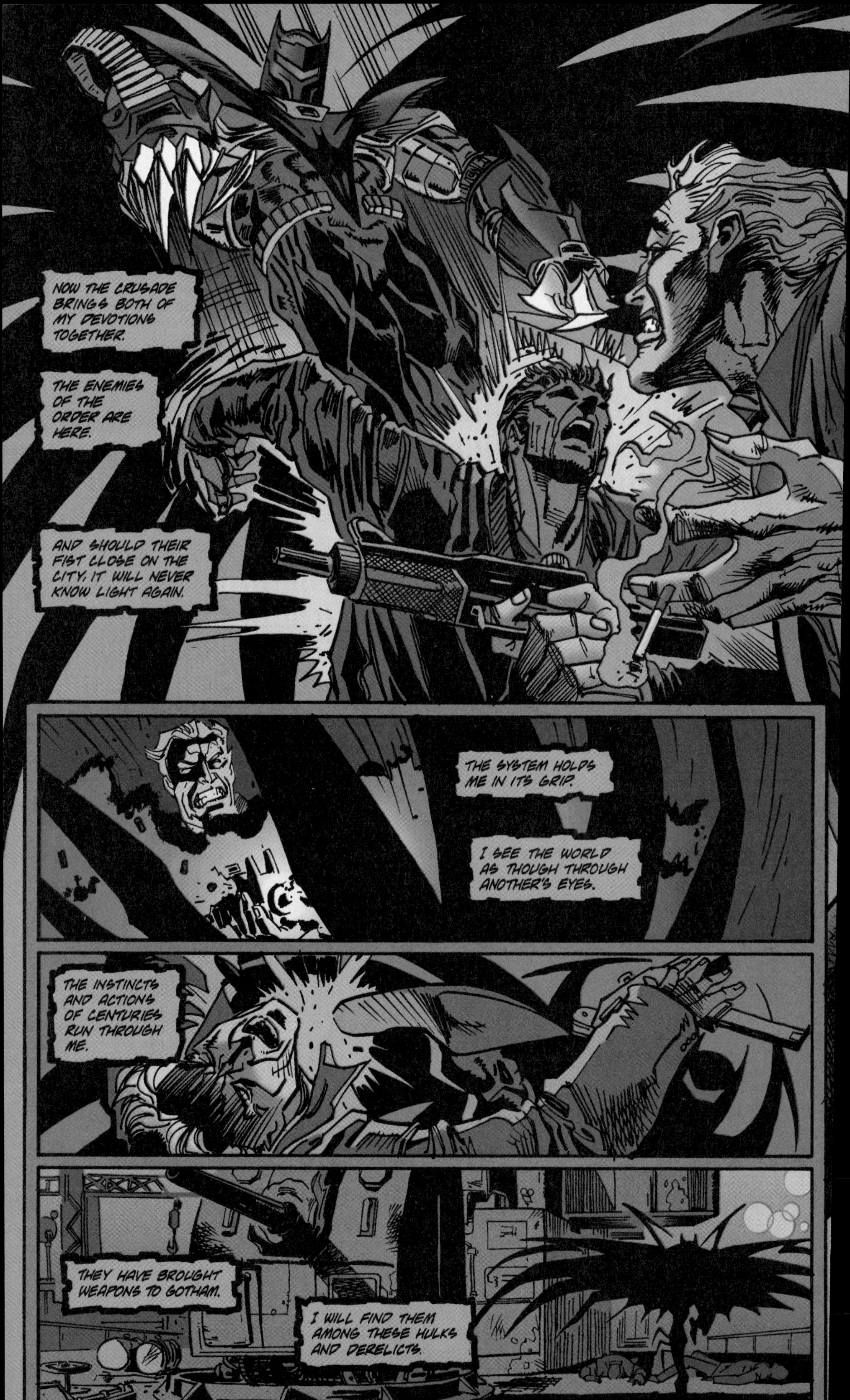
NOW THE CRUSADE BRINGS BOTH OF MY DEVOTIONS TOGETHER.
THE ENEMIES OF THE ORDER ARE HERE.
AND SHOULD THEIR FIST CLOSE ON THE CITY, IT WILL NEVER KNOW LIGHT AGAIN.
THE SYSTEM HOLDS ME IN ITS GRIP.
I SEE THE WORLD AS THOUGH THROUGH ANOTHER'S EYES.
THE INSTINCTS AND ACTIONS OF CENTURIES RUN THROUGH ME.
THEY HAVE BROUGHT WEAPONS TO GOTHAM.
I WILL FIND THEM AMONG THESE HULKS AND DERELICTS.

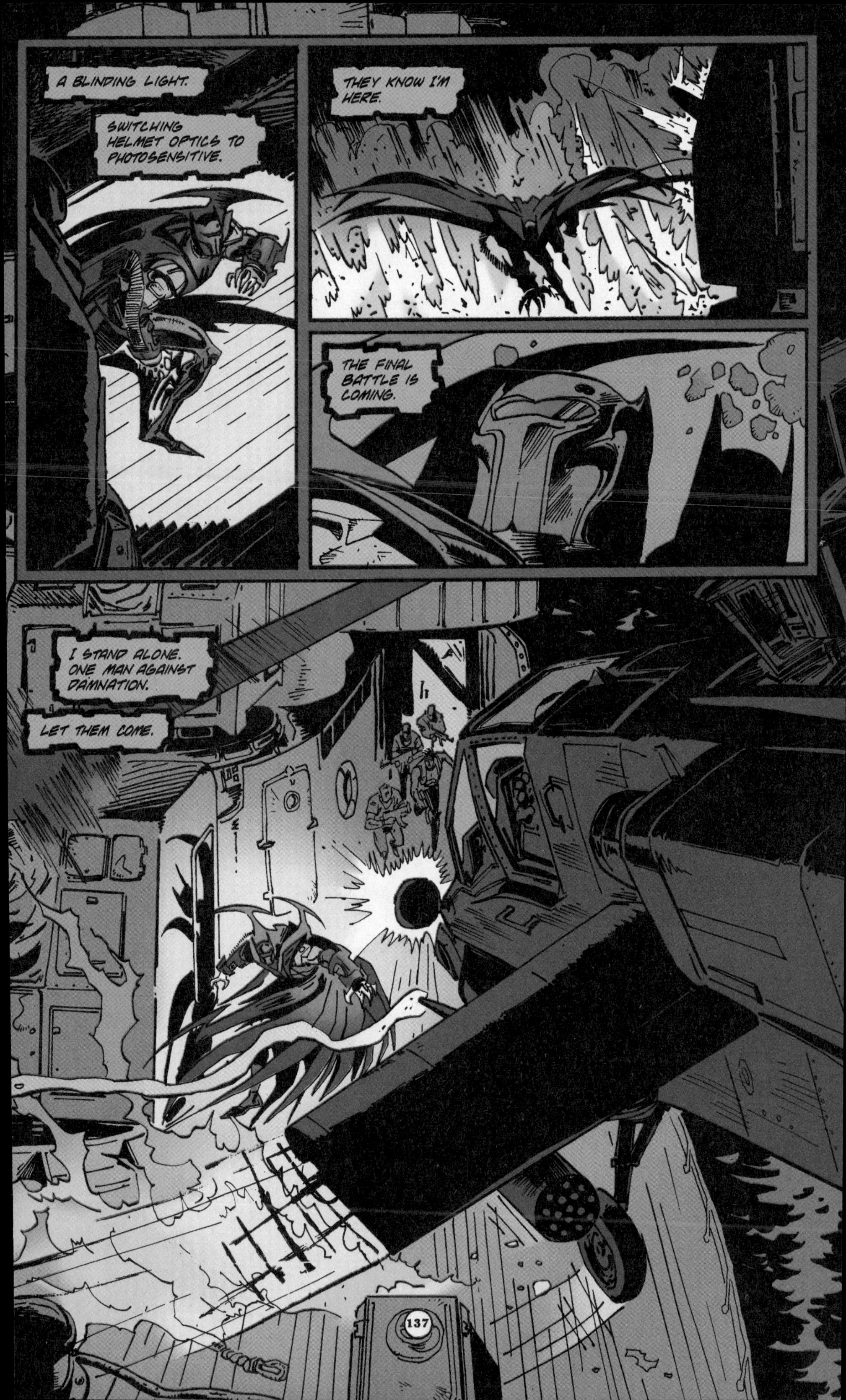

A BLINDING LIGHT.
SWITCHING HELMET OPTICS TO PHOTOSENSITIVE.
THEY KNOW I'M HERE.
THE FINAL BATTLE IS COMING.
I STAND ALONE. ONE MAN AGAINST DAMNATION.
LET THEM COME.

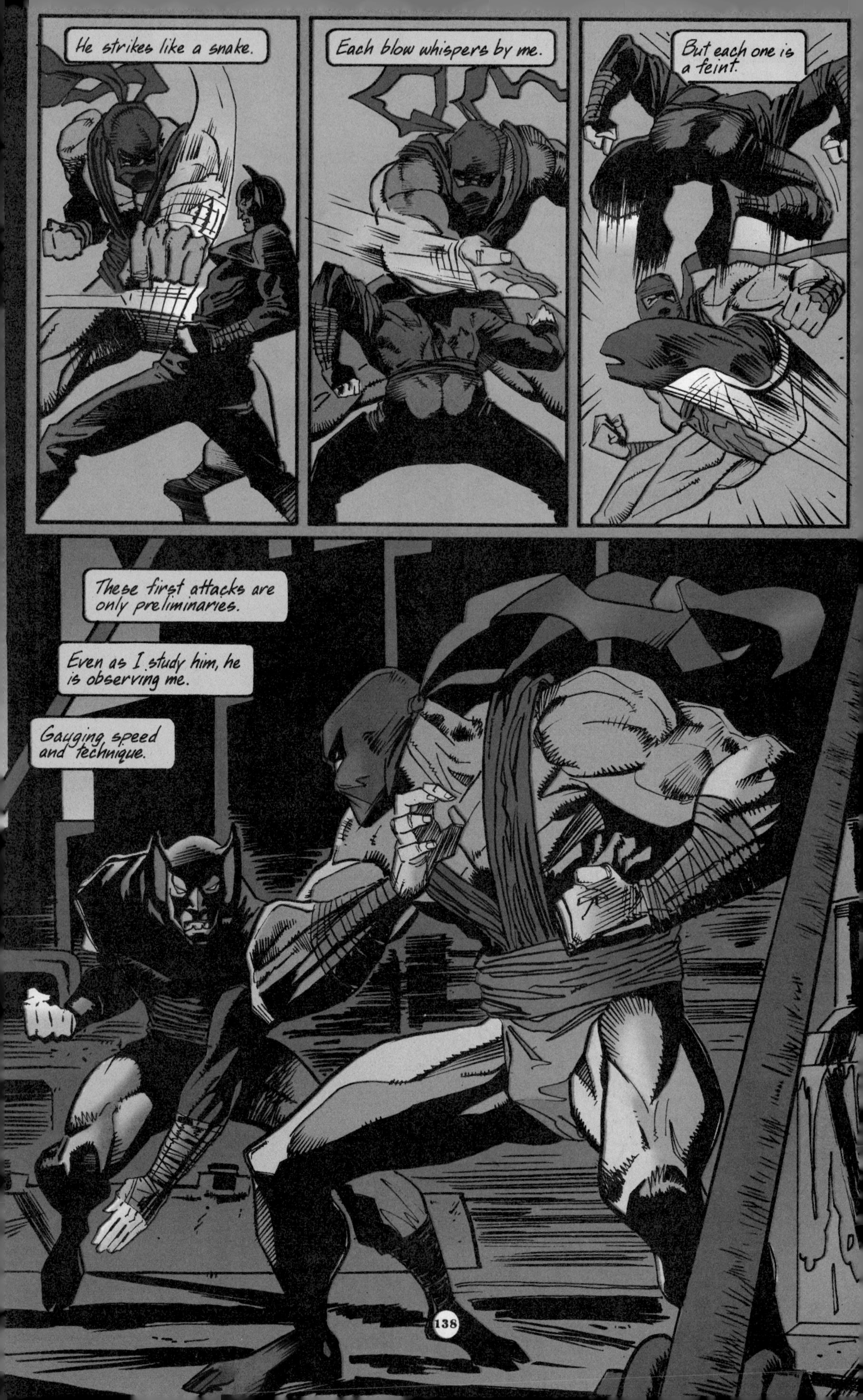
He strikes like a snake.
Each blow whispers by me.
But each one is a feint.
These first attacks are only preliminaries.
Even as I study him, he is observing me.
Gauging speed and technique.

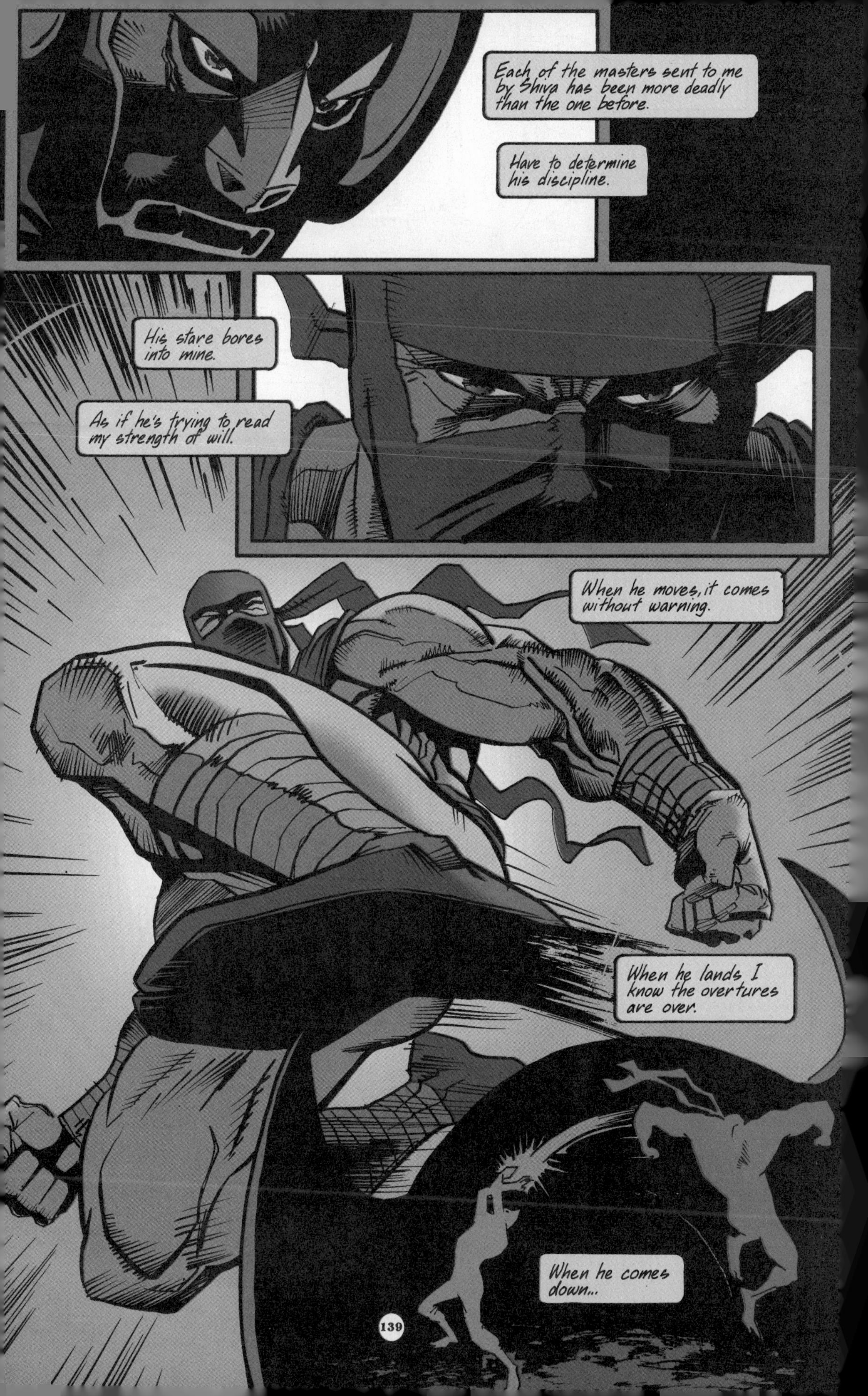
Each of the masters sent to me by Shiva has been more deadly than the one before.
Have to determine his discipline.
His stare bores into mine.
As if he's trying to read my strength of will.
When he moves, it comes without warning.
When he lands I know the overtures are over.
When he comes down...

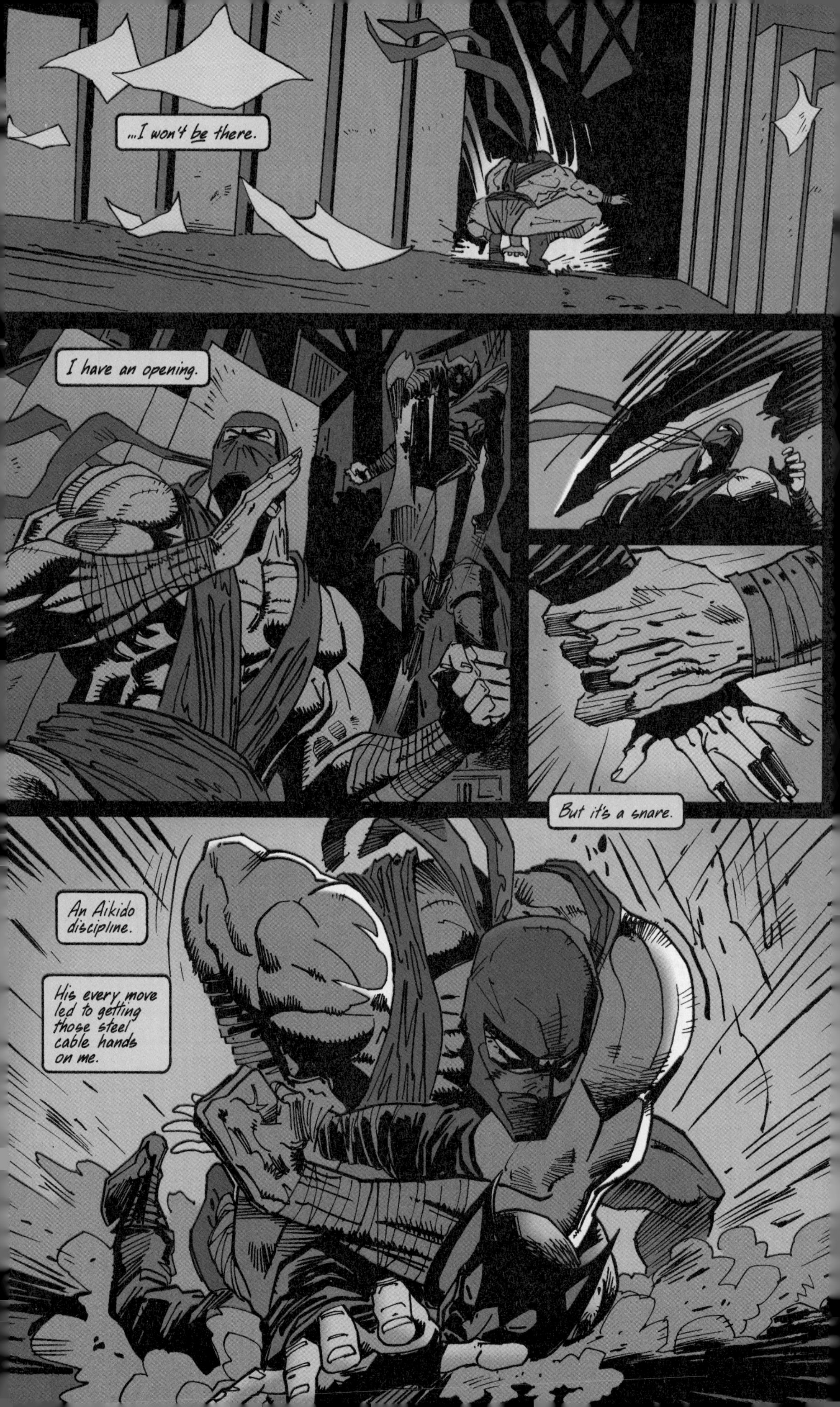
...I won't be there.
I have an opening.
But it's a snare.
An Aikido discipline.
His every move led to getting those steel cable hands on me.

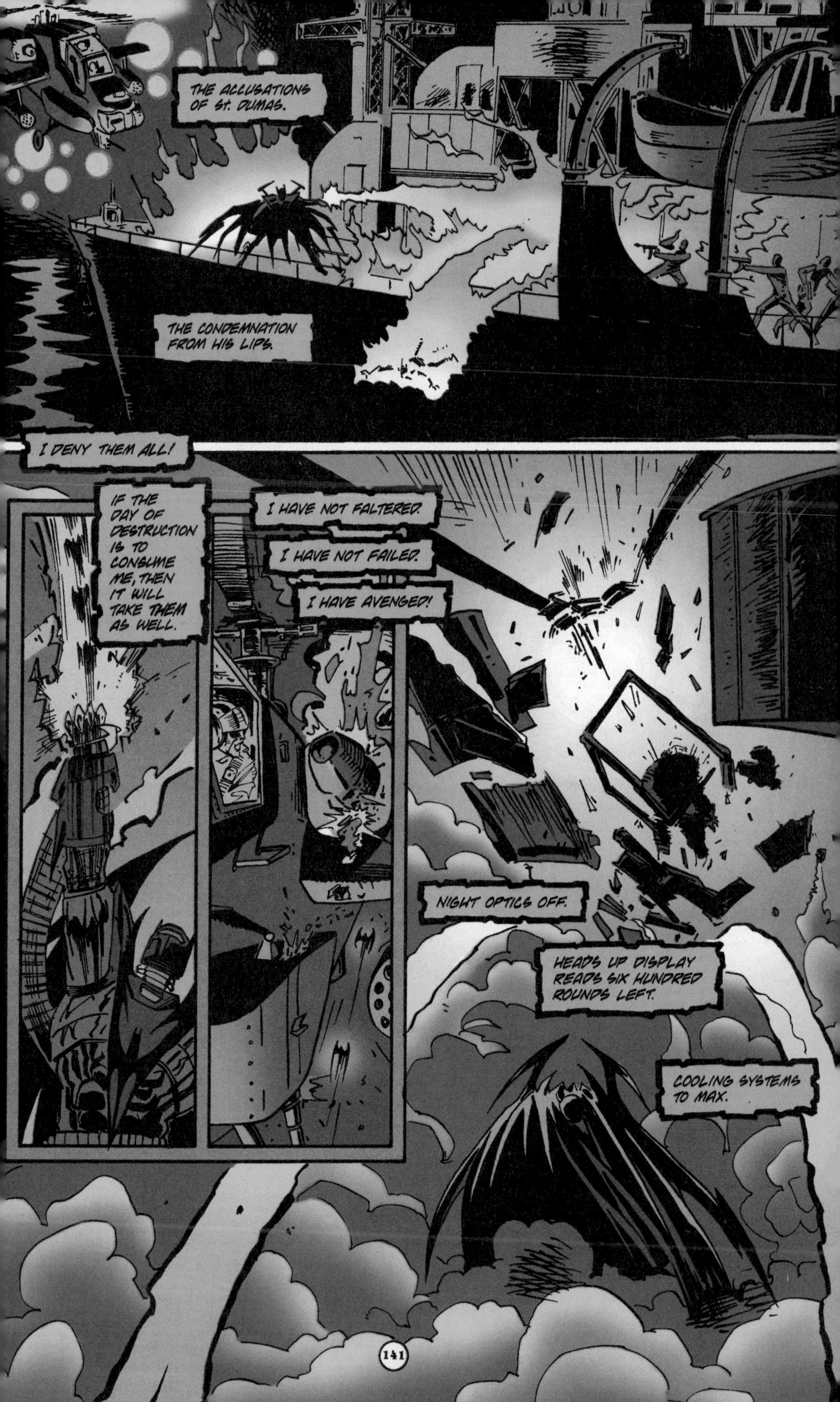

THE ACCUSATIONS OF St. DUMAS.
THE CONDEMNATION FROM HIS LIPS.
I DENY THEM ALL!
IF THE DAY OF DESTRUCTION IS TO CONSUME ME, THEN IT WILL TAKE THEM AS WELL.
I HAVE NOT FALTERED.
I HAVE NOT FAILED.
I HAVE AVENGED!
NIGHT OPTICS OFF.
HEADS UP DISPLAY READS SIX HUNDRED ROUNDS LEFT.
COOLING SYSTEMS TO MAX.

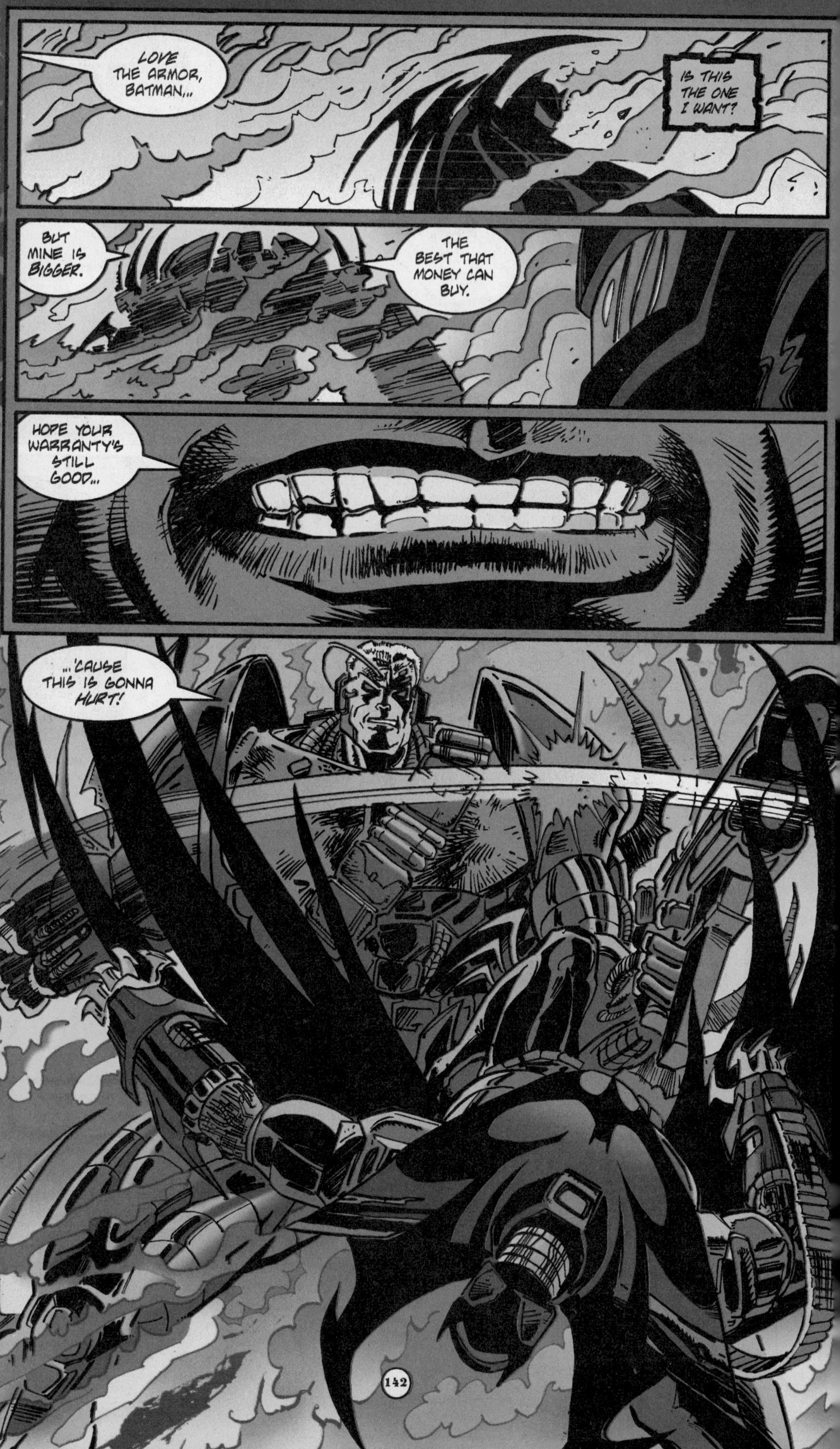
LOVE THE ARMOR, BATMAN...
IS THIS THE ONE I WANT?
BUT MINE IS BIGGER.
THE BEST THAT MONEY CAN BUY.
HOPE YOUR WARRANTY'S STILL GOOD...
...'CAUSE THIS IS GONNA HURT!

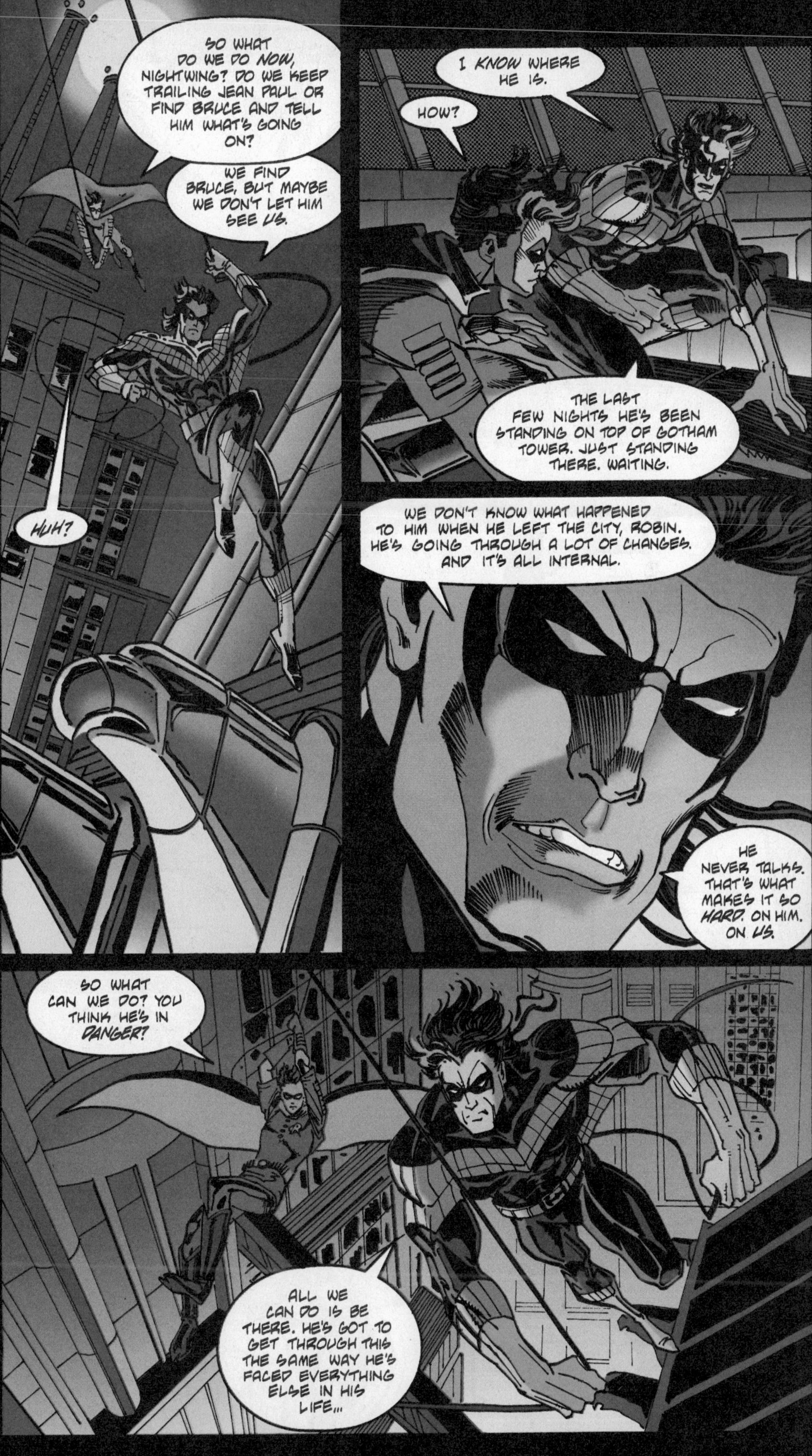
SO WHAT DO WE DO NOW, NIGHTWING? DO WE KEEP TRAILING JEAN PAUL OR FIND BRUCE AND TELL HIM WHAT'S GOING ON?
WE FIND BRUCE, BUT MAYBE WE DON'T LET HIM SEE US.
HUH?
I KNOW WHERE HE IS.
HOW?
THE LAST FEW NIGHTS HE'S BEEN STANDING ON TOP OF GOTHAM TOWER. JUST STANDING THERE. WAITING.
WE DON'T KNOW WHAT HAPPENED TO HIM WHEN HE LEFT THE CITY, ROBIN. HE'S GOING THROUGH A LOT OF CHANGES. AND IT'S ALL INTERNAL.
HE NEVER TALKS. THAT'S WHAT MAKES IT SO HARD. ON HIM. ON US.
SO WHAT CAN WE DO? YOU THINK HE'S IN DANGER?
ALL WE CAN DO IS BE THERE. HE'S GOT TO GET THROUGH THIS THE SAME WAY HE'S FACED EVERYTHING ELSE IN HIS LIFE...

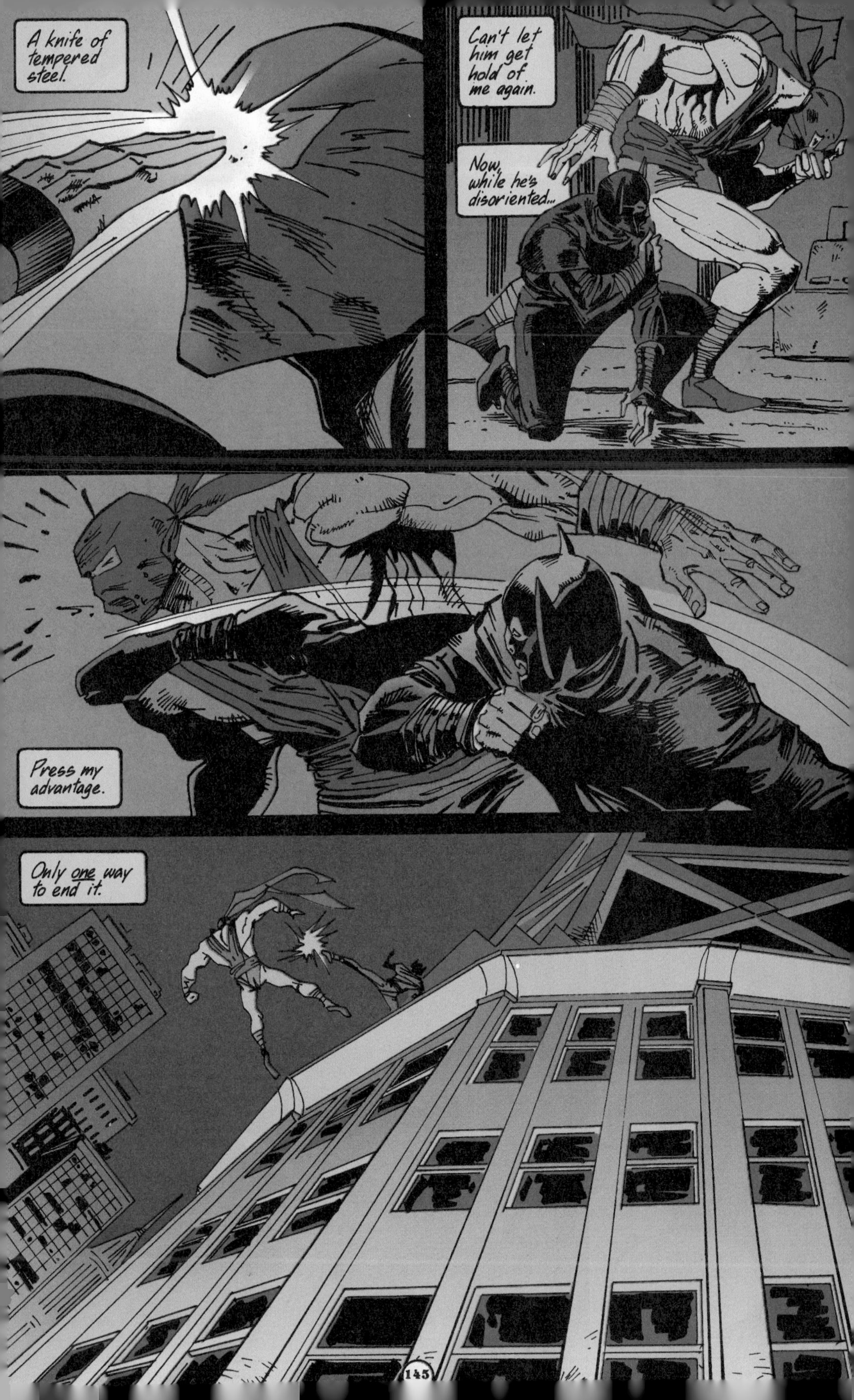
A knife of tempered steel.
Can't let him get hold of me again.
Now, while he's disoriented...
Press my advantage.
Only one way to end it.

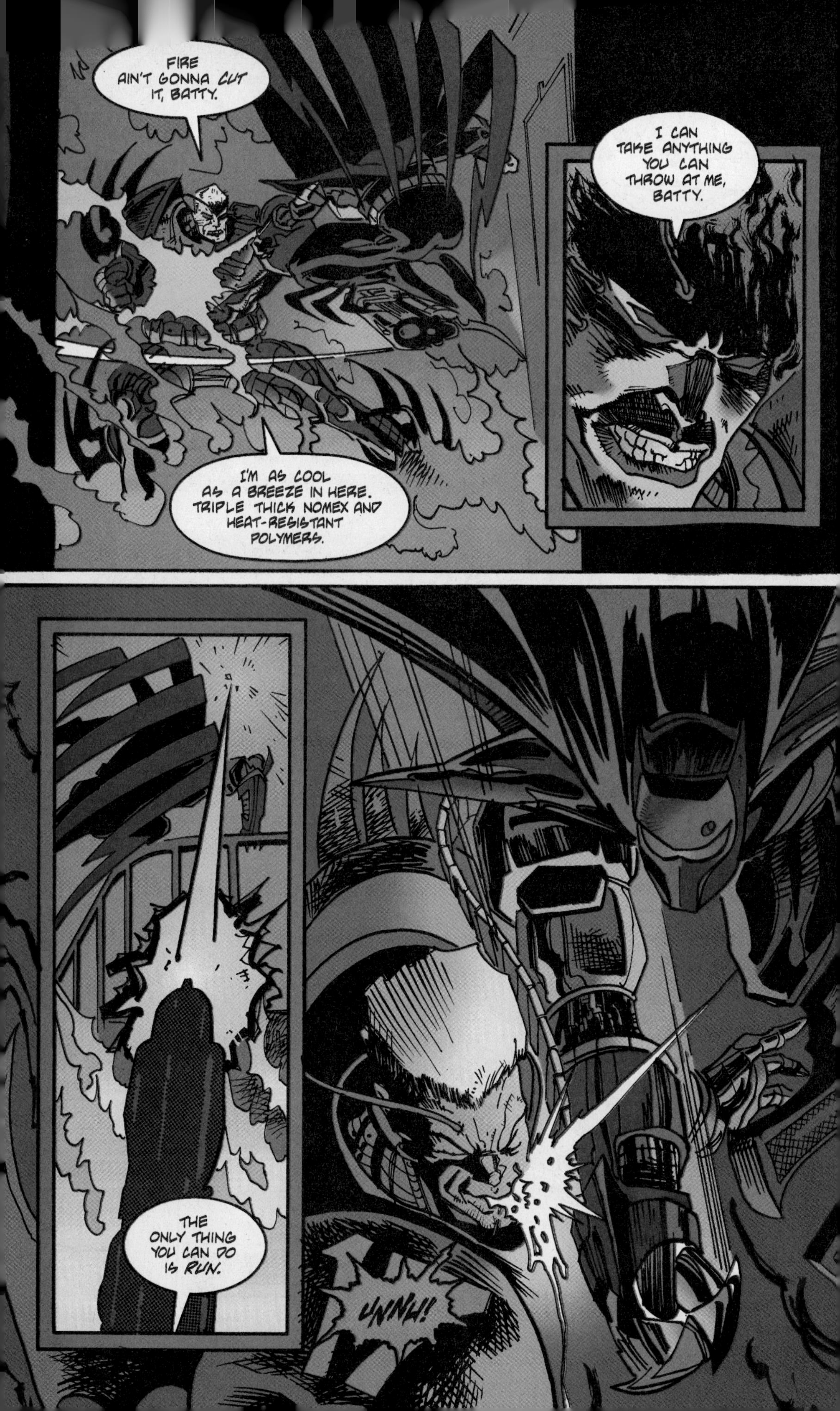
FIRE AIN'T GONNA CUT IT, BATTY.
I'M AS COOL AS A BREEZE IN HERE. TRIPLE THICK NOMEX AND HEAT-RESISTANT POLYMERS.
I CAN TAKE ANYTHING YOU CAN THROW AT ME, BATTY.
THE ONLY THING YOU CAN DO IS RUN.
UNNH!!

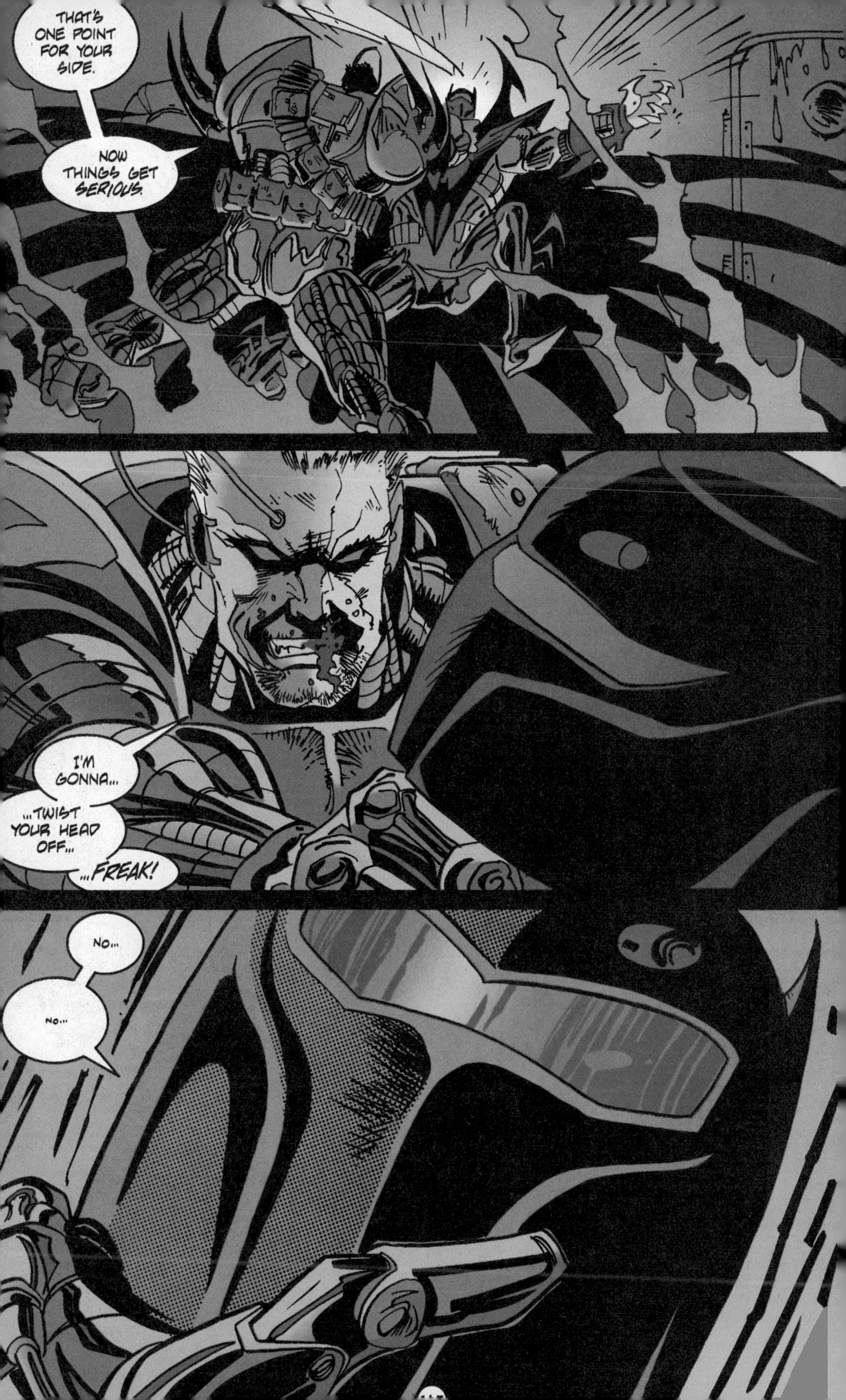
THAT'S ONE POINT FOR YOUR SIDE.
NOW THINGS GET SERIOUS.
I'M GONNA...
...TWIST YOUR HEAD OFF...
...FREAK!
NO...
NO...

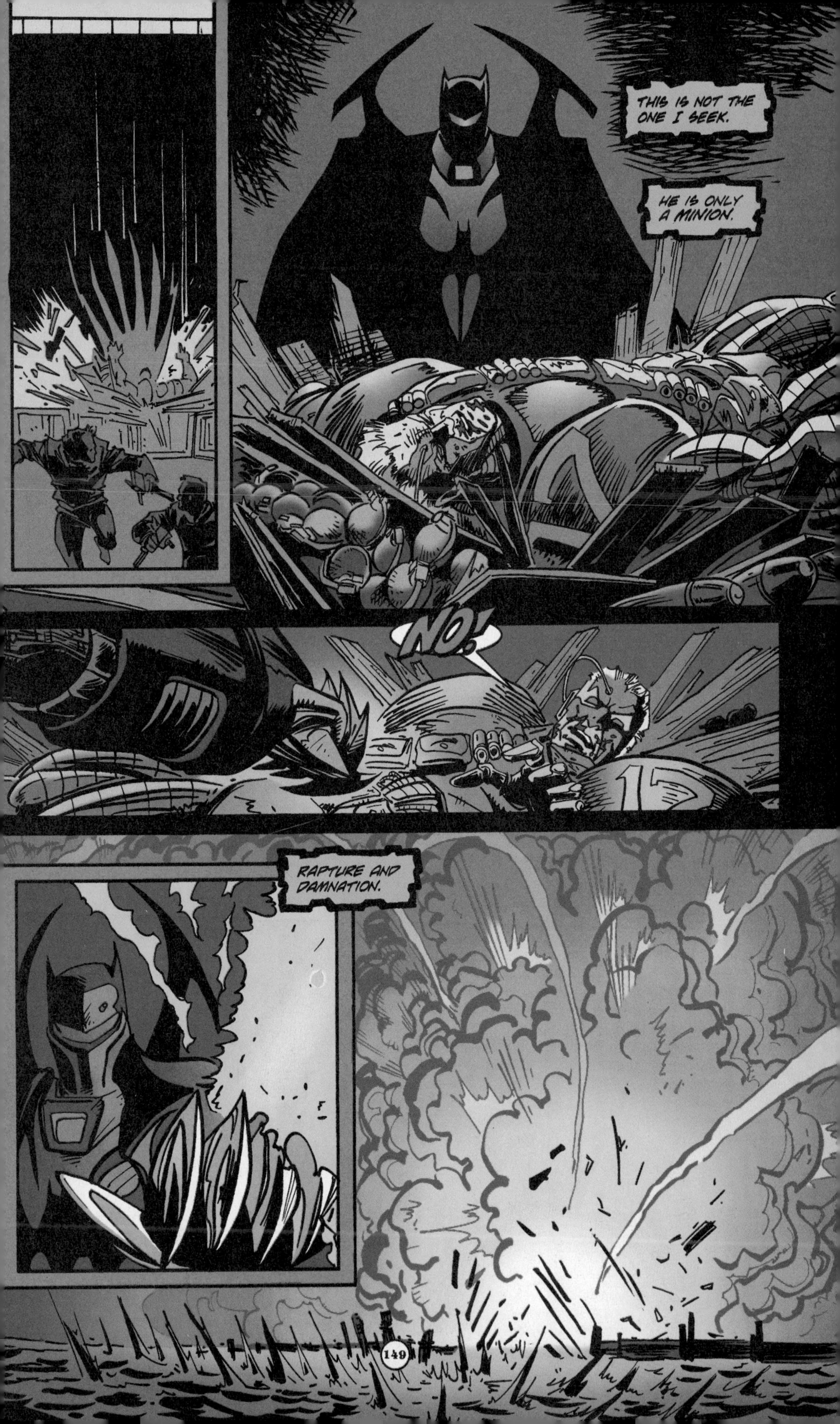
THIS IS NOT THE ONE I SEEK.
HE IS ONLY A MINION.
NO!
RAPTURE AND DAMNATION.

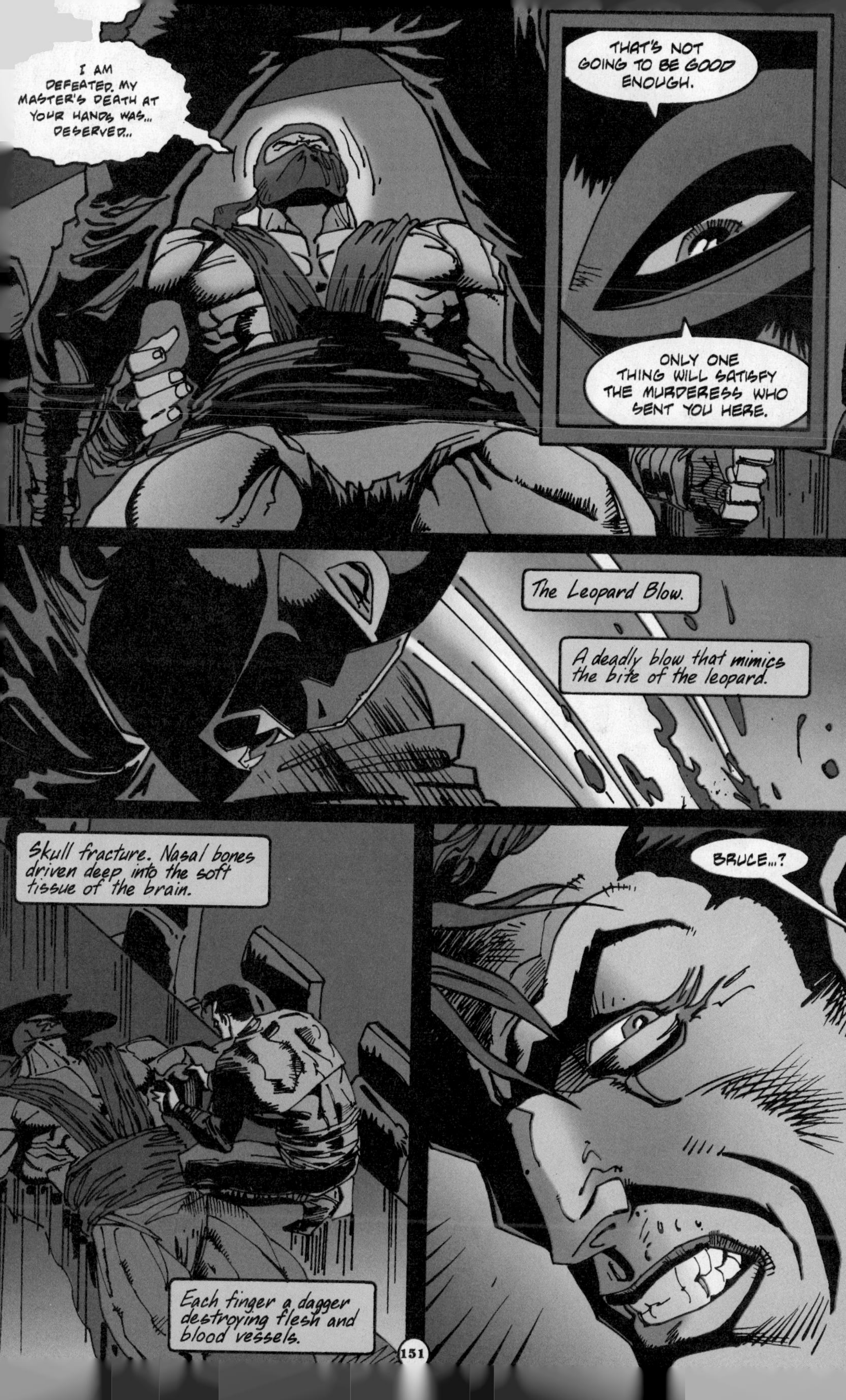
I AM DEFEATED. MY MASTER'S DEATH AT YOUR HANDS WAS... DESERVED...
THAT'S NOT GOING TO BE GOOD ENOUGH.
ONLY ONE THING WILL SATISFY THE MURDERESS WHO SENT YOU HERE.
The Leopard Blow.
A deadly blow that mimics the bite of the leopard.
Skull fracture. Nasal bones driven deep into the soft tissue of the brain.
Each finger a dagger destroying flesh and blood vessels.
BRUCE...?

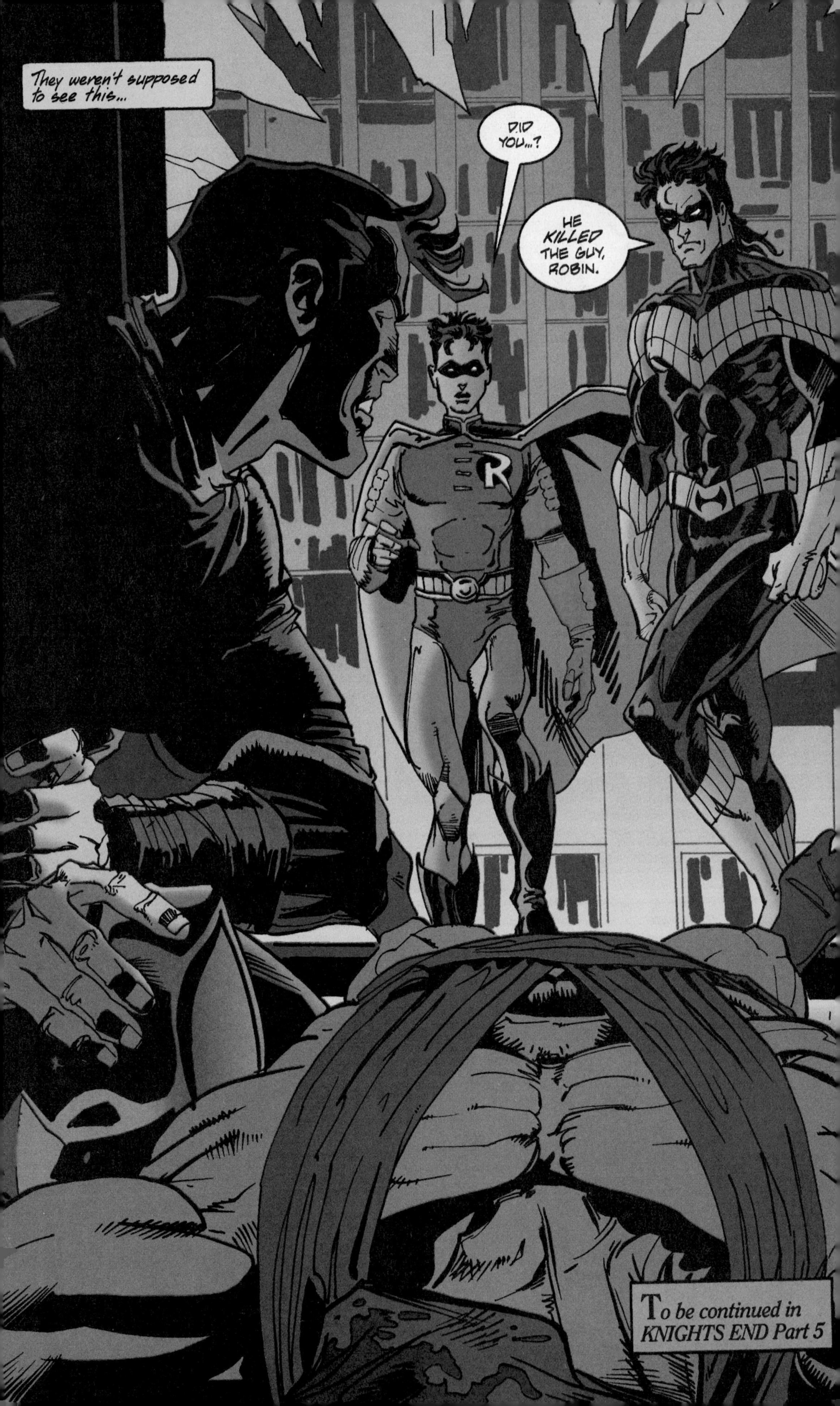
They weren't supposed to see this...
DID YOU...?
HE KILLED THE GUY, ROBIN.
To be continued in KNIGHTS END Part 5

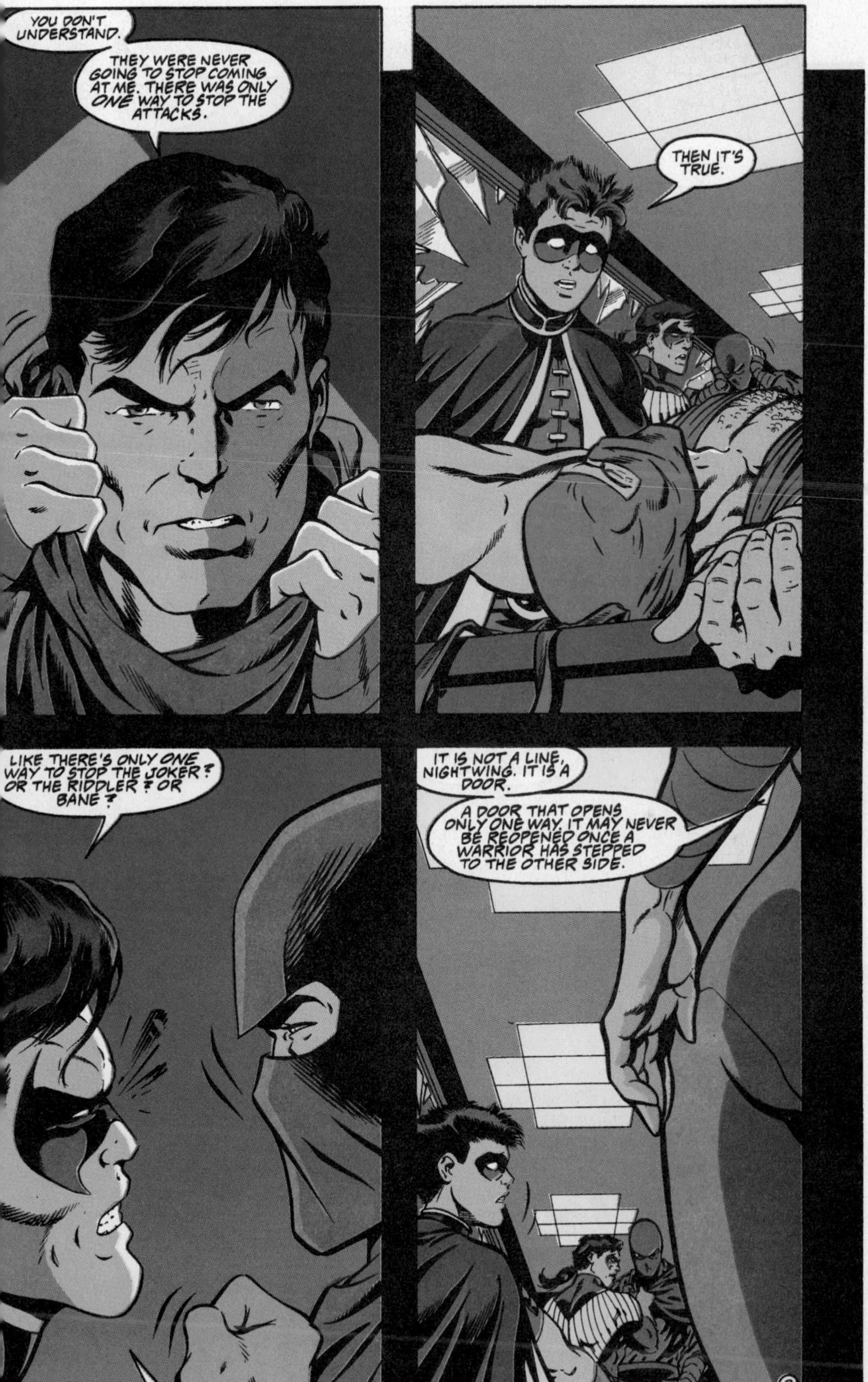
YOU DON'T UNDERSTAND.
THEY WERE NEVER GOING TO STOP COMING AT ME. THERE WAS ONLY ONE WAY TO STOP THE ATTACKS.
THEN IT'S TRUE.
LIKE THERE'S ONLY ONE WAY TO STOP THE JOKER? OR THE RIDDLER? OR BANE?
WHAT'S SO DIFFERENT THIS TIME? WHY CROSS THE LINE FOR THIS GUY?
IT IS NOT A LINE, NIGHTWING. IT IS A DOOR.
A DOOR THAT OPENS ONLY ONE WAY. IT MAY NEVER BE REOPENED ONCE A WARRIOR HAS STEPPED TO THE OTHER SIDE.
3

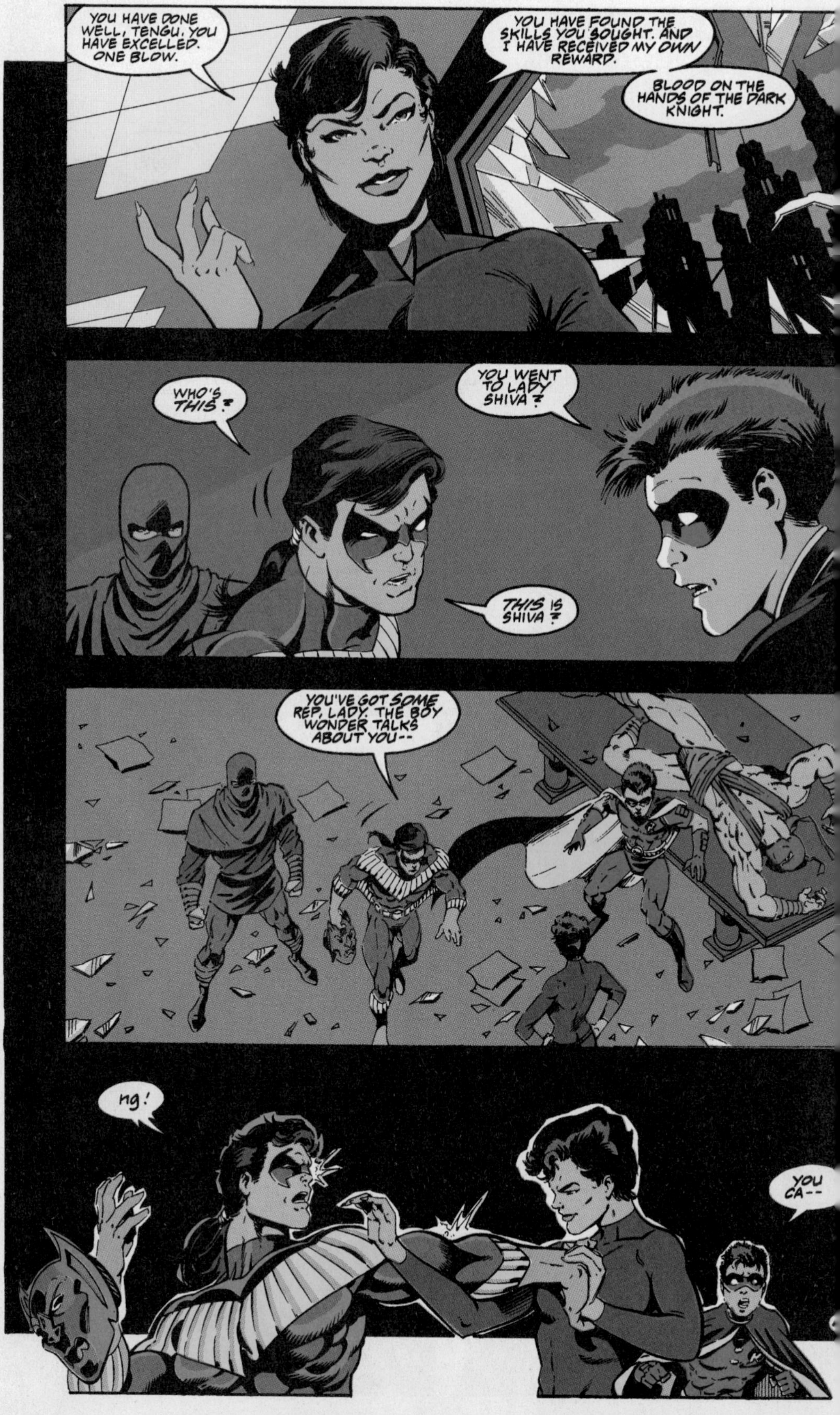
YOU HAVE DONE WELL, TENGU. YOU HAVE EXCELLED. ONE BLOW.
YOU HAVE FOUND THE SKILLS YOU SOUGHT. AND I HAVE RECEIVED MY OWN REWARD.
BLOOD ON THE HANDS OF THE DARK KNIGHT.
WHO'S THIS?
YOU WENT TO LADY SHIVA?
THIS IS SHIVA?
YOU'VE GOT SOME REP, LADY. THE BOY WONDER TALKS ABOUT YOU--
ng!
YOU CA--

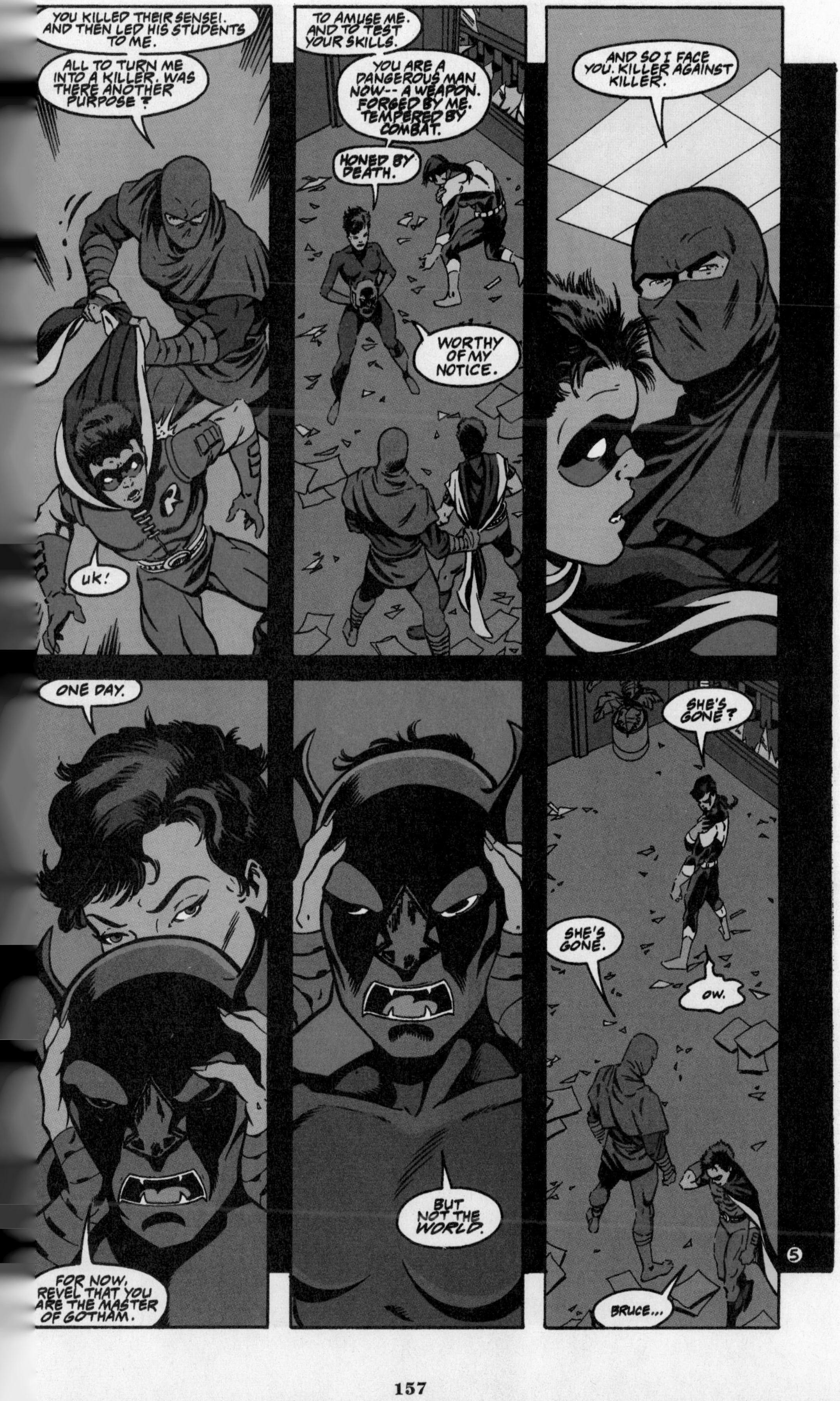
YOU KILLED THEIR SENSEI. AND THEN LED HIS STUDENTS TO ME.
ALL TO TURN ME INTO A KILLER. WAS THERE ANOTHER PURPOSE?
UK!
TO AMUSE ME. AND TO TEST YOUR SKILLS.
YOU ARE A DANGEROUS MAN NOW-- A WEAPON. FORGED BY ME. TEMPERED BY COMBAT.
HONED BY DEATH.
WORTHY OF MY NOTICE.
AND SO I FACE YOU. KILLER AGAINST KILLER.
ONE DAY.
FOR NOW, REVEL THAT YOU ARE THE MASTER OF GOTHAM.
BUT NOT THE WORLD.
SHE'S GONE?
SHE'S GONE.
OW.
BRUCE...
5

158

159

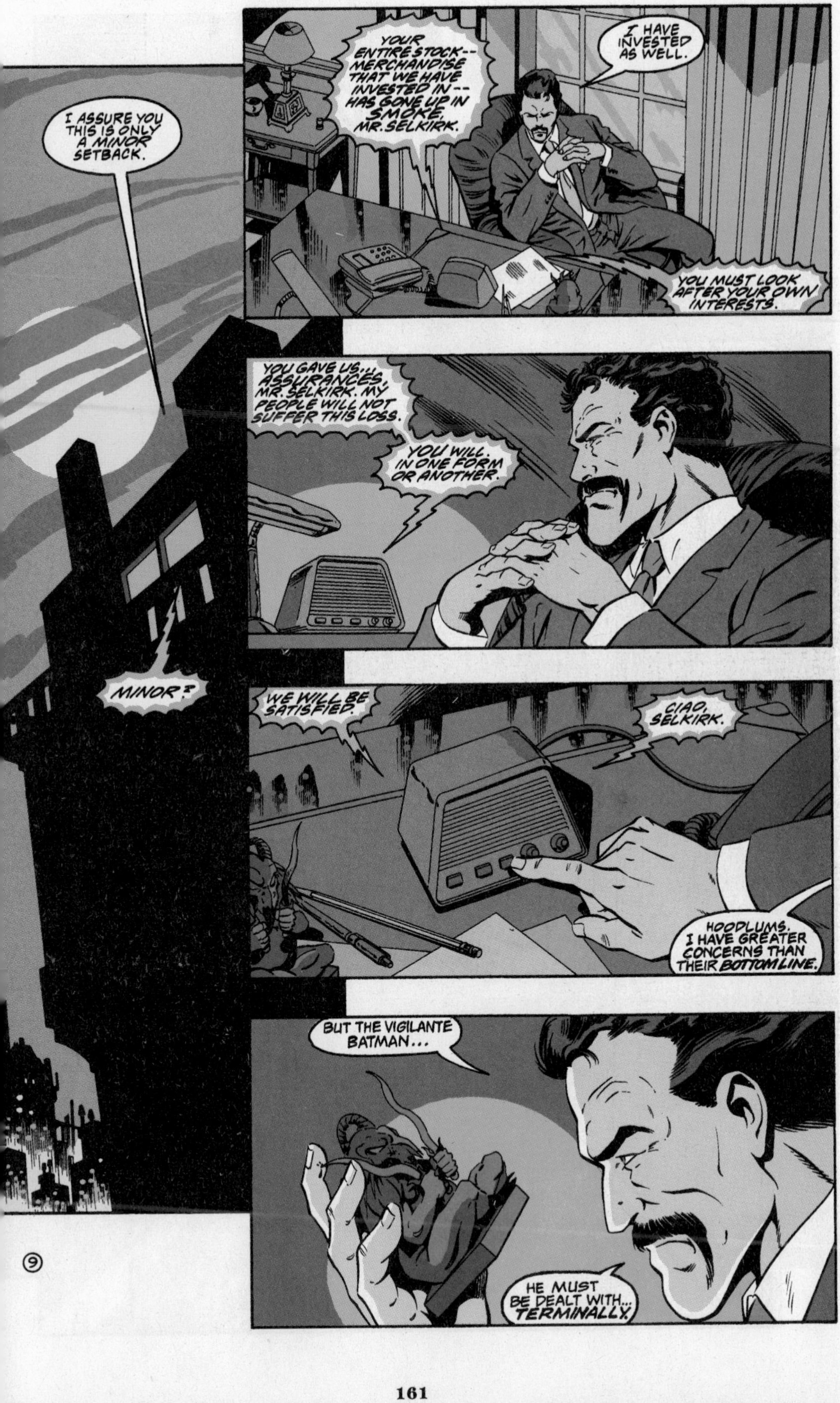
YOUR ENTIRE STOCK-- MERCHANDISE THAT WE HAVE INVESTED IN-- HAS GONE UP IN SMOKE, MR. SELKIRK.
I HAVE INVESTED AS WELL.
YOU MUST LOOK AFTER YOUR OWN INTERESTS.
I ASSURE YOU THIS IS ONLY A MINOR SETBACK.
MINOR?
YOU GAVE US... ASSURANCES, MR. SELKIRK. MY PEOPLE WILL NOT SUFFER THIS LOSS.
YOU WILL. IN ONE FORM OR ANOTHER.
WE WILL BE SATISFIED.
CIAO, SELKIRK.
HOODLUMS. I HAVE GREATER CONCERNS THAN THEIR BOTTOM LINE.
BUT THE VIGILANTE BATMAN...
HE MUST BE DEALT WITH... TERMINALLY.
9

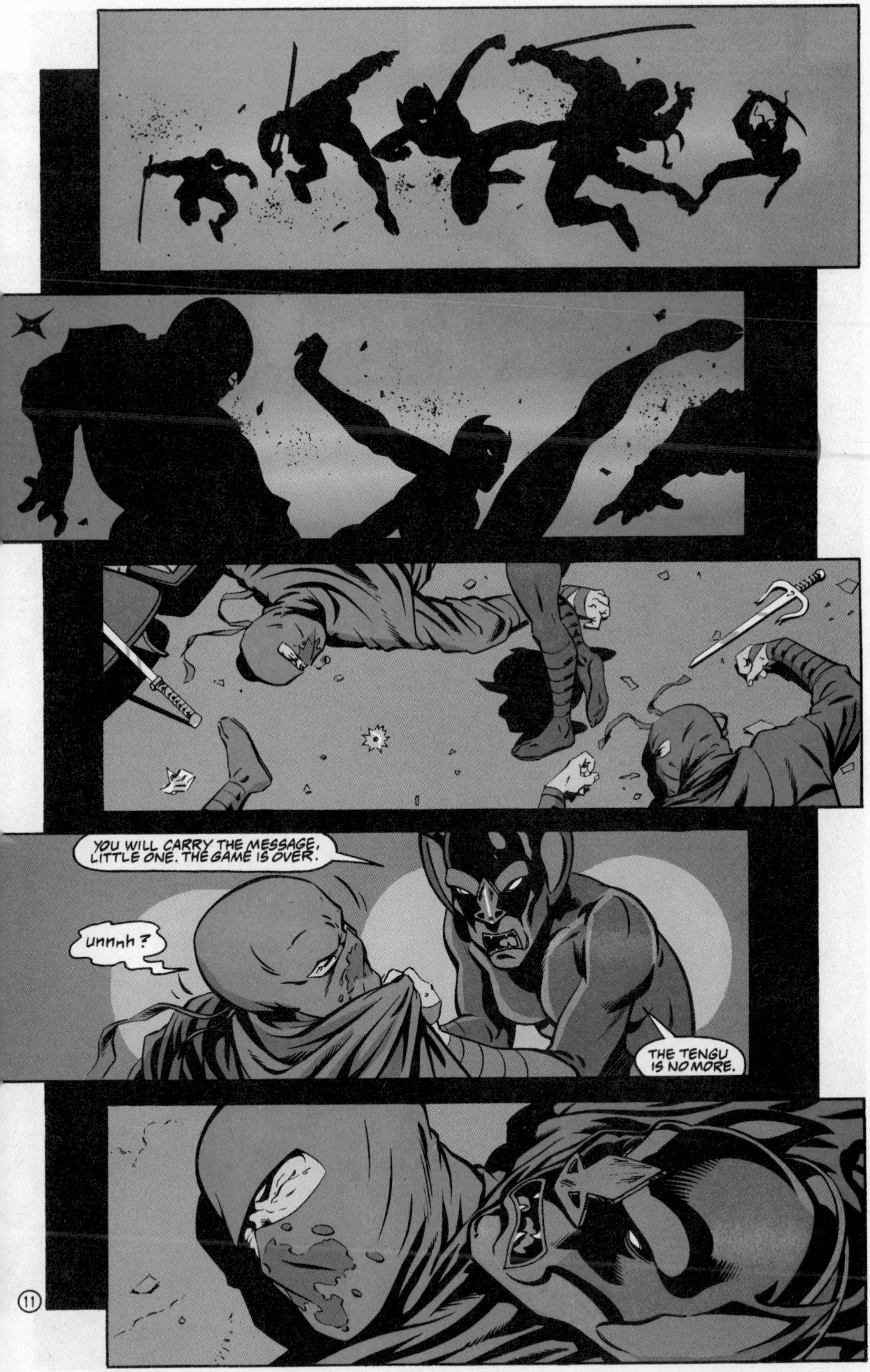
YOU WILL CARRY THE MESSAGE, LITTLE ONE. THE GAME IS OVER.
unnnh ?
THE TENGU IS NO MORE.
11

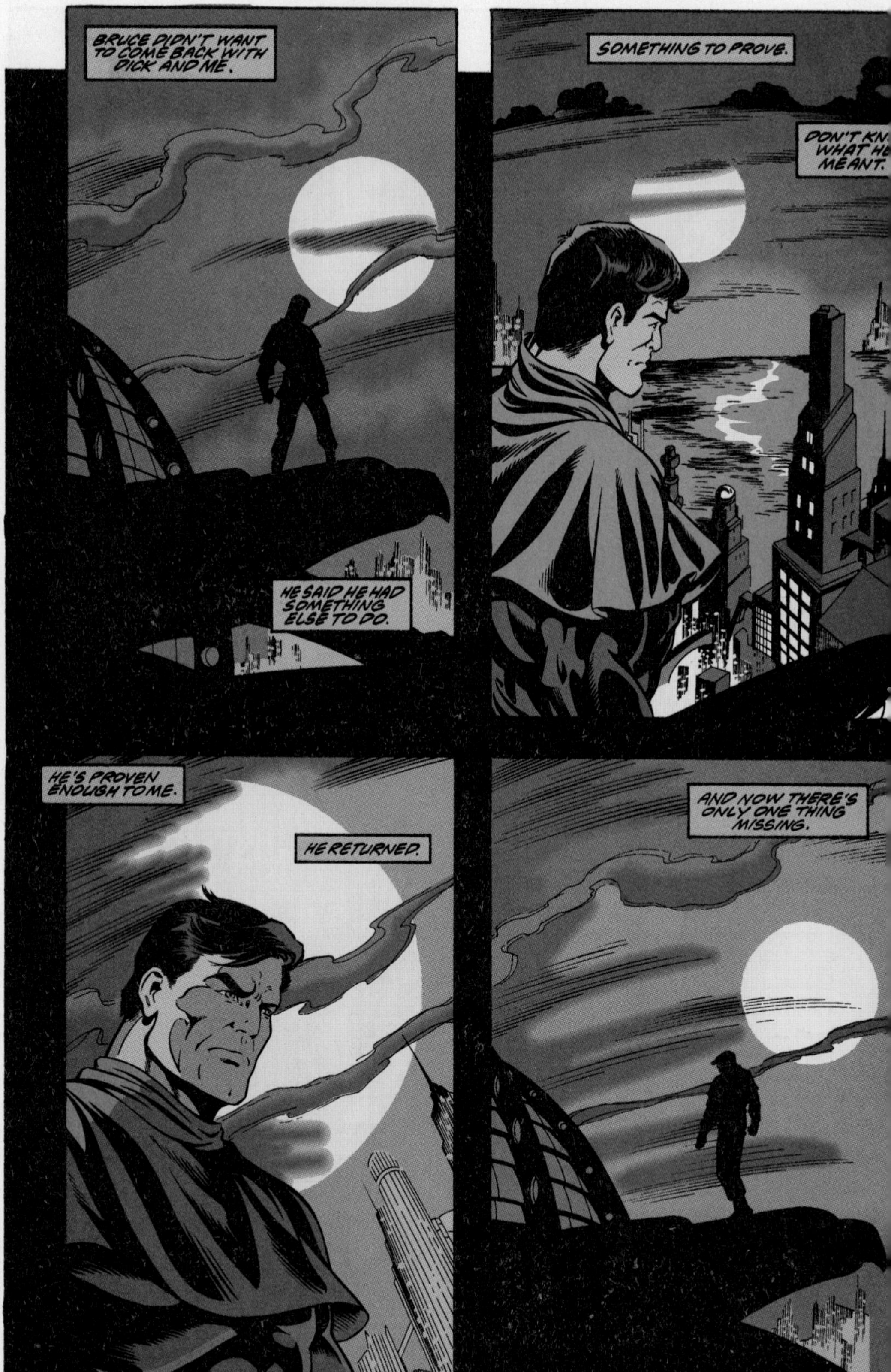
BRUCE DIDN'T WANT TO COME BACK WITH DICK AND ME.
HE SAID HE HAD SOMETHING ELSE TO DO.
SOMETHING TO PROVE.
DON'T KN
WHAT HE
MEANT.
HE'S PROVEN ENOUGH TO ME.
HE RETURNED.
AND NOW THERE'S ONLY ONE THING MISSING.

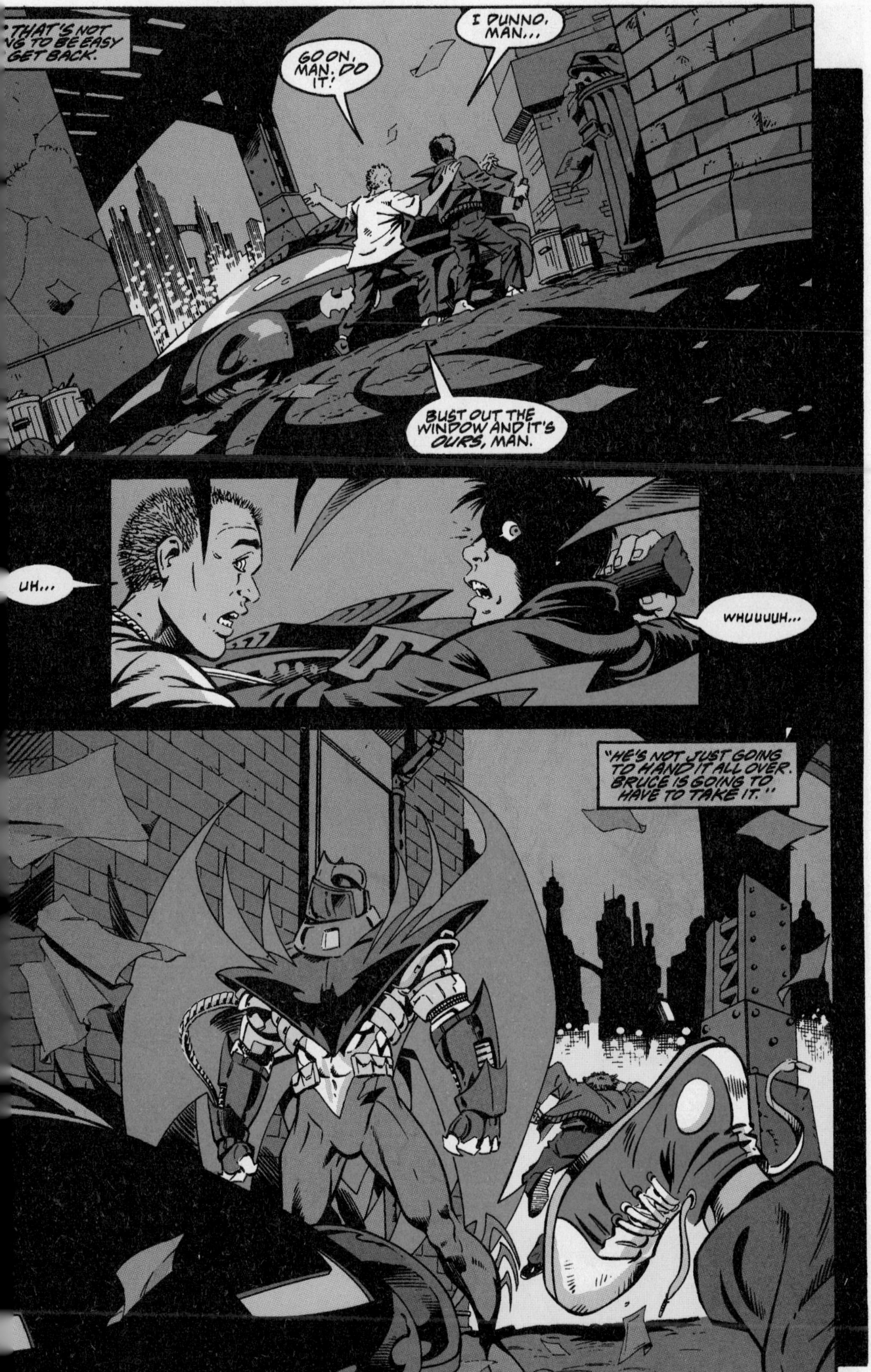
THAT'S NOT
NG TO BE EASY
GET BACK.
GO ON, MAN. DO IT!
I DUNNO, MAN...
BUST OUT THE WINDOW AND IT'S OURS, MAN.
UH...
WHUUUUH...
"HE'S NOT JUST GOING TO HAND IT ALL OVER. BRUCE IS GOING TO HAVE TO TAKE IT."

166

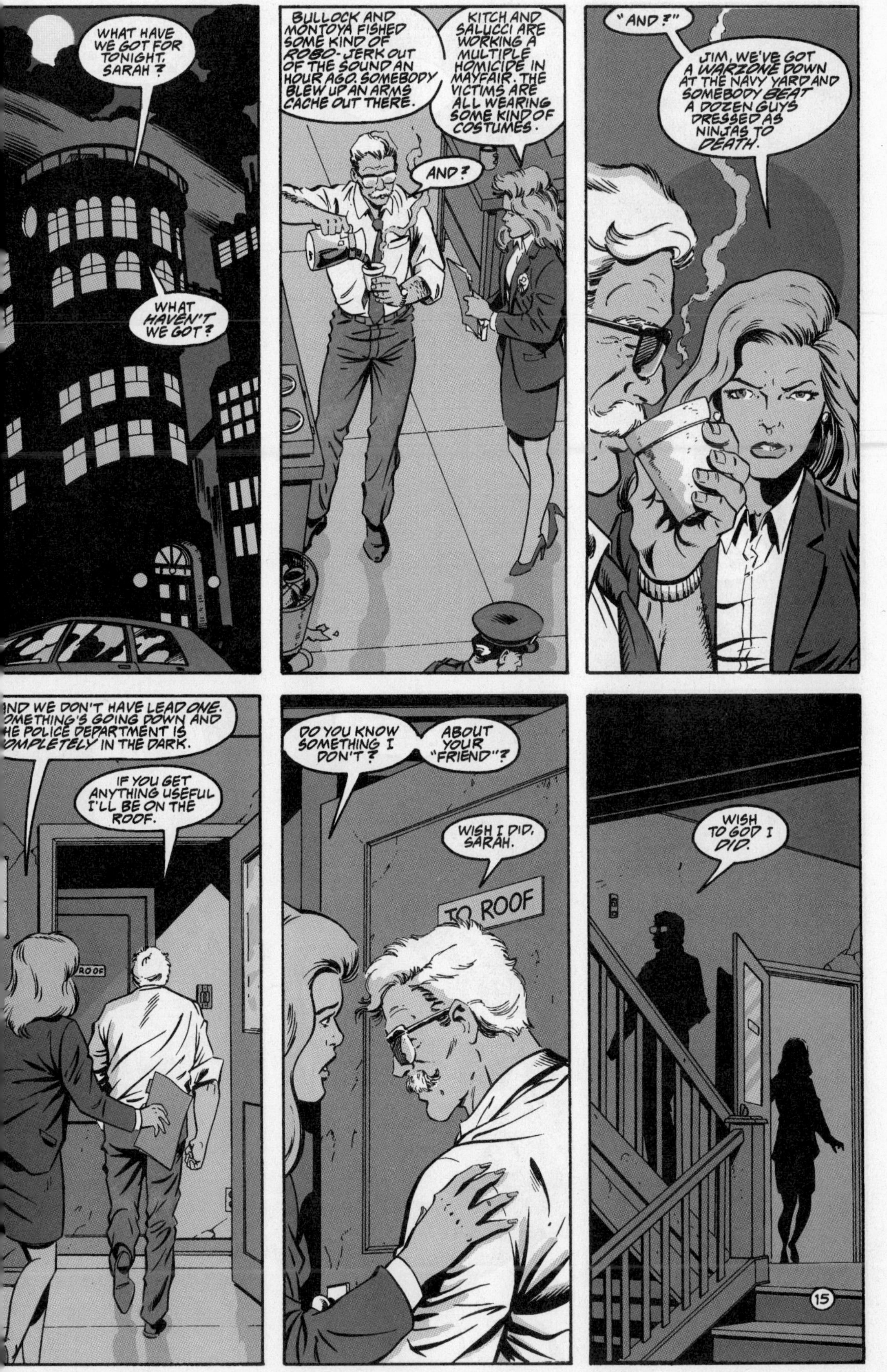
WHAT HAVE WE GOT FOR TONIGHT, SARAH?
WHAT HAVEN'T WE GOT?
BULLOCK AND MONTOYA FISHED SOME KIND OF ROBO-JERK OUT OF THE SOUND AN HOUR AGO. SOMEBODY BLEW UP AN ARMS CACHE OUT THERE.
KITCH AND SALUCCI ARE WORKING A MULTIPLE HOMICIDE IN MAYFAIR. THE VICTIMS ARE ALL WEARING SOME KIND OF COSTUMES.
AND?
"AND?"
JIM, WE'VE GOT A WARZONE DOWN AT THE NAVY YARD AND SOMEBODY BEAT A DOZEN GUYS DRESSED AS NINJAS TO DEATH.
ND WE DON'T HAVE LEAD ONE. OMETHING'S GOING DOWN AND HE POLICE DEPARTMENT IS OMPLETELY IN THE DARK.
IF YOU GET ANYTHING USEFUL I'LL BE ON THE ROOF.
ROOF
DO YOU KNOW SOMETHING I DON'T?
ABOUT YOUR "FRIEND"?
WISH I DID, SARAH.
TO ROOF
WISH TO GOD I DID.
15

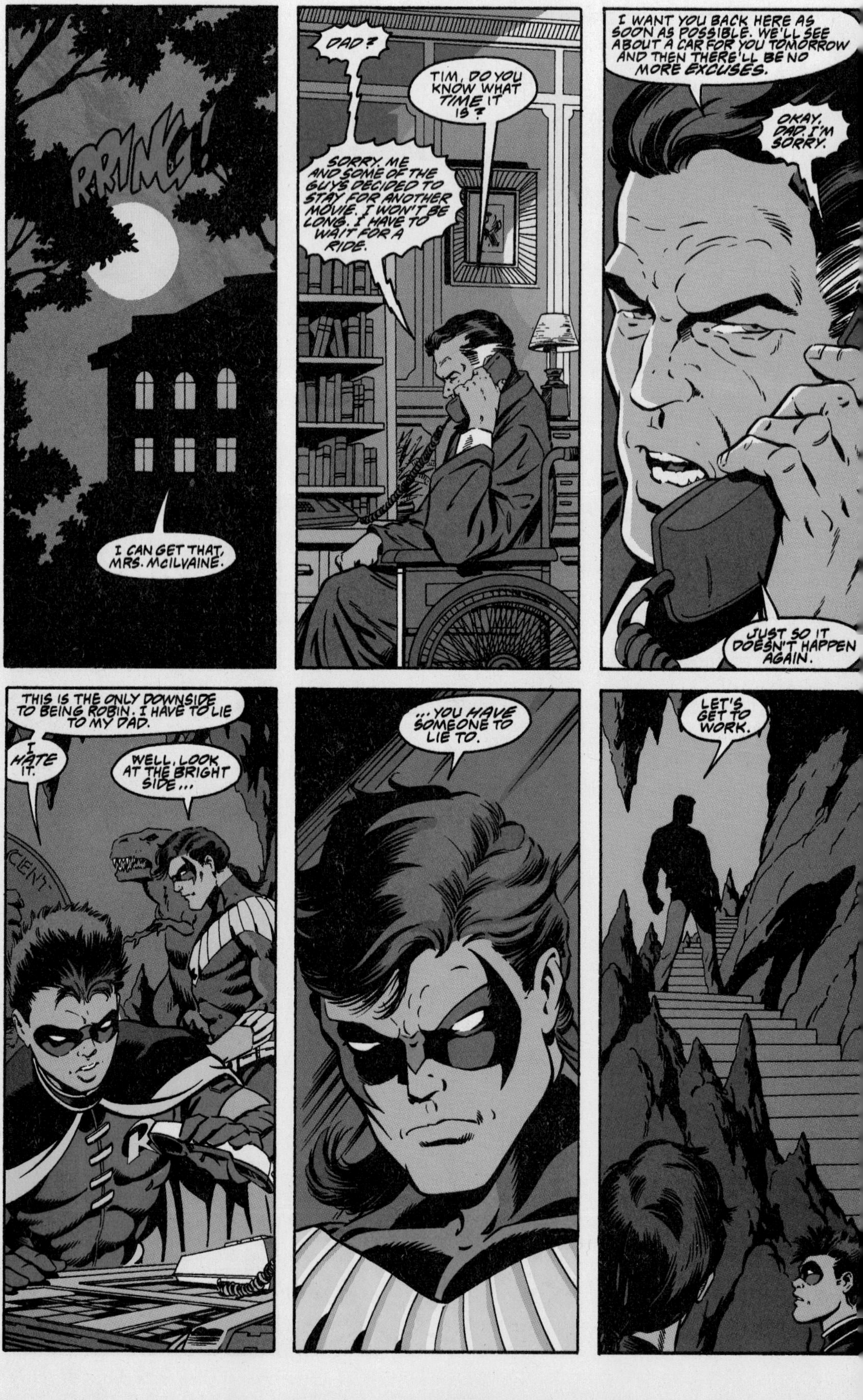
RRING!
I CAN GET THAT, MRS. McILVAINE.
DAD?
TIM, DO YOU KNOW WHAT TIME IT IS?
SORRY. ME AND SOME OF THE GUYS DECIDED TO STAY FOR ANOTHER MOVIE. I WON'T BE LONG. I HAVE TO WAIT FOR A RIDE.
I WANT YOU BACK HERE AS SOON AS POSSIBLE. WE'LL SEE ABOUT A CAR FOR YOU TOMORROW AND THEN THERE'LL BE NO MORE EXCUSES.
OKAY, DAD. I'M SORRY.
JUST SO IT DOESN'T HAPPEN AGAIN.
THIS IS THE ONLY DOWNSIDE TO BEING ROBIN. I HAVE TO LIE TO MY DAD.
I HATE IT.
WELL, LOOK AT THE BRIGHT SIDE...
...YOU HAVE SOMEONE TO LIE TO.
LET'S GET TO WORK.

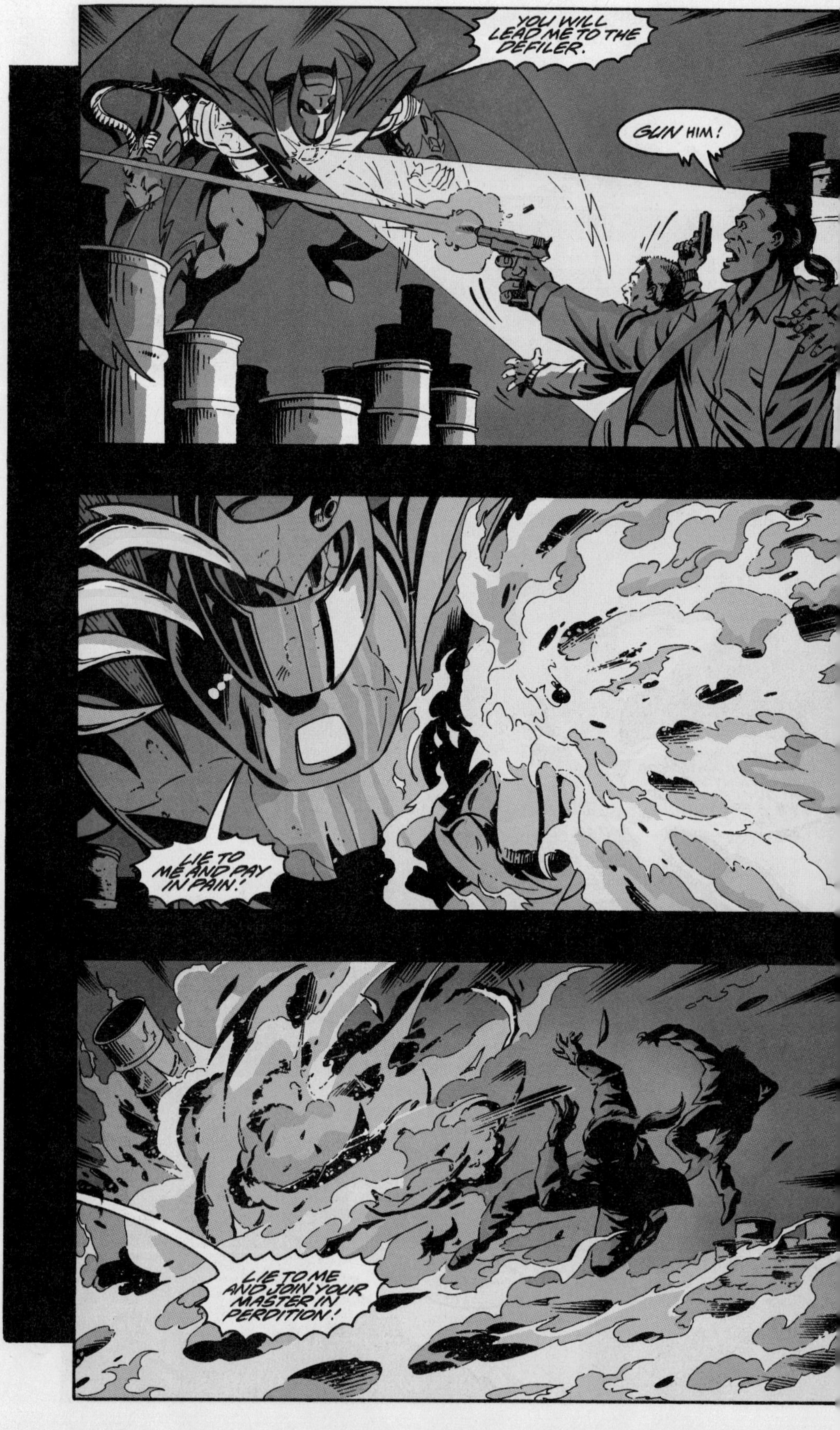
YOU WILL LEAD ME TO THE DEFILER.
GUN HIM!
LIE TO ME AND PAY IN PAIN!
LIE TO ME AND JOIN YOUR MASTER IN PERDITION!

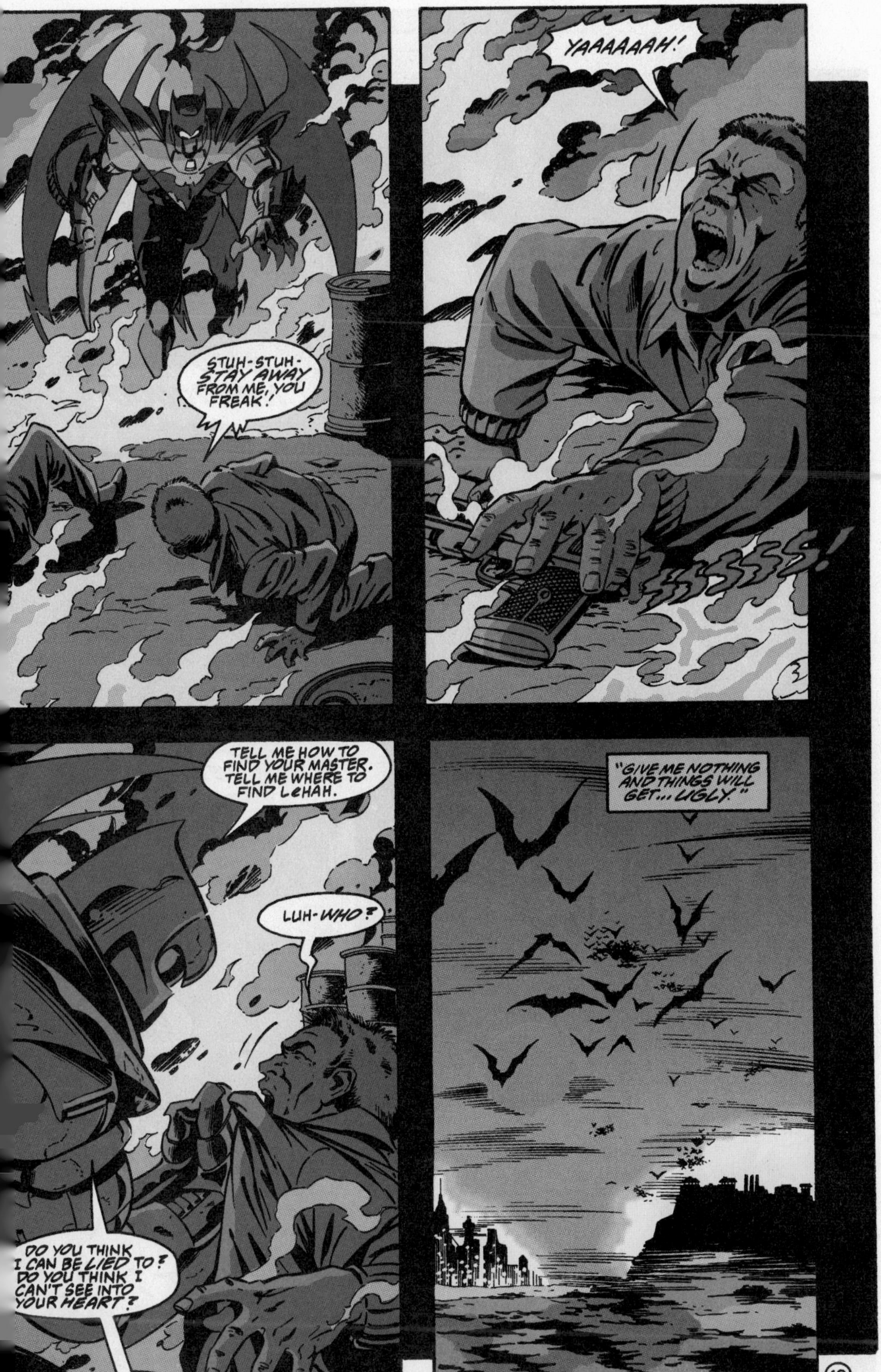
STUH-STUH-STAY AWAY FROM ME, YOU FREAK!
YAAAAAAH!
SSSSSS!
TELL ME HOW TO FIND YOUR MASTER. TELL ME WHERE TO FIND LeHAH.
LUH-WHO?
DO YOU THINK I CAN BE LIED TO? DO YOU THINK I CAN'T SEE INTO YOUR HEART?
GIVE ME LeHAH AND I WILL GIVE YOU MERCY.
"GIVE ME NOTHING AND THINGS WILL GET... UGLY."
19

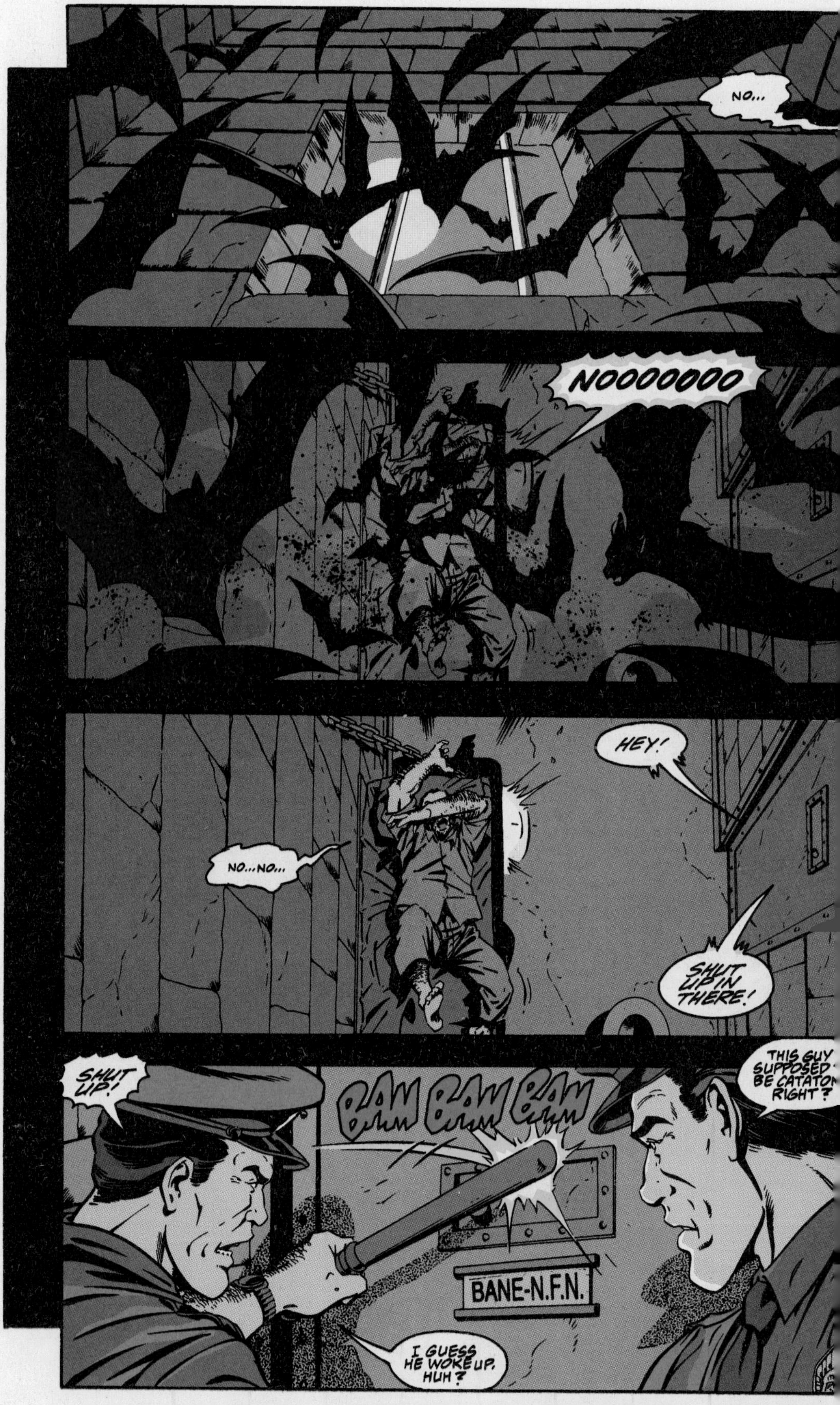
NO...
NOOOOOOO
HEY!
NO...NO...
SHUT UP IN THERE!
SHUT UP!
BAM BAM BAM
THIS GUY SUPPOSED BE CATATON RIGHT?
BANE-N.F.N.
I GUESS HE WOKE UP, HUH?

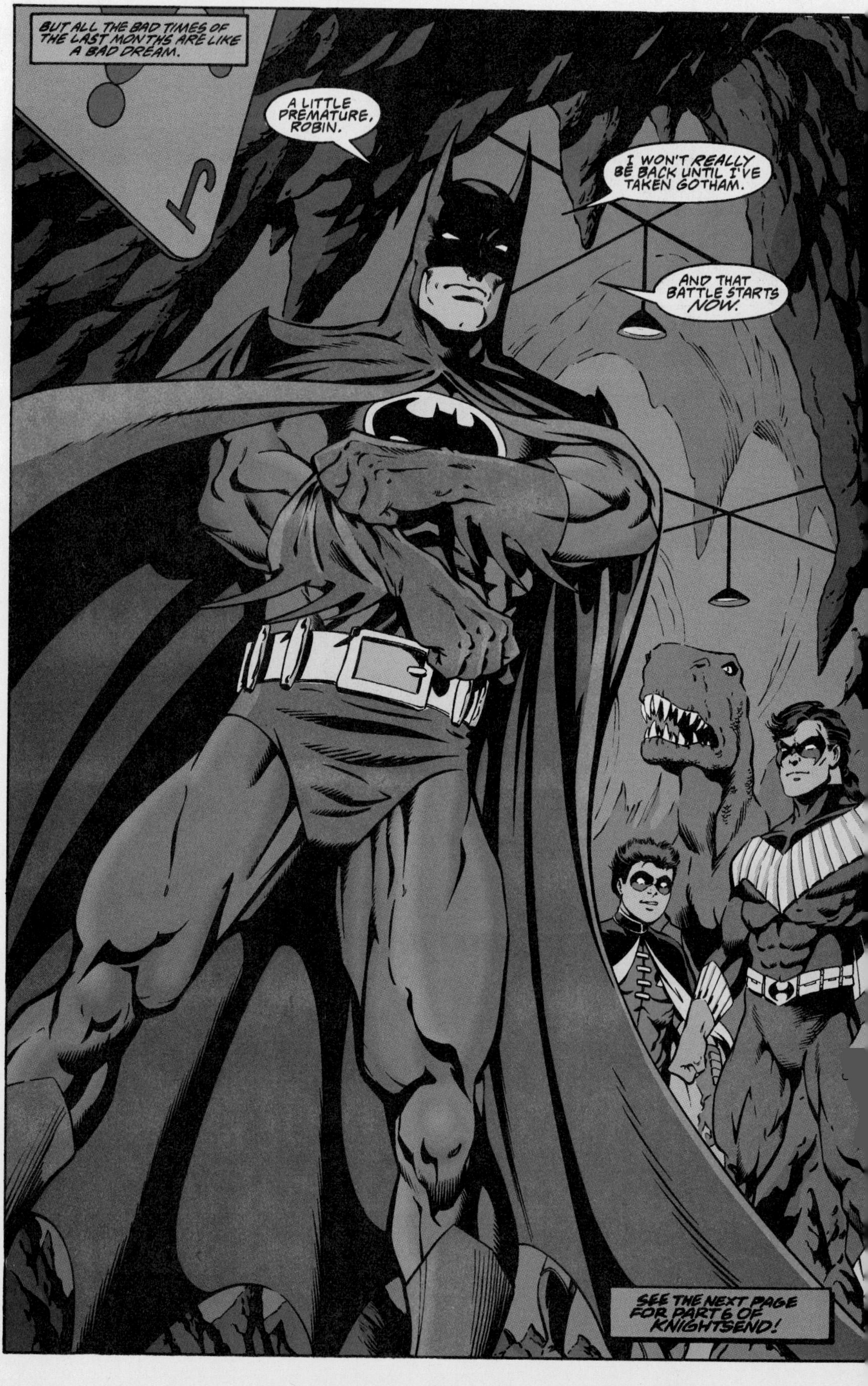
BUT ALL THE BAD TIMES OF THE LAST MONTHS ARE LIKE A BAD DREAM.
A LITTLE PREMATURE, ROBIN.
I WON'T REALLY BE BACK UNTIL I'VE TAKEN GOTHAM.
AND THAT BATTLE STARTS NOW.
SEE THE NEXT PAGE FOR PART 6 OF KNIGHTSEND!

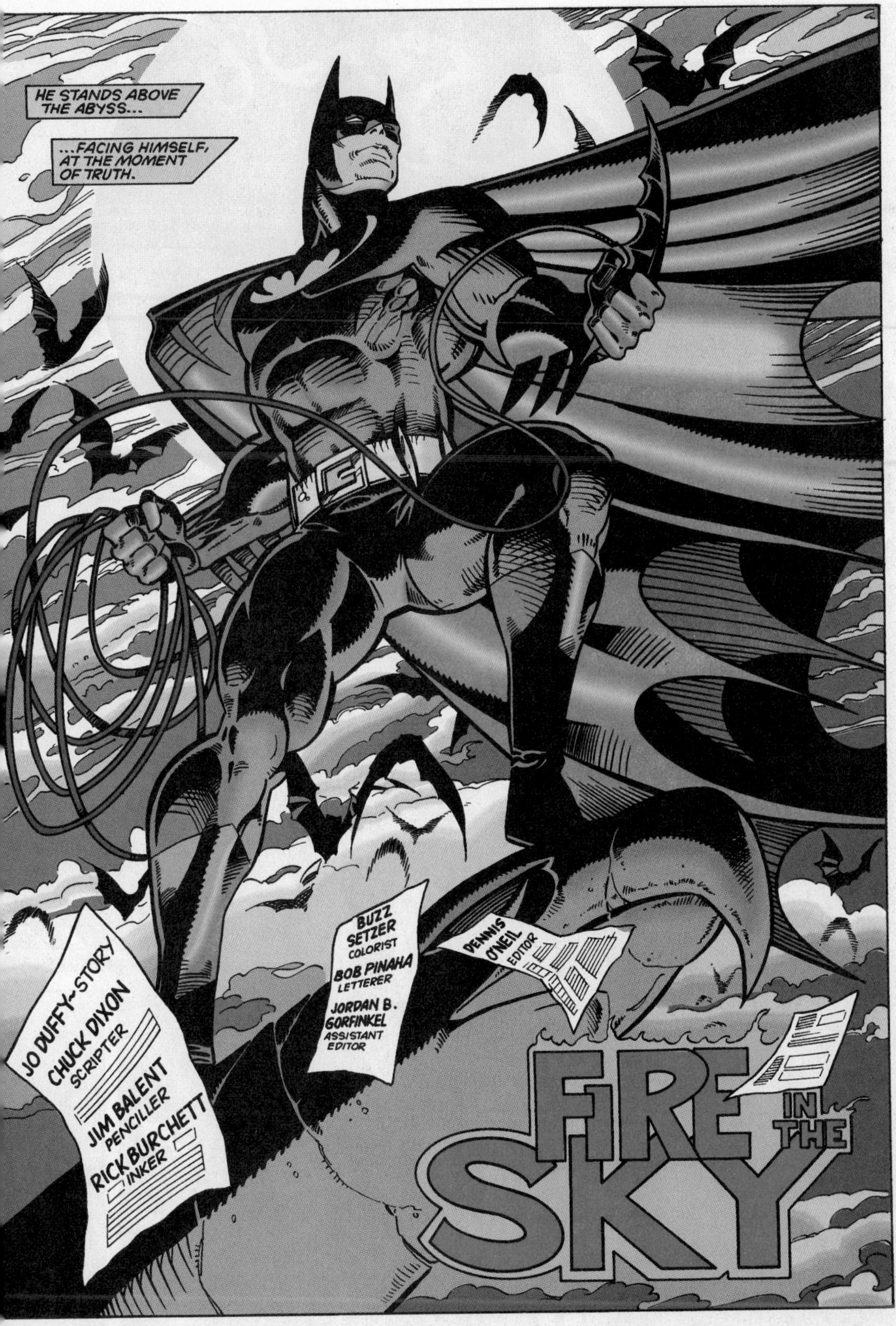
HE STANDS ABOVE THE ABYSS...
...FACING HIMSELF, AT THE MOMENT OF TRUTH.
JO DUFFY-STORY
CHUCK DIXON SCRIPTER
JIM BALENT PENCILLER
RICK BURCHETT INKER
BUZZ SETZER COLORIST
BOB PINAHA LETTERER
JORDAN B. GORFINKEL ASSISTANT EDITOR
DENNIS O'NEIL EDITOR
FIRE IN THE SKY

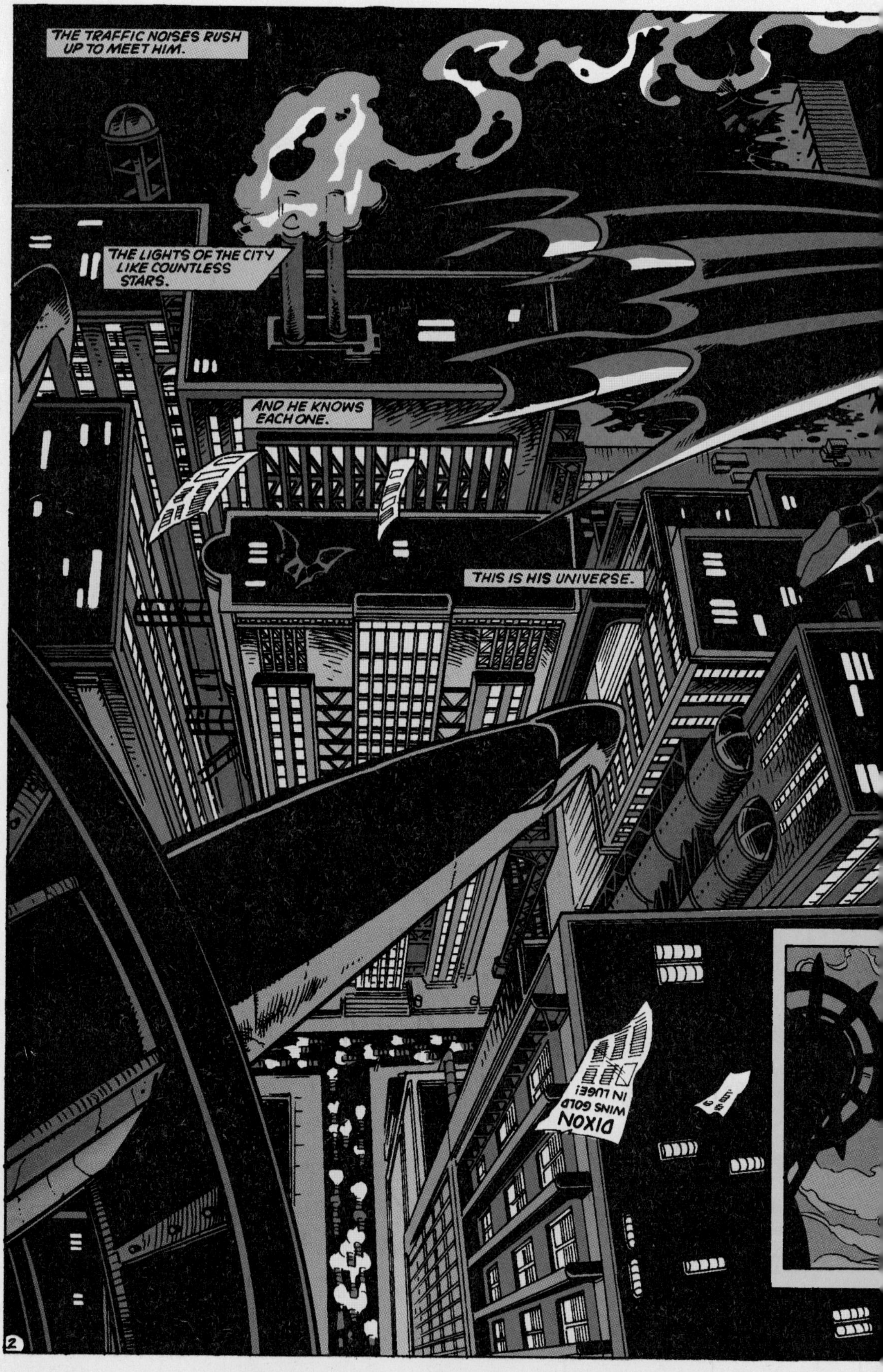
THE TRAFFIC NOISES RUSH UP TO MEET HIM.
THE LIGHTS OF THE CITY LIKE COUNTLESS STARS.
AND HE KNOWS EACH ONE.
THIS IS HIS UNIVERSE.
DIXON WINS GOLD IN LUGE!

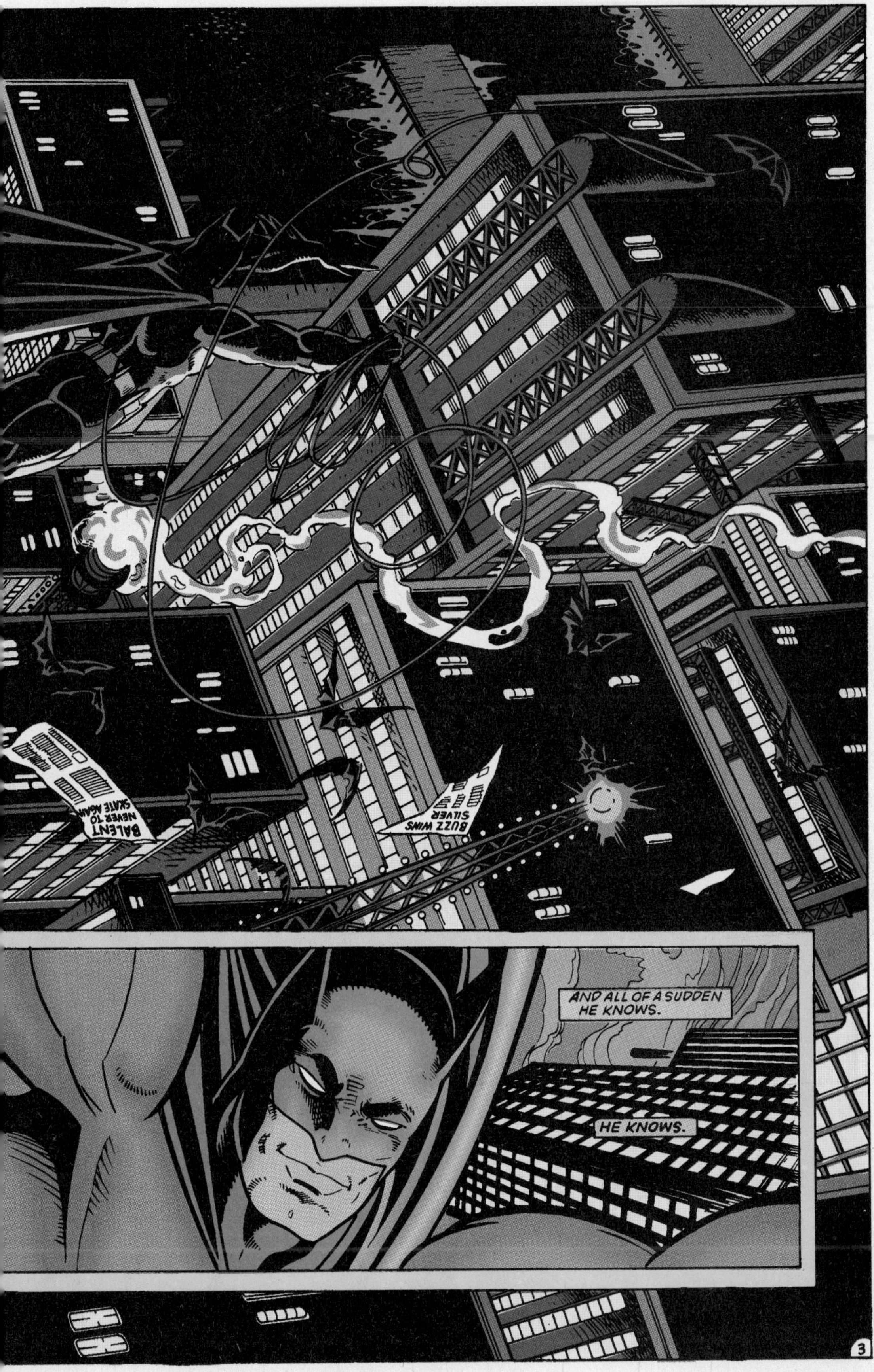
BALENT NEVER TO SKATE AGAIN
BUZZ WINS SILVER
AND ALL OF A SUDDEN HE KNOWS.
HE KNOWS.
3

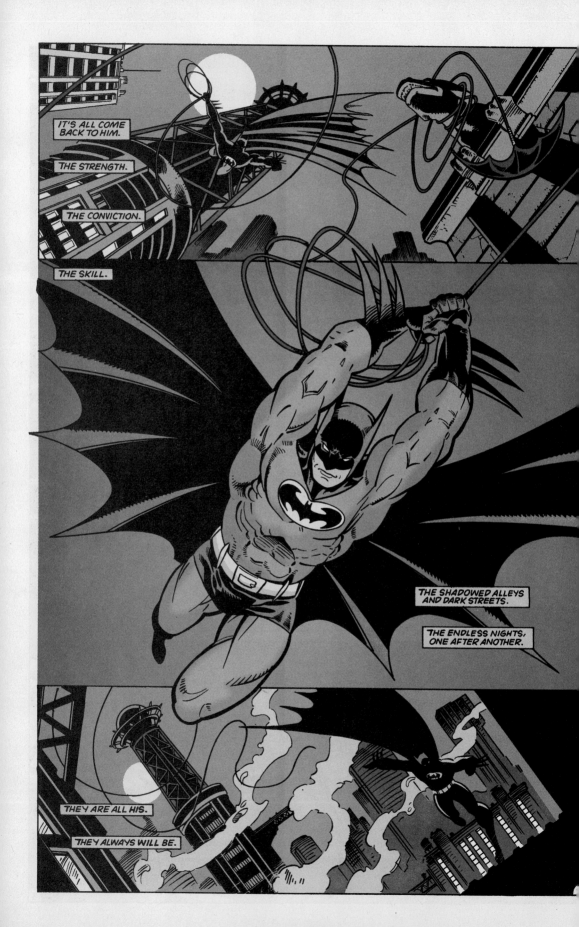

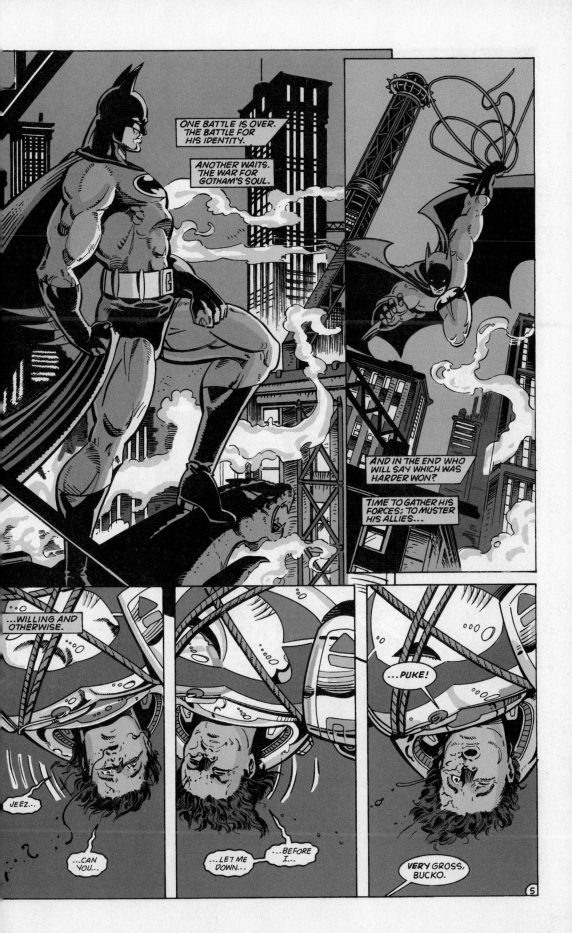

ONE BATTLE IS OVER. THE BATTLE FOR HIS IDENTITY.

ANOTHER WAITS. THE WAR FOR GOTHAM'S SOUL.

AND IN THE END WHO WILL SAY WHICH WAS HARDER WON?

TIME TO GATHER HIS FORCES; TO MUSTER HIS ALLIES...

...WILLING AND OTHERWISE.

JEEZ...

...CAN YOU...

...LET ME DOWN...

...BEFORE I...

...PUKE!

VERY GROSS, BUCKO.

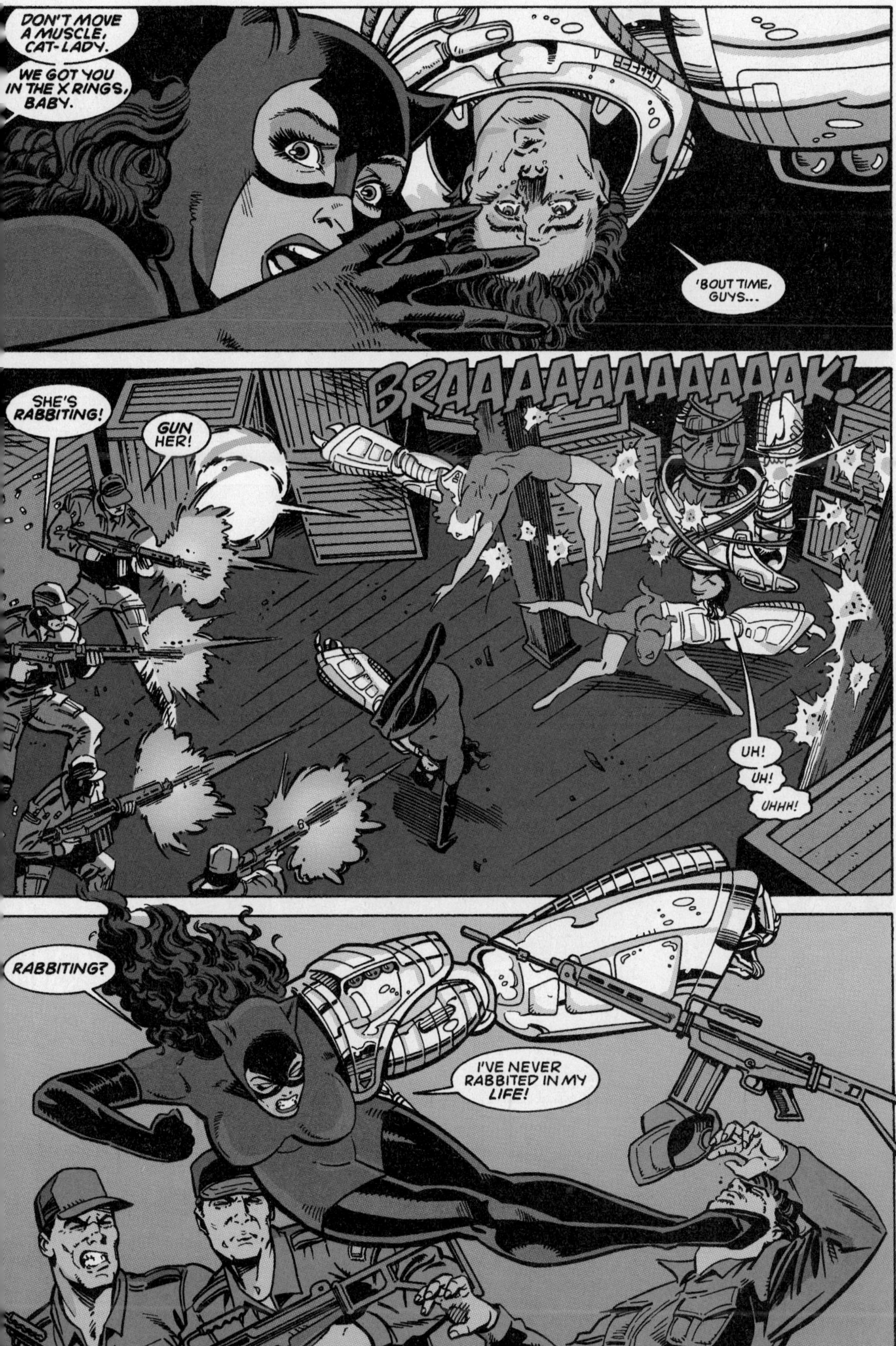
DON'T MOVE A MUSCLE, CAT-LADY.
WE GOT YOU IN THE X RINGS, BABY.
'BOUT TIME, GUYS...
BRAAAAAAAAAAAK!
SHE'S RABBITING!
GUN HER!
UH!
UH!
UHHH!
RABBITING?
I'VE NEVER RABBITED IN MY LIFE!
7

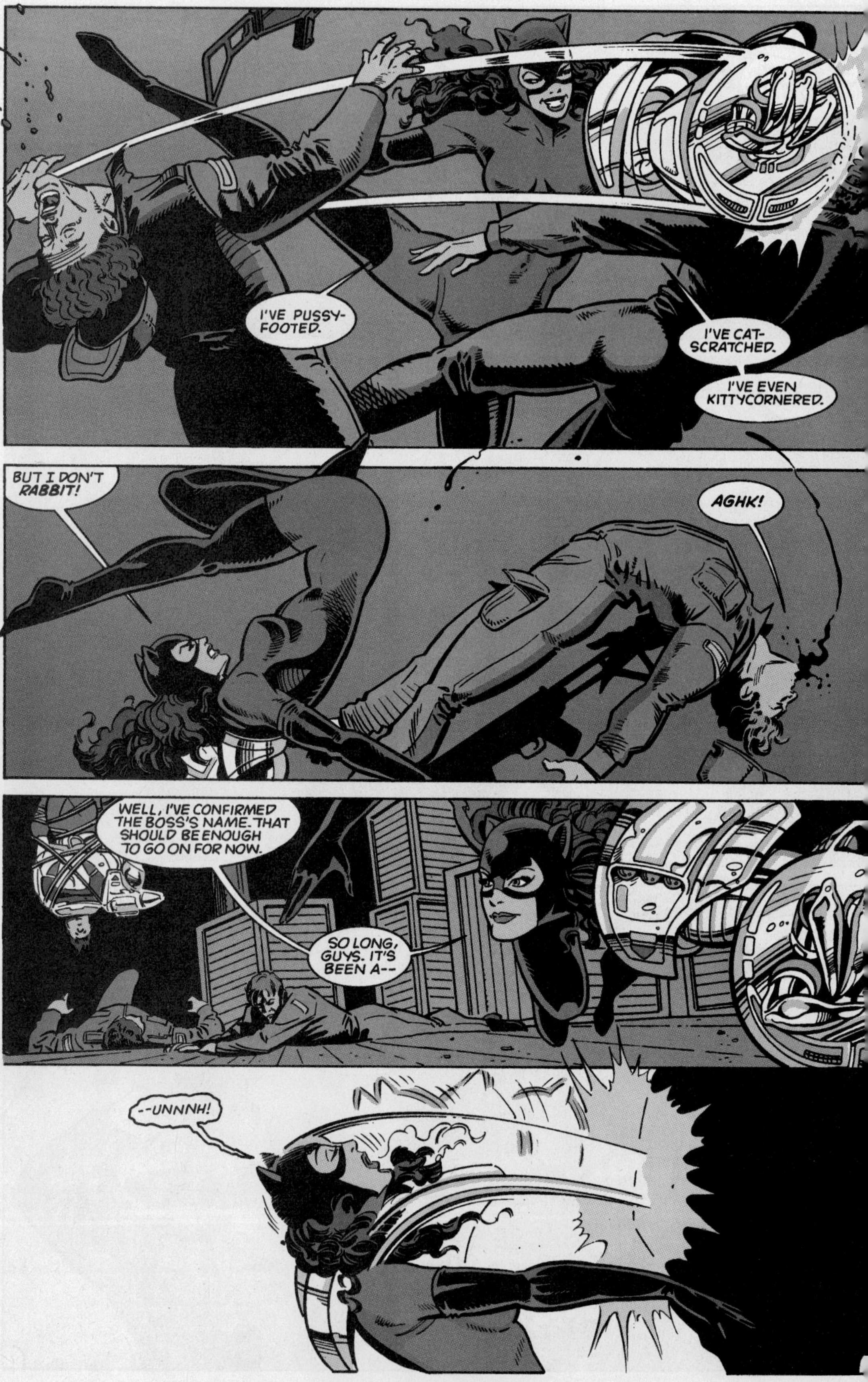
I'VE PUSSY-FOOTED.
I'VE CAT-SCRATCHED.
I'VE EVEN KITTYCORNERED.
BUT I DON'T RABBIT!
AGHK!
WELL, I'VE CONFIRMED THE BOSS'S NAME. THAT SHOULD BE ENOUGH TO GO ON FOR NOW.
SO LONG, GUYS. IT'S BEEN A--
--UNNNH!

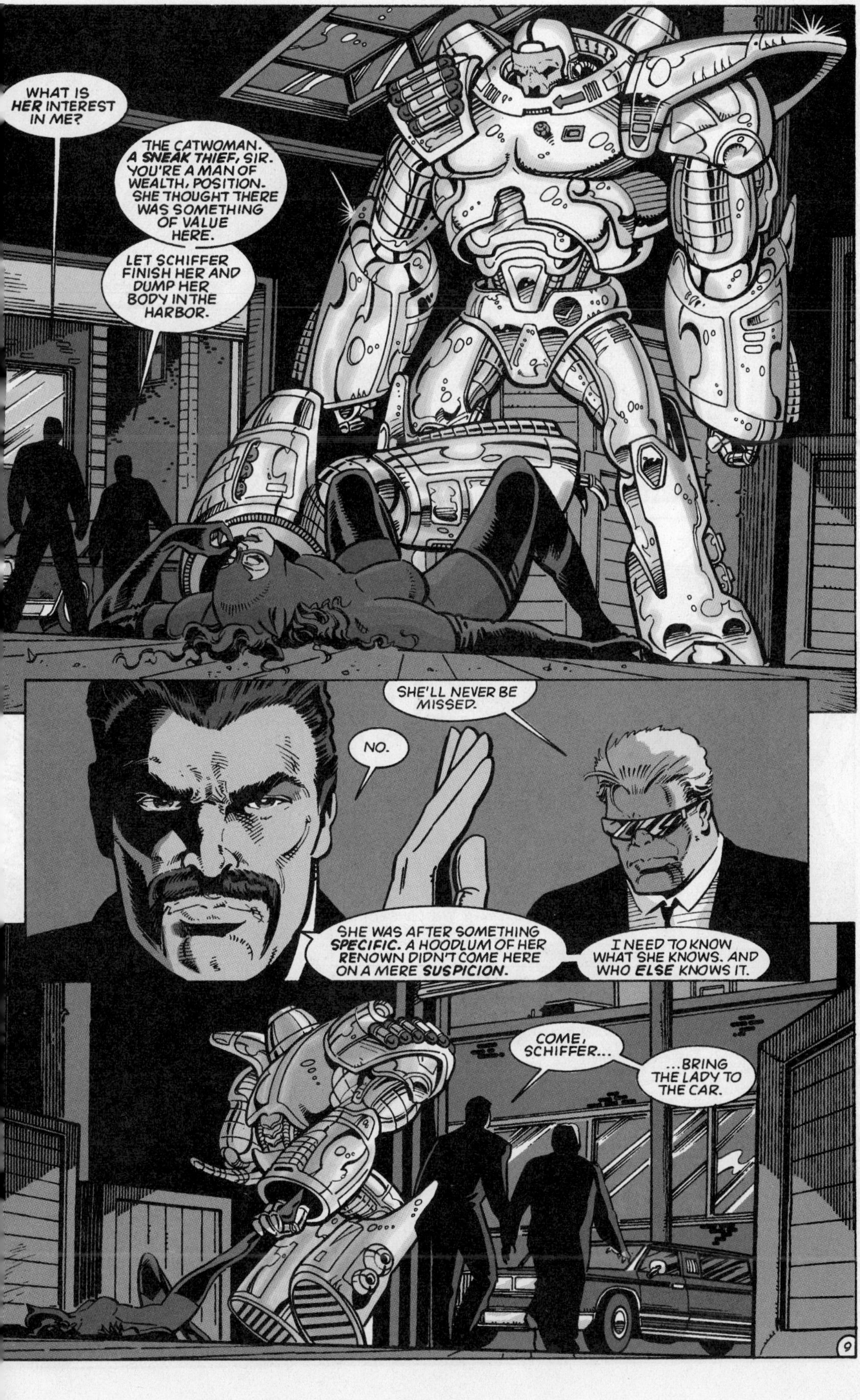
WHAT IS HER INTEREST IN ME?
THE CATWOMAN. A SNEAK THIEF, SIR. YOU'RE A MAN OF WEALTH, POSITION. SHE THOUGHT THERE WAS SOMETHING OF VALUE HERE.
LET SCHIFFER FINISH HER AND DUMP HER BODY IN THE HARBOR.
SHE'LL NEVER BE MISSED.
NO.
SHE WAS AFTER SOMETHING SPECIFIC. A HOODLUM OF HER RENOWN DIDN'T COME HERE ON A MERE SUSPICION.
I NEED TO KNOW WHAT SHE KNOWS. AND WHO ELSE KNOWS IT.
COME, SCHIFFER...
...BRING THE LADY TO THE CAR.
9

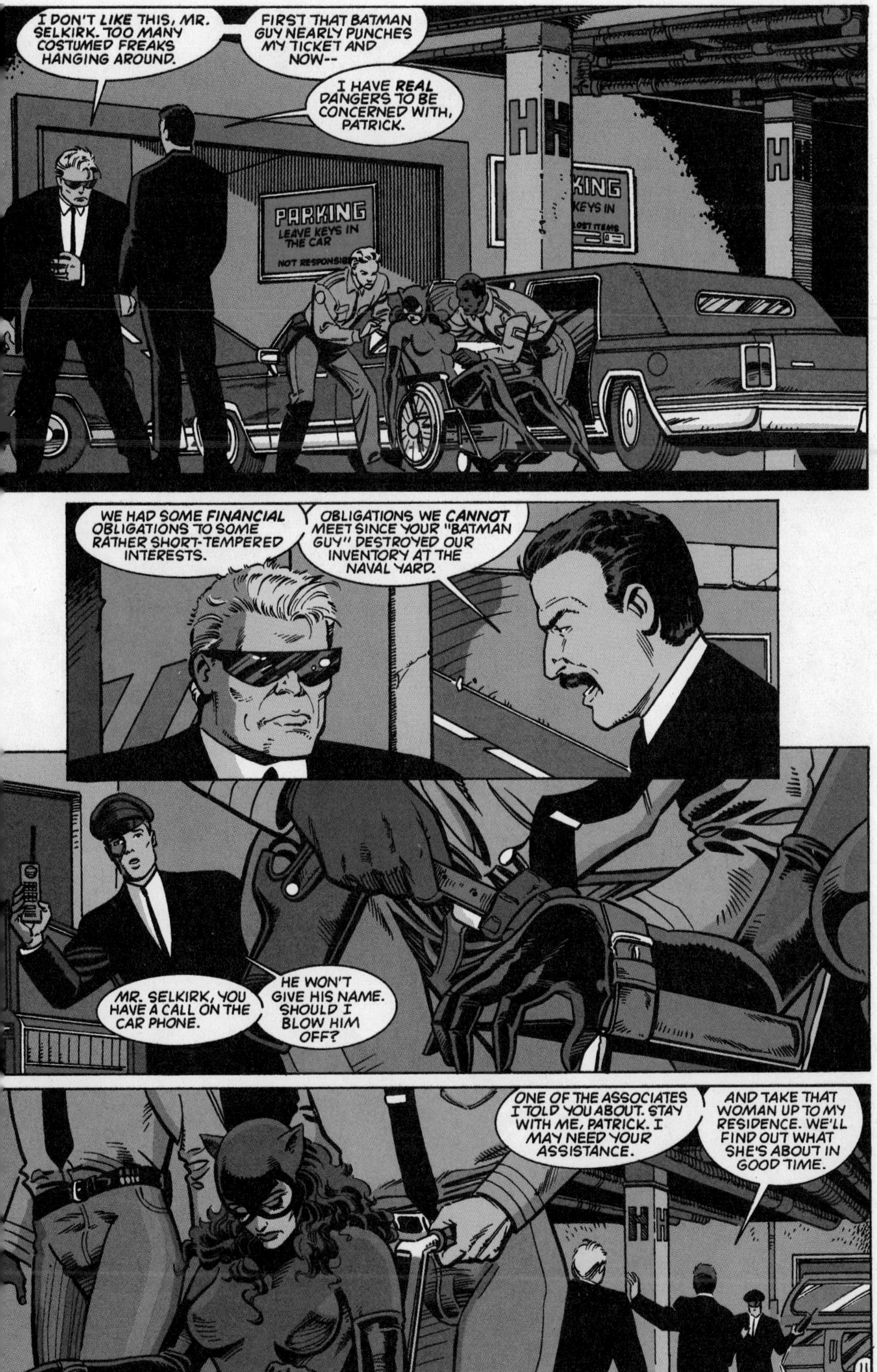
I DON'T LIKE THIS, MR. SELKIRK. TOO MANY COSTUMED FREAKS HANGING AROUND.
FIRST THAT BATMAN GUY NEARLY PUNCHES MY TICKET AND NOW--
I HAVE REAL DANGERS TO BE CONCERNED WITH, PATRICK.
PARKING LEAVE KEYS IN THE CAR NOT RESPONSIBLE
WE HAD SOME FINANCIAL OBLIGATIONS TO SOME RATHER SHORT-TEMPERED INTERESTS.
OBLIGATIONS WE CANNOT MEET SINCE YOUR "BATMAN GUY" DESTROYED OUR INVENTORY AT THE NAVAL YARD.
MR. SELKIRK, YOU HAVE A CALL ON THE CAR PHONE.
HE WON'T GIVE HIS NAME. SHOULD I BLOW HIM OFF?
ONE OF THE ASSOCIATES I TOLD YOU ABOUT. STAY WITH ME, PATRICK. I MAY NEED YOUR ASSISTANCE.
AND TAKE THAT WOMAN UP TO MY RESIDENCE. WE'LL FIND OUT WHAT SHE'S ABOUT IN GOOD TIME.
11

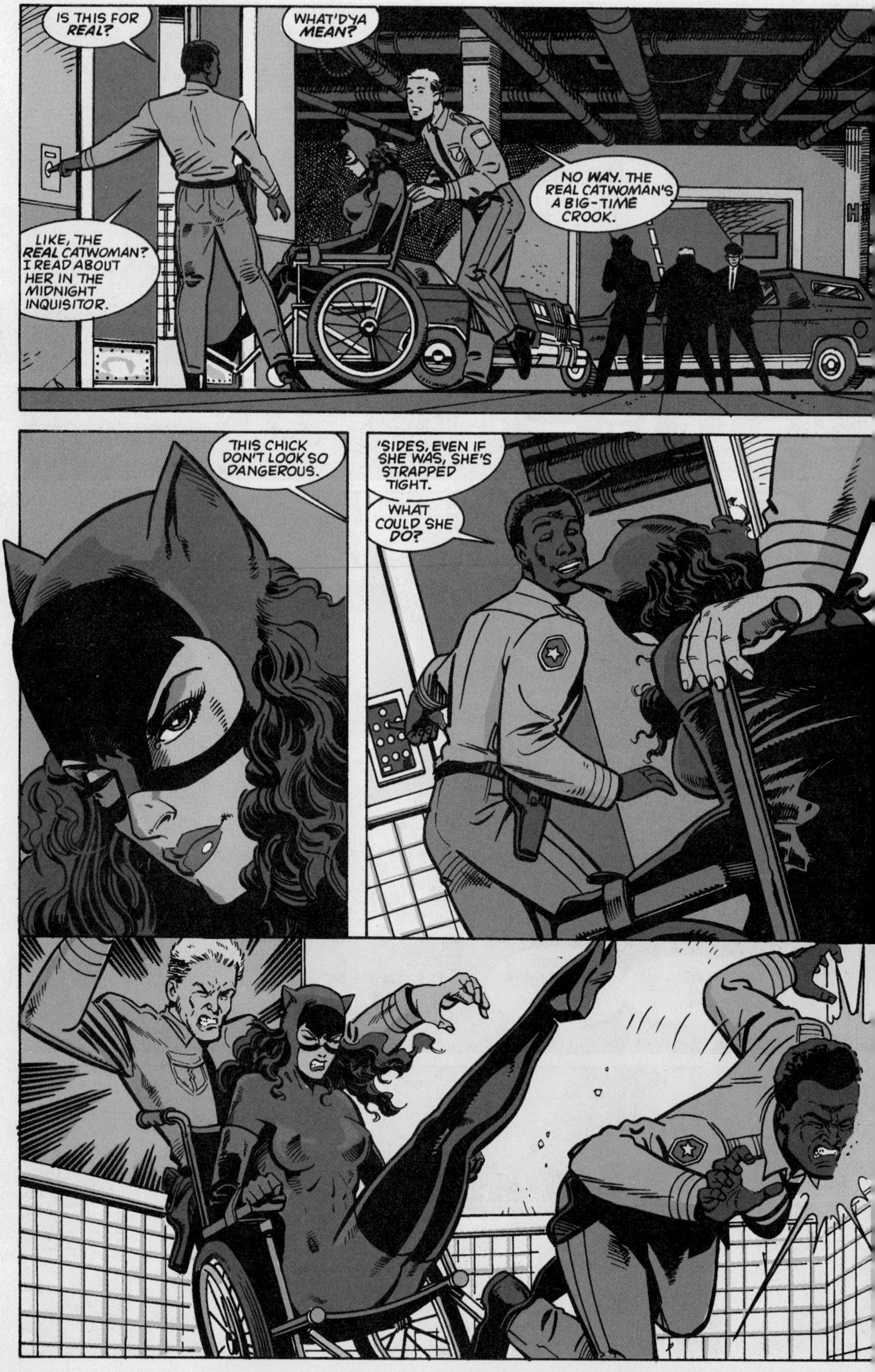
IS THIS FOR REAL?
WHAT'DYA MEAN?
LIKE, THE REAL CATWOMAN? I READ ABOUT HER IN THE MIDNIGHT INQUISITOR.
NO WAY. THE REAL CATWOMAN'S A BIG-TIME CROOK.
THIS CHICK DON'T LOOK SO DANGEROUS.
'SIDES, EVEN IF SHE WAS, SHE'S STRAPPED TIGHT.
WHAT COULD SHE DO?

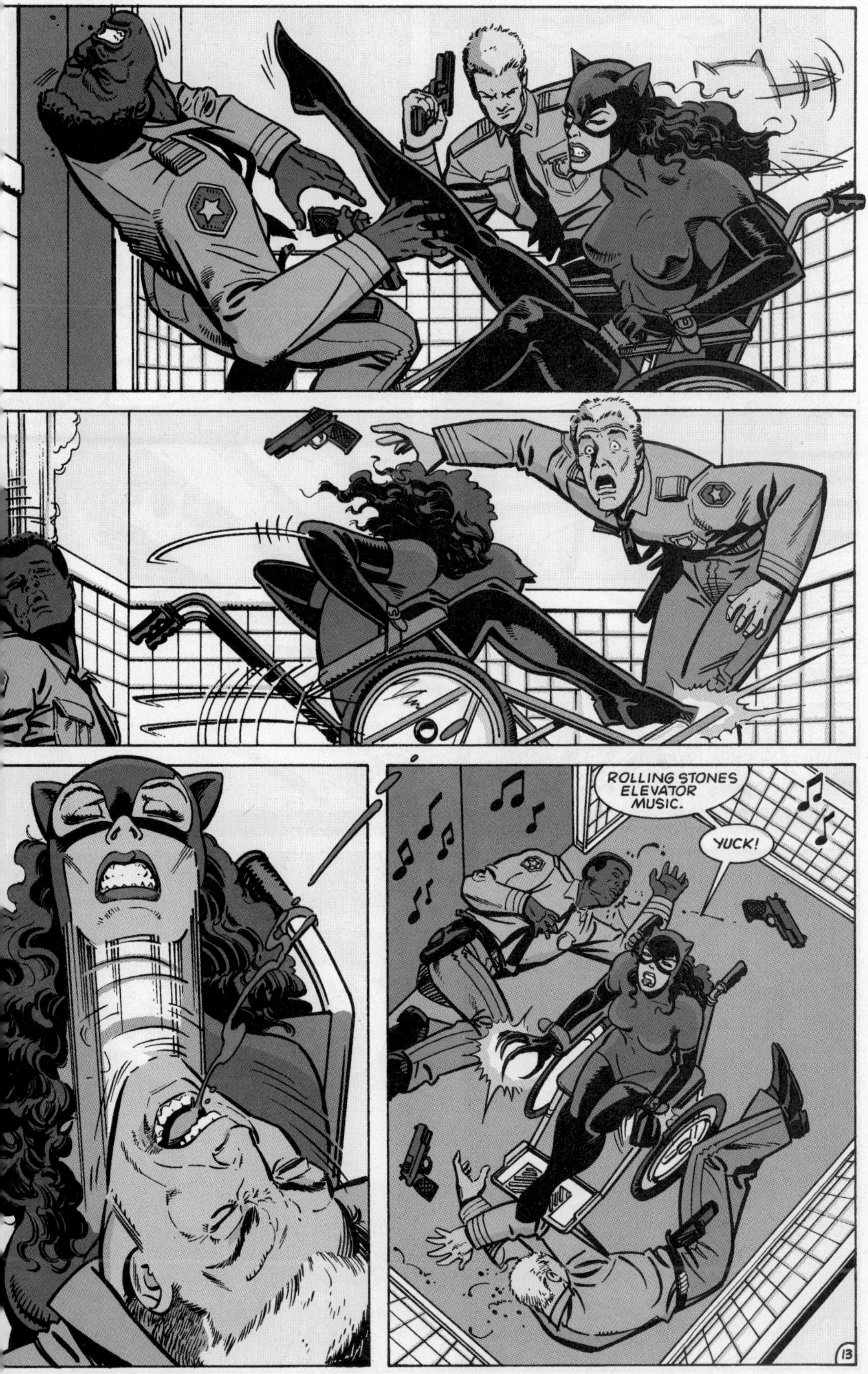
ROLLING STONES ELEVATOR MUSIC.
YUCK!
13

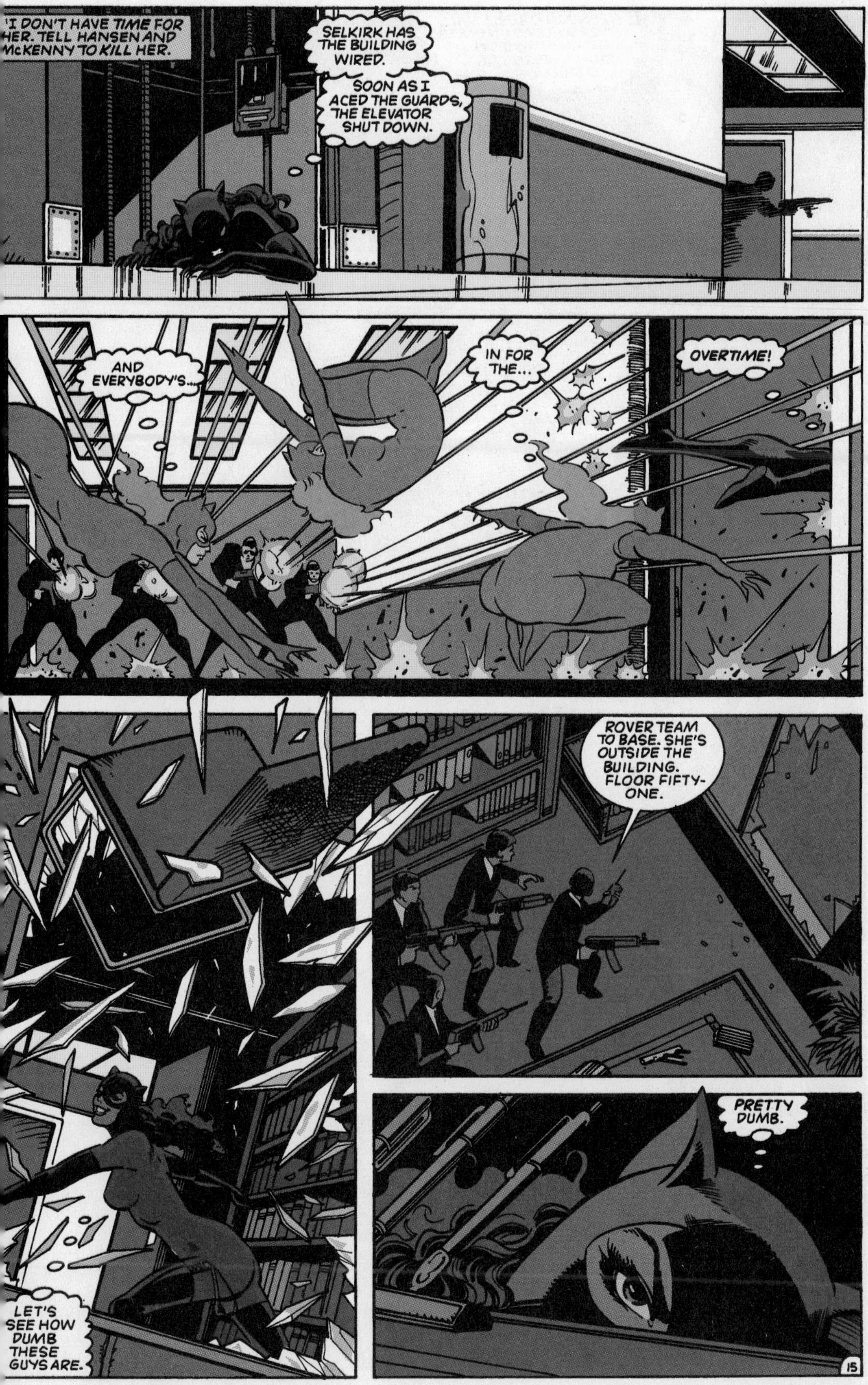
I DON'T HAVE TIME FOR HER. TELL HANSEN AND McKENNY TO KILL HER.
SELKIRK HAS THE BUILDING WIRED.
SOON AS I ACED THE GUARDS, THE ELEVATOR SHUT DOWN.
AND EVERYBODY'S...
IN FOR THE...
OVERTIME!
LET'S SEE HOW DUMB THESE GUYS ARE.
ROVER TEAM TO BASE. SHE'S OUTSIDE THE BUILDING. FLOOR FIFTY-ONE.
PRETTY DUMB.
15

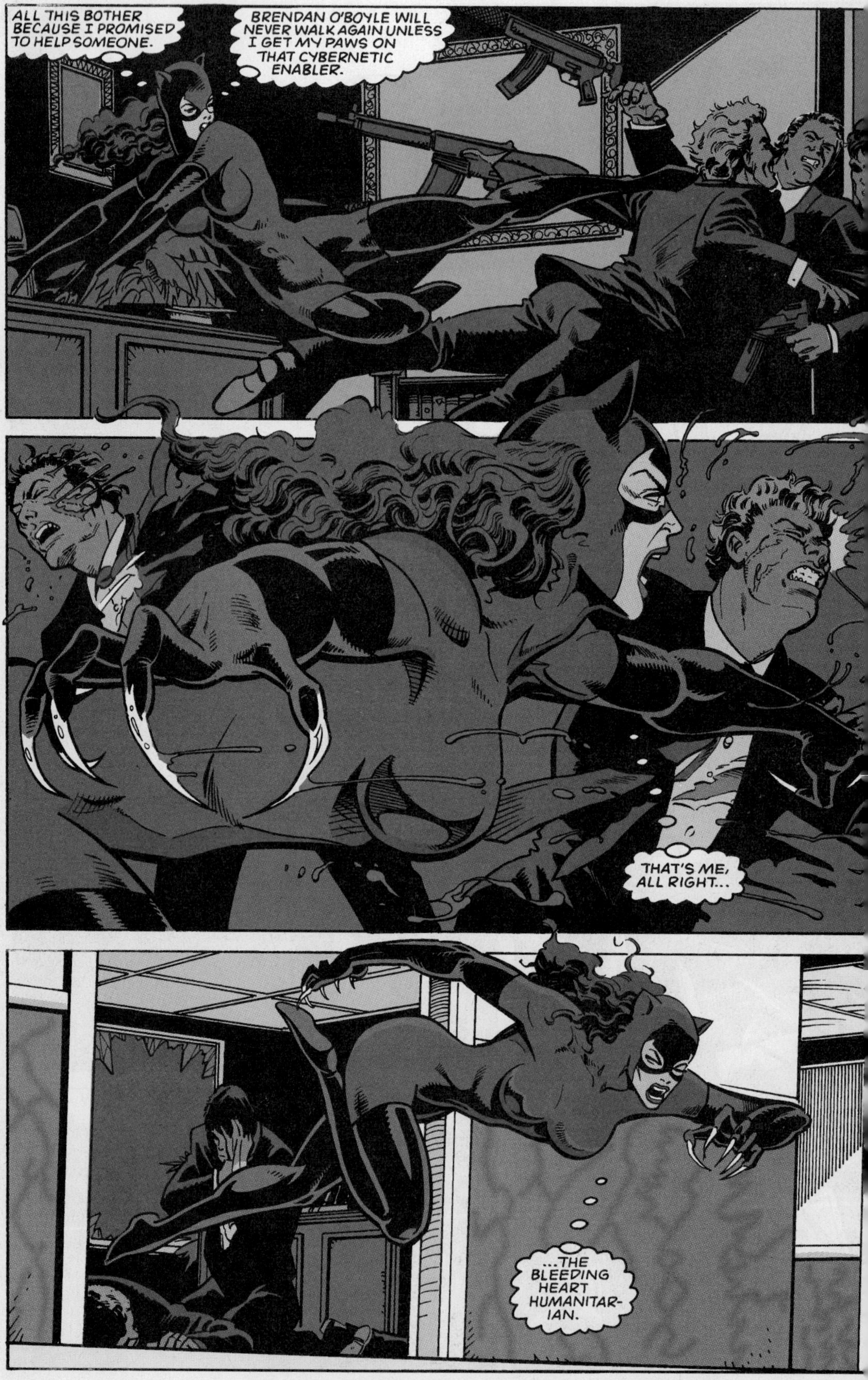
ALL THIS BOTHER BECAUSE I PROMISED TO HELP SOMEONE.
BRENDAN O'BOYLE WILL NEVER WALK AGAIN UNLESS I GET MY PAWS ON THAT CYBERNETIC ENABLER.
THAT'S ME, ALL RIGHT...
...THE BLEEDING HEART HUMANITAR-IAN.

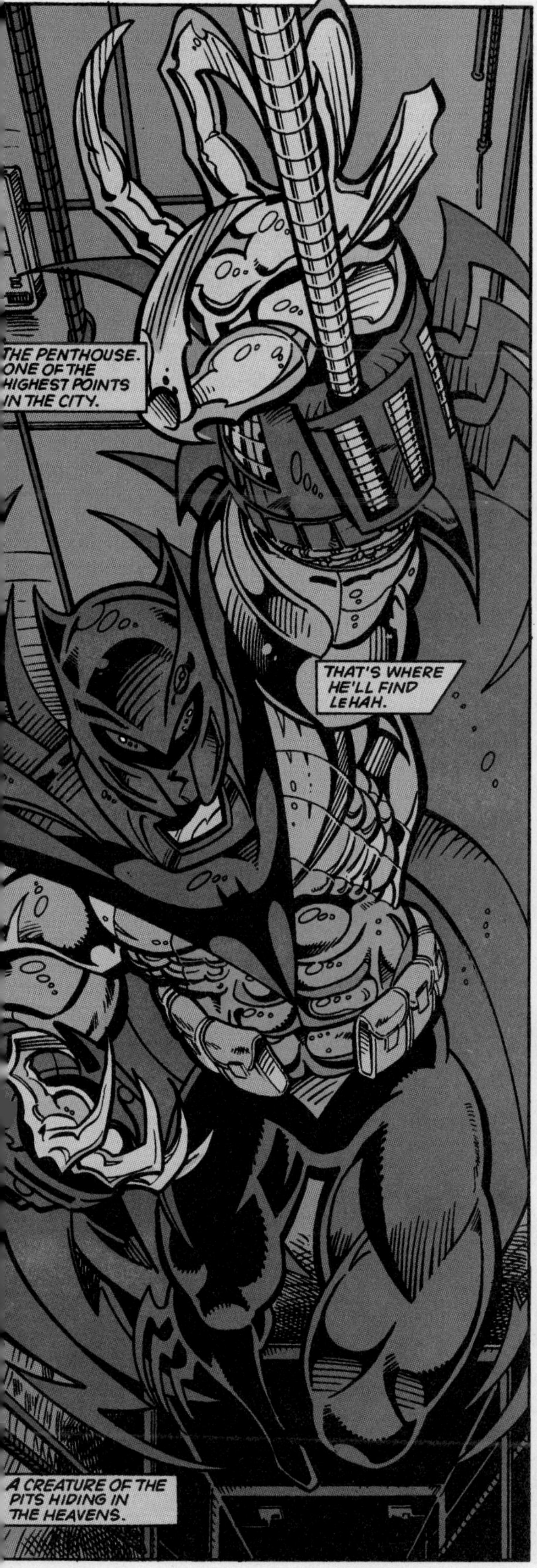
THE PENTHOUSE. ONE OF THE HIGHEST POINTS IN THE CITY.
THAT'S WHERE HE'LL FIND LEHAH.
A CREATURE OF THE PITS HIDING IN THE HEAVENS.

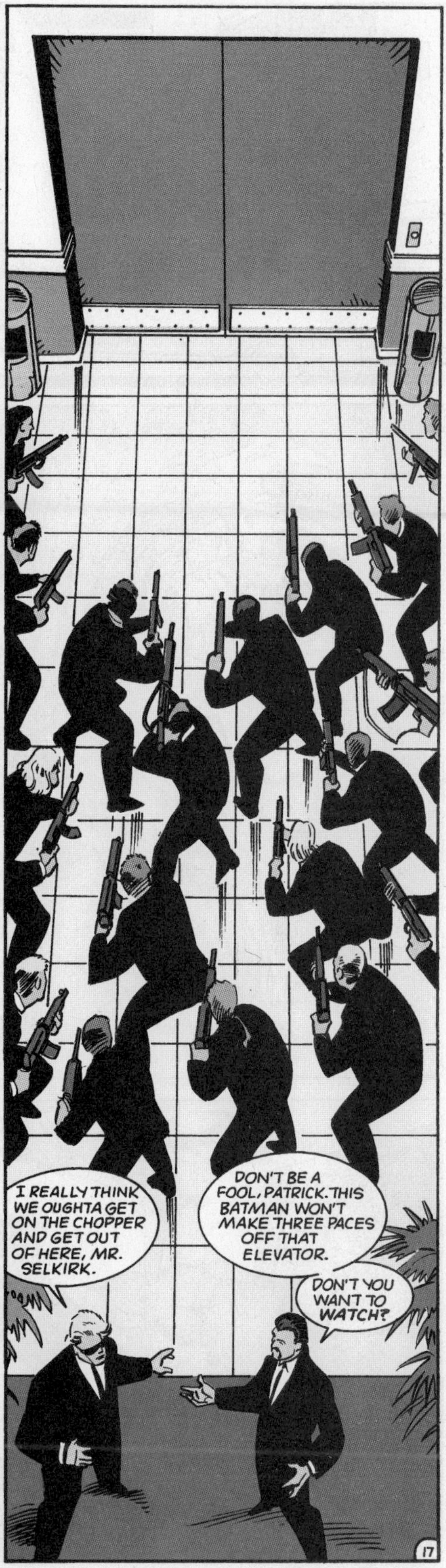
I REALLY THINK WE OUGHTA GET ON THE CHOPPER AND GET OUT OF HERE, MR. SELKIRK.
DON'T BE A FOOL, PATRICK. THIS BATMAN WON'T MAKE THREE PACES OFF THAT ELEVATOR.
DON'T YOU WANT TO WATCH?
17

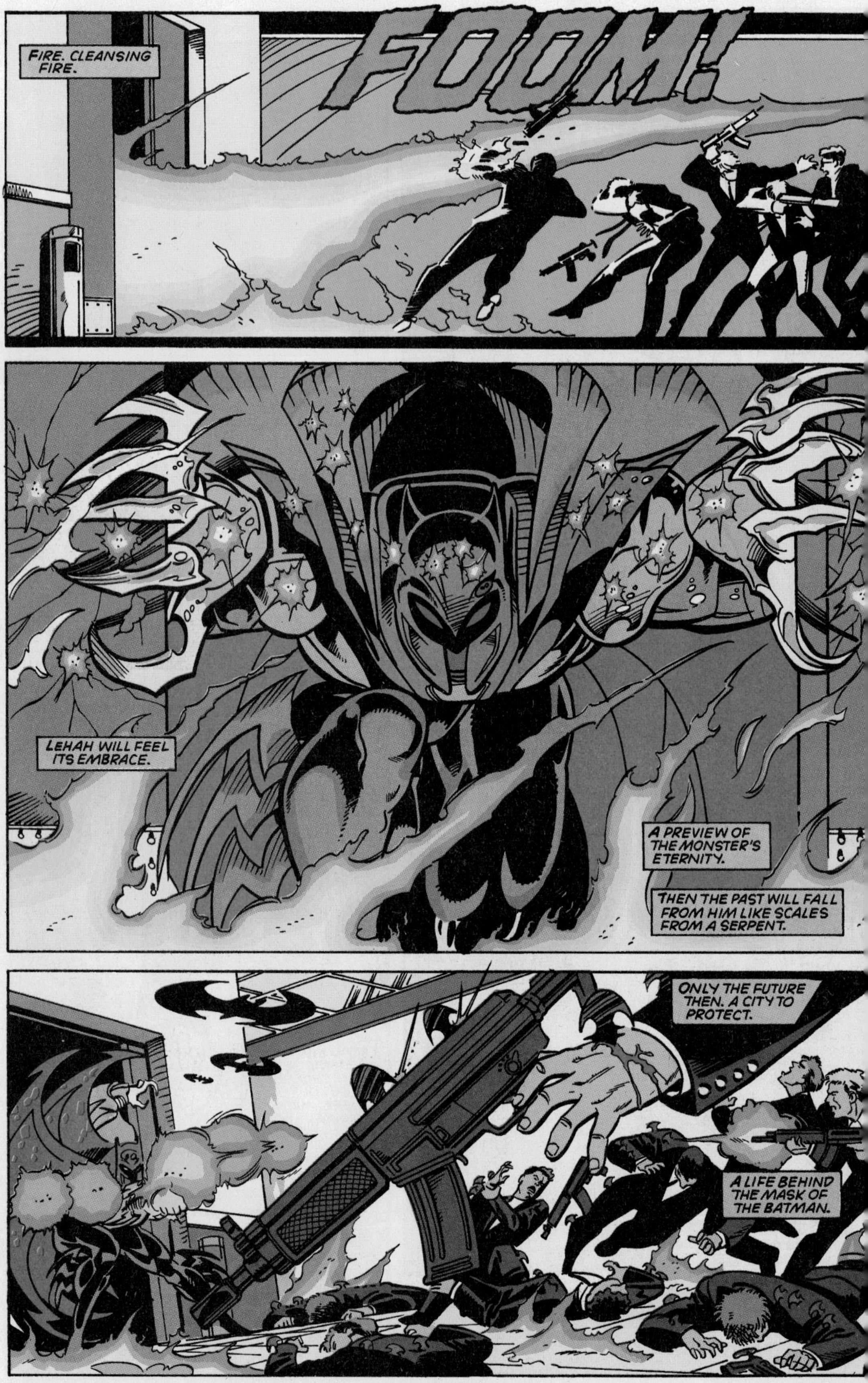
FIRE. CLEANSING FIRE.
FOOM!
LEHAH WILL FEEL ITS EMBRACE.
A PREVIEW OF THE MONSTER'S ETERNITY.
THEN THE PAST WILL FALL FROM HIM LIKE SCALES FROM A SERPENT.
ONLY THE FUTURE THEN. A CITY TO PROTECT.
A LIFE BEHIND THE MASK OF THE BATMAN.

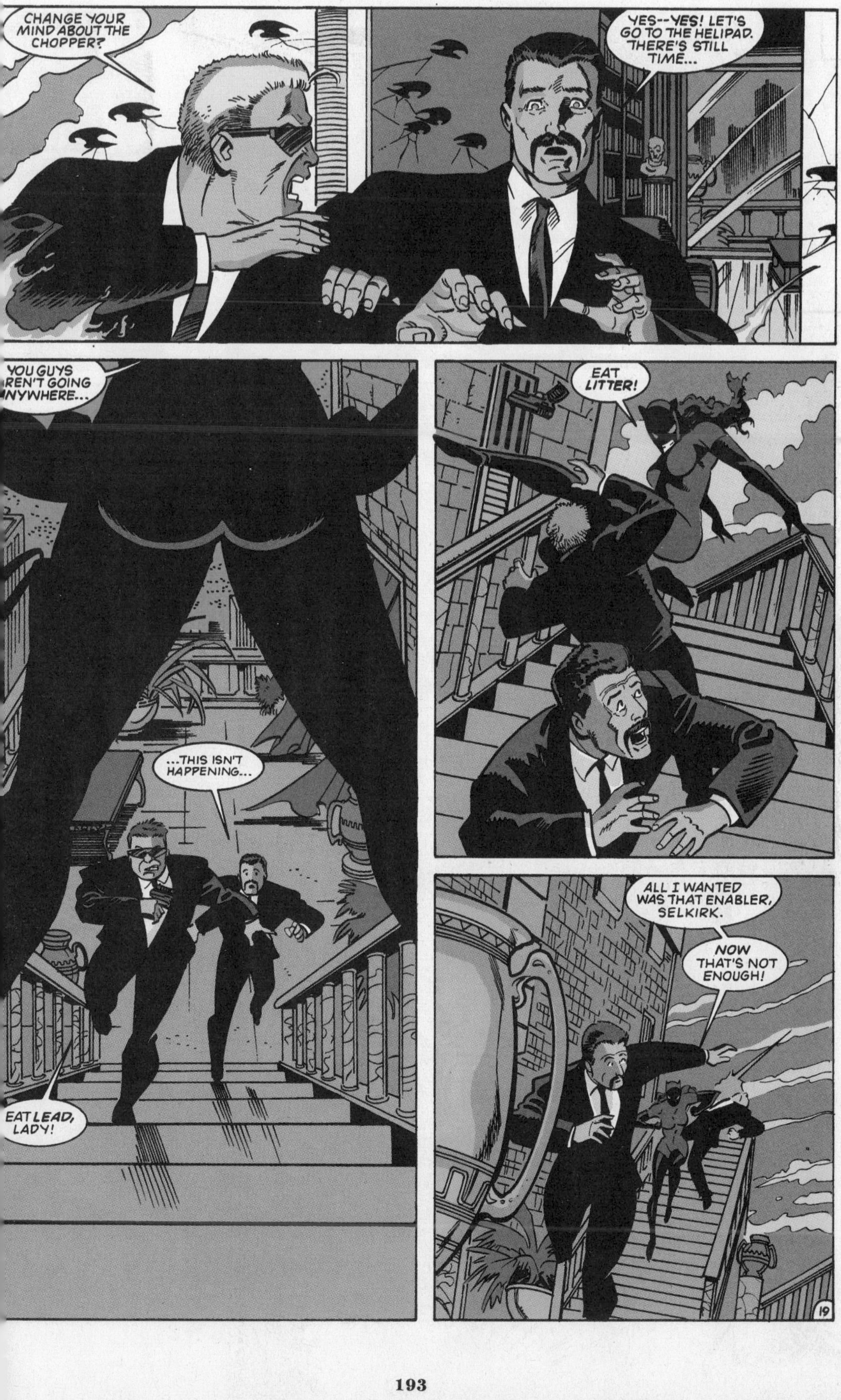
CHANGE YOUR MIND ABOUT THE CHOPPER?
YES--YES! LET'S GO TO THE HELIPAD. THERE'S STILL TIME...
YOU GUYS RENT'T GOING NYWHERE...
...THIS ISN'T HAPPENING...
EAT LEAD, LADY!
EAT LITTER!
ALL I WANTED WAS THAT ENABLER, SELKIRK.
NOW THAT'S NOT ENOUGH!
19

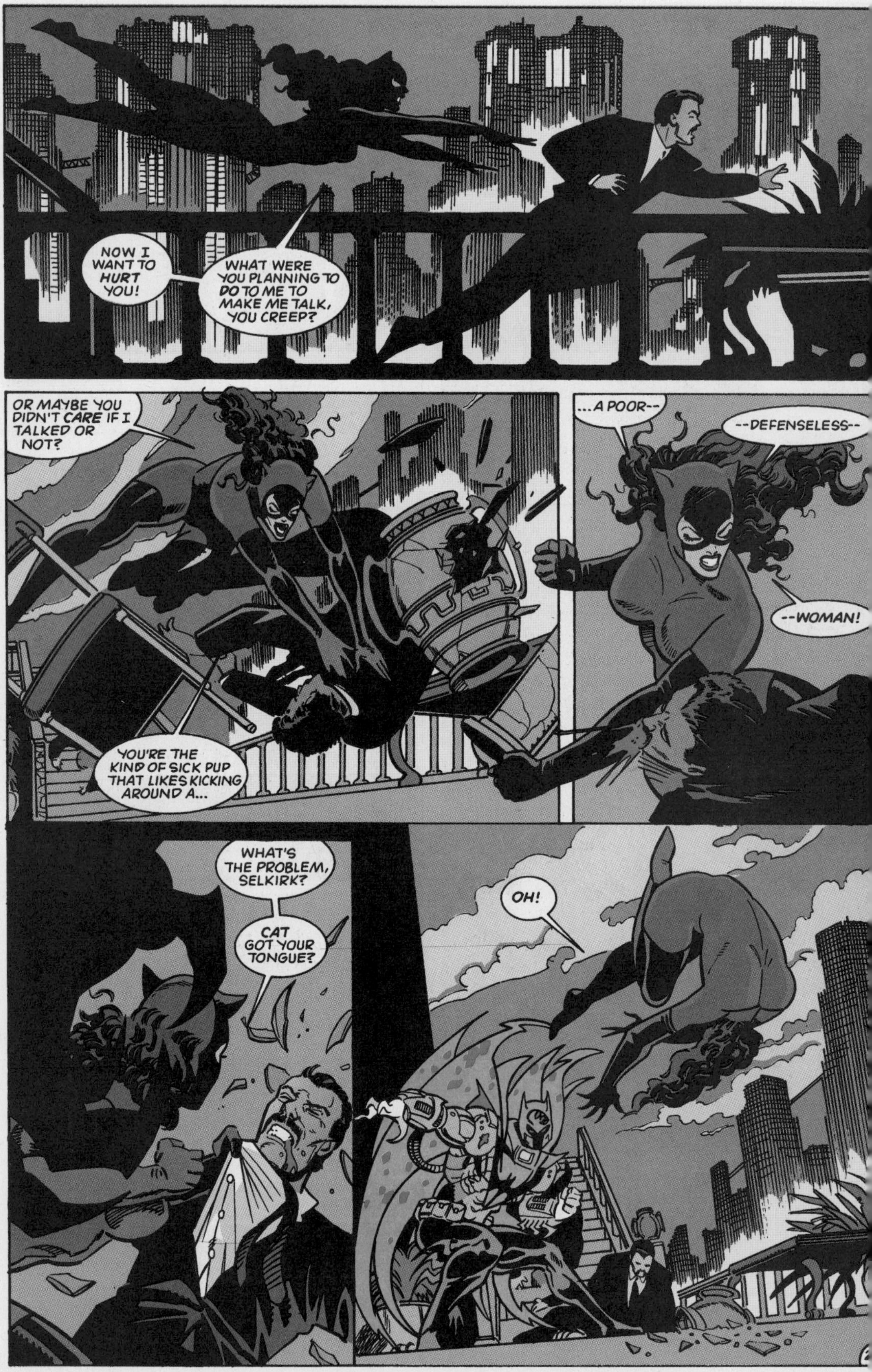
WHAT WERE YOU PLANNING TO DO TO ME TO MAKE ME TALK, YOU CREEP?
NOW I WANT TO HURT YOU!
OR MAYBE YOU DIDN'T CARE IF I TALKED OR NOT?
YOU'RE THE KIND OF SICK PUP THAT LIKES KICKING AROUND A...
...A POOR--
--DEFENSELESS--
--WOMAN!
WHAT'S THE PROBLEM, SELKIRK?
CAT GOT YOUR TONGUE?
OH!

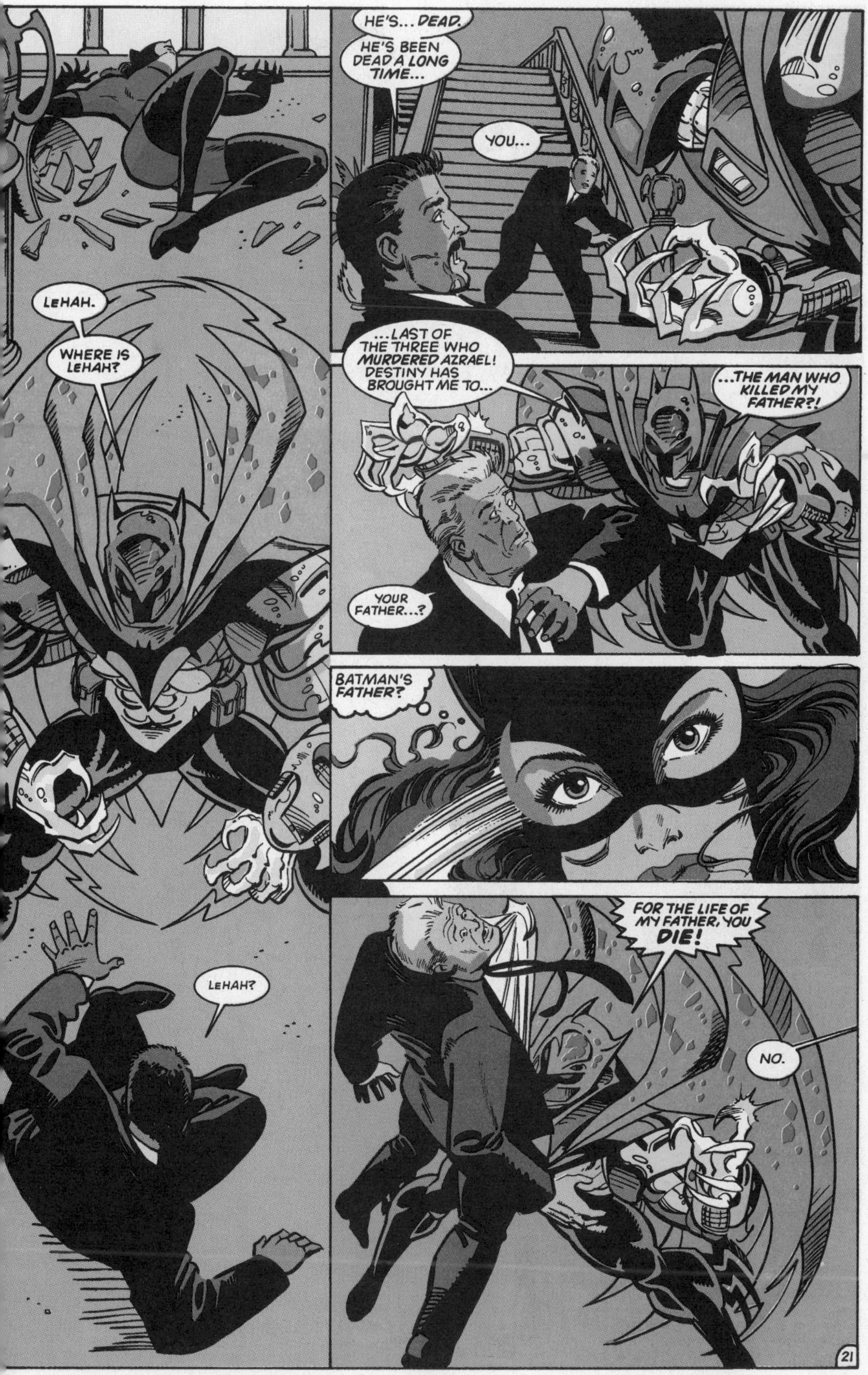
HE'S... DEAD.
HE'S BEEN DEAD A LONG TIME...
YOU...
LEHAH.
WHERE IS LEHAH?
...LAST OF THE THREE WHO MURDERED AZRAEL! DESTINY HAS BROUGHT ME TO...
...THE MAN WHO KILLED MY FATHER?!
YOUR FATHER...?
BATMAN'S FATHER?
LEHAH?
FOR THE LIFE OF MY FATHER, YOU DIE!
NO.
21

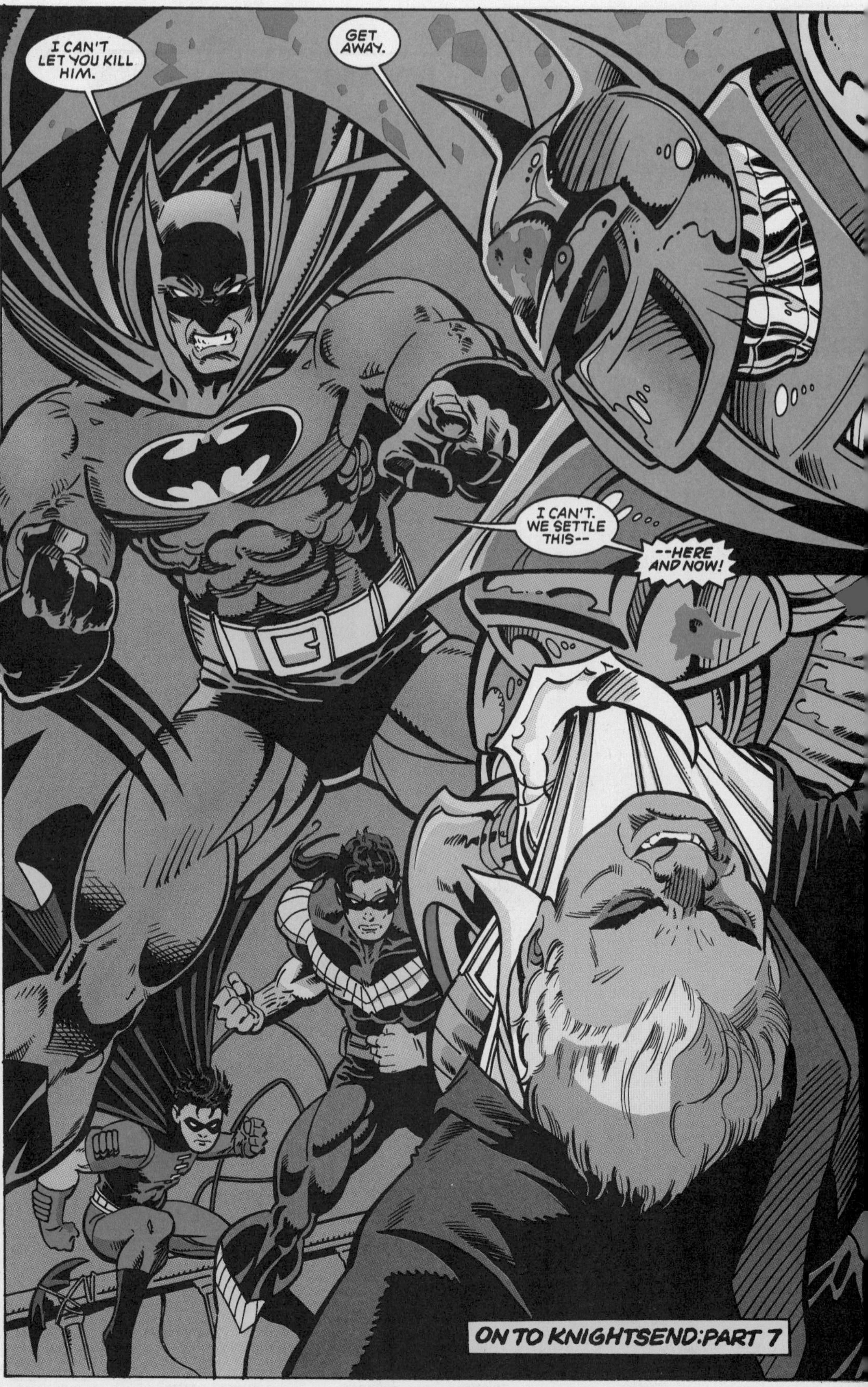
I CAN'T LET YOU KILL HIM.
GET AWAY.
I CAN'T. WE SETTLE THIS--
--HERE AND NOW!
ON TO KNIGHTSEND: PART 7

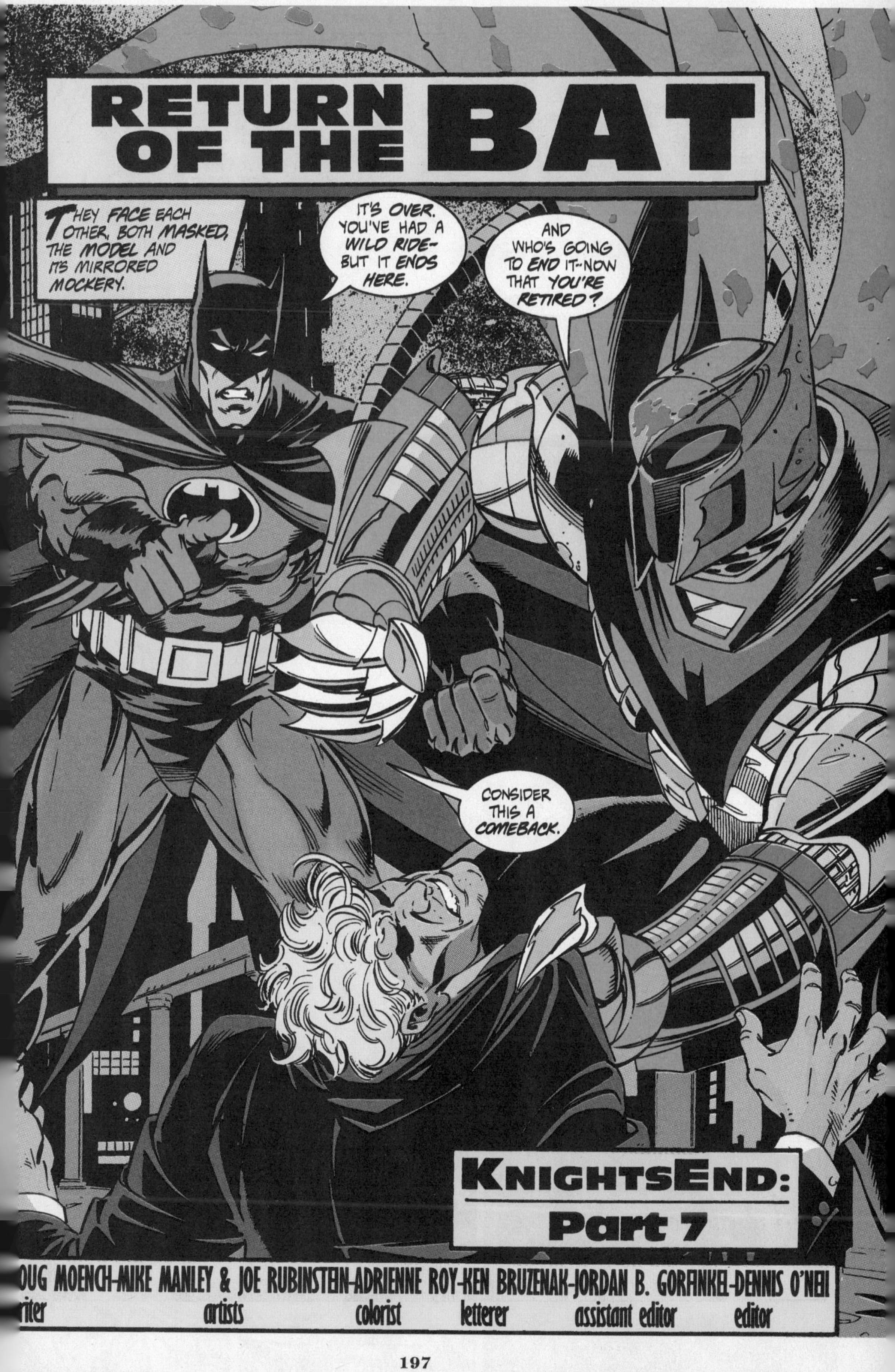
RETURN OF THE BAT
THEY FACE EACH OTHER, BOTH MASKED, THE MODEL AND ITS MIRRORED MOCKERY.
IT'S OVER. YOU'VE HAD A WILD RIDE-- BUT IT ENDS HERE.
AND WHO'S GOING TO END IT--NOW THAT YOU'RE RETIRED?
CONSIDER THIS A COMEBACK.
KNIGHTSEND: Part 7
OUG MOENCH-MIKE MANLEY & JOE RUBINSTEIN-ADRIENNE ROY-KEN BRUZENAK-JORDAN B. GORFINKEL-DENNIS O'NEI
riter artists colorist letterer assistant editor editor

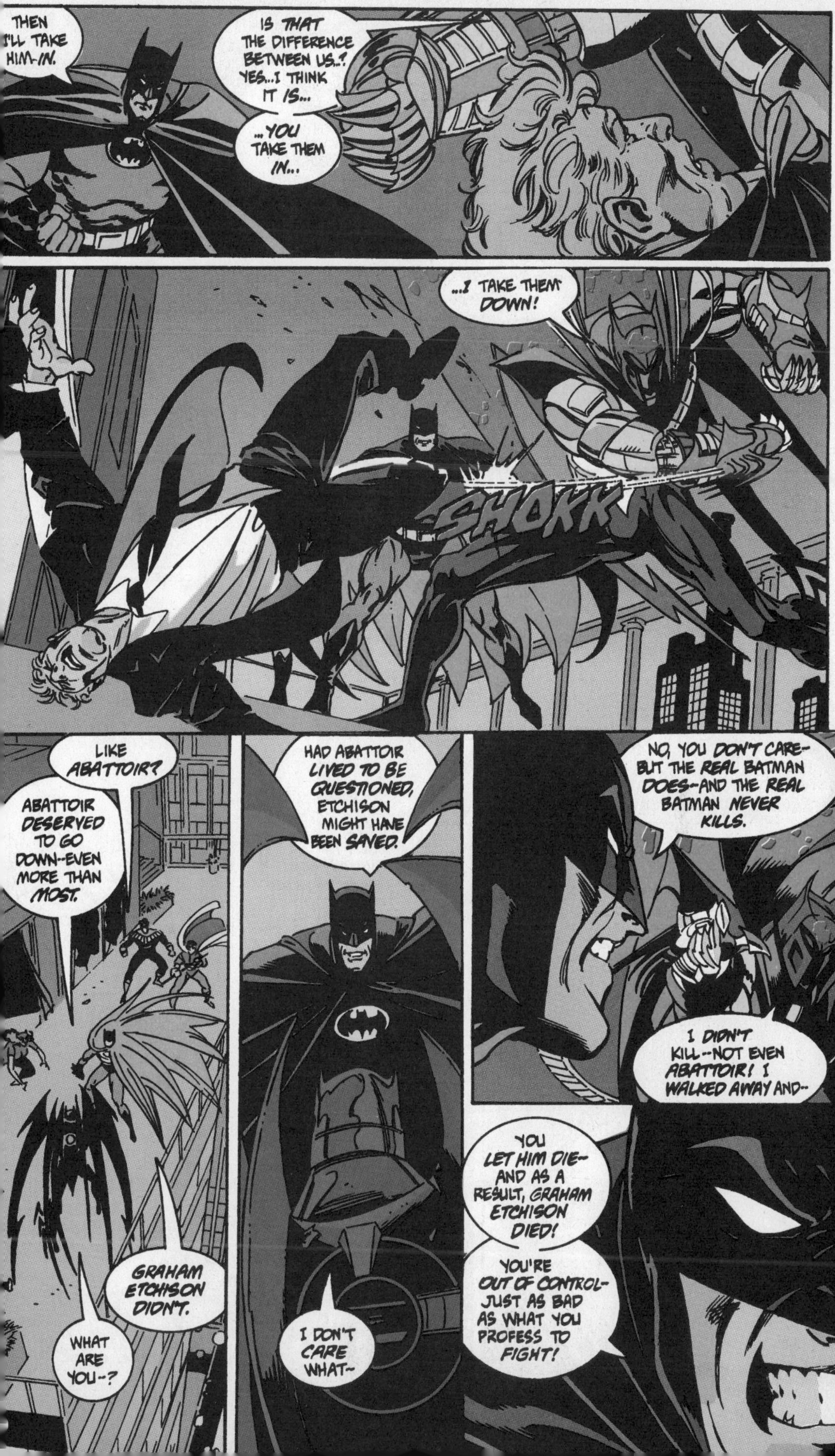
THEN I'LL TAKE HIM-IN.
IS THAT THE DIFFERENCE BETWEEN US..? YES...I THINK IT IS...
...YOU TAKE THEM IN...
...I TAKE THEM DOWN!
SHOKK
LIKE ABATTOIR?
ABATTOIR DESERVED TO GO DOWN--EVEN MORE THAN MOST.
GRAHAM ETCHISON DIDN'T.
WHAT ARE YOU--?
HAD ABATTOIR LIVED TO BE QUESTIONED, ETCHISON MIGHT HAVE BEEN SAVED.
I DON'T CARE WHAT-
NO, YOU DON'T CARE-BUT THE REAL BATMAN DOES--AND THE REAL BATMAN NEVER KILLS.
I DIDN'T KILL--NOT EVEN ABATTOIR! I WALKED AWAY AND--
YOU LET HIM DIE--AND AS A RESULT, GRAHAM ETCHISON DIED!
YOU'RE OUT OF CONTROL-JUST AS BAD AS WHAT YOU PROFESS TO FIGHT!

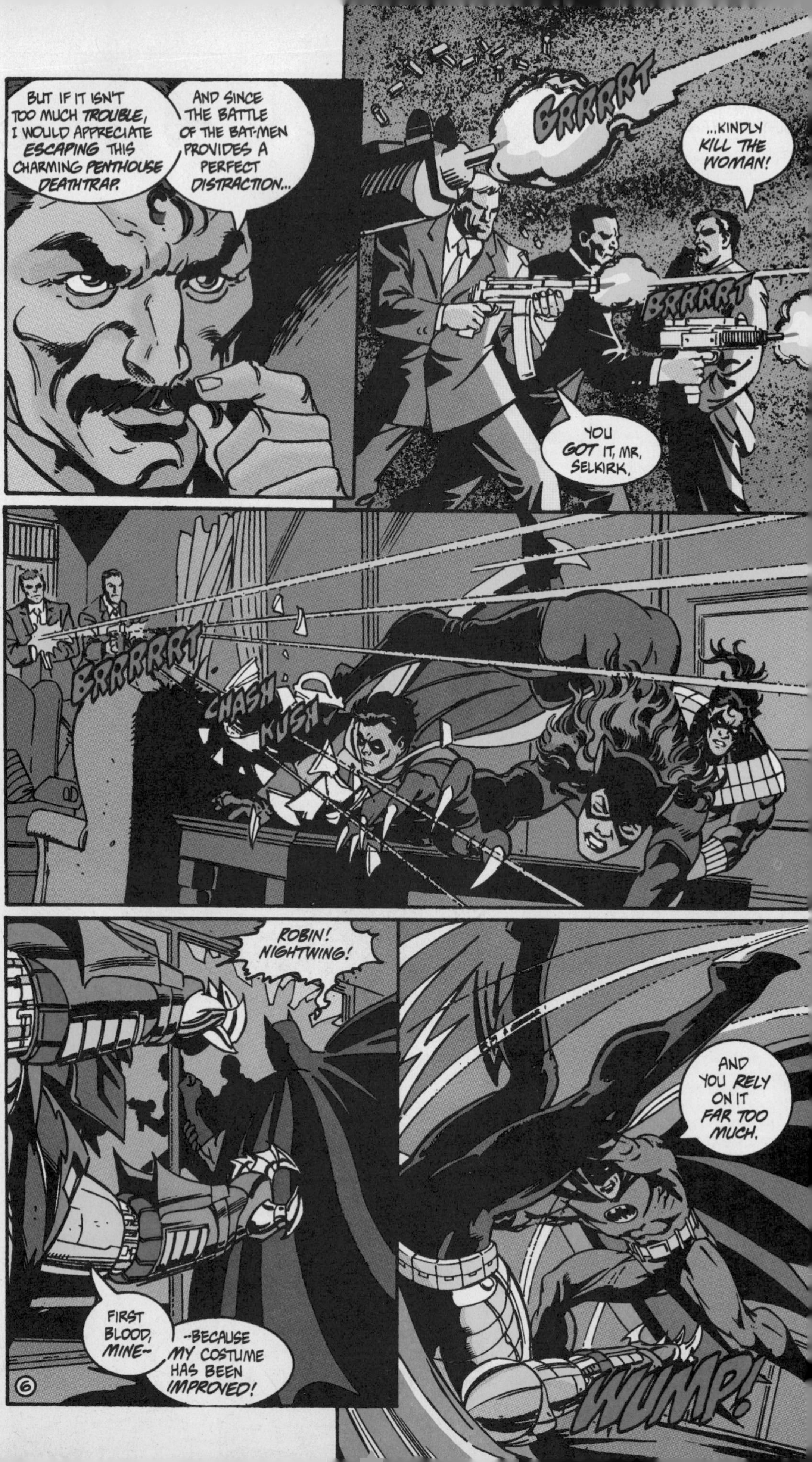
BUT IF IT ISN'T TOO MUCH TROUBLE, I WOULD APPRECIATE ESCAPING THIS CHARMING PENTHOUSE DEATHTRAP.
AND SINCE THE BATTLE OF THE BAT-MEN PROVIDES A PERFECT DISTRACTION...
BRRRRT
...KINDLY KILL THE WOMAN!
BRRRRT
YOU GOT IT, MR. SELKIRK.
BRRRRRRT
CHASH
KUSH
ROBIN! NIGHTWING!
AND YOU RELY ON IT FAR TOO MUCH.
FIRST BLOOD, MINE--
--BECAUSE MY COSTUME HAS BEEN IMPROVED!
6
WUMP!

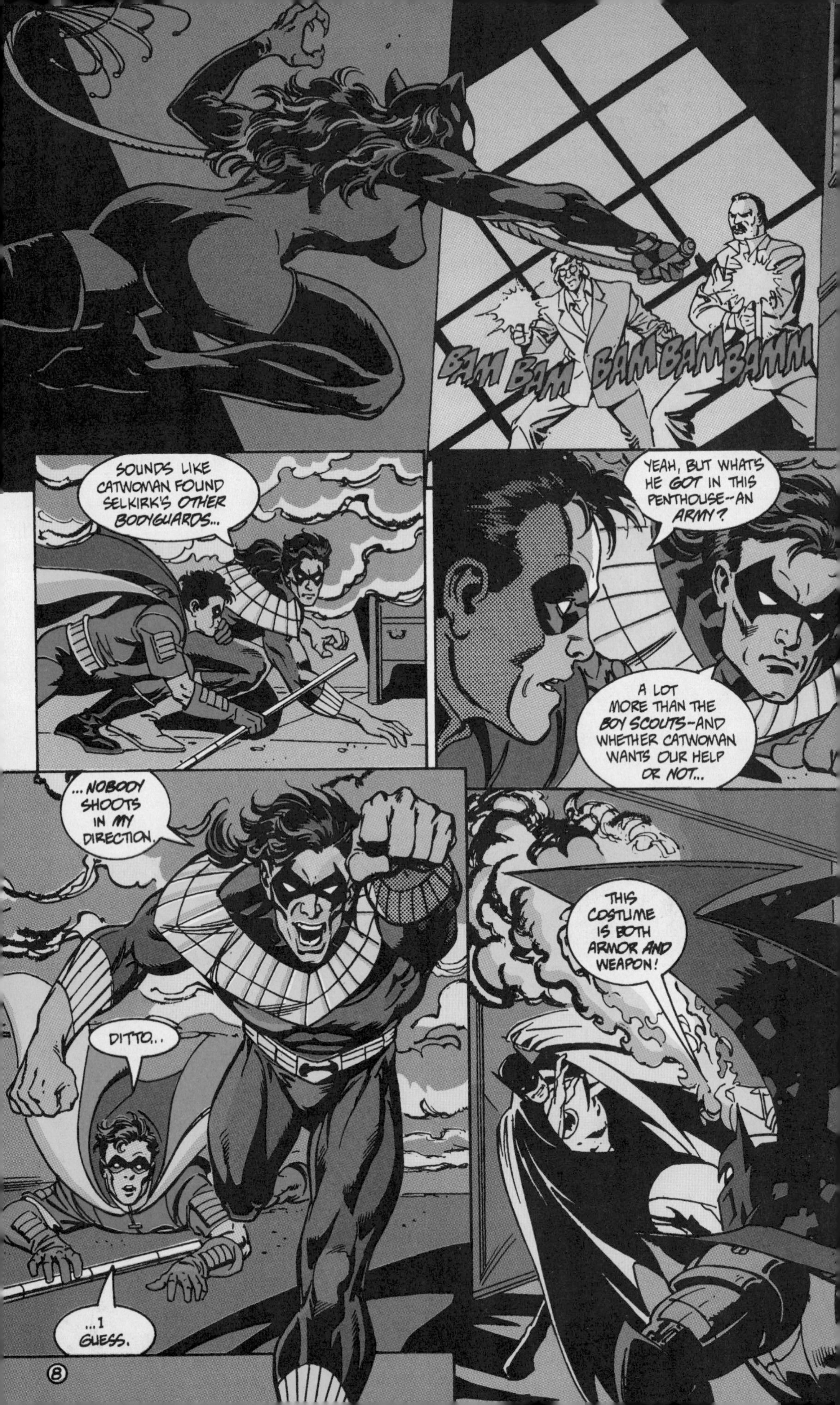
BAM BAM BAM BAM BAMM
SOUNDS LIKE CATWOMAN FOUND SELKIRK'S OTHER BODYGUARDS...
YEAH, BUT WHAT'S HE GOT IN THIS PENTHOUSE--AN ARMY?
A LOT MORE THAN THE BOY SCOUTS--AND WHETHER CATWOMAN WANTS OUR HELP OR NOT...
...NOBODY SHOOTS IN MY DIRECTION.
DITTO...
...I GUESS.
THIS COSTUME IS BOTH ARMOR AND WEAPON!

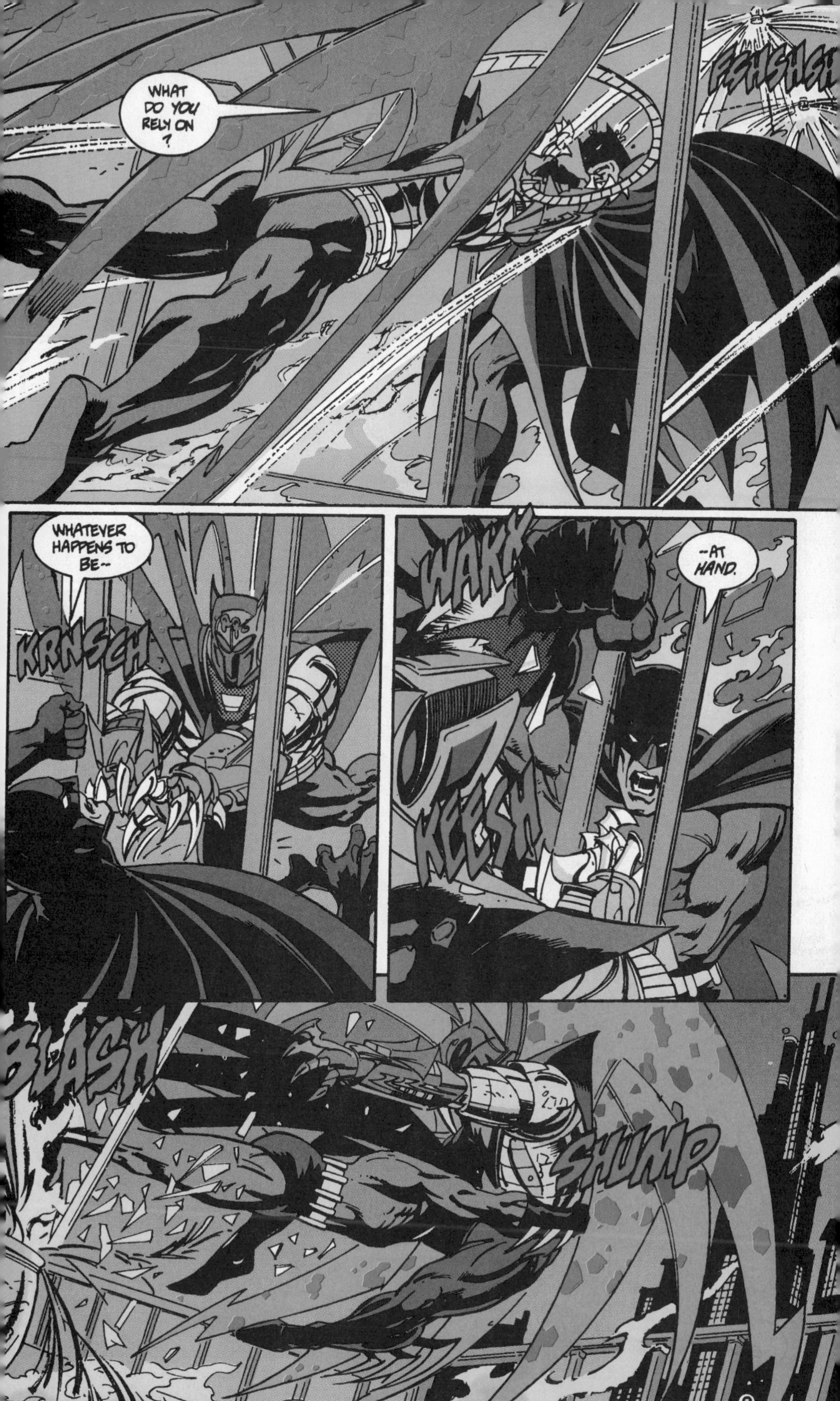
FSHSHSH
WHAT DO YOU RELY ON ?
WHATEVER HAPPENS TO BE--
KRNSCH
WAKK
--AT HAND.
KEESH
BLASH
SHUMP

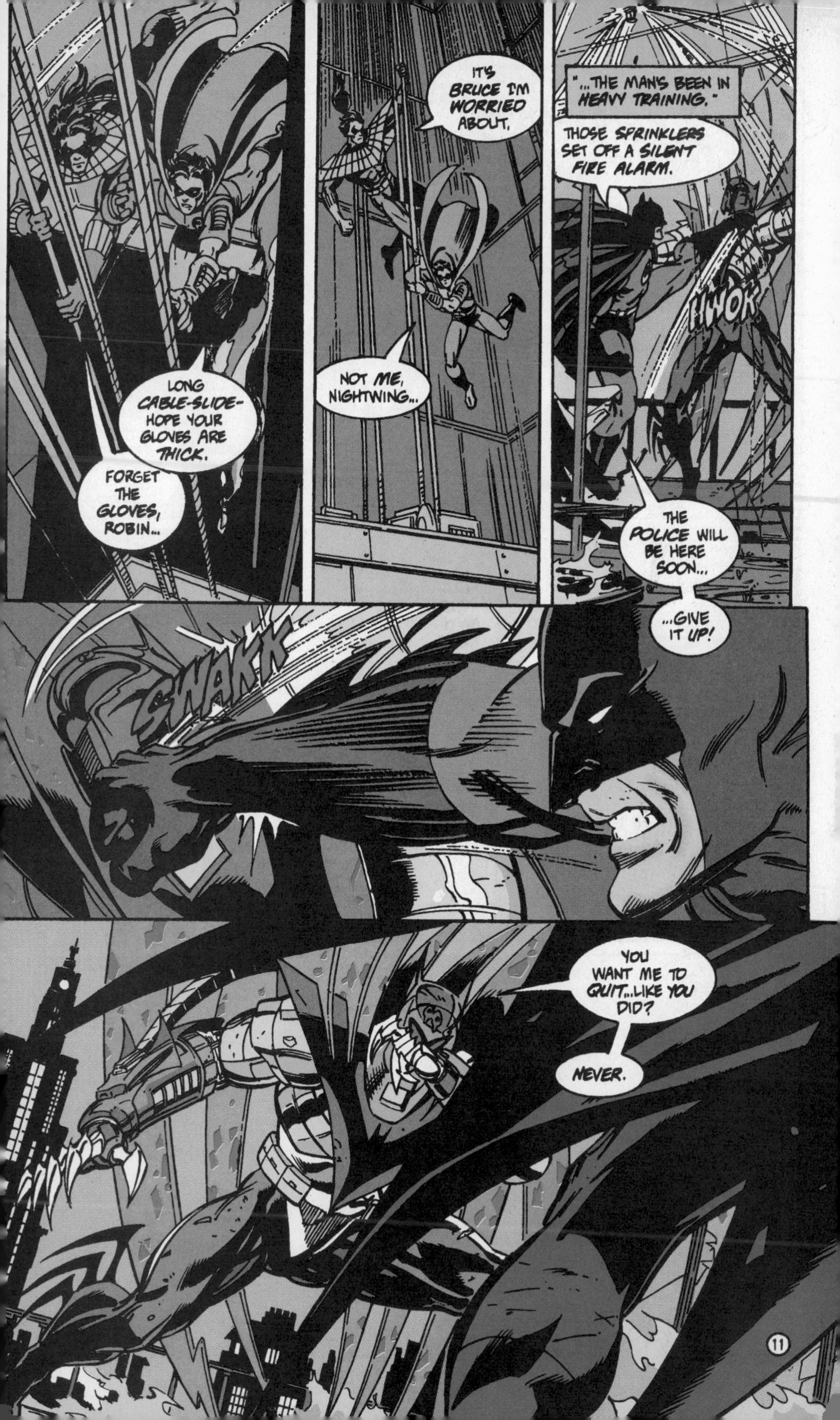
LONG CABLE-SLIDE- HOPE YOUR GLOVES ARE THICK.
FORGET THE GLOVES, ROBIN...
IT'S BRUCE I'M WORRIED ABOUT.
NOT ME, NIGHTWING...
"...THE MAN'S BEEN IN HEAVY TRAINING."
THOSE SPRINKLERS SET OFF A SILENT FIRE ALARM.
WOK
THE POLICE WILL BE HERE SOON...
...GIVE IT UP!
SWAKK
YOU WANT ME TO QUIT...LIKE YOU DID?
NEVER.

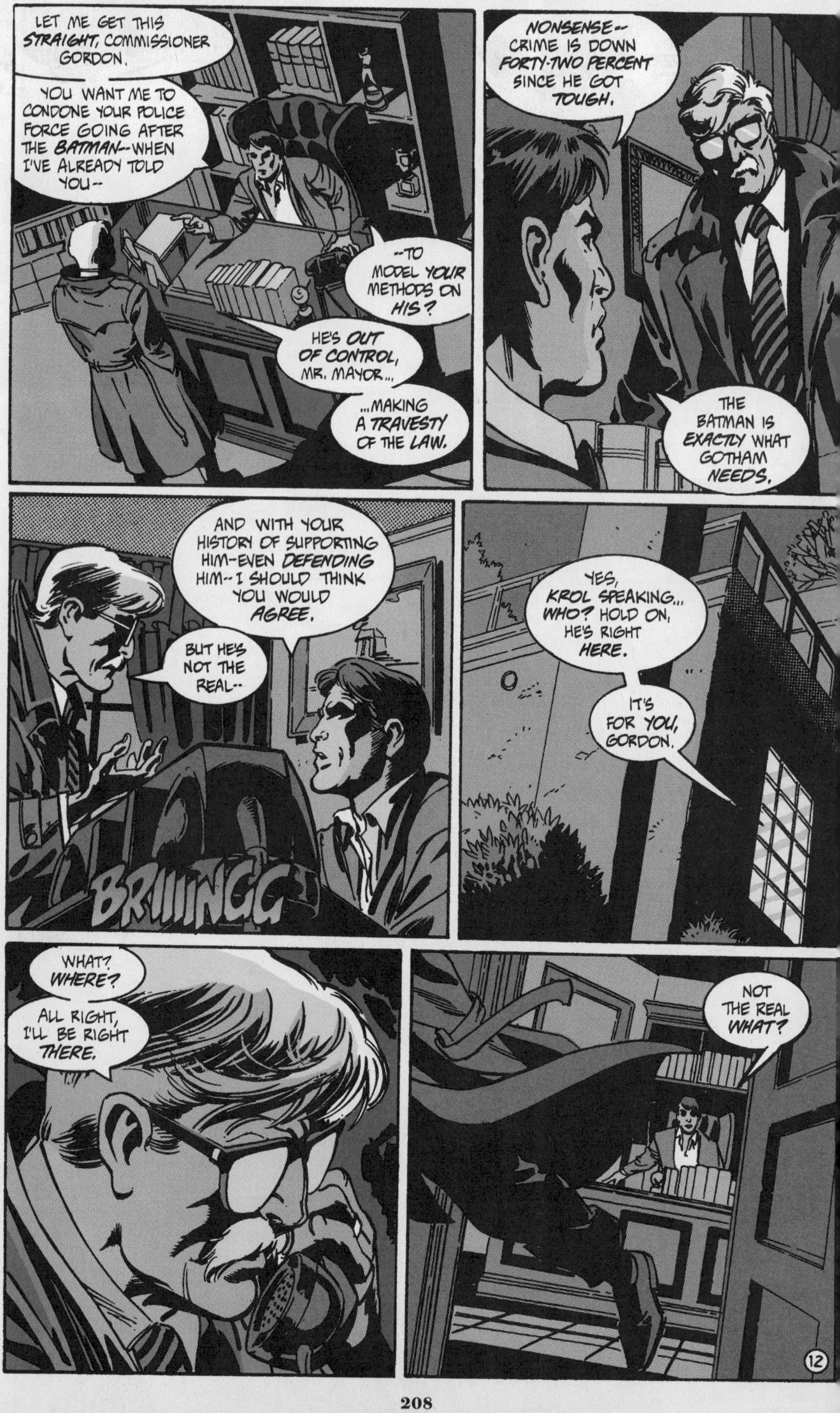
LET ME GET THIS STRAIGHT, COMMISSIONER GORDON.
YOU WANT ME TO CONDONE YOUR POLICE FORCE GOING AFTER THE BATMAN--WHEN I'VE ALREADY TOLD YOU--
--TO MODEL YOUR METHODS ON HIS?
HE'S OUT OF CONTROL, MR. MAYOR...
...MAKING A TRAVESTY OF THE LAW.
NONSENSE--CRIME IS DOWN FORTY-TWO PERCENT SINCE HE GOT TOUGH.
THE BATMAN IS EXACTLY WHAT GOTHAM NEEDS.
AND WITH YOUR HISTORY OF SUPPORTING HIM--EVEN DEFENDING HIM--I SHOULD THINK YOU WOULD AGREE.
BUT HE'S NOT THE REAL--
BRIIIINGG
YES, KROL SPEAKING... WHO? HOLD ON, HE'S RIGHT HERE.
IT'S FOR YOU, GORDON.
WHAT? WHERE?
ALL RIGHT, I'LL BE RIGHT THERE.
NOT THE REAL WHAT?
12

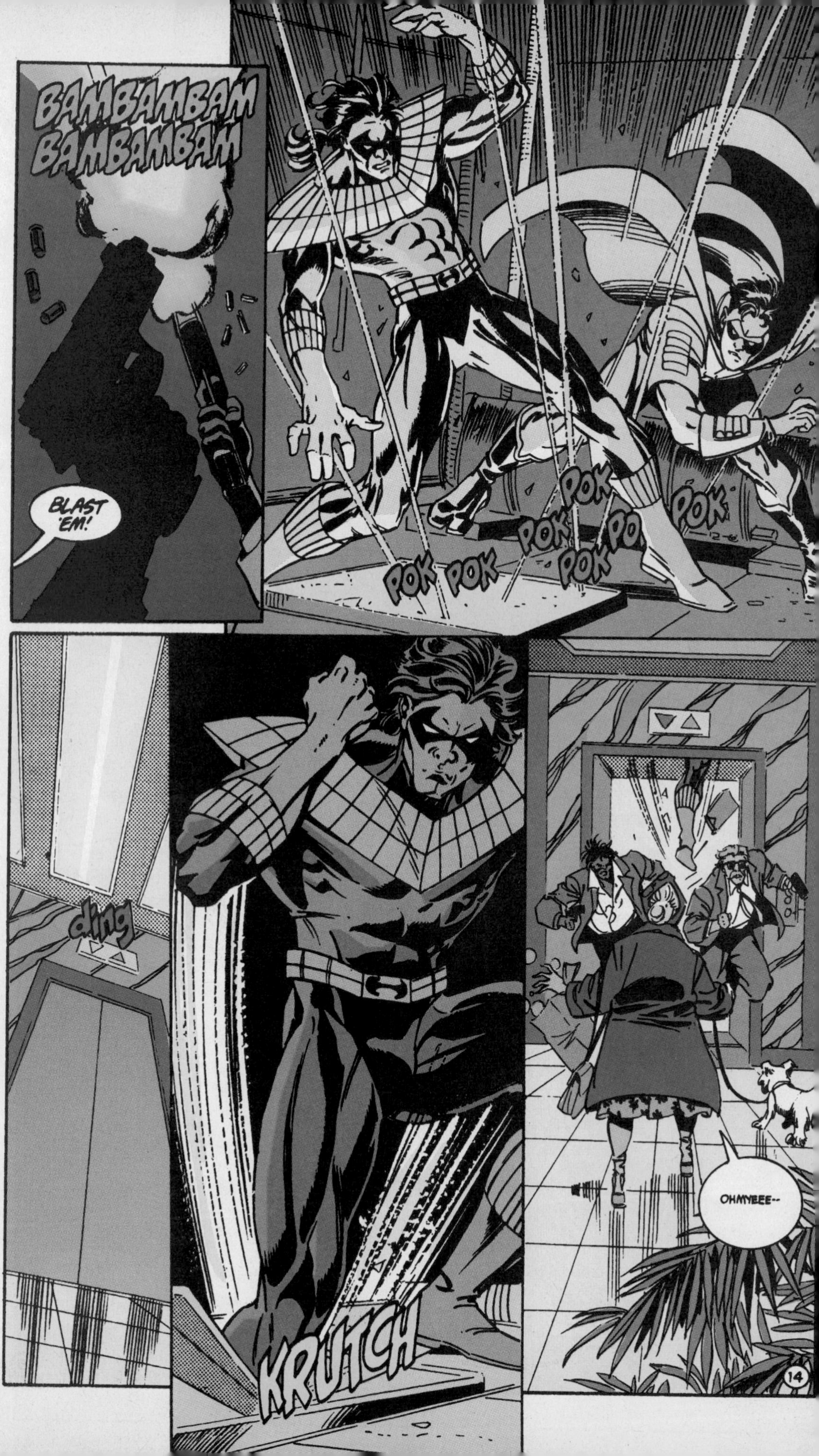
BAMBAMBAM
BAMBAMBAM
BLAST 'EM!
POK POK POK POK POK POK POK
ding
KRUTCH
OHMYEEE--

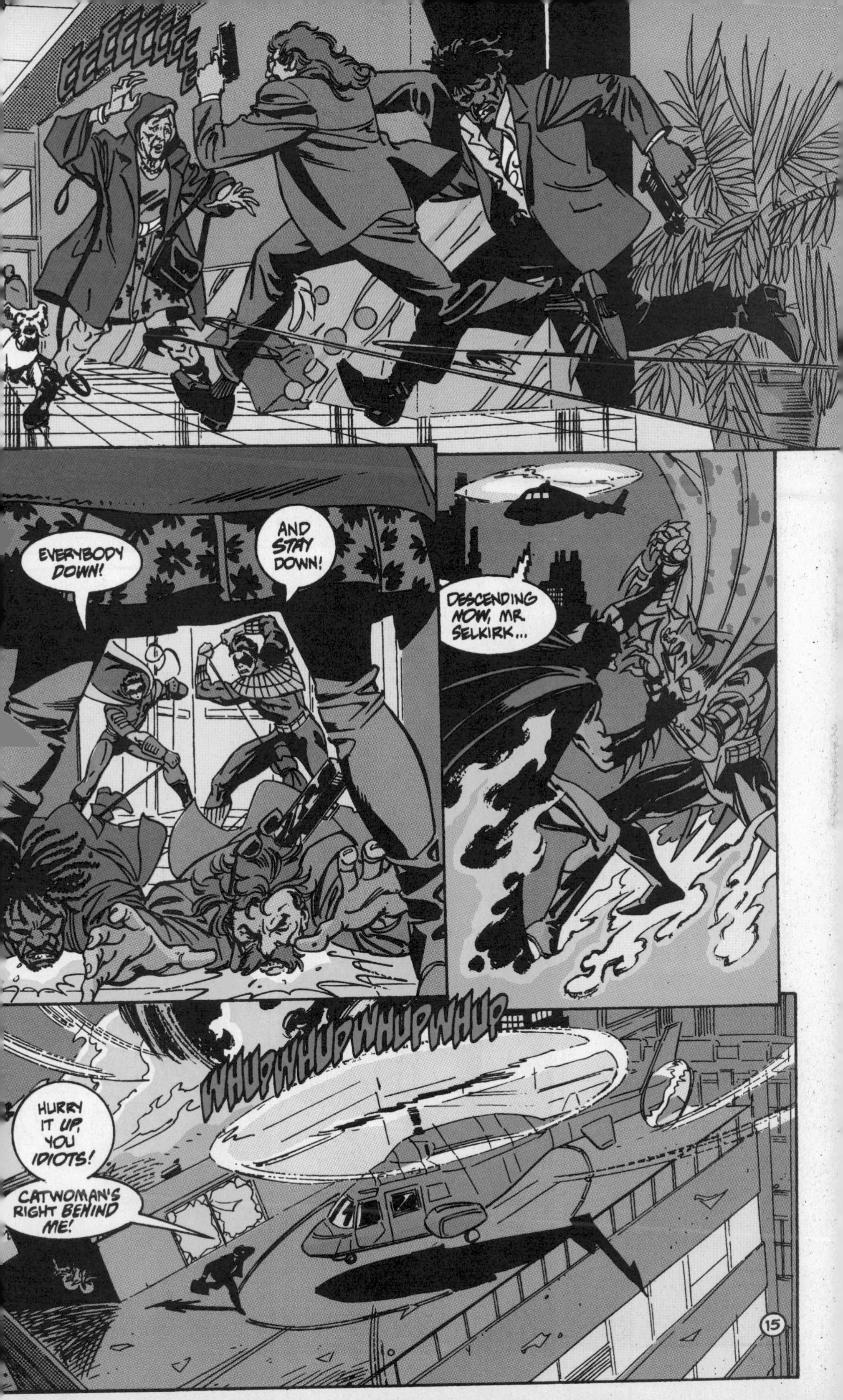
EEEEEEEEE
EVERYBODY DOWN!
AND STAY DOWN!
DESCENDING NOW, MR SELKIRK...
WHUPWHUPWHUPWHUP
HURRY IT UP, YOU IDIOTS!
CATWOMAN'S RIGHT BEHIND ME!
15

SELKIRRRK!

CERTAINLY *TOOK* YOU LONG ENOUGH!

NOW LET'S *GO!* LIFT *OFF!*

...BUT SWING AROUND TO THE *TERRACE* SIDE FOR A BIT OF *UNFINISHED* BUSINESS.

WHUP-WHUP-WHUP

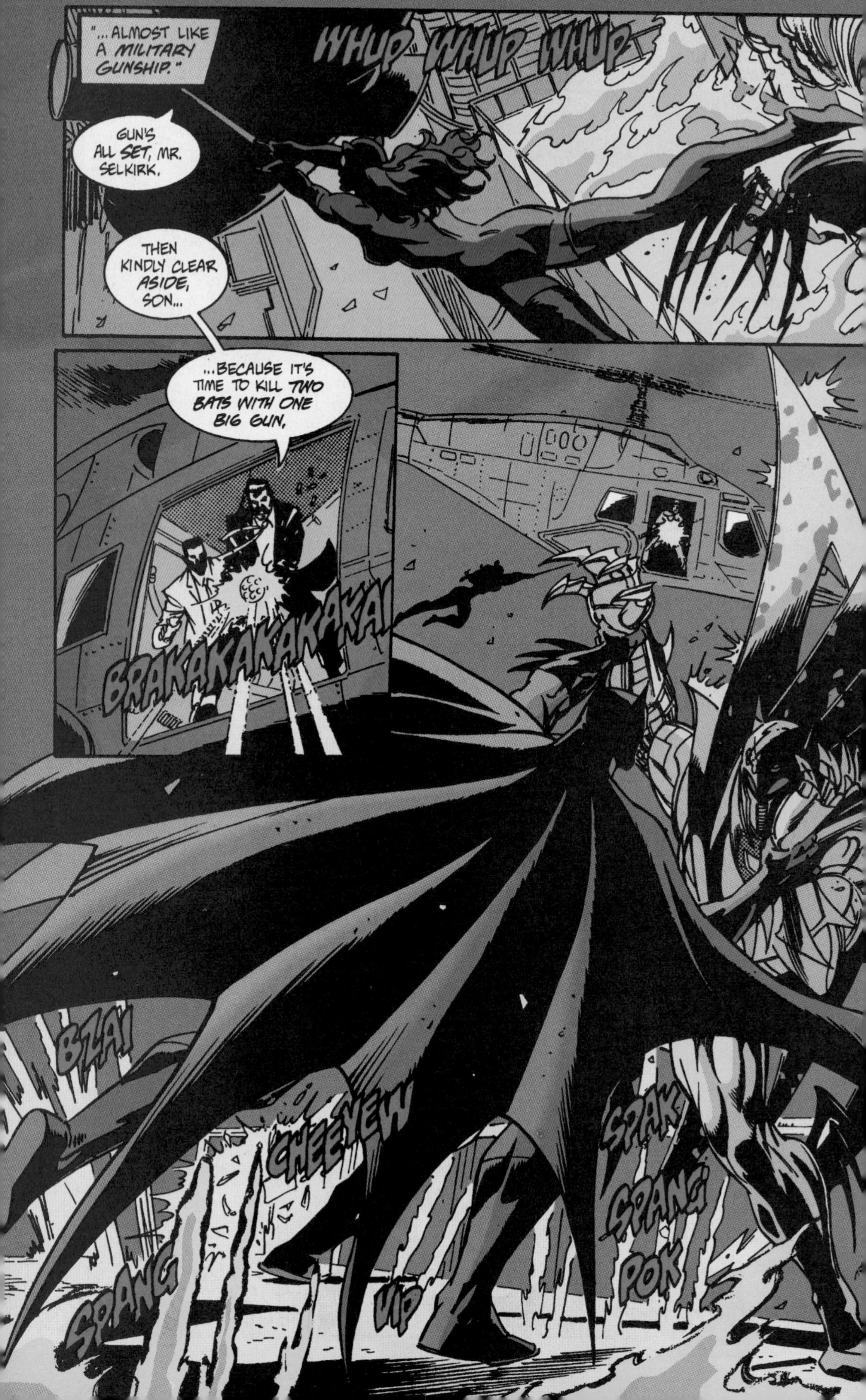

"...ALMOST LIKE A MILITARY GUNSHIP."
WHUP WHUP WHUP
GUN'S ALL SET, MR. SELKIRK.
THEN KINDLY CLEAR ASIDE, SON...
...BECAUSE IT'S TIME TO KILL TWO BATS WITH ONE BIG GUN.
BRAKAKAKAKAKAKAKAI
BZAI
CHEEYEW
SPAK
SPANG
POK
SPANG
VIP

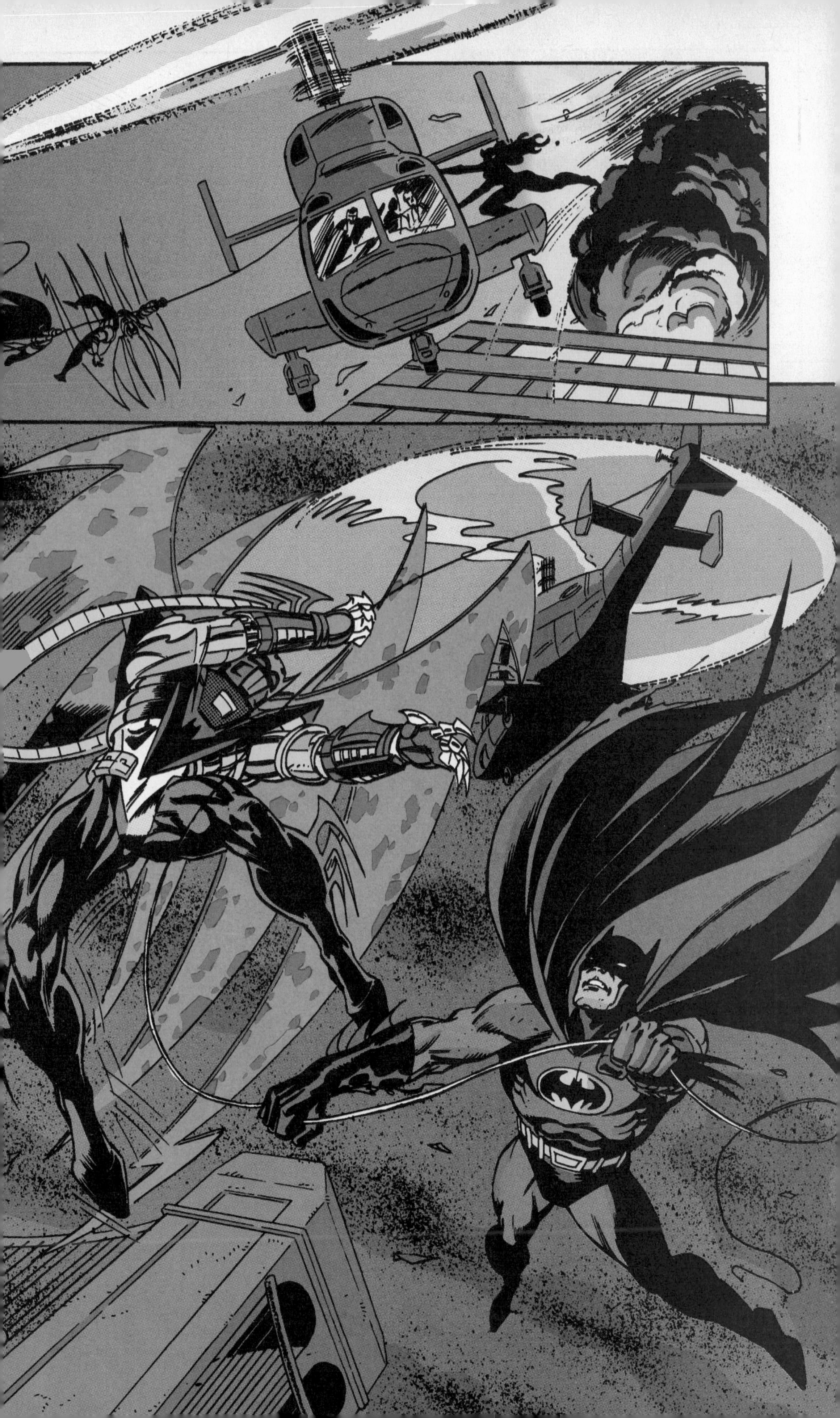

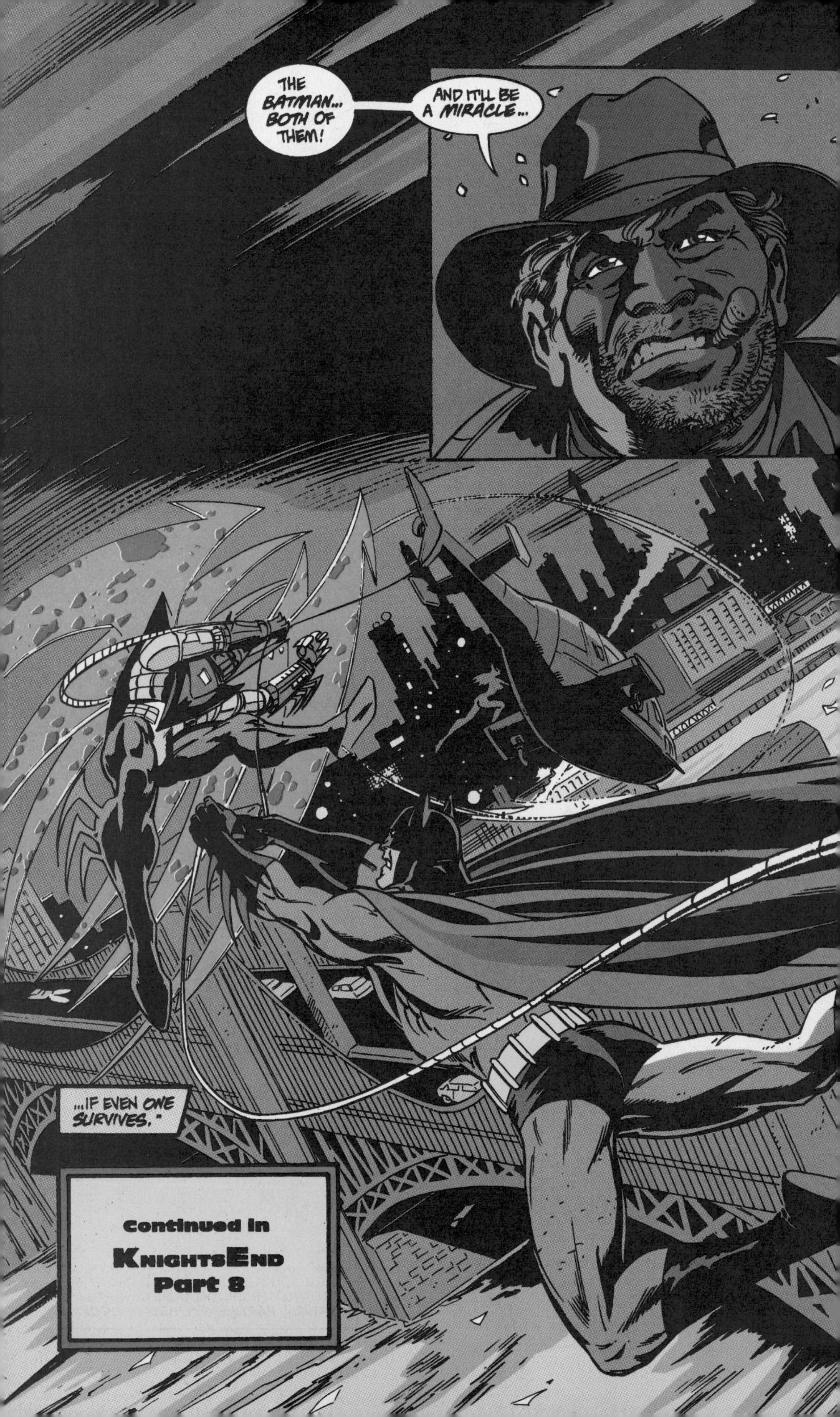
THE BATMAN... BOTH OF THEM!
AND IT'LL BE A MIRACLE...
...IF EVEN ONE SURVIVES."
Continued in
KnightsEnd
Part 8

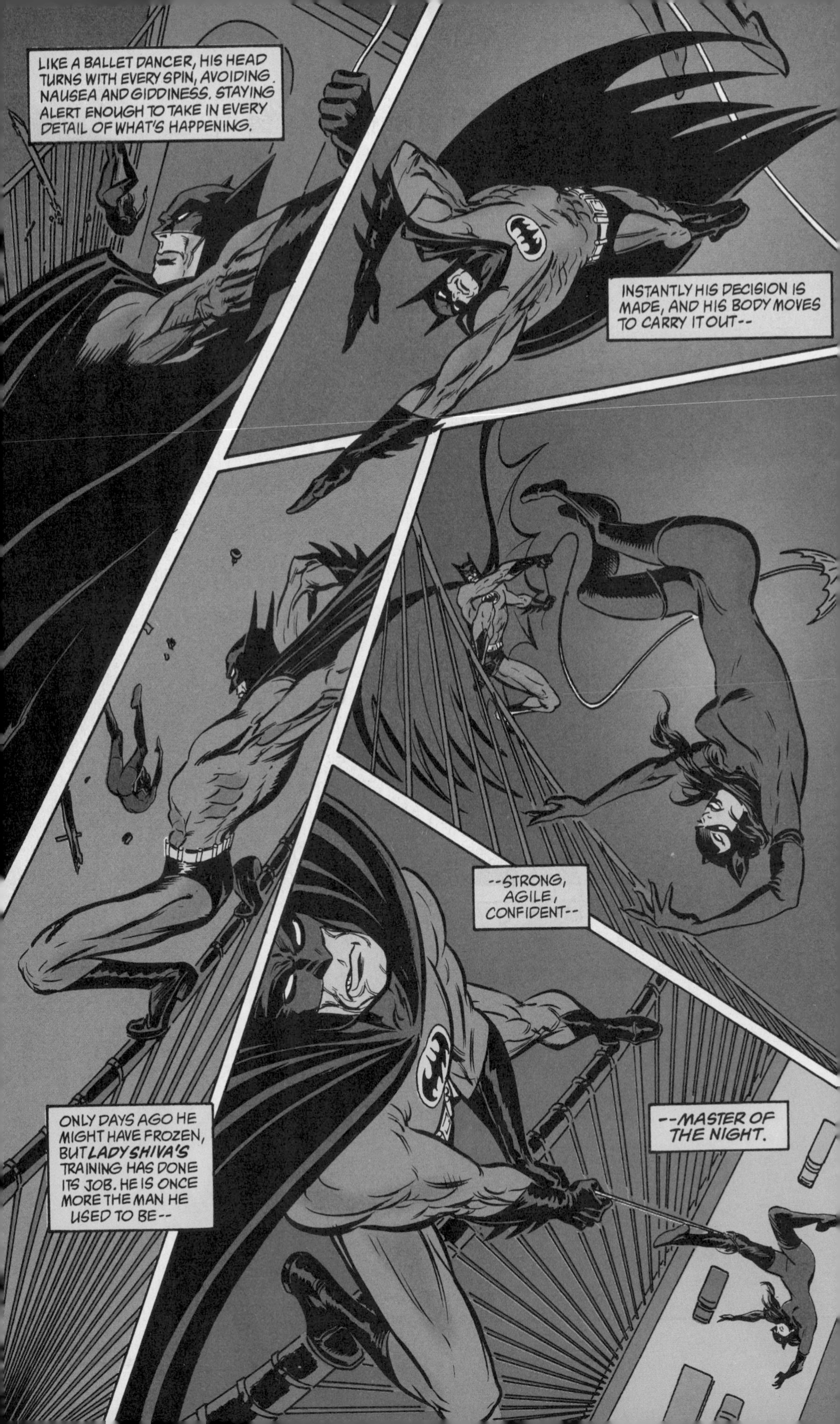
LIKE A BALLET DANCER, HIS HEAD TURNS WITH EVERY SPIN, AVOIDING NAUSEA AND GIDDINESS, STAYING ALERT ENOUGH TO TAKE IN EVERY DETAIL OF WHAT'S HAPPENING.
INSTANTLY HIS DECISION IS MADE, AND HIS BODY MOVES TO CARRY IT OUT--
--STRONG, AGILE, CONFIDENT--
ONLY DAYS AGO HE MIGHT HAVE FROZEN, BUT LADY SHIVA'S TRAINING HAS DONE ITS JOB. HE IS ONCE MORE THE MAN HE USED TO BE--
--MASTER OF THE NIGHT.

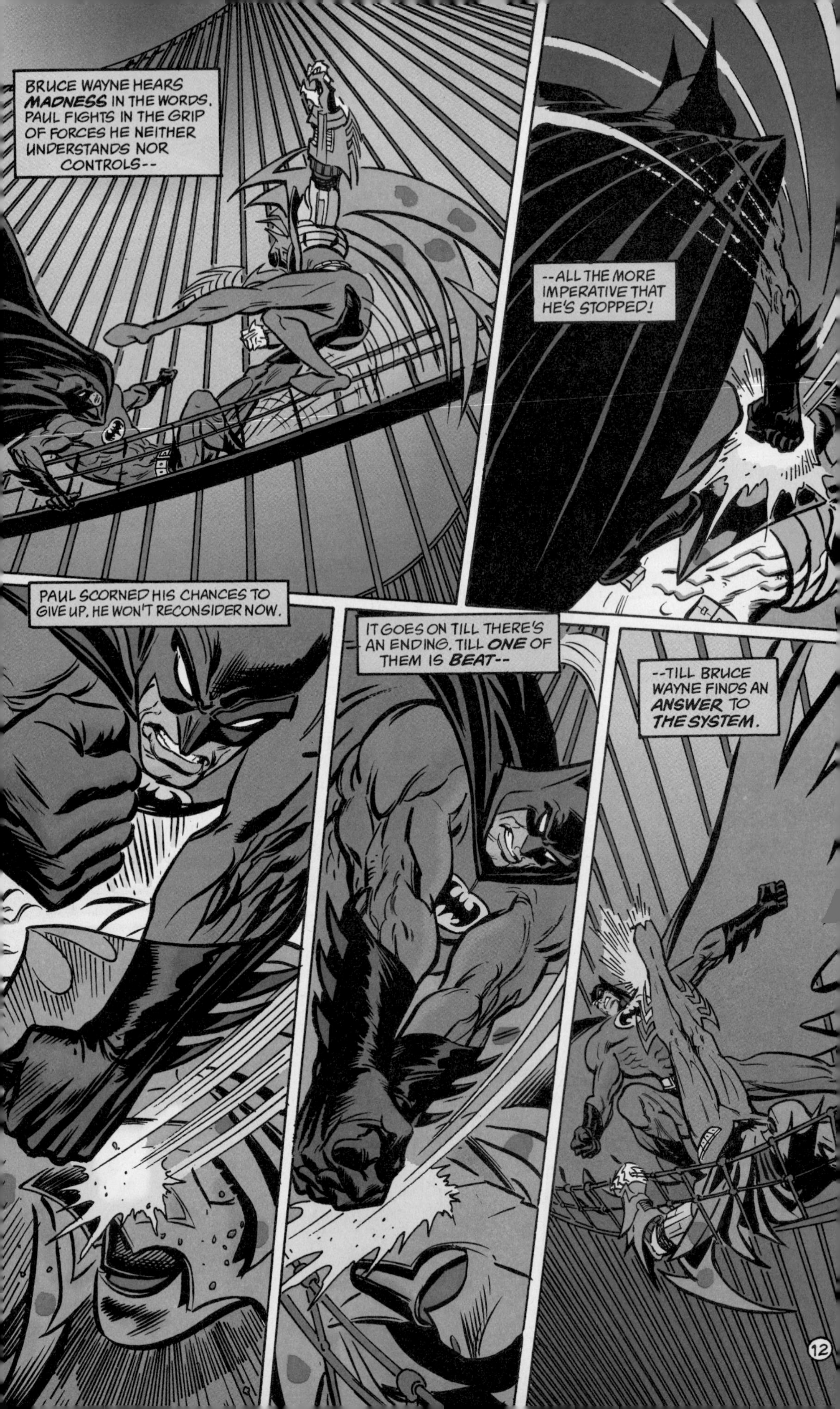
BRUCE WAYNE HEARS MADNESS IN THE WORDS. PAUL FIGHTS IN THE GRIP OF FORCES HE NEITHER UNDERSTANDS NOR CONTROLS--
--ALL THE MORE IMPERATIVE THAT HE'S STOPPED!
PAUL SCORNED HIS CHANCES TO GIVE UP. HE WON'T RECONSIDER NOW.
IT GOES ON TILL THERE'S AN ENDING. TILL ONE OF THEM IS BEAT--
--TILL BRUCE WAYNE FINDS AN ANSWER TO THE SYSTEM.
12

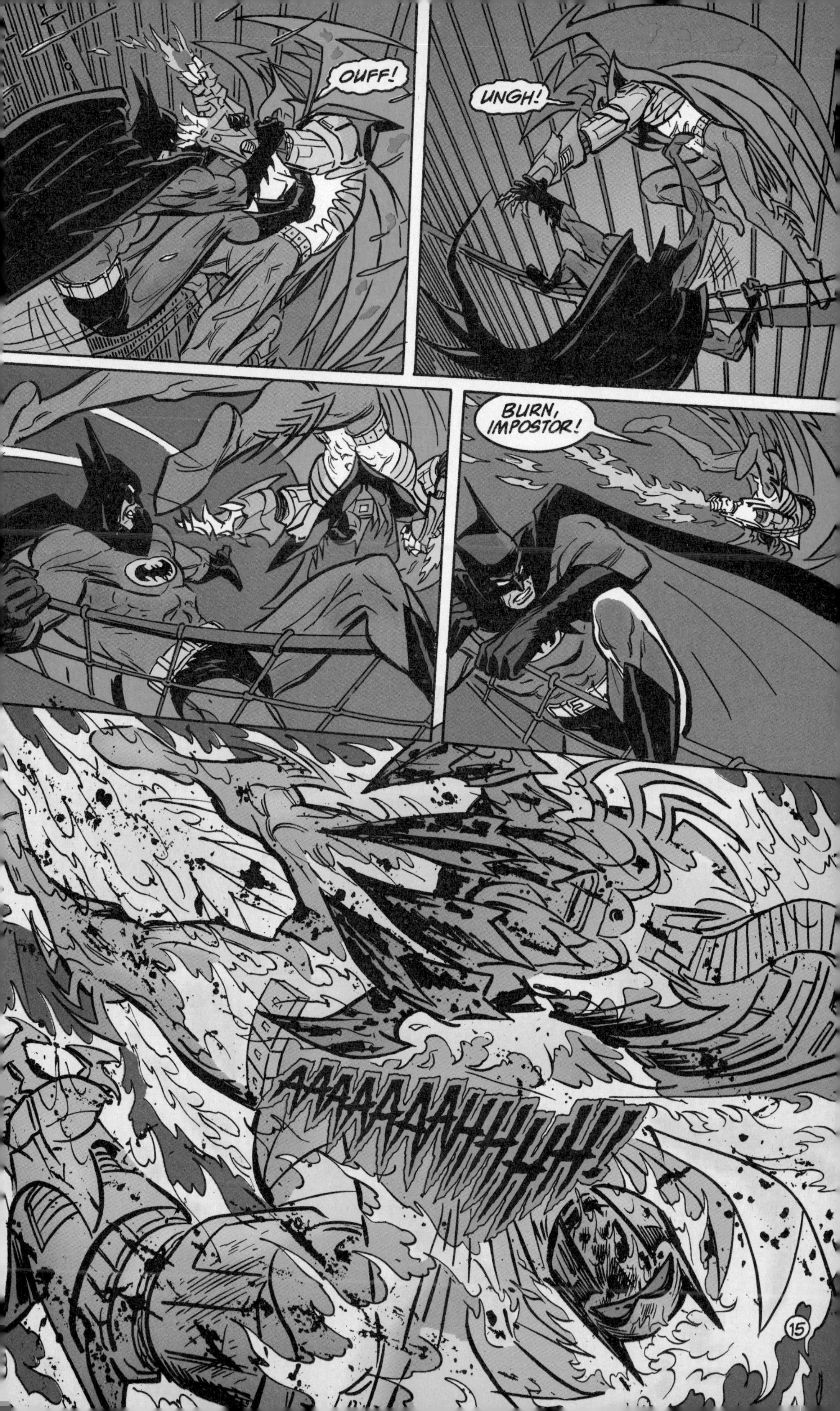
OUFF!
UNGH!
BURN, IMPOSTOR!
AAAAAAAHHHH!
15

YOURS, I
BELIEVE.

THANKS.

AREN'T YOU HEADING
THE WRONG WAY?

THERE
ARE MEN STILL
INSIDE!

DOESN'T MATTER.
I CAN'T LET THEM
DIE.

SELKIRK
AND HIS MOOKS?
MEN?

OH NO--
BATMAN AND
CATWOMAN!

DAMN!

RESCUE WORK'S
NOT IN YOUR LINE.
WHAT'S YOUR
ANGLE?

SELKIRK
HAS SOMETHING
I NEED. ONCE I
HAVE IT, I DON'T
CARE WHAT
HAPPENS TO
HIM!

IF THE TINGLE SHE FELT
THE FIRST TIME SHE'D
SEEN HIM LEFT HER IN ANY
DOUBT, IT FADES NOW.
THE MAN IN THE METAL
COSTUME WOULD NEVER
RISK HIS LIFE FOR SCUM--

--SHE KNOWS
THE REAL BATMAN IS
BACK.

17

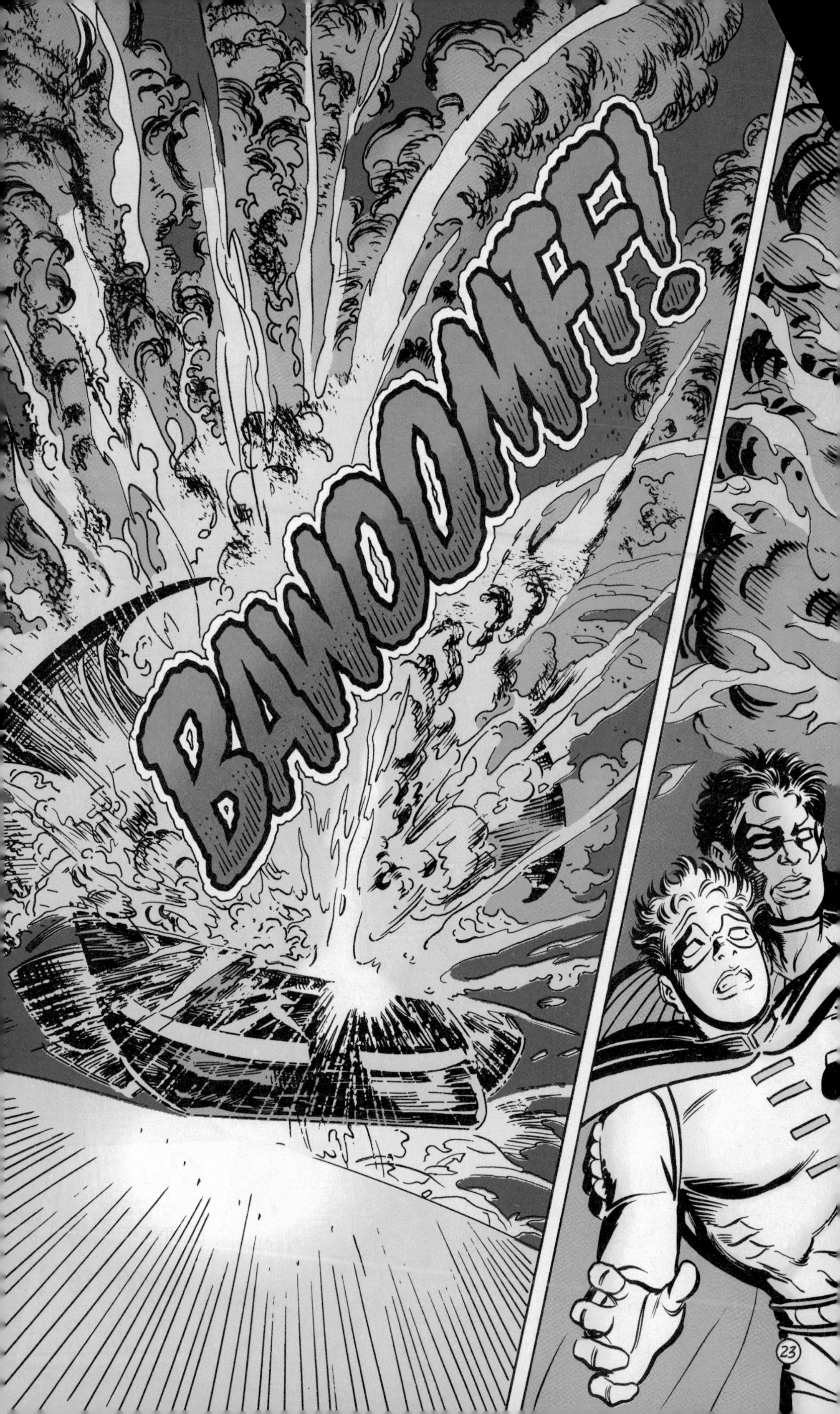
BAWOOMF!

FLESH and STEEL

CHUCK DIXON · GRAHAM NOLAN · SCOTT HANNA
writer · penciller · inker
ADRIENNE ROY · JOHN COSTANZA · DARREN VINCENZO
colorist · letterer · assistant editor
SCOTT PETERSON · BATMAN created by
editor · BOB KANE

YOU KILLED HIM!

YOU KILLED THE BATMAN!

HE SHOULD NEVER HAVE CROSSED THE PUNISHING ANGEL! NOW HE HAS PROVED WITH HIS LIFE--

THERE IS ONLY ONE TRUE BATMAN!

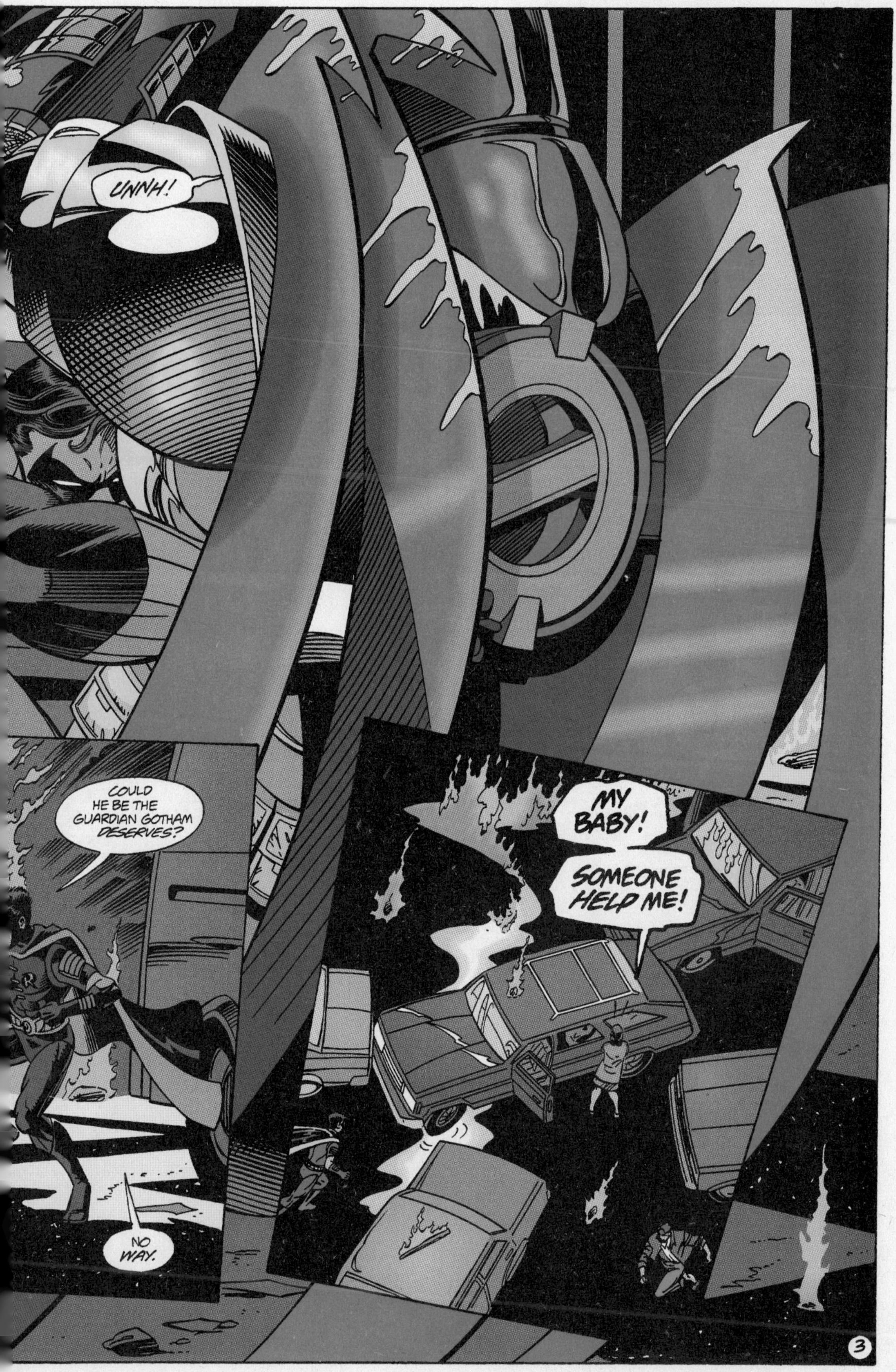
UNNH!
COULD HE BE THE GUARDIAN GOTHAM *DESERVES?*
NO WAY.
MY BABY!
SOMEONE HELP ME!
3

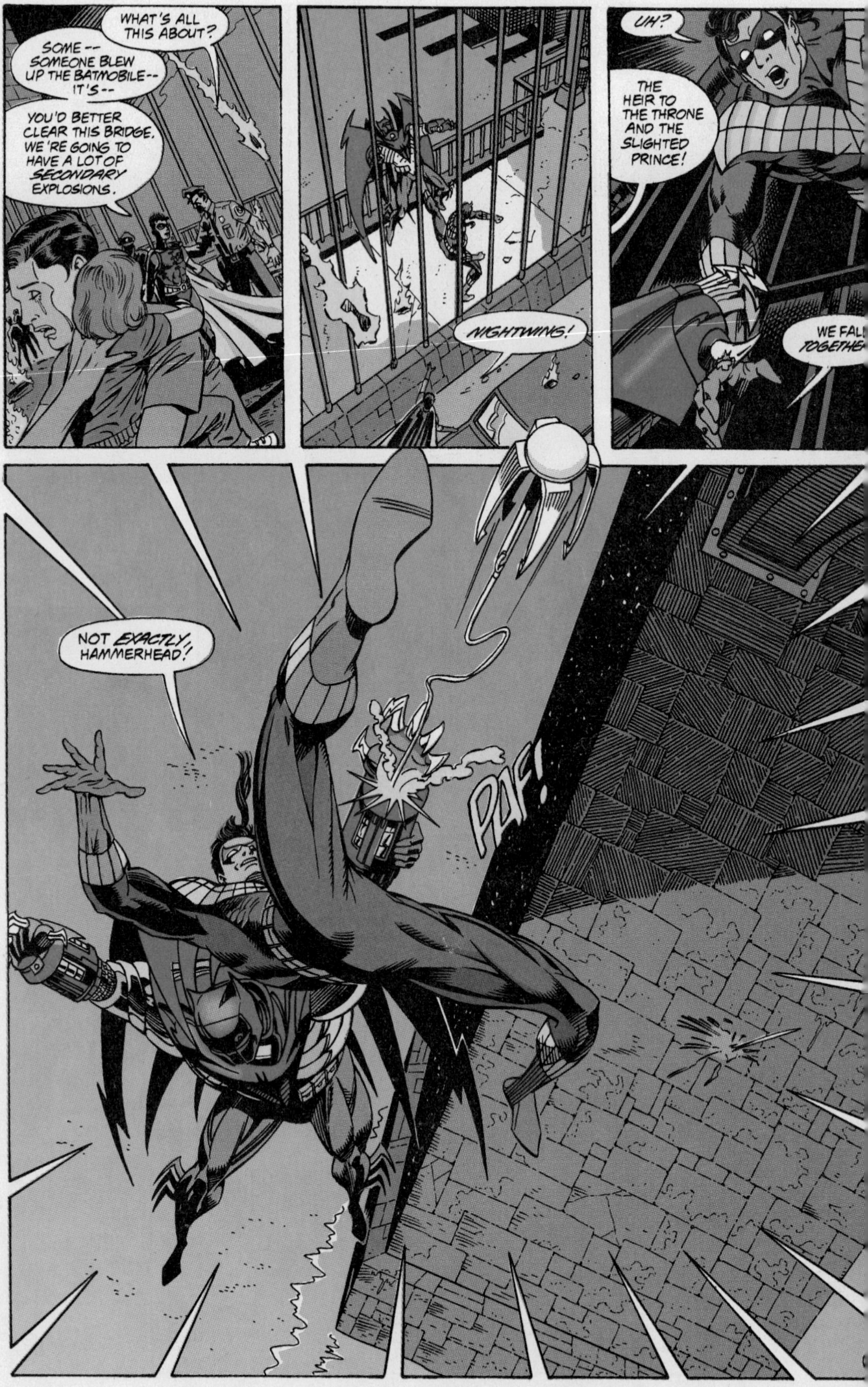
WHAT'S ALL THIS ABOUT?
SOME -- SOMEONE BLEW UP THE BATMOBILE-- IT'S --
YOU'D BETTER CLEAR THIS BRIDGE. WE'RE GOING TO HAVE A LOT OF SECONDARY EXPLOSIONS.
NIGHTWING!
UH?
THE HEIR TO THE THRONE AND THE SLIGHTED PRINCE!
WE FAL TOGETHE
NOT EXACTLY, HAMMERHEAD!
POF!

ADDERLY, WHAT THE HELL'S GOING ON HERE?

I WAS LATE ON THE SCENE, SGT. BULLOCK. BUT WE GOT WITNESSES SAW EVERYTHING BUT *FLYING SAUCERS* HERE.

WE *SAW* THE CHOPPER CRASH.

THAT WAS JUST THE *BEGINNING.*

COUPLE PEOPLE SAY THEY SAW *TWO* BATMANS. I MEAN, BAT*MEN*, RIGHT? THEN SOME CAR EXPLODED BIGTIME AND IT *REALLY* HIT THE FAN.

SO WHAT DO *YOU* GUYS KNOW?

NOT A DAMN THING. JUST KEEP THE *GAWKERS* OFF THE BRIDGE, OKAY?

SO WHAT IS GOING ON, HARV?

FROM WHERE *I* STAND, MONTOYA?

IT LOOKS LIKE THE COSTUMED GEEKS ARE FIGHTING TO SEE WHO GETS TO BE GOTHAM'S NUMBER ONE MASKED MAN.

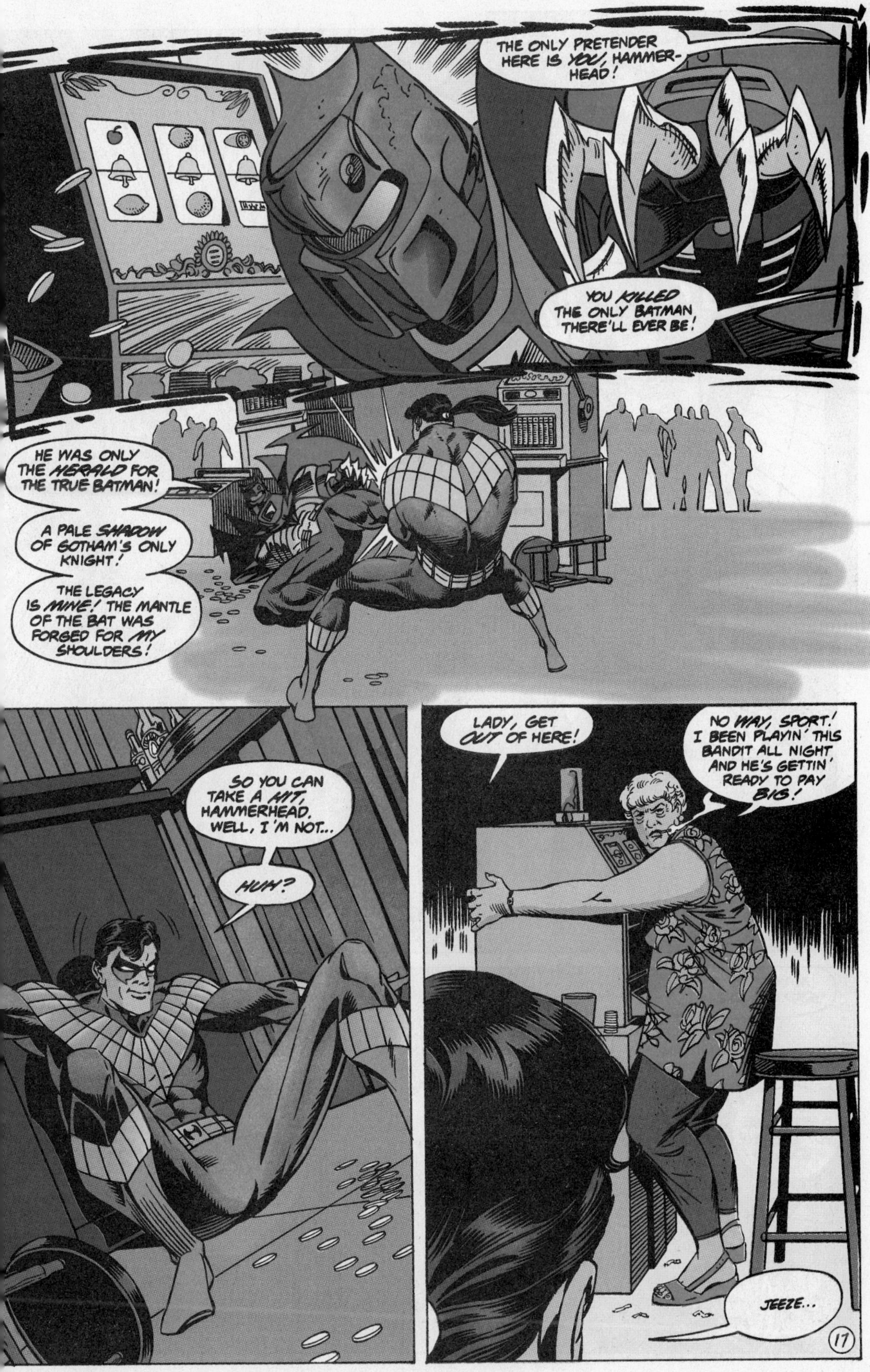
THE ONLY PRETENDER HERE IS YOU, HAMMER-HEAD!
YOU KILLED THE ONLY BATMAN THERE'LL EVER BE!
HE WAS ONLY THE HERALD FOR THE TRUE BATMAN!
A PALE SHADOW OF GOTHAM'S ONLY KNIGHT!
THE LEGACY IS MINE! THE MANTLE OF THE BAT WAS FORGED FOR MY SHOULDERS!
SO YOU CAN TAKE A HIT, HAMMERHEAD. WELL, I'M NOT...
HUH?
LADY, GET OUT OF HERE!
NO WAY, SPORT! I BEEN PLAYIN' THIS BANDIT ALL NIGHT AND HE'S GETTIN' READY TO PAY BIG!
JEEZE...
17

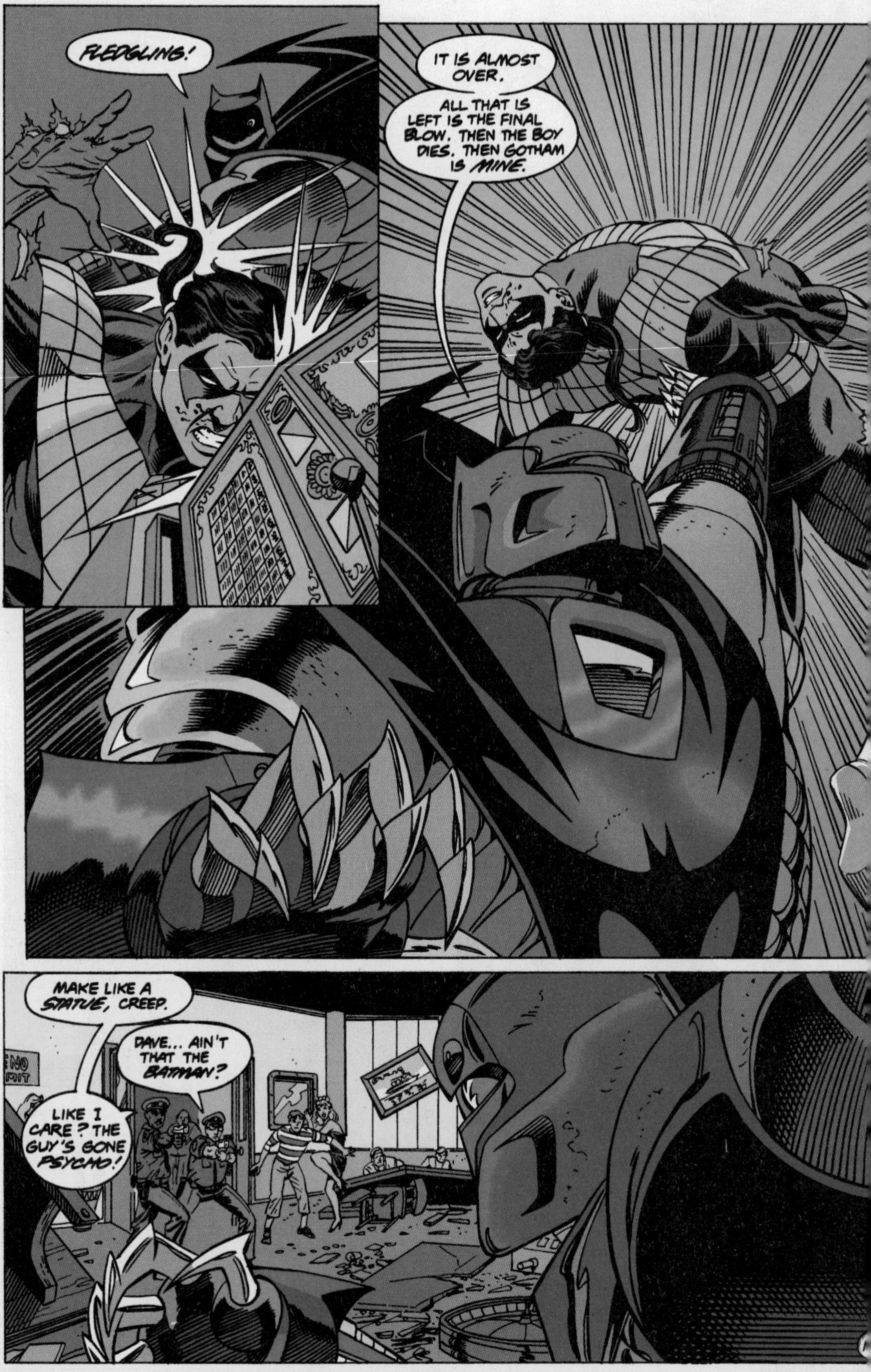
FLEDGLING!
IT IS ALMOST OVER.
ALL THAT IS LEFT IS THE FINAL BLOW. THEN THE BOY DIES. THEN GOTHAM IS MINE.
MAKE LIKE A STATUE, CREEP.
DAVE... AIN'T THAT THE BATMAN?
LIKE I CARE? THE GUY'S GONE PSYCHO!

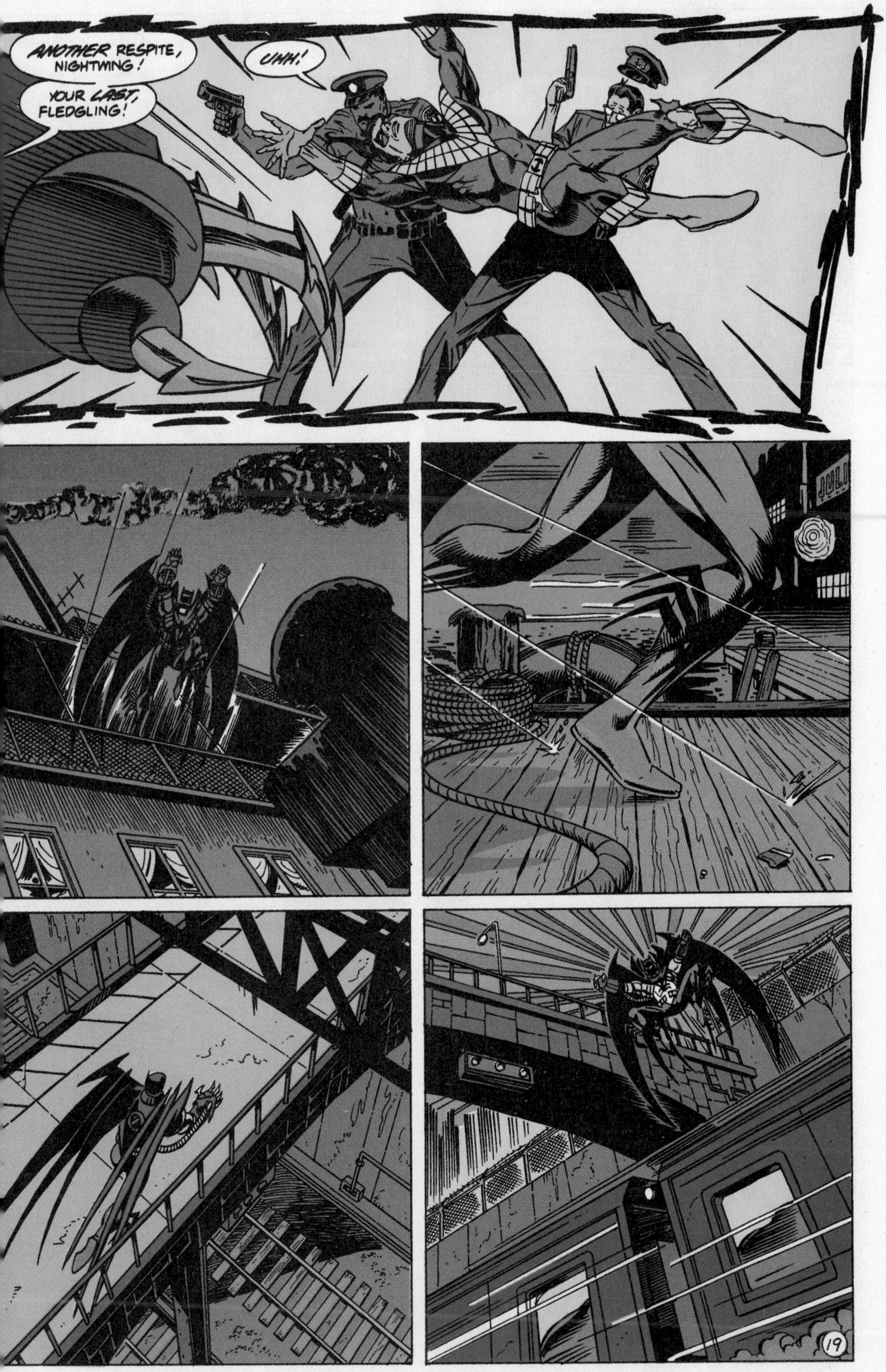
ANOTHER RESPITE, NIGHTWING!
UNH!
YOUR LAST, FLEDGLING!
19

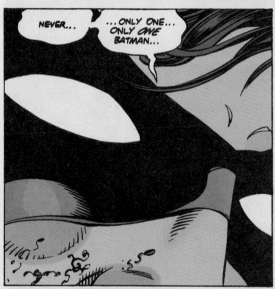

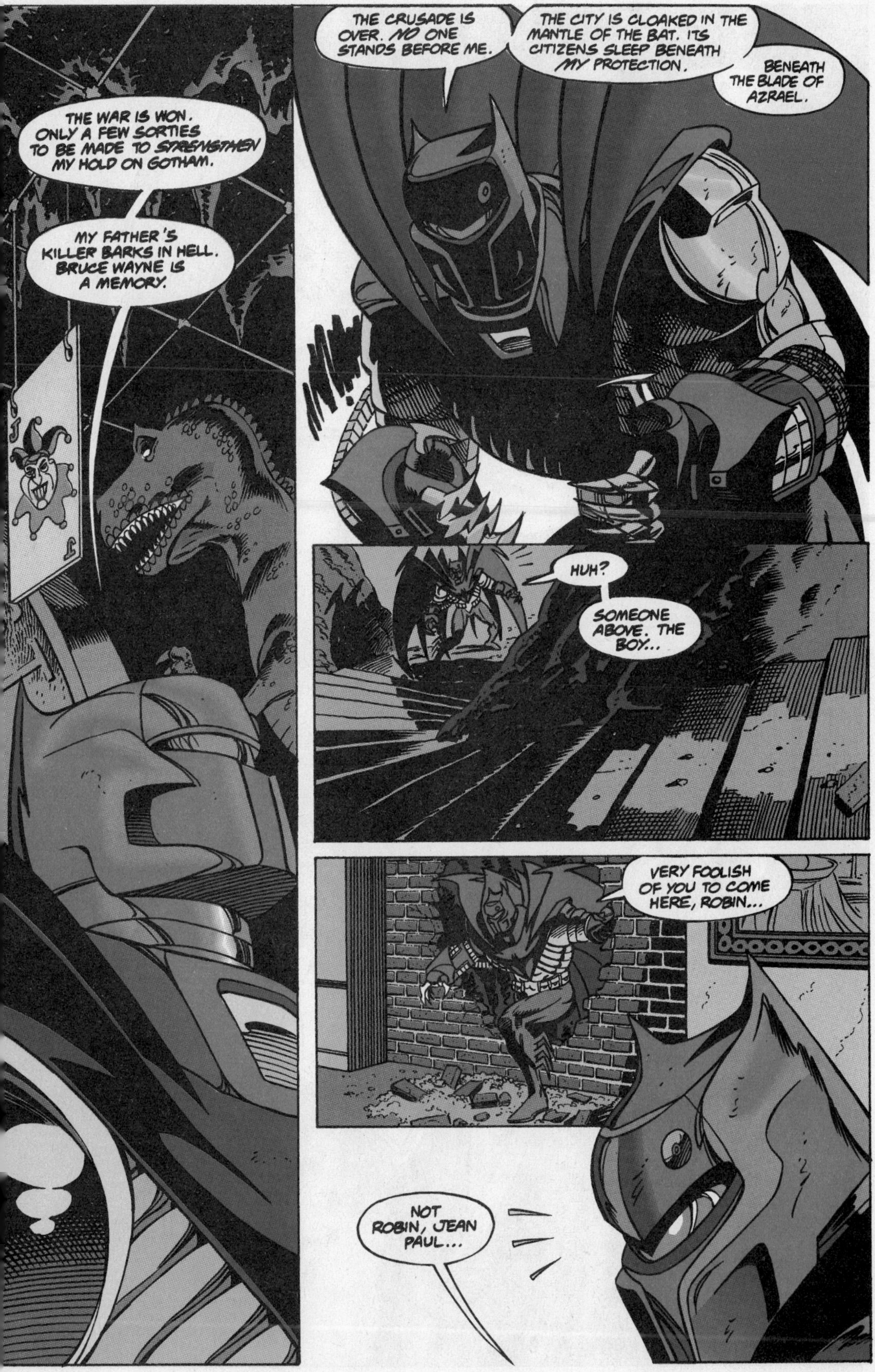
THE WAR IS WON. ONLY A FEW SORTIES TO BE MADE TO STRENGTHEN MY HOLD ON GOTHAM.
MY FATHER'S KILLER BARKS IN HELL. BRUCE WAYNE IS A MEMORY.
THE CRUSADE IS OVER. NO ONE STANDS BEFORE ME.
THE CITY IS CLOAKED IN THE MANTLE OF THE BAT. ITS CITIZENS SLEEP BENEATH MY PROTECTION.
BENEATH THE BLADE OF AZRAEL.
HUH?
SOMEONE ABOVE. THE BOY...
VERY FOOLISH OF YOU TO COME HERE, ROBIN...
NOT ROBIN, JEAN PAUL...

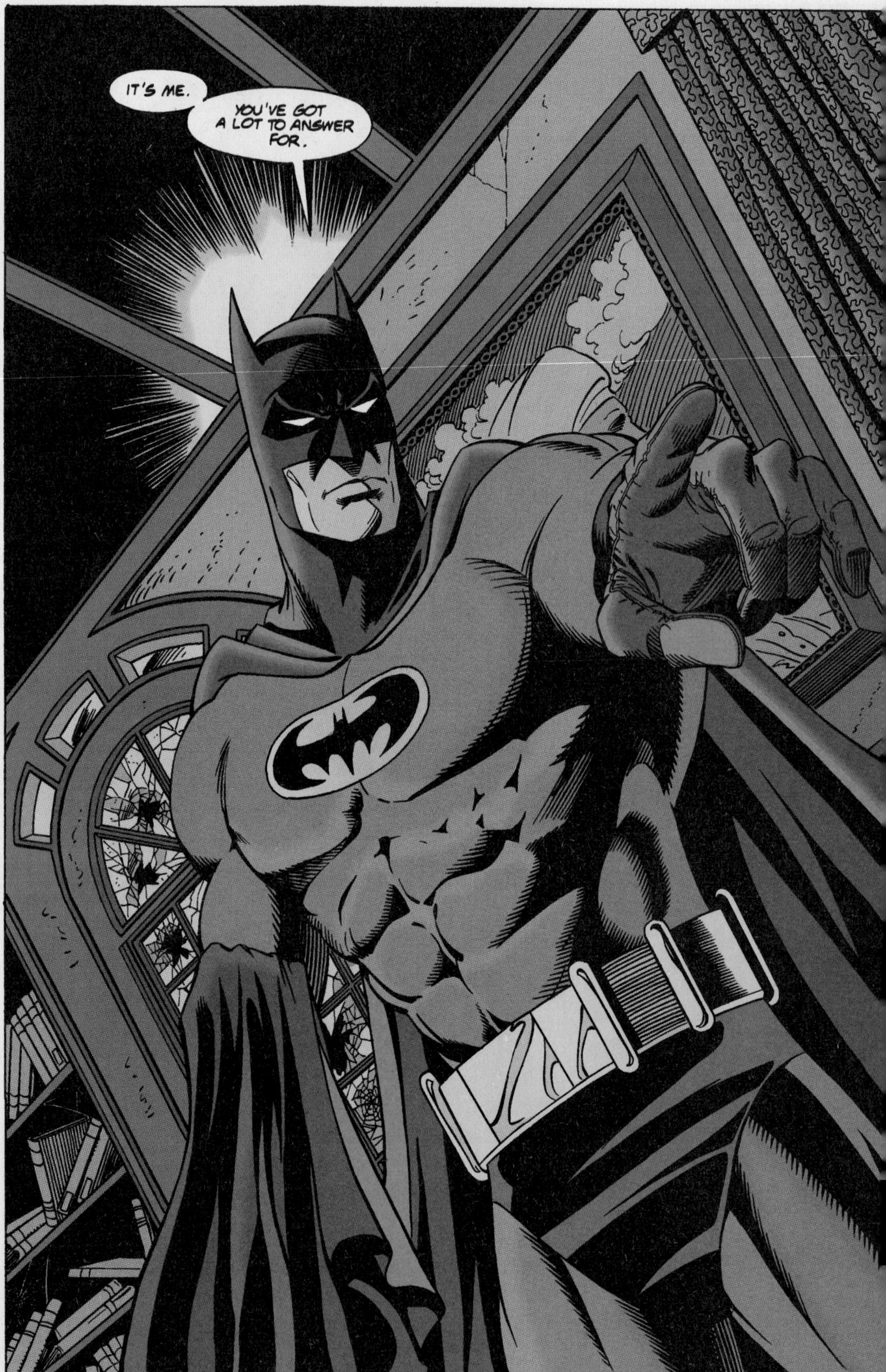
IT'S ME.
YOU'VE GOT A LOT TO ANSWER FOR.

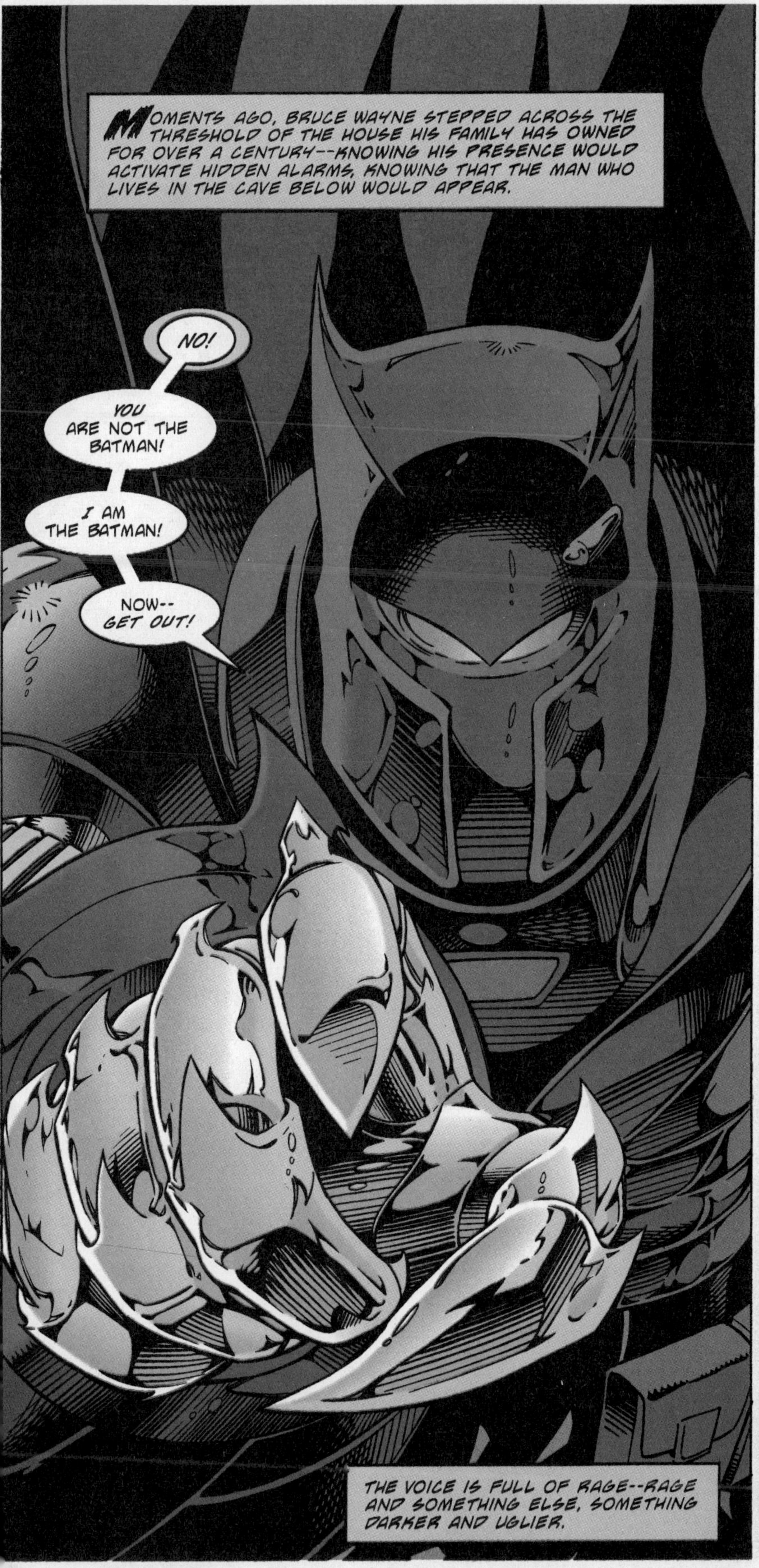
MOMENTS AGO, BRUCE WAYNE STEPPED ACROSS THE THRESHOLD OF THE HOUSE HIS FAMILY HAS OWNED FOR OVER A CENTURY--KNOWING HIS PRESENCE WOULD ACTIVATE HIDDEN ALARMS, KNOWING THAT THE MAN WHO LIVES IN THE CAVE BELOW WOULD APPEAR.
NO!
YOU ARE NOT THE BATMAN!
I AM THE BATMAN!
NOW-- GET OUT!
THE VOICE IS FULL OF RAGE--RAGE AND SOMETHING ELSE, SOMETHING DARKER AND UGLIER.

CLIMAX

writer
DENNY O'NEIL

penciller
BARRY KITSON

inker
SCOTT HANNA

letterer
WILLIE SCHUBERT

colorist
DIGITAL CHAMELEON

assistant editor
CHUCK KIM

associate editor
JIM SPIVEY

editor
ARCHIE GOODWIN

BATMAN created
by BOB KANE

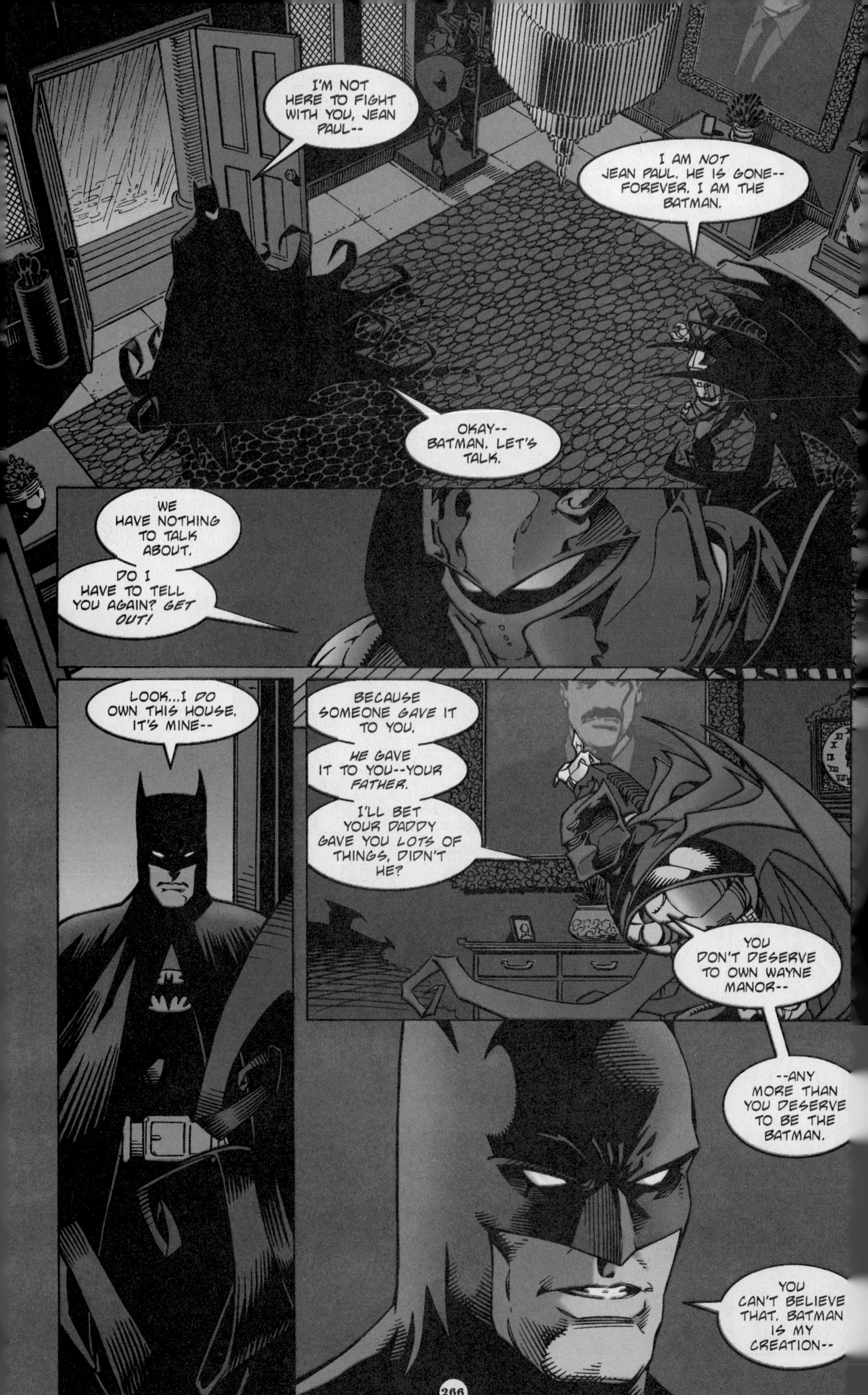
I'M NOT HERE TO FIGHT WITH YOU, JEAN PAUL--
I AM NOT JEAN PAUL. HE IS GONE-- FOREVER. I AM THE BATMAN.
OKAY-- BATMAN. LET'S TALK.
WE HAVE NOTHING TO TALK ABOUT.
DO I HAVE TO TELL YOU AGAIN? GET OUT!
LOOK...I DO OWN THIS HOUSE. IT'S MINE--
BECAUSE SOMEONE GAVE IT TO YOU.
HE GAVE IT TO YOU--YOUR FATHER.
I'LL BET YOUR DADDY GAVE YOU LOTS OF THINGS, DIDN'T HE?
YOU DON'T DESERVE TO OWN WAYNE MANOR--
--ANY MORE THAN YOU DESERVE TO BE THE BATMAN.
YOU CAN'T BELIEVE THAT. BATMAN IS MY CREATION--

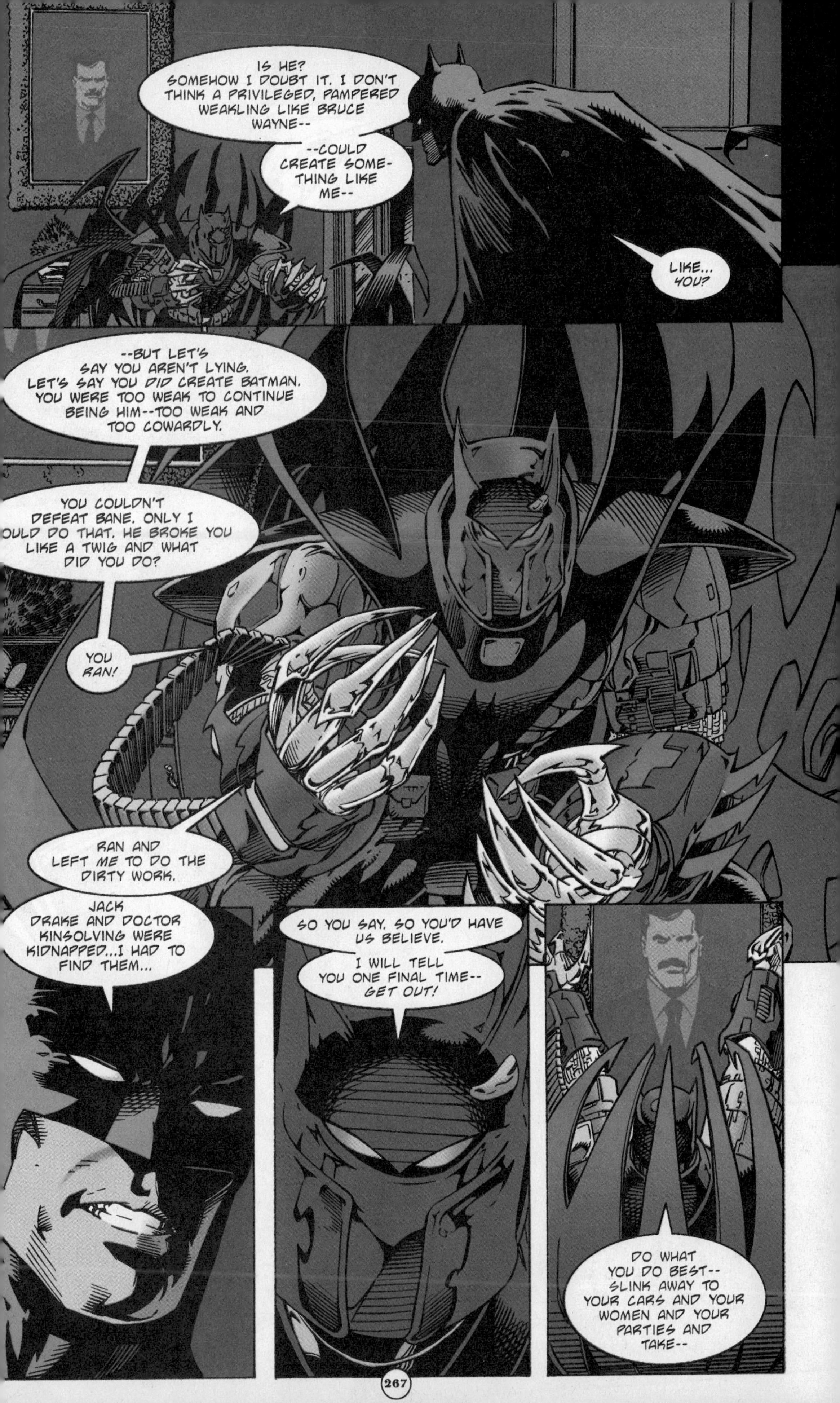
IS HE? SOMEHOW I DOUBT IT. I DON'T THINK A PRIVILEGED, PAMPERED WEAKLING LIKE BRUCE WAYNE--
--COULD CREATE SOME-THING LIKE ME--
LIKE... YOU?
--BUT LET'S SAY YOU AREN'T LYING. LET'S SAY YOU *DID* CREATE BATMAN. YOU WERE TOO WEAK TO CONTINUE BEING HIM--TOO WEAK AND TOO COWARDLY.
YOU COULDN'T DEFEAT BANE. ONLY I OULD DO THAT. HE BROKE YOU LIKE A TWIG AND WHAT DID YOU DO?
YOU RAN!
RAN AND LEFT ME TO DO THE DIRTY WORK.
JACK DRAKE AND DOCTOR KINSOLVING WERE KIDNAPPED...I HAD TO FIND THEM...
SO YOU SAY. SO YOU'D HAVE US BELIEVE.
I WILL TELL YOU ONE FINAL TIME-- *GET OUT!*
DO WHAT YOU DO BEST-- SLINK AWAY TO YOUR CARS AND YOUR WOMEN AND YOUR PARTIES AND TAKE--

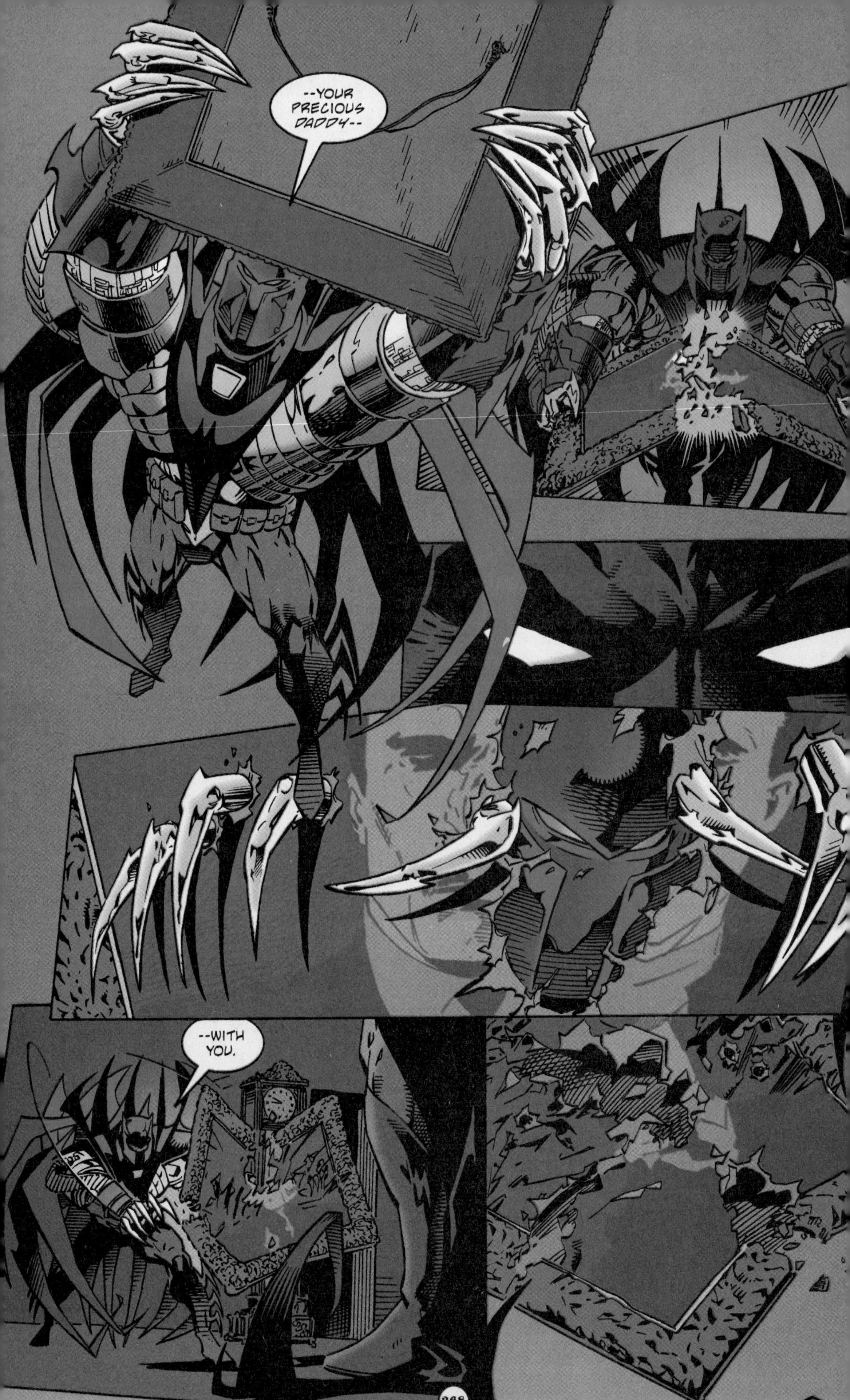
--YOUR PRECIOUS DADDY--
--WITH YOU.

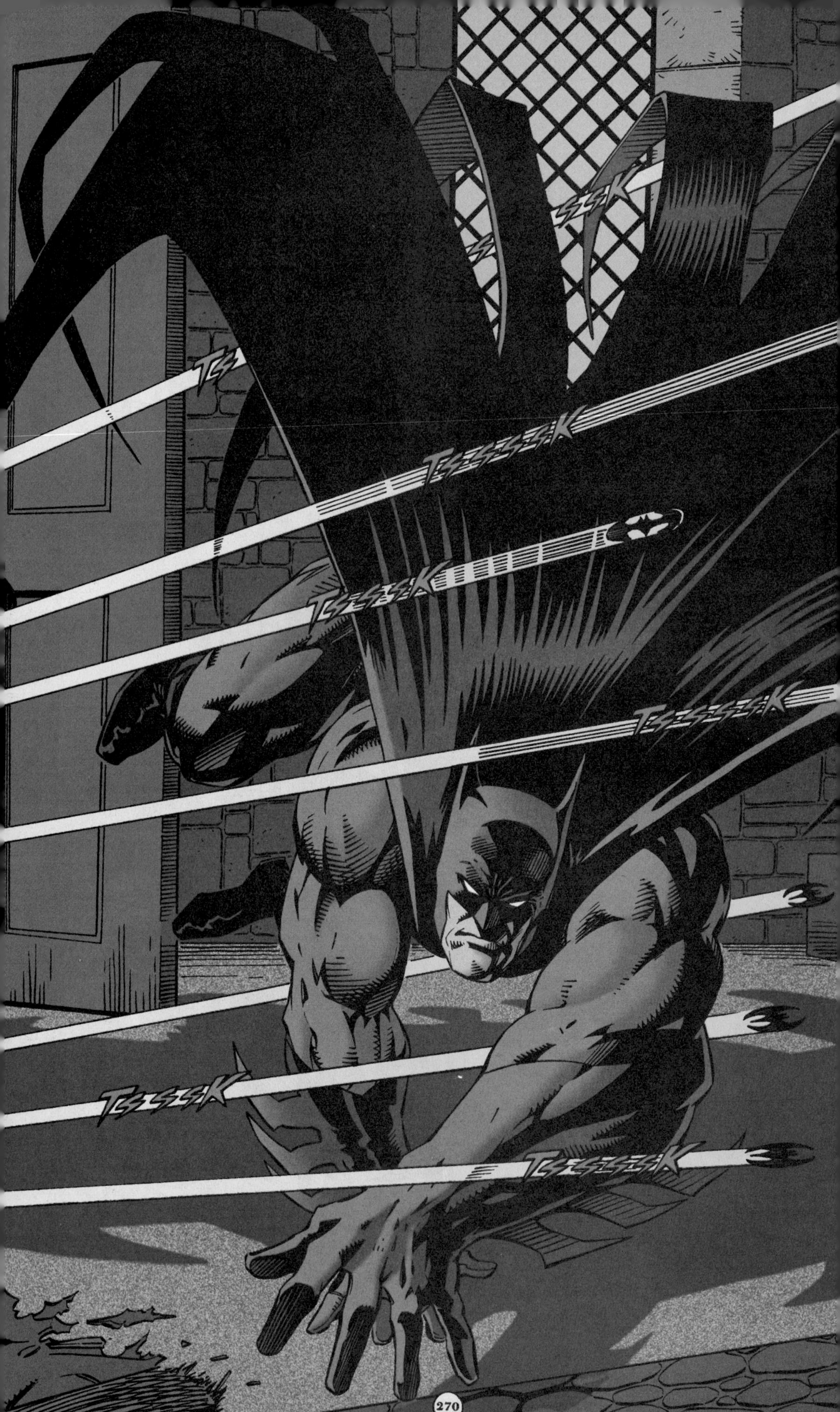
TSSSSSK
TSSSSK
TSSSSSSK
TSSSSK
TSSSSSSK

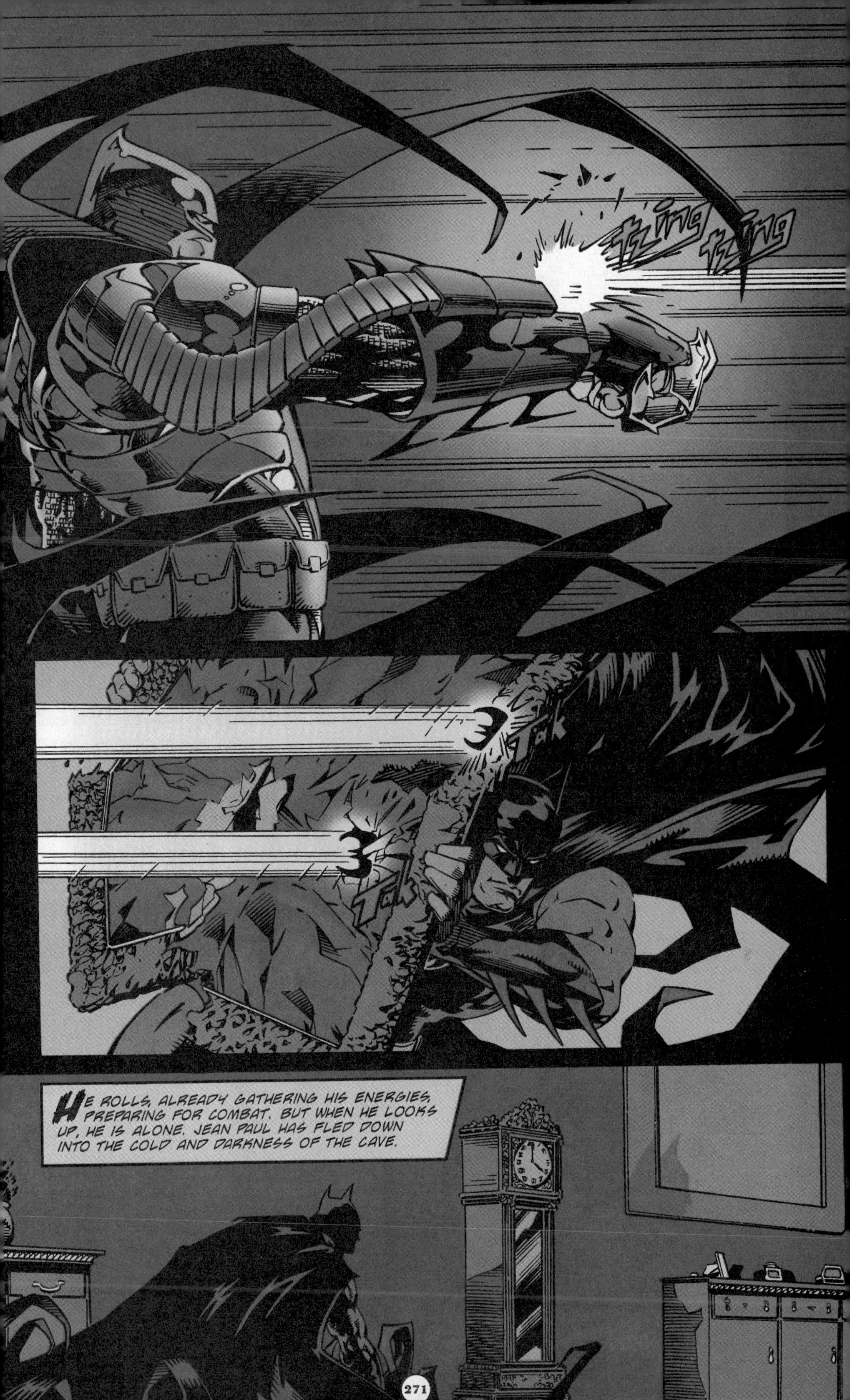

tzing tzing
HE ROLLS, ALREADY GATHERING HIS ENERGIES, PREPARING FOR COMBAT. BUT WHEN HE LOOKS UP, HE IS ALONE. JEAN PAUL HAS FLED DOWN INTO THE COLD AND DARKNESS OF THE CAVE.

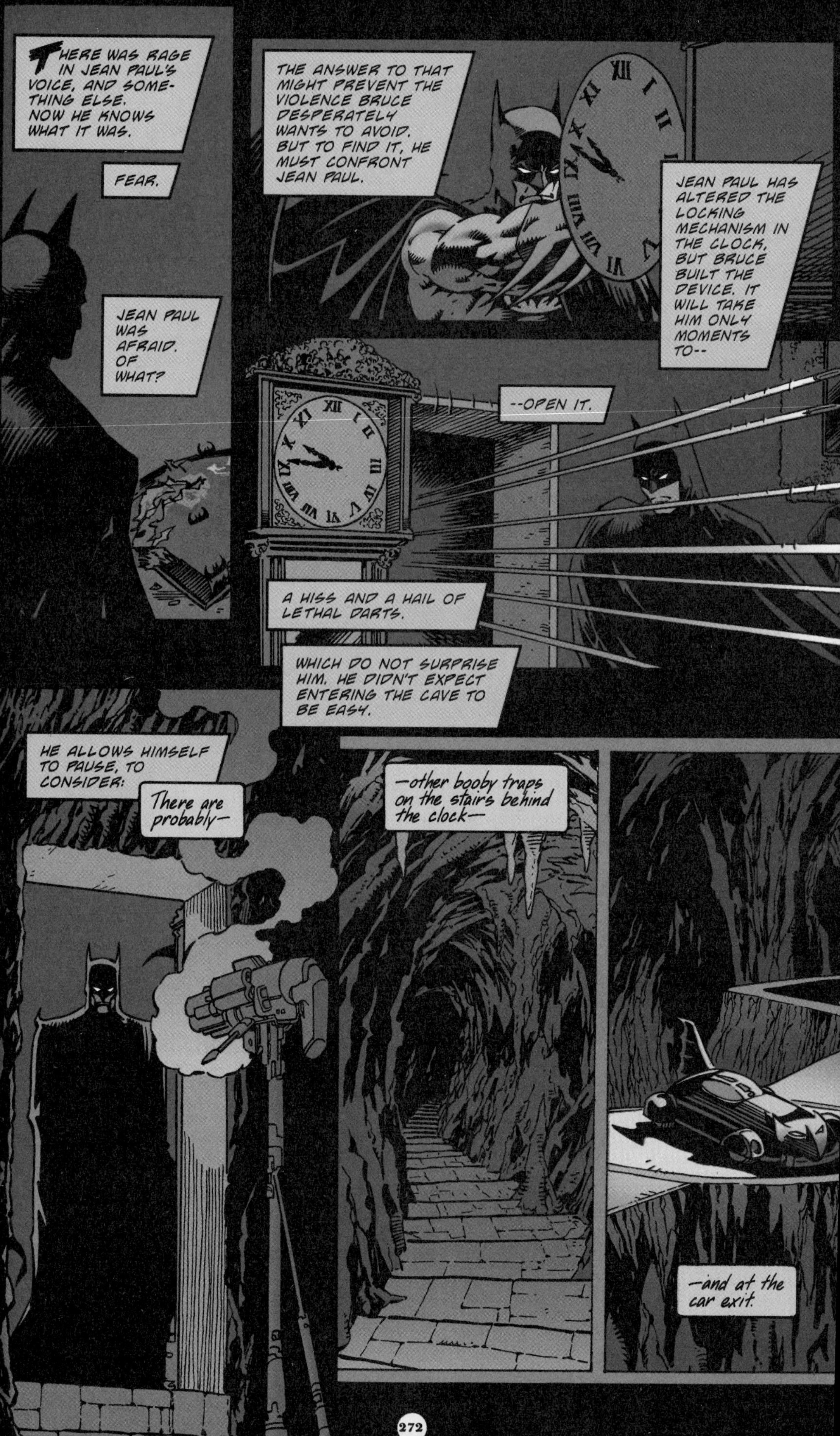
THERE WAS RAGE IN JEAN PAUL'S VOICE, AND SOMETHING ELSE. NOW HE KNOWS WHAT IT WAS.
FEAR.
JEAN PAUL WAS AFRAID. OF WHAT?
THE ANSWER TO THAT MIGHT PREVENT THE VIOLENCE BRUCE DESPERATELY WANTS TO AVOID. BUT TO FIND IT, HE MUST CONFRONT JEAN PAUL.
JEAN PAUL HAS ALTERED THE LOCKING MECHANISM IN THE CLOCK, BUT BRUCE BUILT THE DEVICE. IT WILL TAKE HIM ONLY MOMENTS TO--
--OPEN IT.
A HISS AND A HAIL OF LETHAL DARTS.
WHICH DO NOT SURPRISE HIM. HE DIDN'T EXPECT ENTERING THE CAVE TO BE EASY.
HE ALLOWS HIMSELF TO PAUSE, TO CONSIDER:
There are probably—
—other booby traps on the stairs behind the clock—
—and at the car exit.

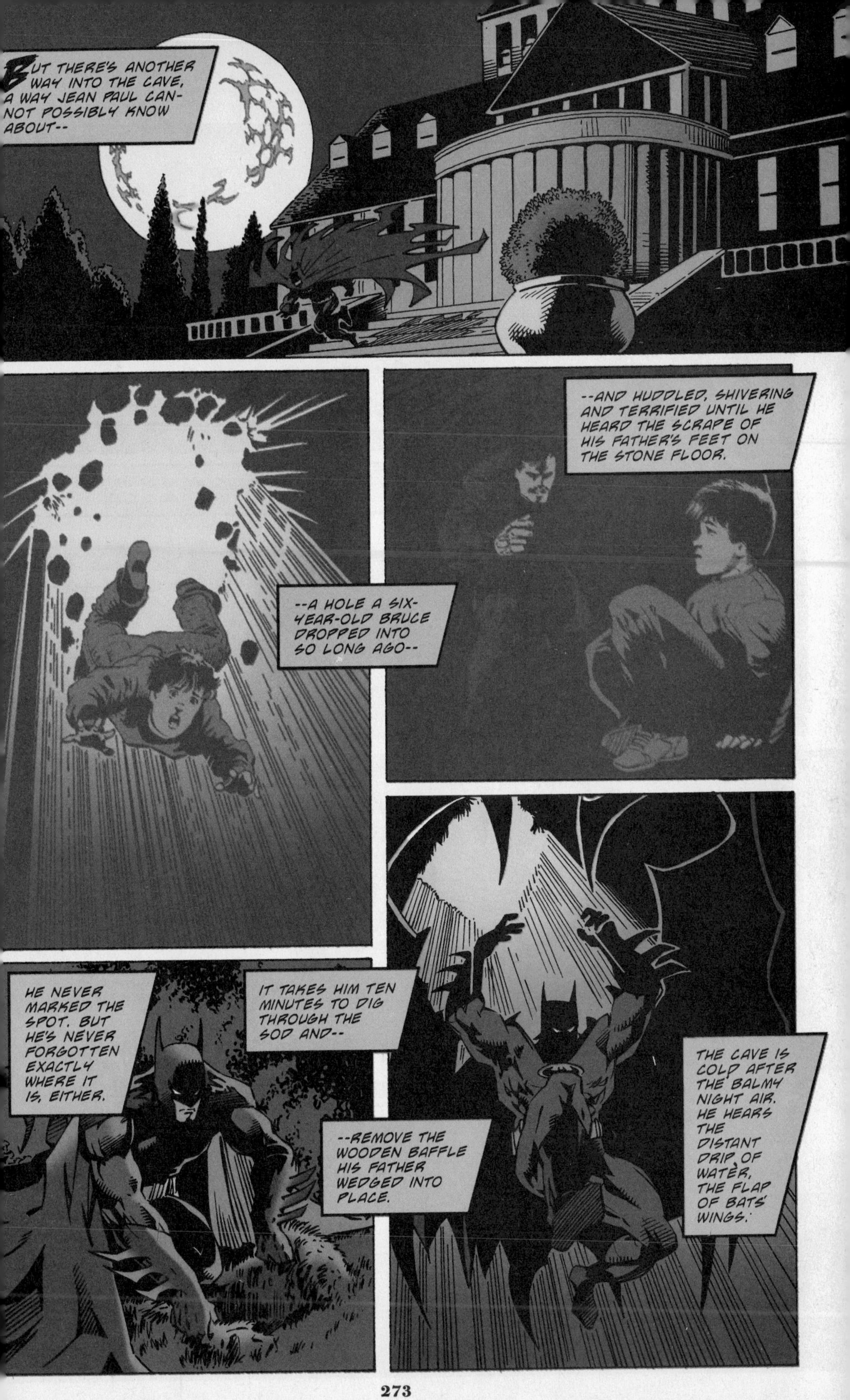
BUT THERE'S ANOTHER WAY INTO THE CAVE, A WAY JEAN PAUL CANNOT POSSIBLY KNOW ABOUT--
--A HOLE A SIX-YEAR-OLD BRUCE DROPPED INTO SO LONG AGO--
--AND HUDDLED, SHIVERING AND TERRIFIED UNTIL HE HEARD THE SCRAPE OF HIS FATHER'S FEET ON THE STONE FLOOR.
HE NEVER MARKED THE SPOT. BUT HE'S NEVER FORGOTTEN EXACTLY WHERE IT IS, EITHER.
IT TAKES HIM TEN MINUTES TO DIG THROUGH THE SOD AND--
--REMOVE THE WOODEN BAFFLE HIS FATHER WEDGED INTO PLACE.
THE CAVE IS COLD AFTER THE BALMY NIGHT AIR. HE HEARS THE DISTANT DRIP OF WATER, THE FLAP OF BATS' WINGS.

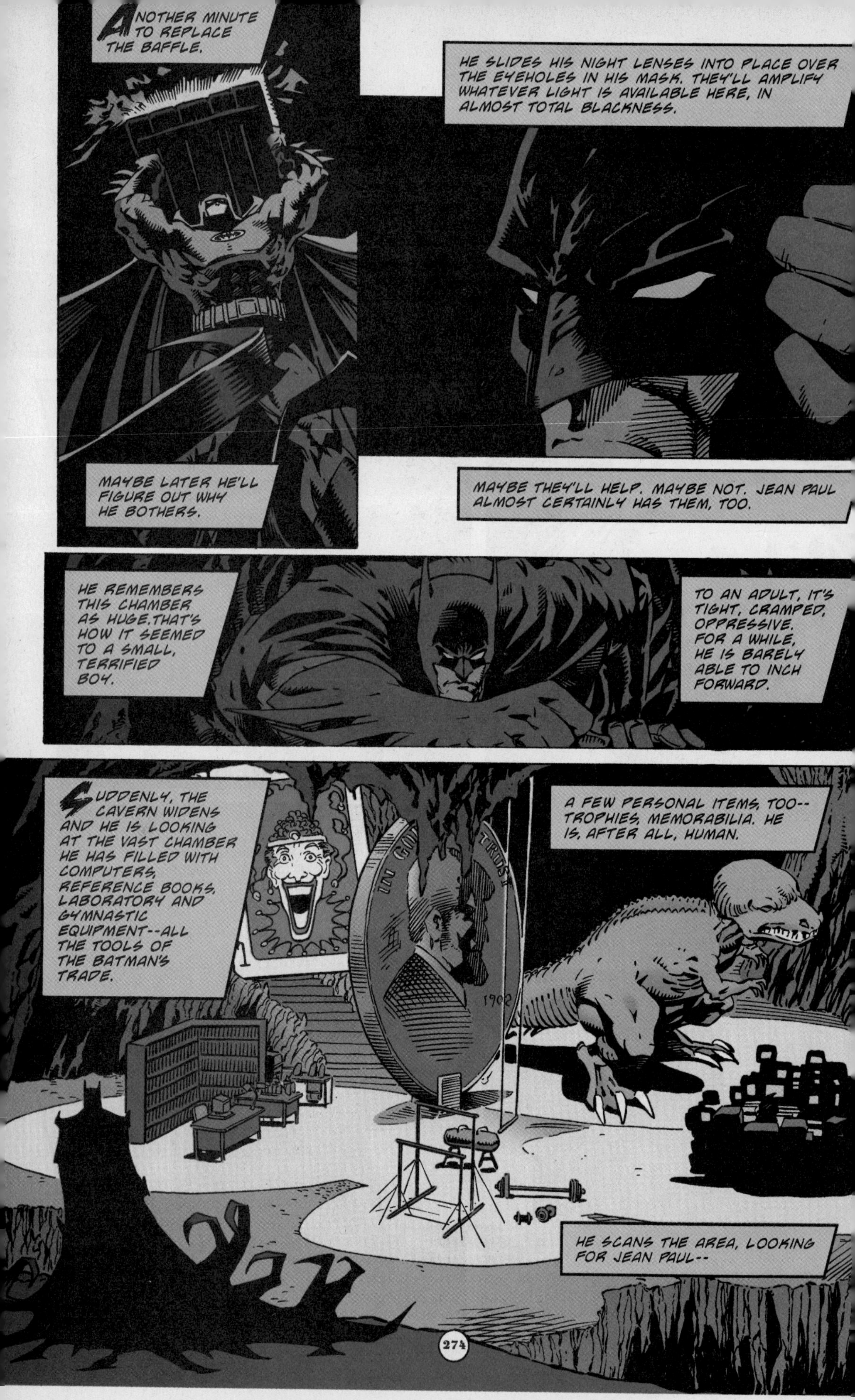
ANOTHER MINUTE TO REPLACE THE BAFFLE.
MAYBE LATER HE'LL FIGURE OUT WHY HE BOTHERS.
HE SLIDES HIS NIGHT LENSES INTO PLACE OVER THE EYEHOLES IN HIS MASK. THEY'LL AMPLIFY WHATEVER LIGHT IS AVAILABLE HERE, IN ALMOST TOTAL BLACKNESS.
MAYBE THEY'LL HELP. MAYBE NOT. JEAN PAUL ALMOST CERTAINLY HAS THEM, TOO.
HE REMEMBERS THIS CHAMBER AS HUGE. THAT'S HOW IT SEEMED TO A SMALL, TERRIFIED BOY.
TO AN ADULT, IT'S TIGHT, CRAMPED, OPPRESSIVE. FOR A WHILE, HE IS BARELY ABLE TO INCH FORWARD.
SUDDENLY, THE CAVERN WIDENS AND HE IS LOOKING AT THE VAST CHAMBER HE HAS FILLED WITH COMPUTERS, REFERENCE BOOKS, LABORATORY AND GYMNASTIC EQUIPMENT--ALL THE TOOLS OF THE BATMAN'S TRADE.
A FEW PERSONAL ITEMS, TOO--TROPHIES, MEMORABILIA. HE IS, AFTER ALL, HUMAN.
HE SCANS THE AREA, LOOKING FOR JEAN PAUL--

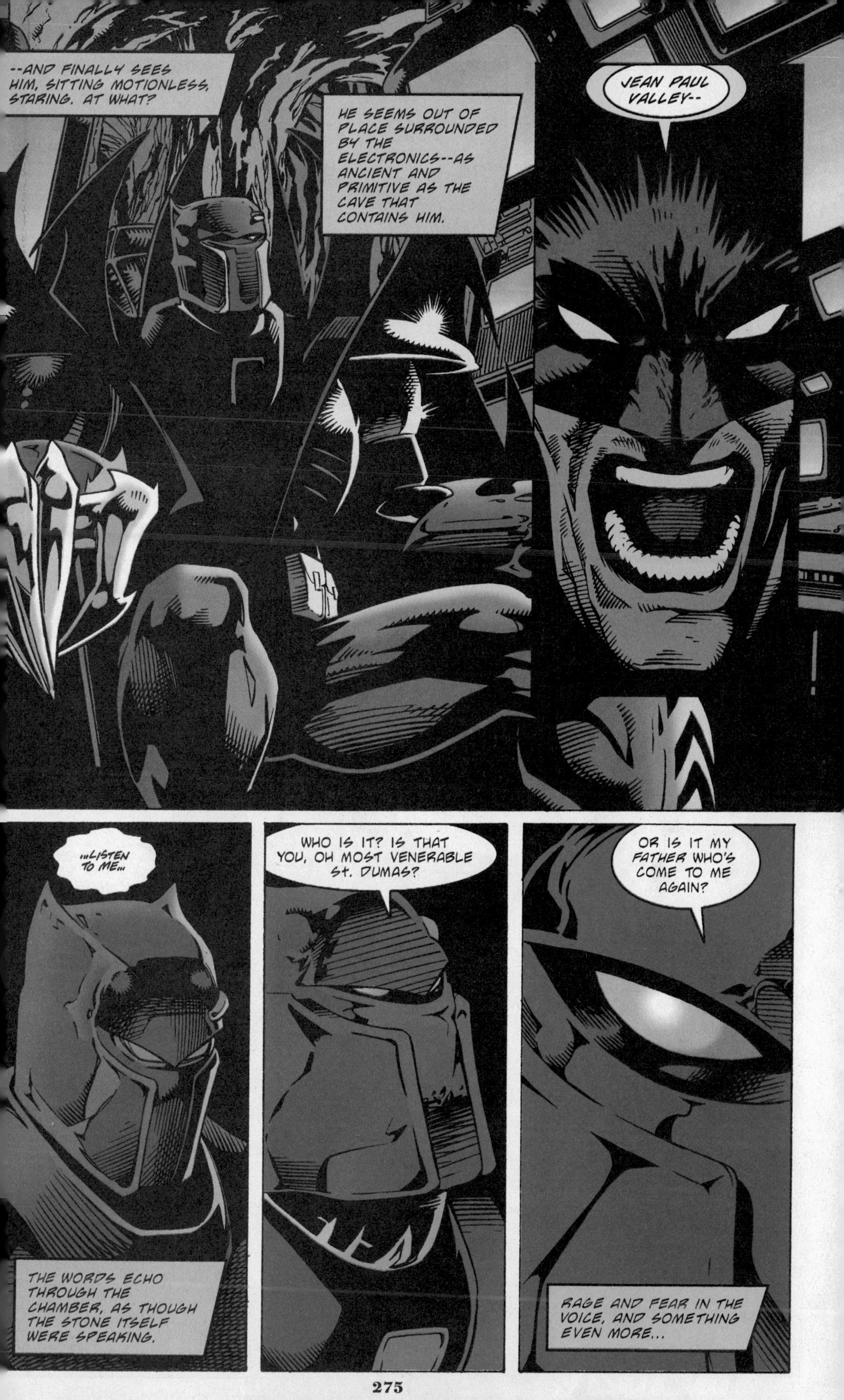
--AND FINALLY SEES HIM, SITTING MOTIONLESS, STARING. AT WHAT?
HE SEEMS OUT OF PLACE SURROUNDED BY THE ELECTRONICS--AS ANCIENT AND PRIMITIVE AS THE CAVE THAT CONTAINS HIM.
JEAN PAUL VALLEY--
...LISTEN TO ME...
THE WORDS ECHO THROUGH THE CHAMBER, AS THOUGH THE STONE ITSELF WERE SPEAKING.
WHO IS IT? IS THAT YOU, OH MOST VENERABLE St. DUMAS?
OR IS IT MY FATHER WHO'S COME TO ME AGAIN?
RAGE AND FEAR IN THE VOICE, AND SOMETHING EVEN MORE...

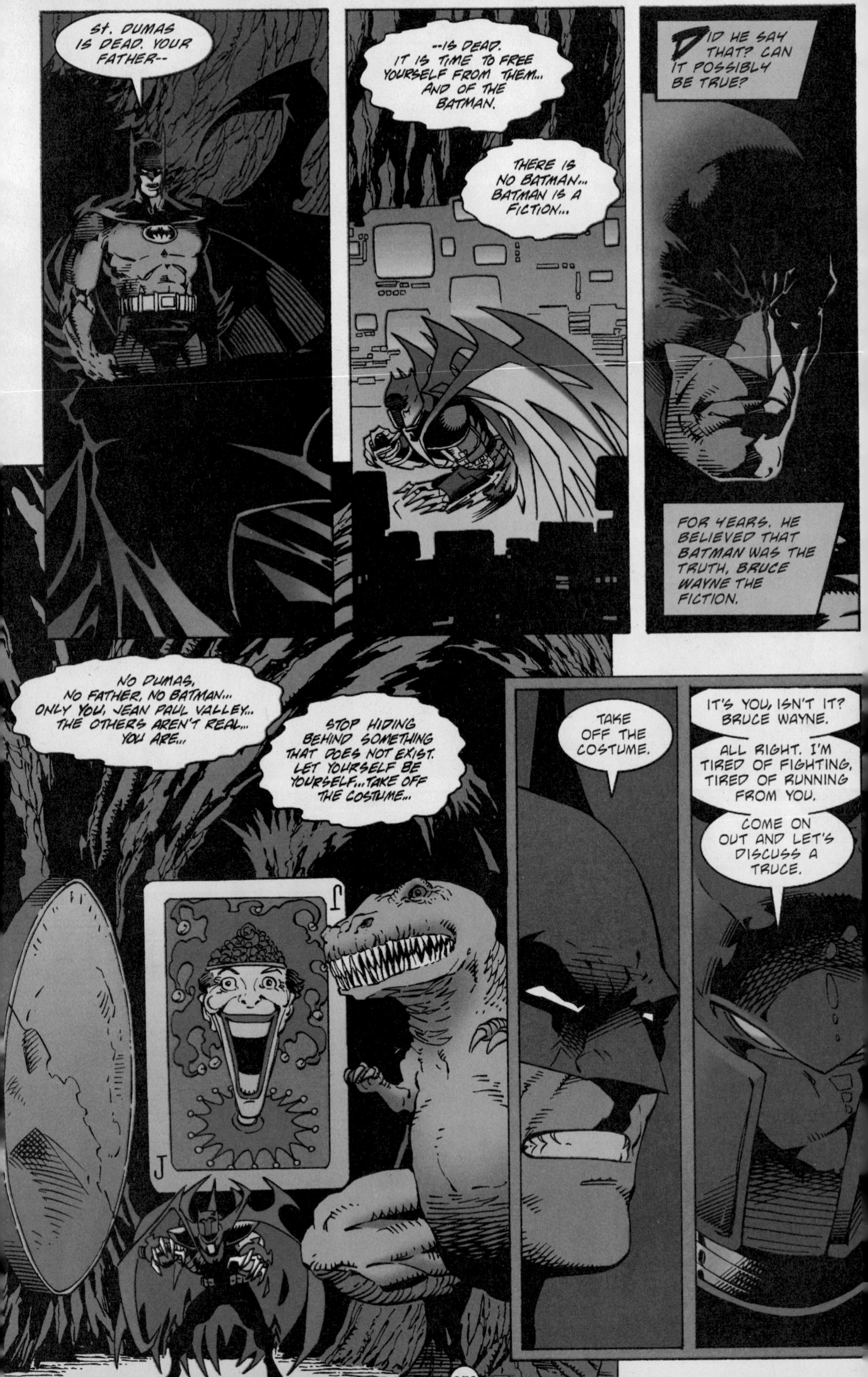
St. DUMAS IS DEAD. YOUR FATHER--
--IS DEAD. IT IS TIME TO FREE YOURSELF FROM THEM... AND OF THE BATMAN.
THERE IS NO BATMAN... BATMAN IS A FICTION...
DID HE SAY THAT? CAN IT POSSIBLY BE TRUE?
FOR YEARS, HE BELIEVED THAT BATMAN WAS THE TRUTH, BRUCE WAYNE THE FICTION.
NO DUMAS, NO FATHER, NO BATMAN... ONLY YOU, JEAN PAUL VALLEY... THE OTHERS AREN'T REAL... YOU ARE...
STOP HIDING BEHIND SOMETHING THAT DOES NOT EXIST. LET YOURSELF BE YOURSELF...TAKE OFF THE COSTUME...
TAKE OFF THE COSTUME.
IT'S YOU, ISN'T IT? BRUCE WAYNE.
ALL RIGHT. I'M TIRED OF FIGHTING, TIRED OF RUNNING FROM YOU.
COME ON OUT AND LET'S DISCUSS A TRUCE.

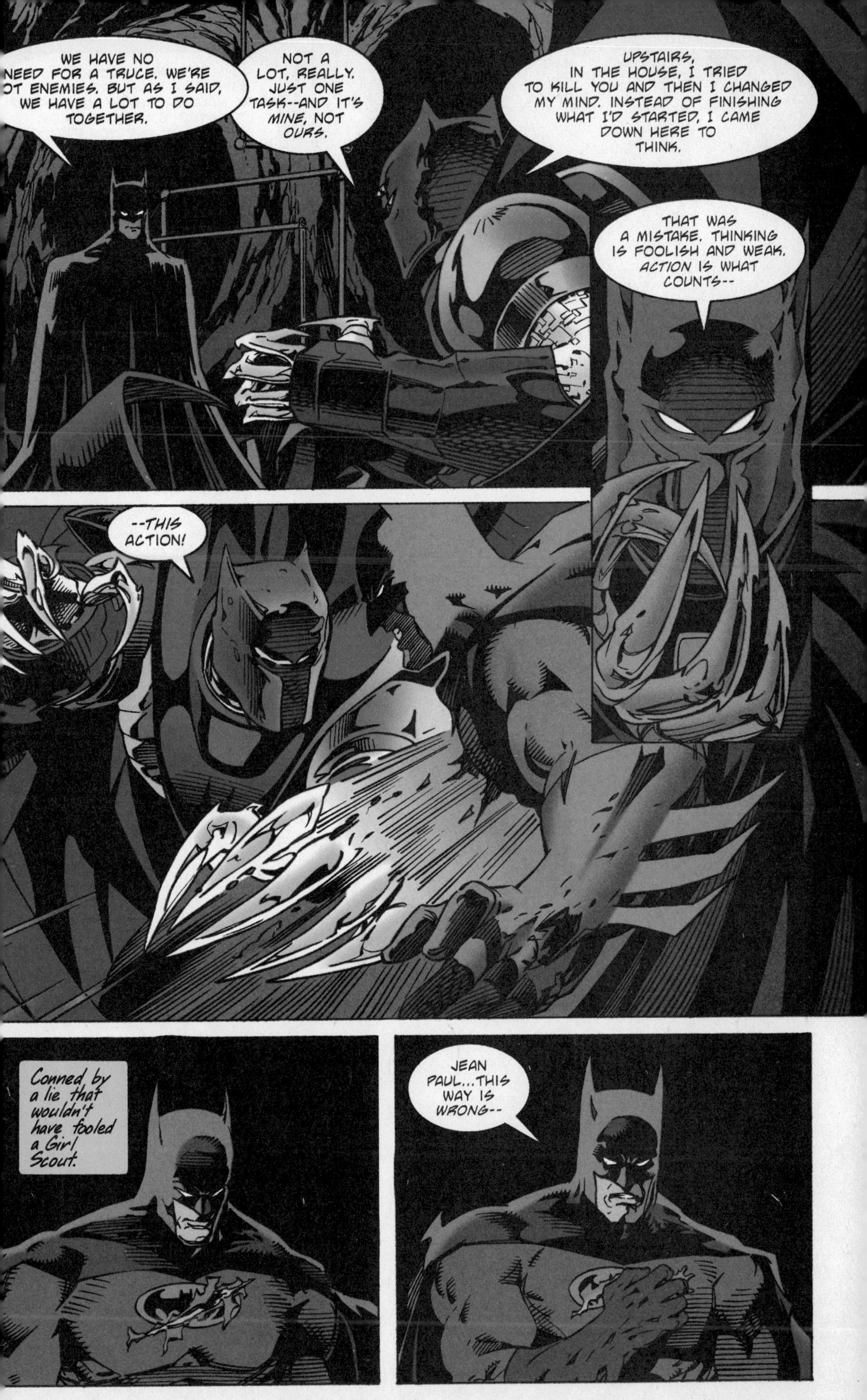
WE HAVE NO NEED FOR A TRUCE. WE'RE OT ENEMIES. BUT AS I SAID, WE HAVE A LOT TO DO TOGETHER.
NOT A LOT, REALLY. JUST ONE TASK--AND IT'S *MINE*, NOT *OURS*.
UPSTAIRS, IN THE HOUSE, I TRIED TO KILL YOU AND THEN I CHANGED MY MIND. INSTEAD OF FINISHING WHAT I'D STARTED, I CAME DOWN HERE TO THINK.
THAT WAS A MISTAKE. THINKING IS FOOLISH AND WEAK. *ACTION* IS WHAT COUNTS--
--*THIS* ACTION!
Conned by a lie that wouldn't have fooled a Girl Scout.
JEAN PAUL...THIS WAY IS *WRONG*--

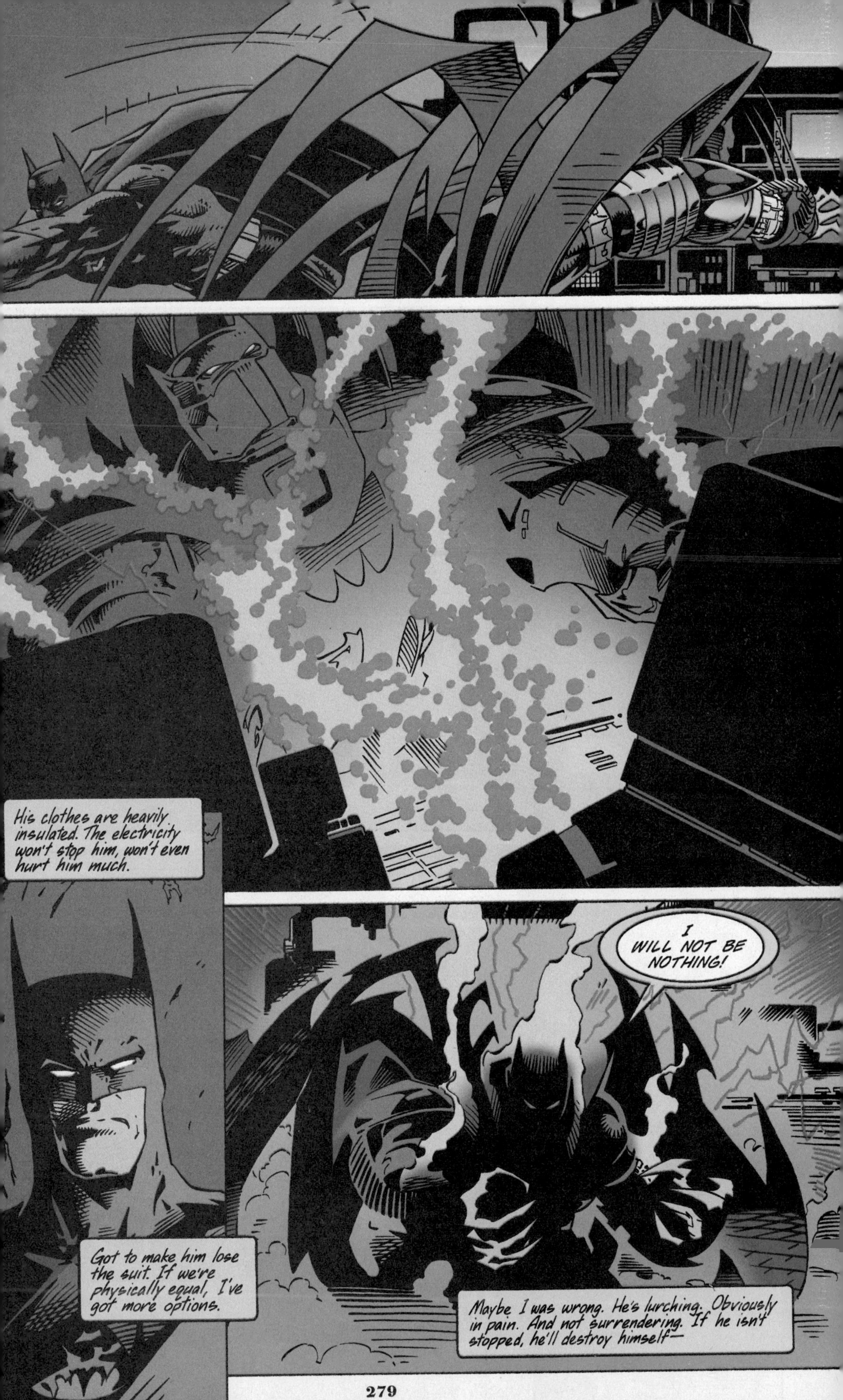
His clothes are heavily insulated. The electricity won't stop him, won't even hurt him much.
Got to make him lose the suit. If we're physically equal, I've got more options.
I WILL NOT BE NOTHING!
Maybe I was wrong. He's lurching. Obviously in pain. And not surrendering. If he isn't stopped, he'll destroy himself—

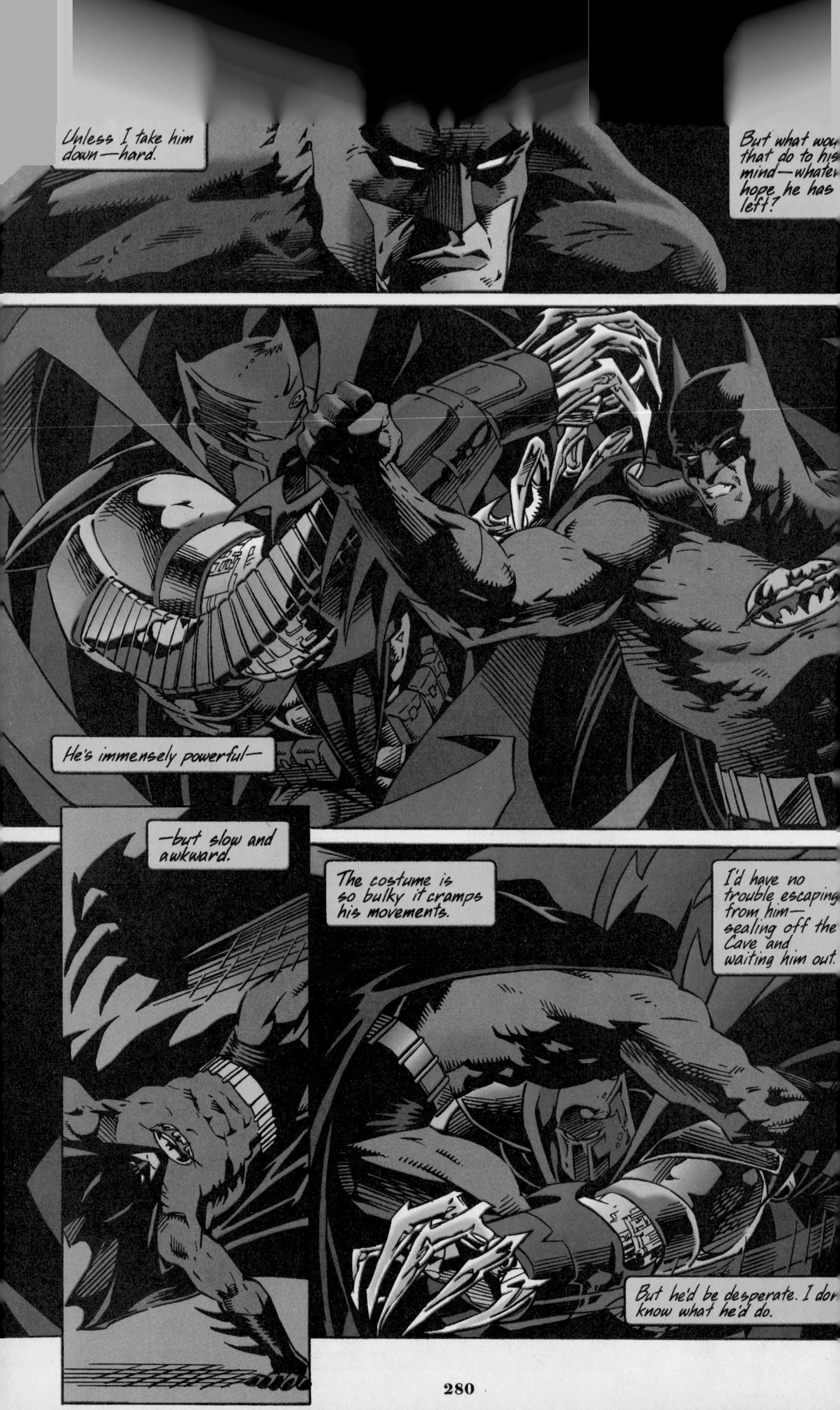
Unless I take him down—hard.
But what wou that do to his mind—whatev hope he has left?
He's immensely powerful—
—but slow and awkward.
The costume is so bulky it cramps his movements.
I'd have no trouble escaping from him—sealing off the Cave and waiting him out.
But he'd be desperate. I dor know what he'd do.

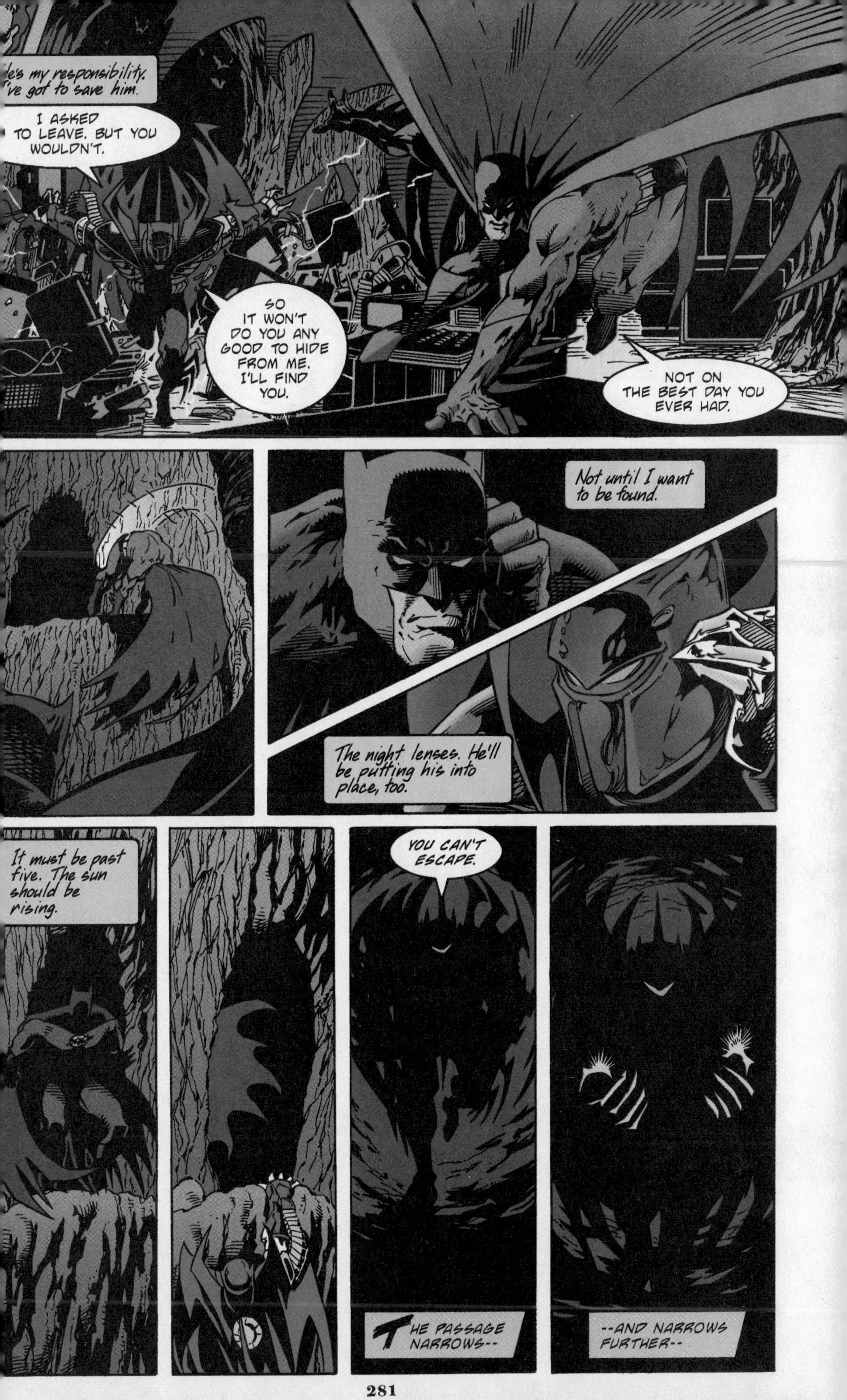

He's my responsibility. I've got to save him.
I ASKED TO LEAVE. BUT YOU WOULDN'T.
SO IT WON'T DO YOU ANY GOOD TO HIDE FROM ME. I'LL FIND YOU.
NOT ON THE BEST DAY YOU EVER HAD.
Not until I want to be found.
The night lenses. He'll be putting his into place, too.
It must be past five. The sun should be rising.
YOU CAN'T ESCAPE.
THE PASSAGE NARROWS--
--AND NARROWS FURTHER--

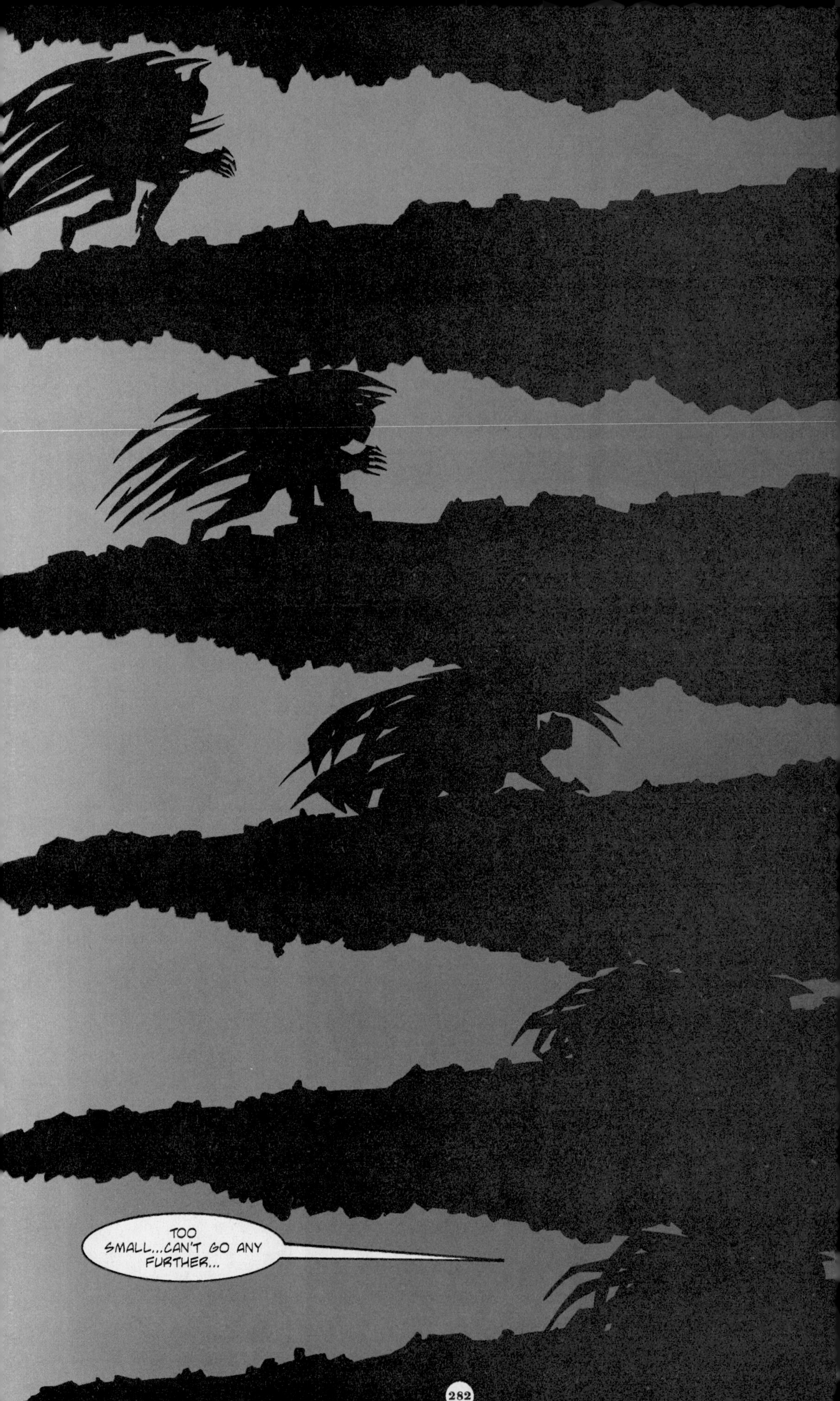
TOO SMALL...CAN'T GO ANY FURTHER...

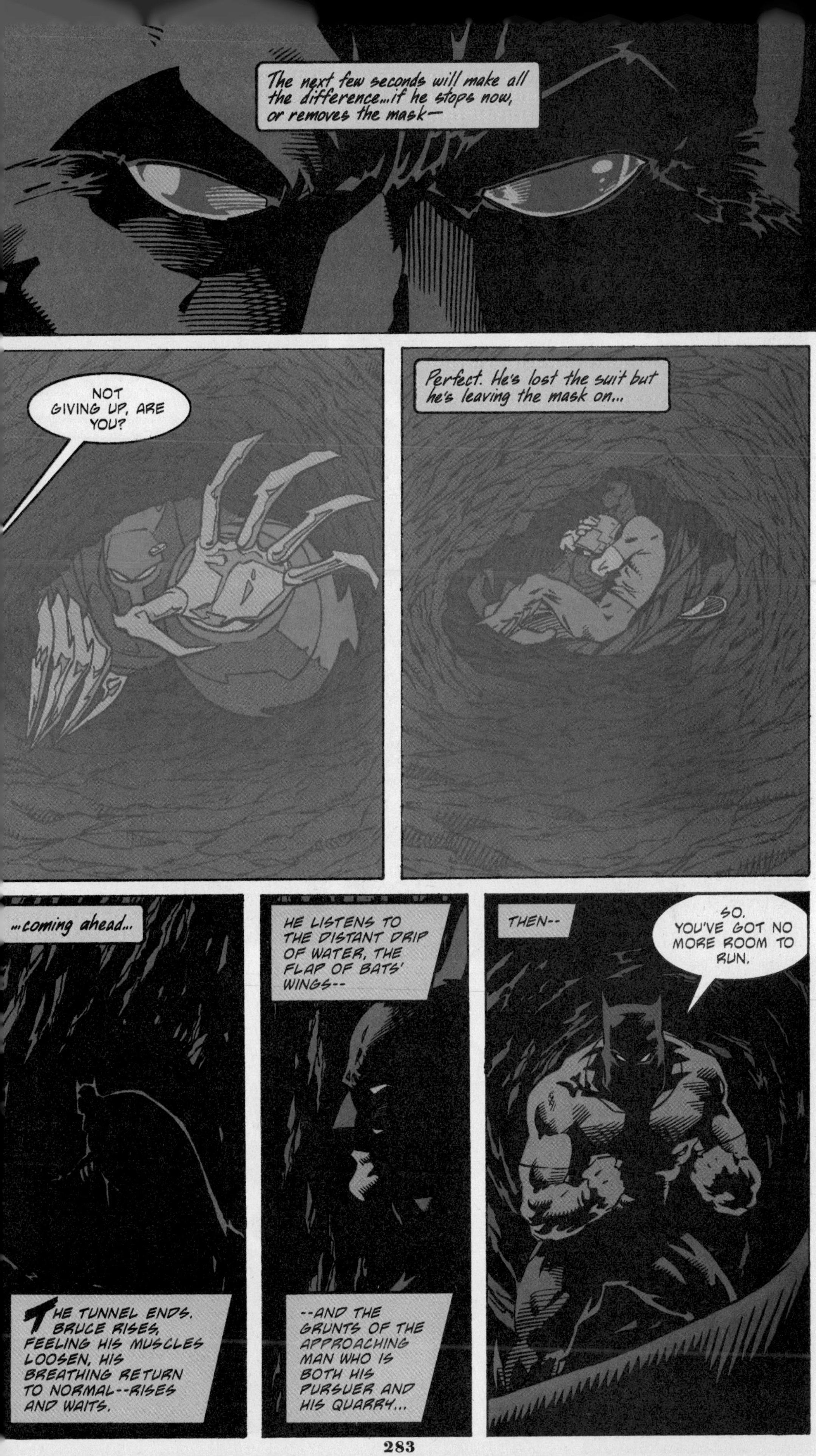

The next few seconds will make all the difference...if he stops now, or removes the mask—
NOT GIVING UP, ARE YOU?
Perfect. He's lost the suit but he's leaving the mask on...
...coming ahead...
THE TUNNEL ENDS. BRUCE RISES, FEELING HIS MUSCLES LOOSEN, HIS BREATHING RETURN TO NORMAL--RISES AND WAITS.
HE LISTENS TO THE DISTANT DRIP OF WATER, THE FLAP OF BATS' WINGS--
--AND THE GRUNTS OF THE APPROACHING MAN WHO IS BOTH HIS PURSUER AND HIS QUARRY...
THEN--
SO. YOU'VE GOT NO MORE ROOM TO RUN.

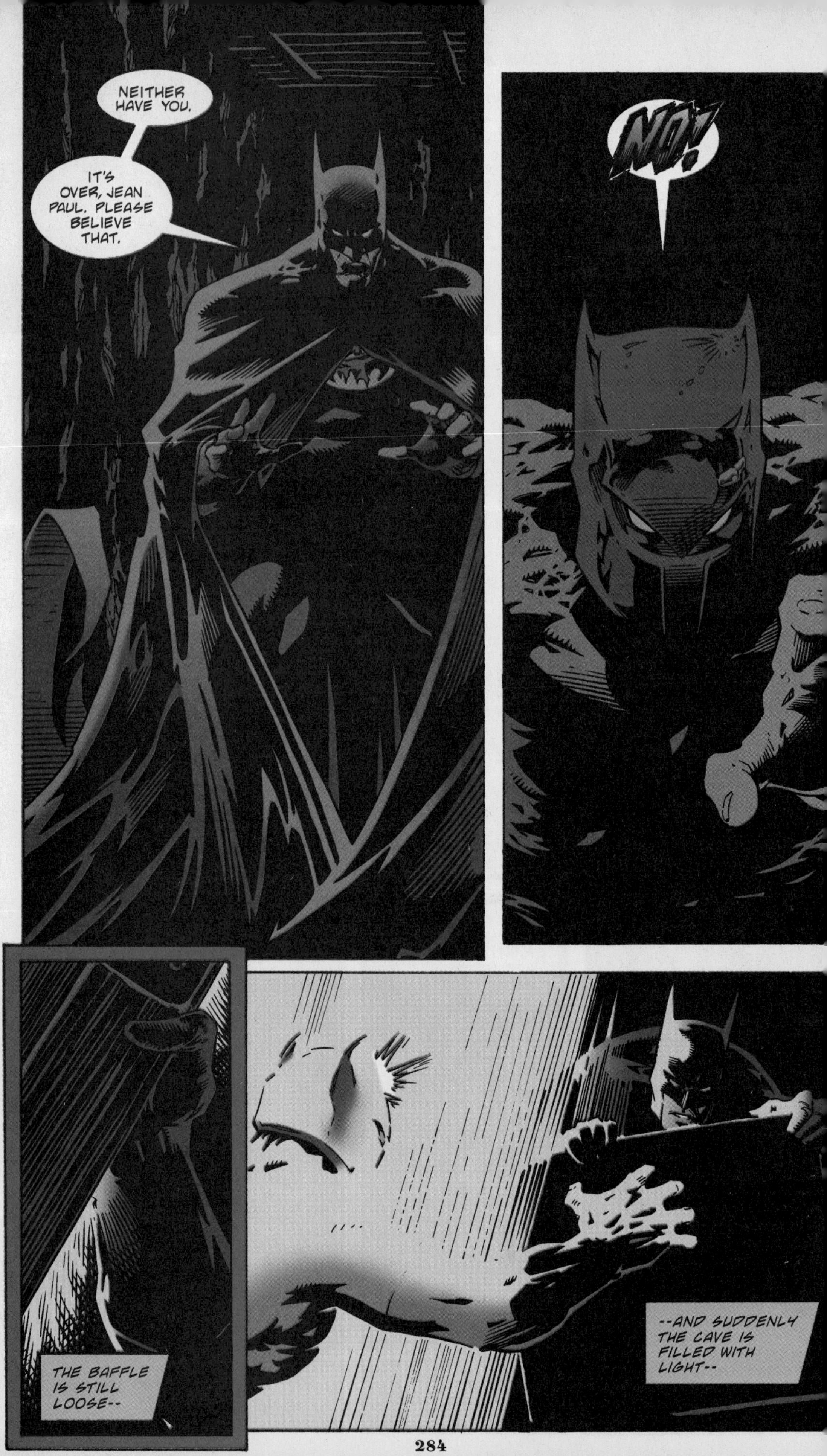
NEITHER HAVE YOU.
IT'S OVER, JEAN PAUL. PLEASE BELIEVE THAT.
NO!
THE BAFFLE IS STILL LOOSE--
--AND SUDDENLY THE CAVE IS FILLED WITH LIGHT--

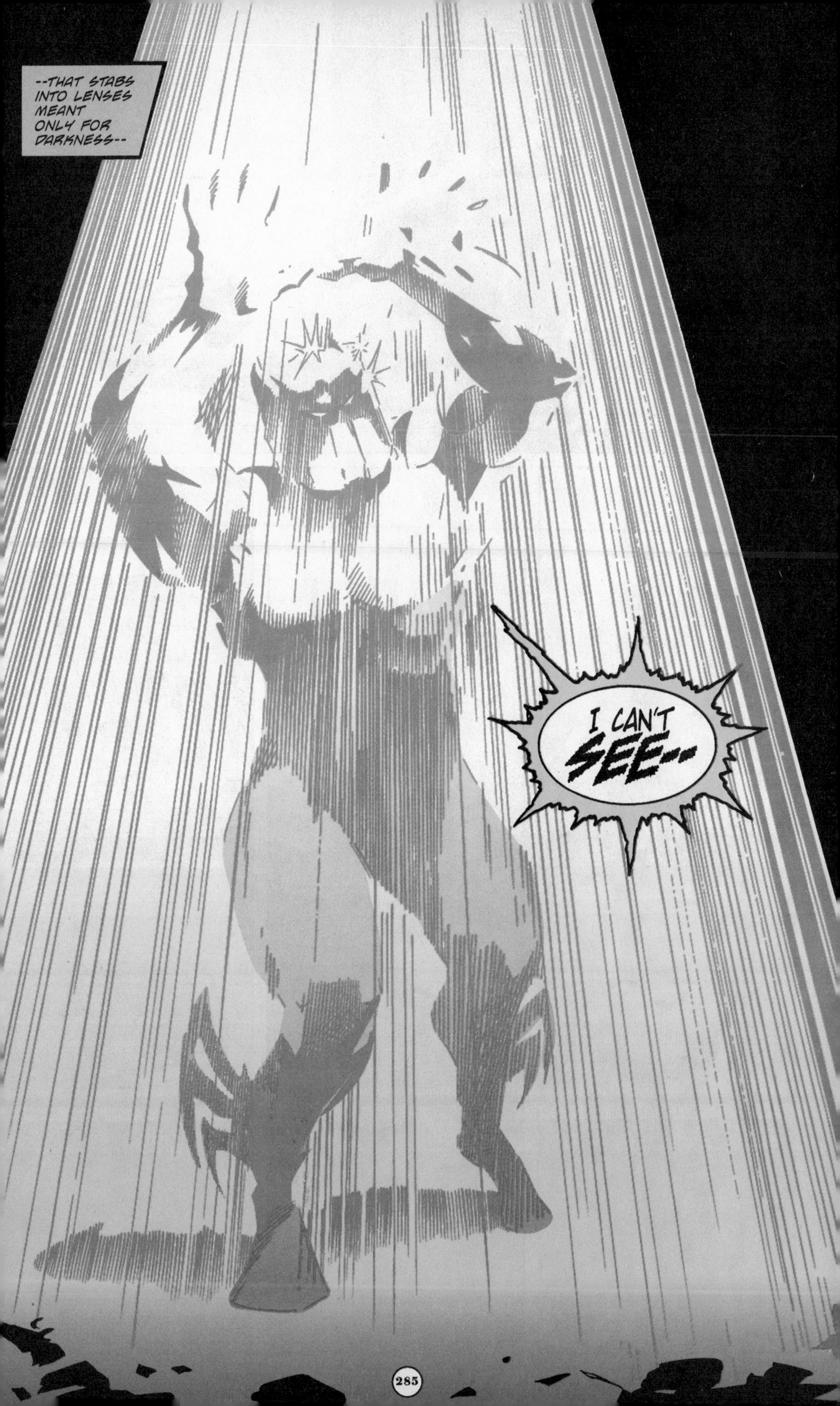
--THAT STABS INTO LENSES MEANT ONLY FOR DARKNESS--
I CAN'T SEE--

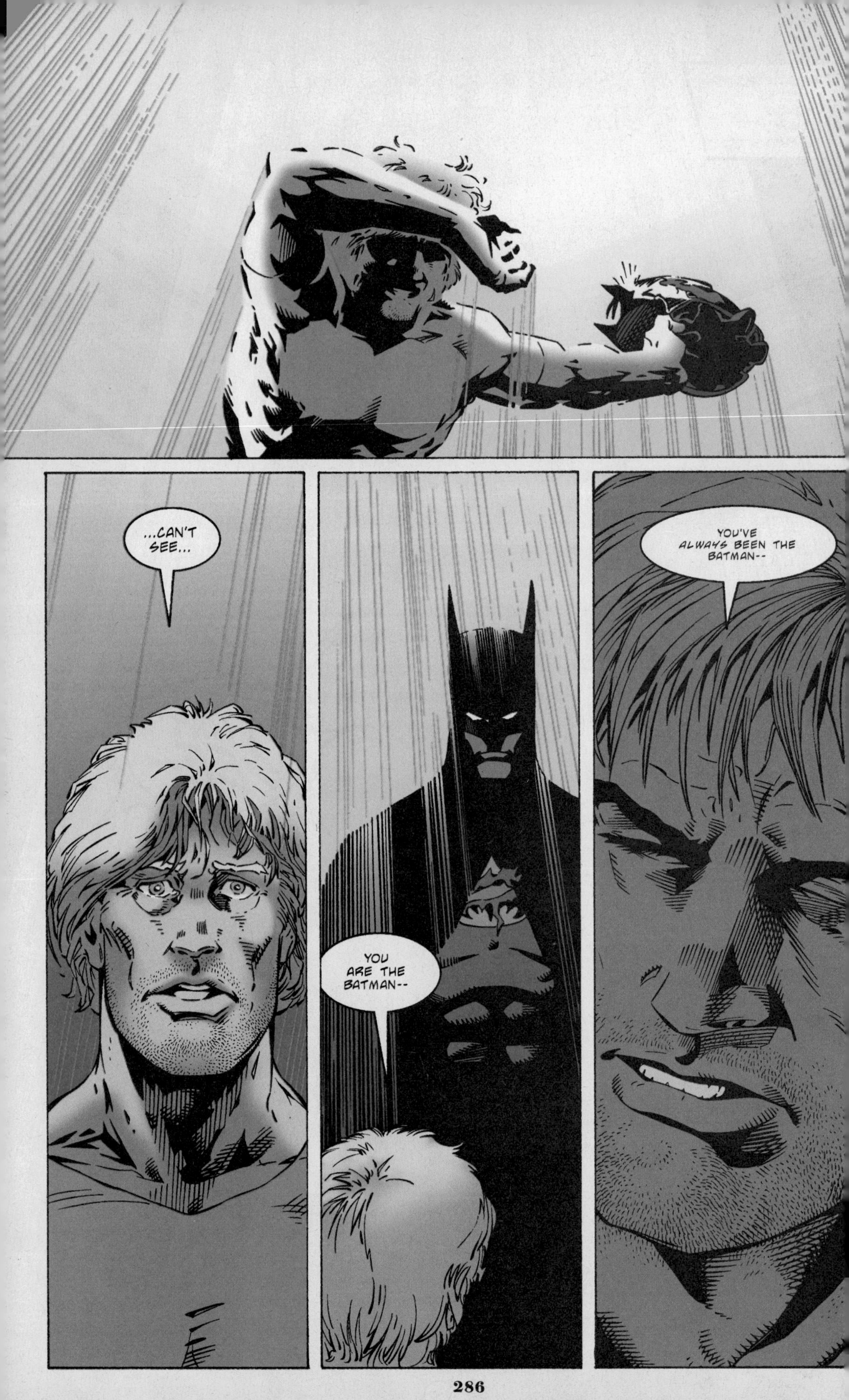
...CAN'T SEE...
YOU ARE THE BATMAN--
YOU'VE ALWAYS BEEN THE BATMAN--

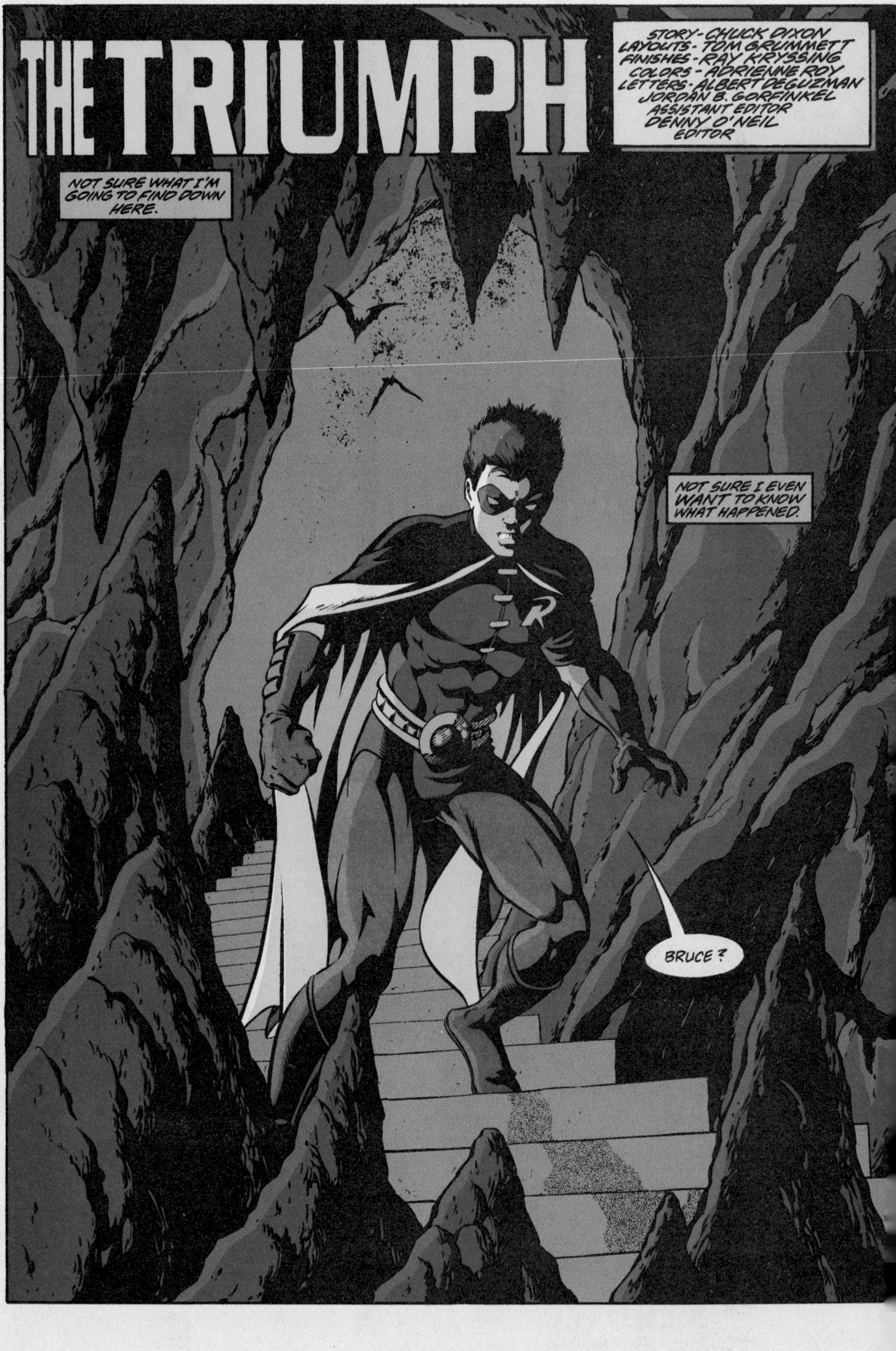
THE TRIUMPH
STORY - CHUCK DIXON
LAYOUTS - TOM GRUMMETT
FINISHES - RAY KRYSSING
COLORS - ADRIENNE ROY
LETTERS - ALBERT DEGUZMAN
JORDAN B. GORFINKEL
ASSISTANT EDITOR
DENNY O'NEIL
EDITOR
NOT SURE WHAT I'M GOING TO FIND DOWN HERE.
NOT SURE I EVEN WANT TO KNOW WHAT HAPPENED.
BRUCE?

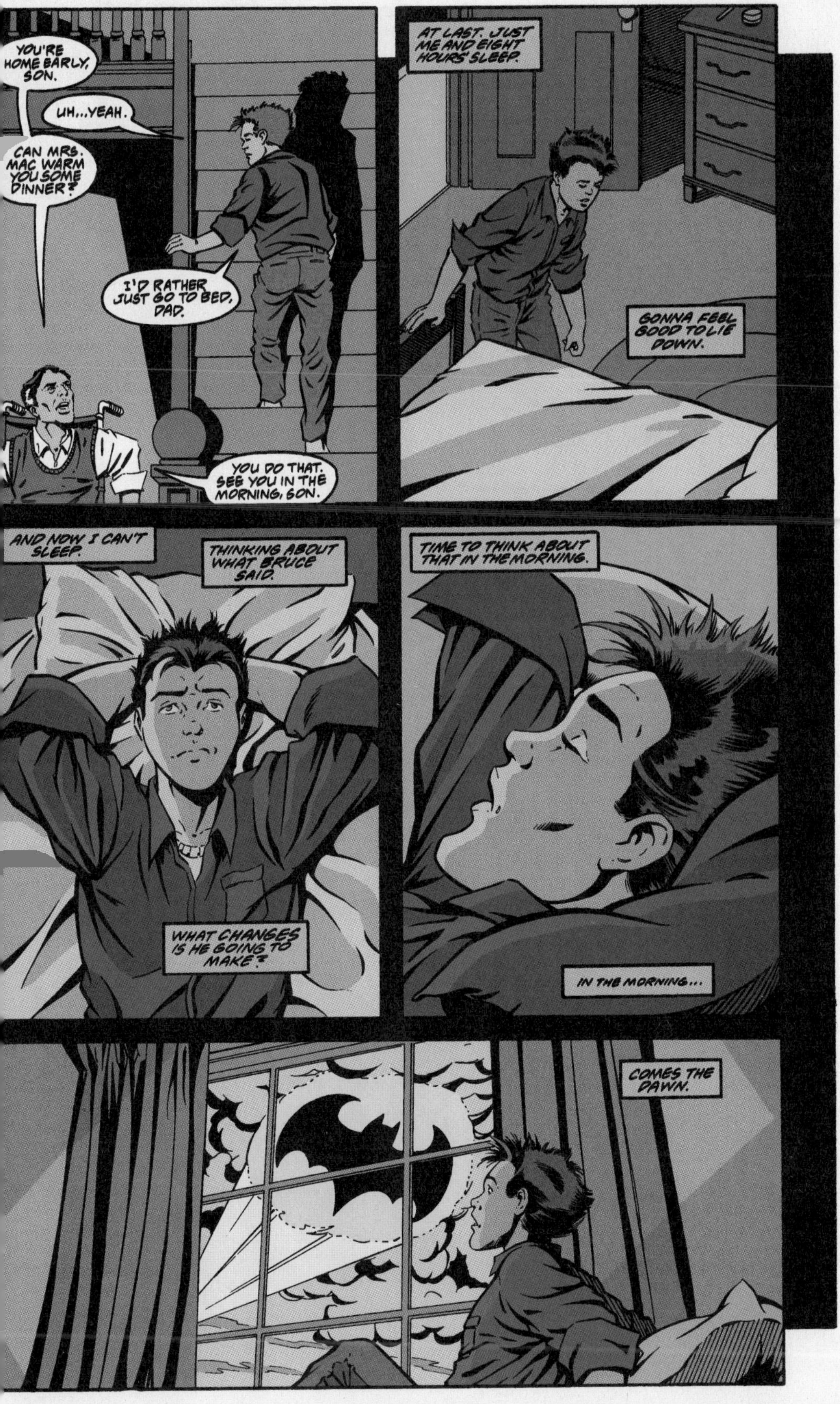
YOU'RE HOME EARLY, SON.
UH...YEAH.
CAN MRS. MAC WARM YOU SOME DINNER?
I'D RATHER JUST GO TO BED, DAD.
YOU DO THAT. SEE YOU IN THE MORNING, SON.
AT LAST. JUST ME AND EIGHT HOURS' SLEEP.
GONNA FEEL GOOD TO LIE DOWN.
AND NOW I CAN'T SLEEP.
THINKING ABOUT WHAT BRUCE SAID.
WHAT CHANGES IS HE GOING TO MAKE?
TIME TO THINK ABOUT THAT IN THE MORNING.
IN THE MORNING...
COMES THE DAWN.

DON'T HAVE TO GUESS WHERE HE'S GONE.

POLICE SCANNERS ARE FULL OF IT.

HOSTAGE SITUATION AT THE MUSEUM OF ANTIQUITIES.

SO WHAT'S THE STORY, COMMISH?

FAILED HEIST AT ONE OF THE EXHIBITS, BULLOCK. NOT SURE HOW MANY PERPS. LOOKS LIKE THEY'VE TAKEN SOME UNIVERSITY STUDENTS HOSTAGE.

BEAUTIFUL. IS TACTICAL PREPARED TO MOVE IN?

HOSTAGE NEGOTIATIONS IS TRYING TO REACH THEM FIRST, RENEE. SO FAR THERE'S NO ANSWER.

I SAW THE SIGNAL. YOU HAD IT REPAIRED.

YES. I ONLY HOPE IT'S NOT A MISTAKE. THERE'RE ALREADY ENOUGH VARIABLES IN THIS SITUATION.

THE MUSEUM'S A MAZE. I WANT TO TRY EVERYTHING ELSE BEFORE WE SEND COPS IN.

AND AFTER LAST NIGHT I'M WONDERING IF WE'LL EVER SEE HIM. AGAIN.

298

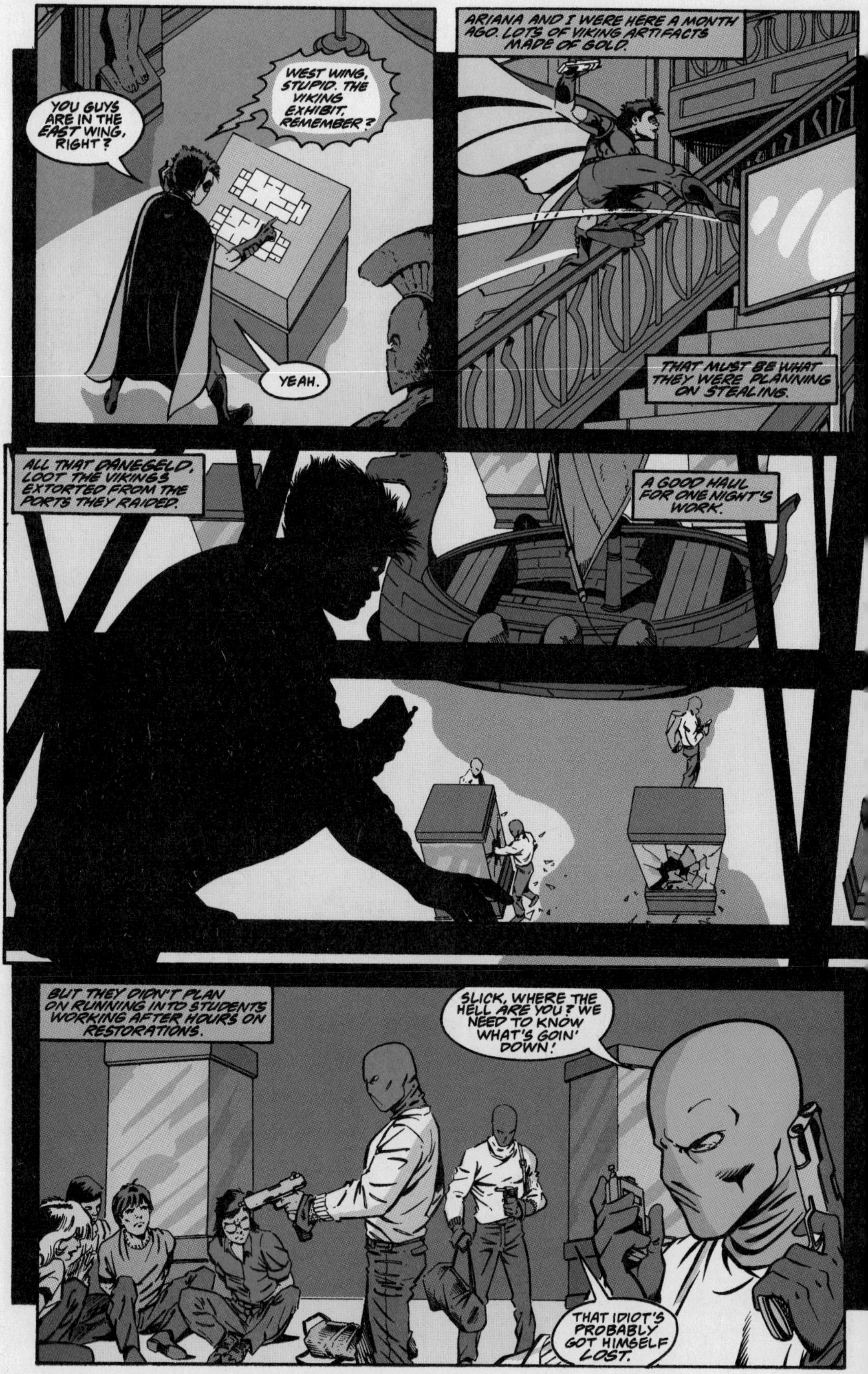

YOU GUYS ARE IN THE EAST WING, RIGHT?
WEST WING, STUPID. THE VIKING EXHIBIT, REMEMBER?
YEAH.
ARIANA AND I WERE HERE A MONTH AGO. LOTS OF VIKING ARTIFACTS MADE OF GOLD.
THAT MUST BE WHAT THEY WERE PLANNING ON STEALING.
ALL THAT DANEGELD, LOOT THE VIKINGS EXTORTED FROM THE PORTS THEY RAIDED.
A GOOD HAUL FOR ONE NIGHT'S WORK.
BUT THEY DIDN'T PLAN ON RUNNING INTO STUDENTS WORKING AFTER HOURS ON RESTORATIONS.
SLICK, WHERE THE HELL ARE YOU? WE NEED TO KNOW WHAT'S GOIN' DOWN!
THAT IDIOT'S PROBABLY GOT HIMSELF LOST.

301

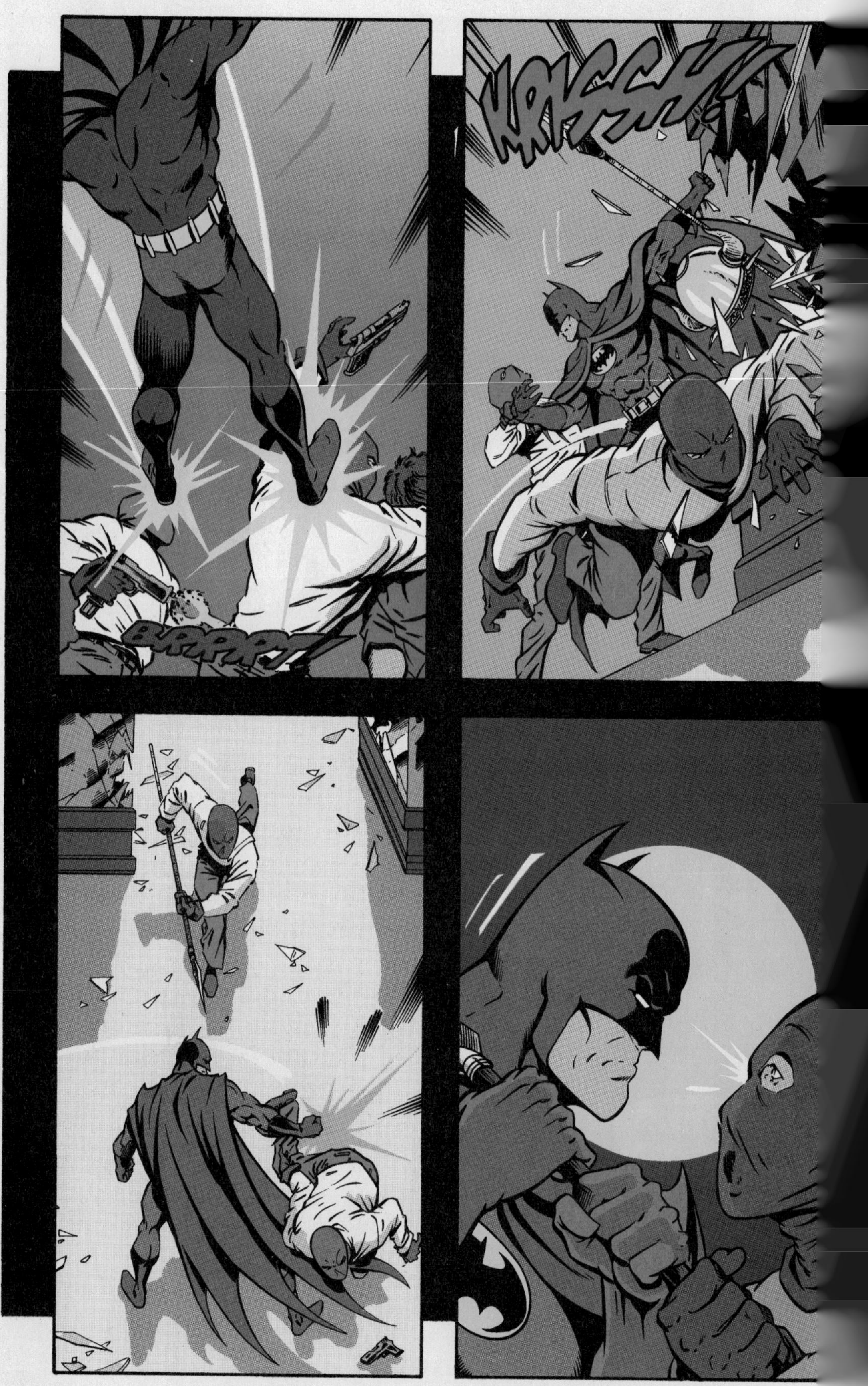

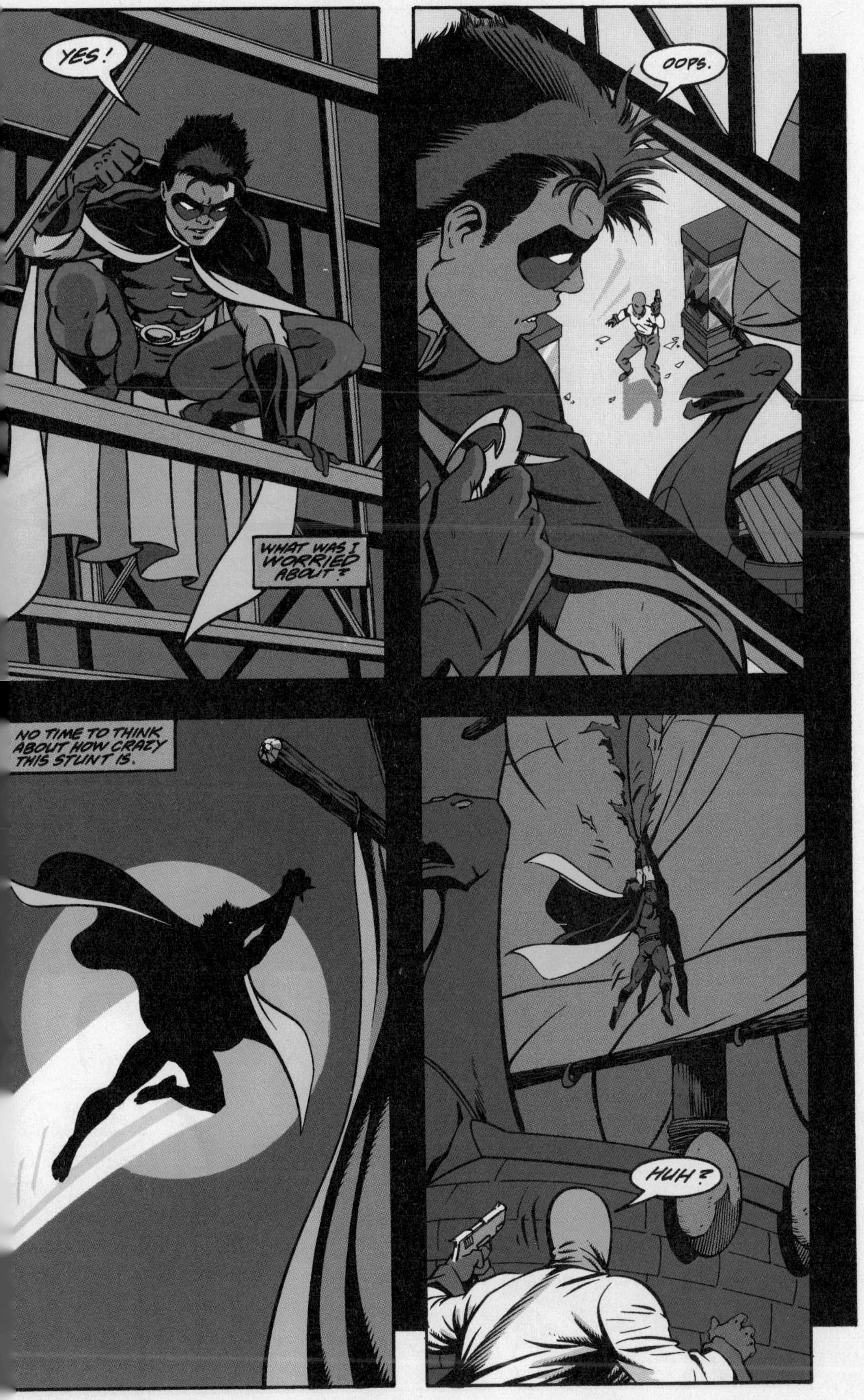
YES!
WHAT WAS I WORRIED ABOUT?
OOPS.
NO TIME TO THINK ABOUT HOW CRAZY THIS STUNT IS.
HUH?

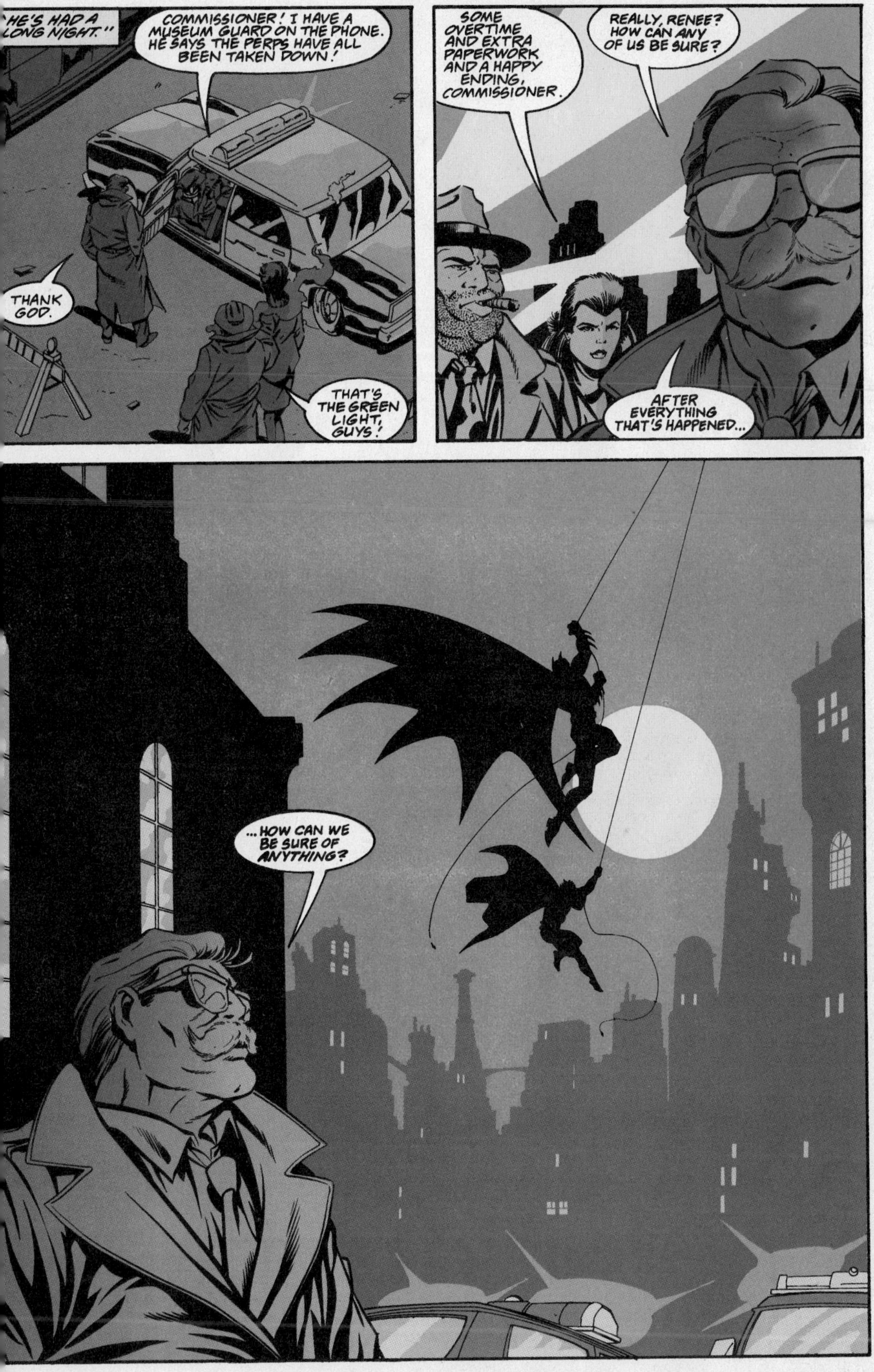
"HE'S HAD A LONG NIGHT."
COMMISSIONER! I HAVE A MUSEUM GUARD ON THE PHONE. HE SAYS THE PERPS HAVE ALL BEEN TAKEN DOWN!
THANK GOD.
THAT'S THE GREEN LIGHT, GUYS!
SOME OVERTIME AND EXTRA PAPERWORK AND A HAPPY ENDING, COMMISSIONER.
REALLY, RENEE? HOW CAN ANY OF US BE SURE?
AFTER EVERYTHING THAT'S HAPPENED...
...HOW CAN WE BE SURE OF ANYTHING?

C O V E R S

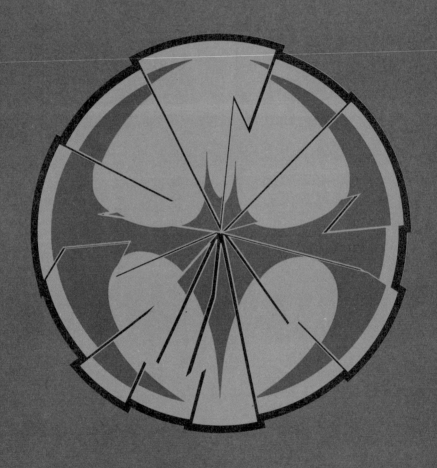

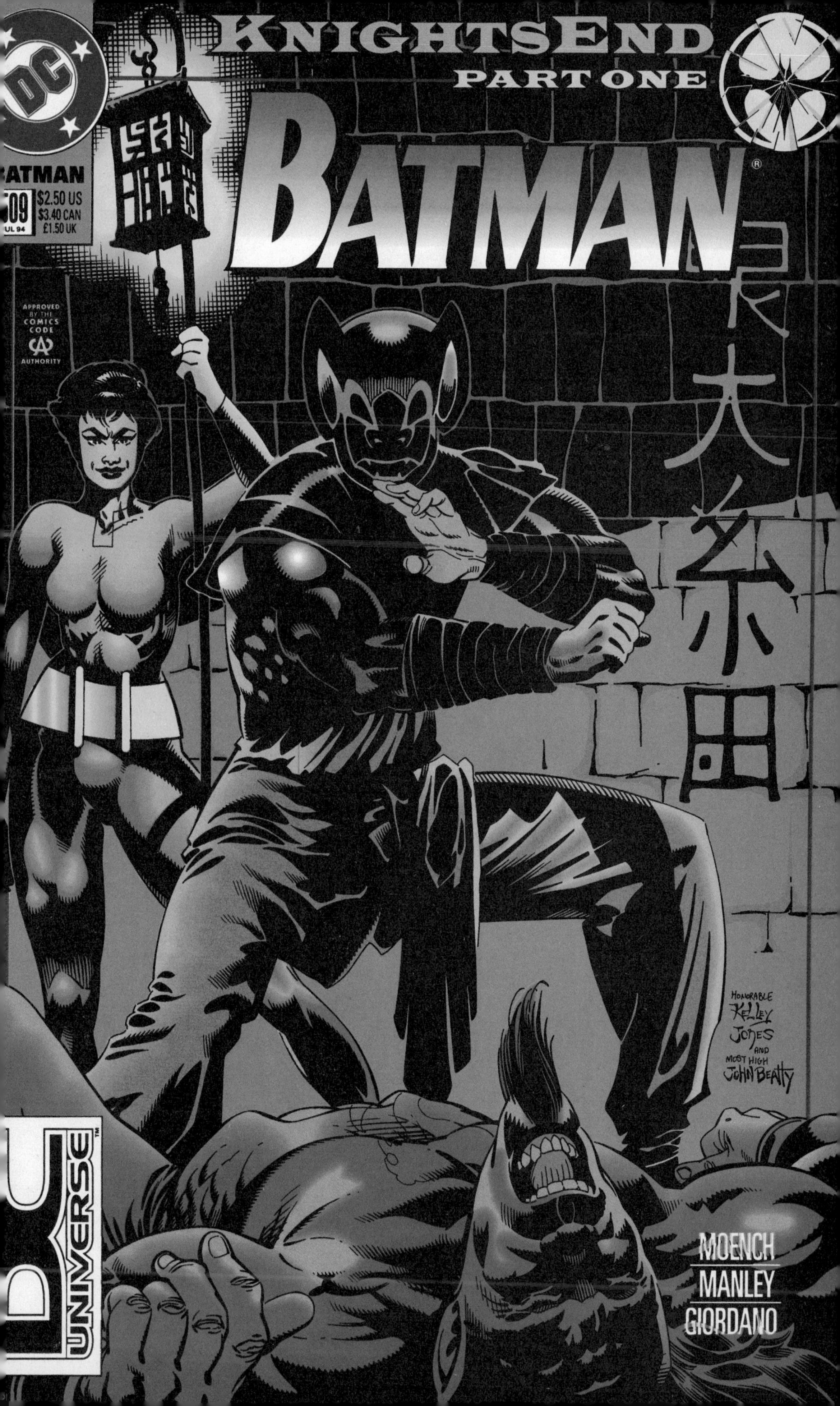

KNIGHTSEND
PART ONE
DC
BATMAN
509
$2.50 US
$3.40 CAN
£1.50 UK
JUL 94
BATMAN
APPROVED BY THE COMICS CODE AUTHORITY
HONORABLE KELLEY JONES AND MOST HIGH JOHN BEATTY
DC UNIVERSE
MOENCH
MANLEY
GIORDANO

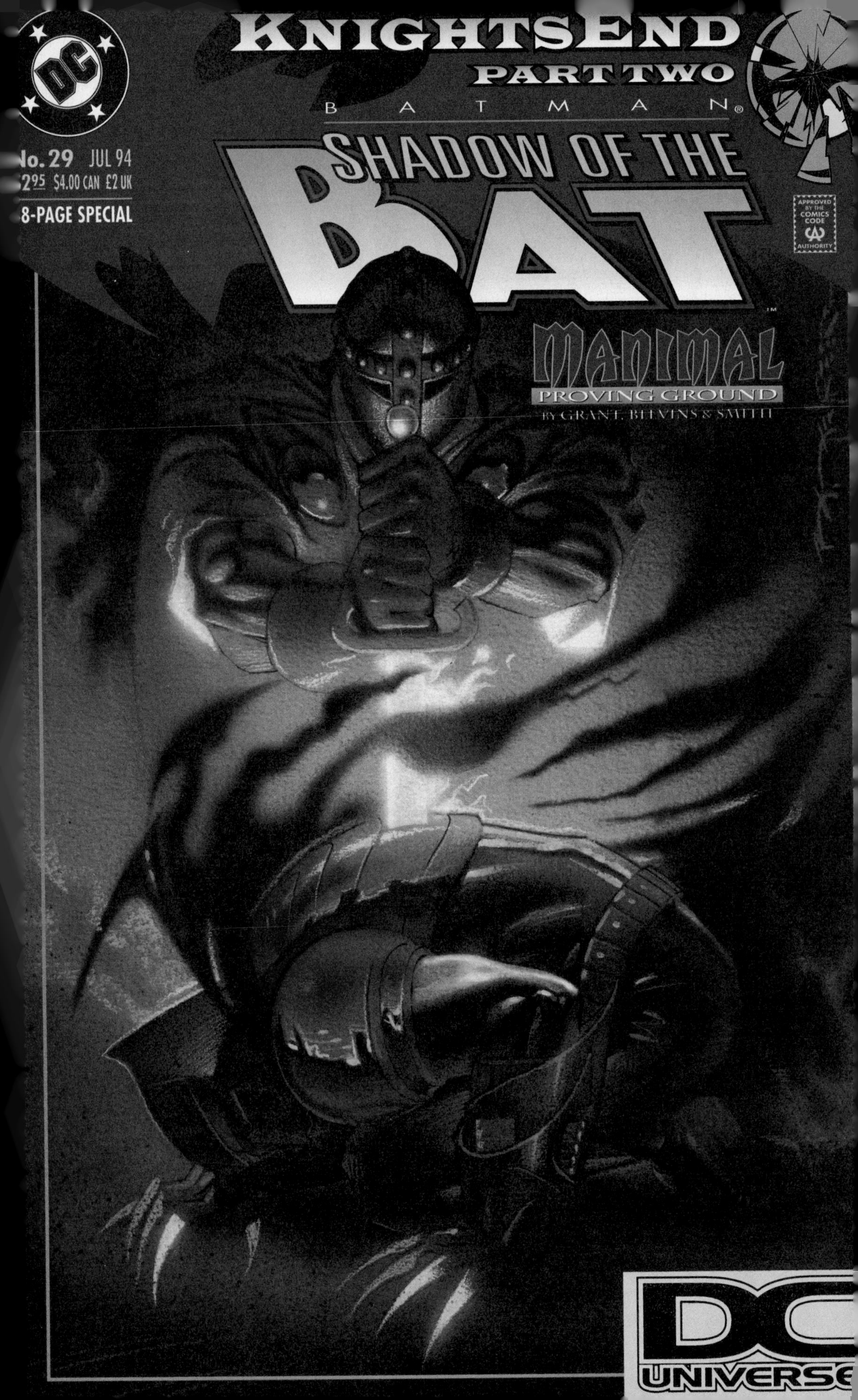
KNIGHTSEND
PART TWO
BATMAN®
SHADOW OF THE BAT™
No. 29 JUL 94
$2.95 $4.00 CAN £2 UK
8-PAGE SPECIAL
APPROVED BY THE COMICS CODE AUTHORITY
MANIMAL
PROVING GROUND
BY GRANT, BLEVINS & SMITH
DC UNIVERSE

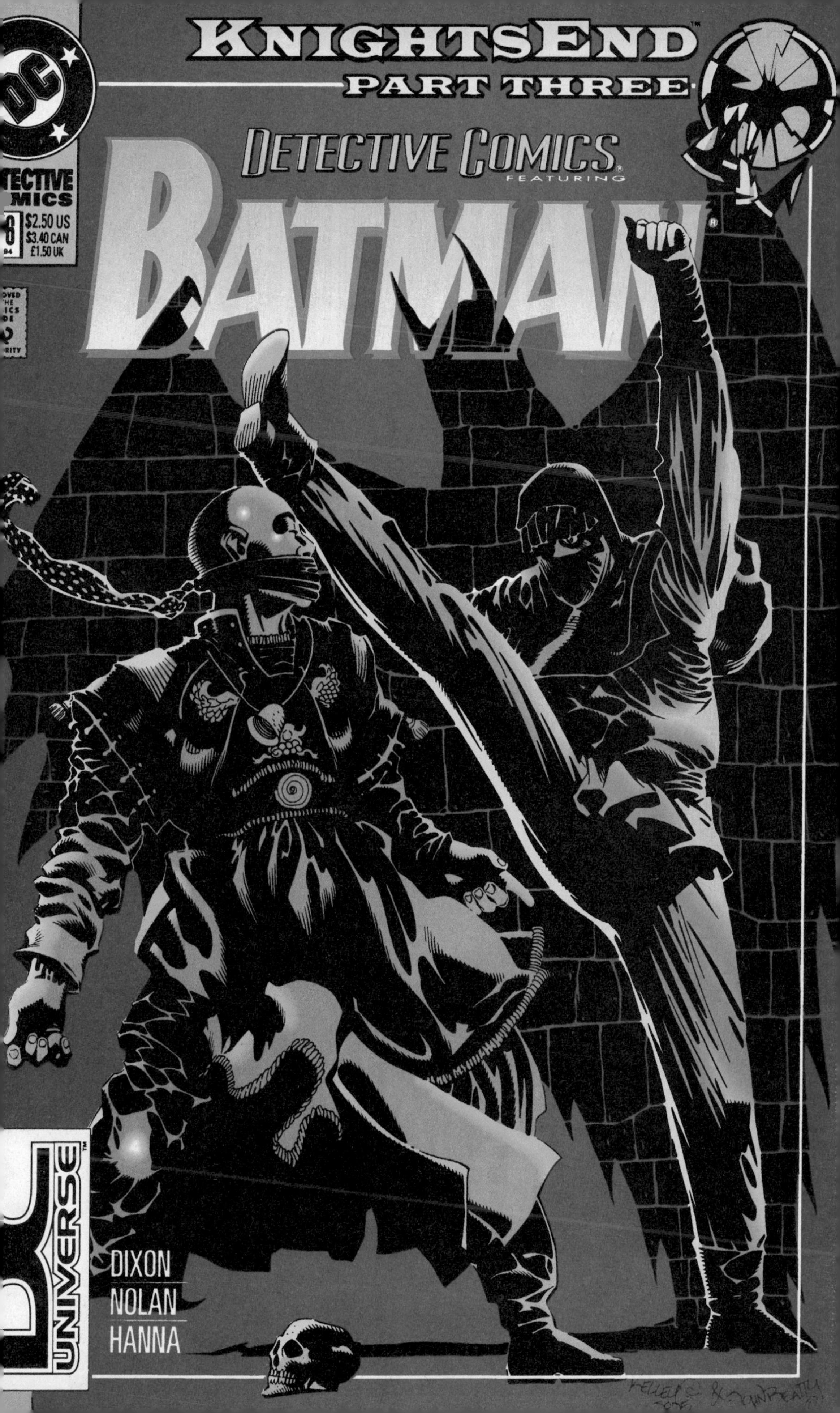
KNIGHTSEND
PART THREE
DETECTIVE COMICS
FEATURING
BATMAN
$2.50 US
$3.40 CAN
£1.50 UK
DC
UNIVERSE
DIXON
NOLAN
HANNA

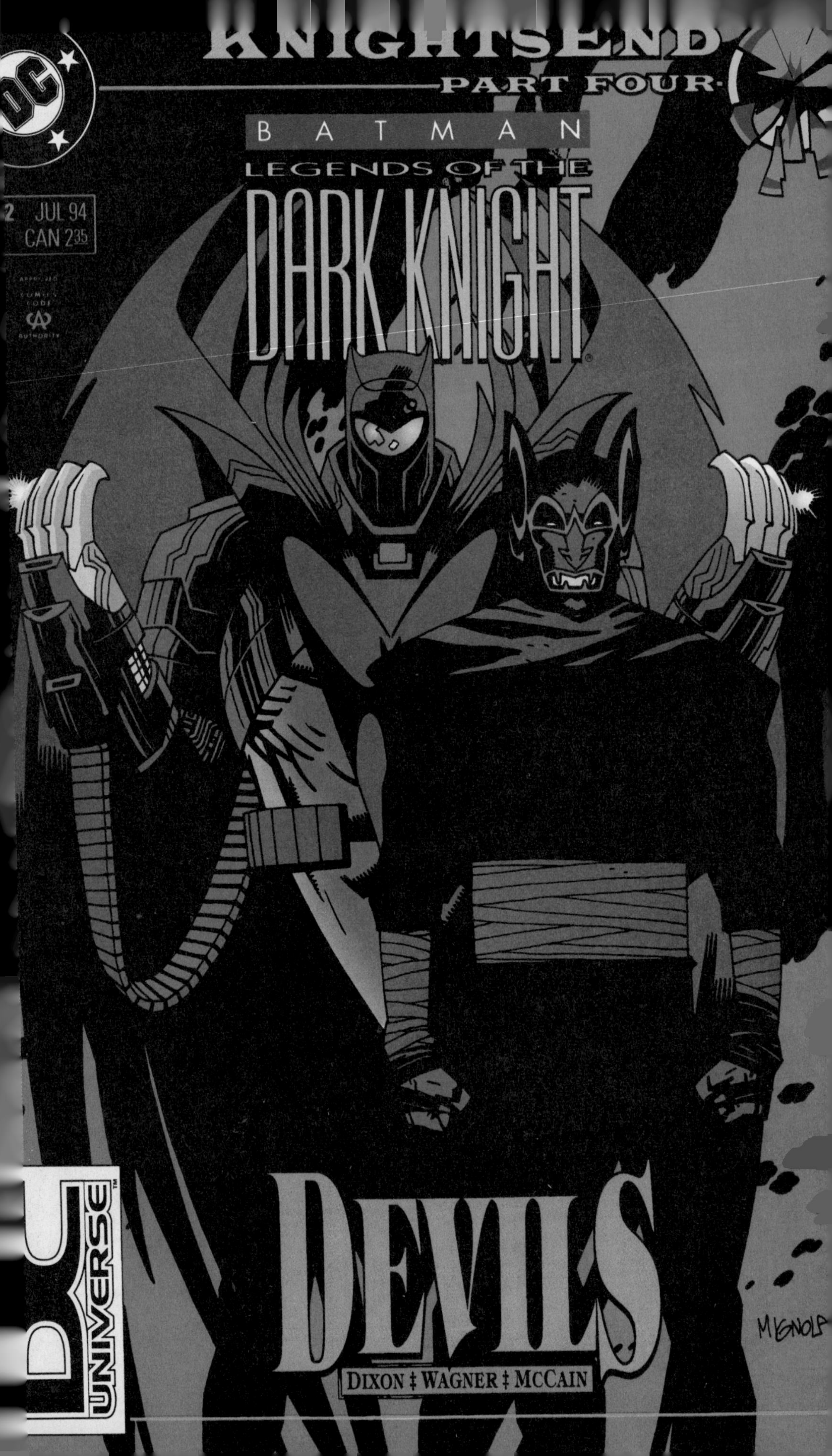
KNIGHTSEND
PART FOUR
BATMAN
LEGENDS OF THE
DARK KNIGHT
2 JUL 94
CAN 2.35
DEVILS
DIXON ‡ WAGNER ‡ McCAIN
MIGNOLA
UNIVERSE

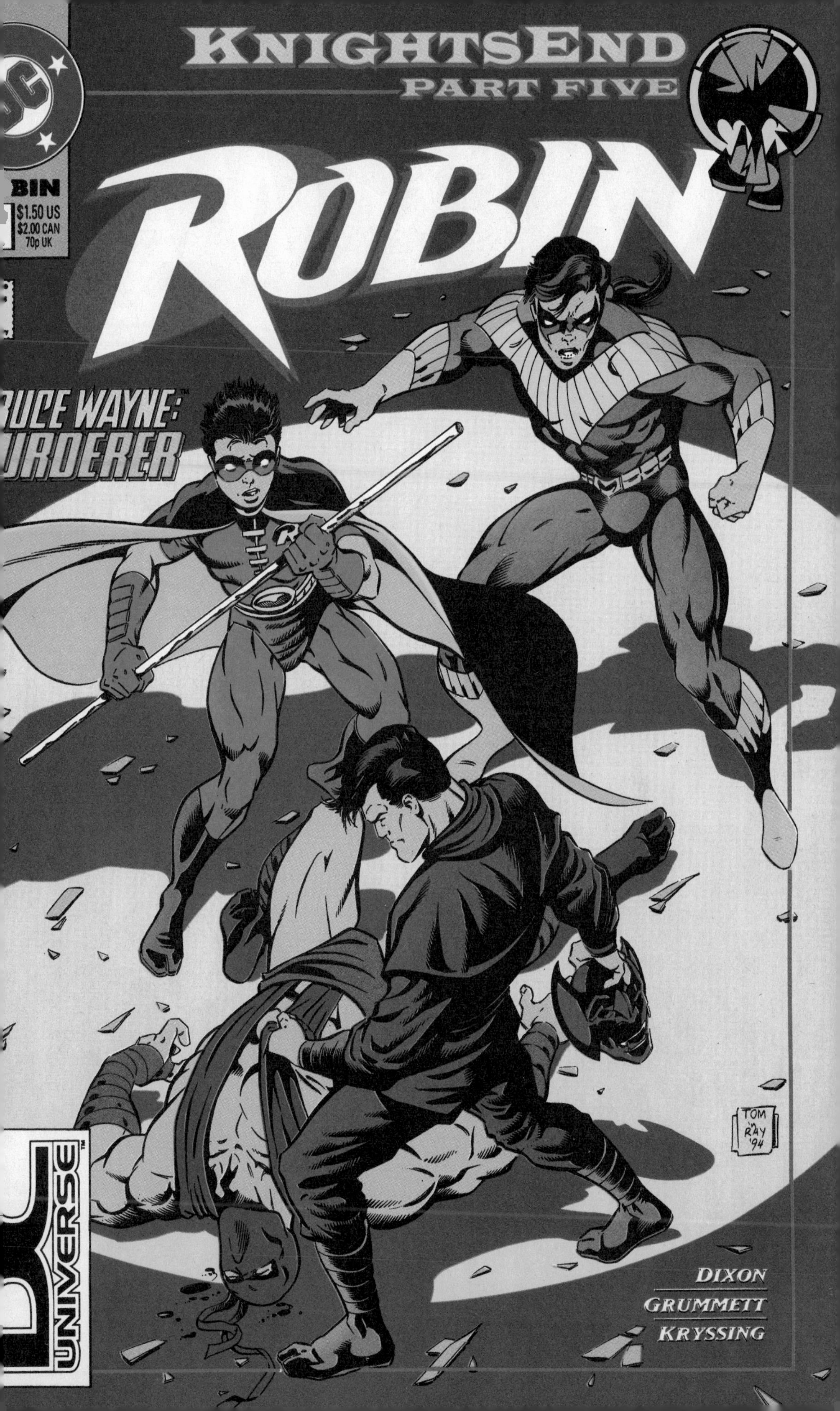

KNIGHTSEND
PART FIVE
ROBIN
BIN
$1.50 US
$2.00 CAN
70p UK
UCE WAYNE:
URDERER
TOM 'n RAY '94
UNIVERSE
DIXON
GRUMMETT
KRYSSING

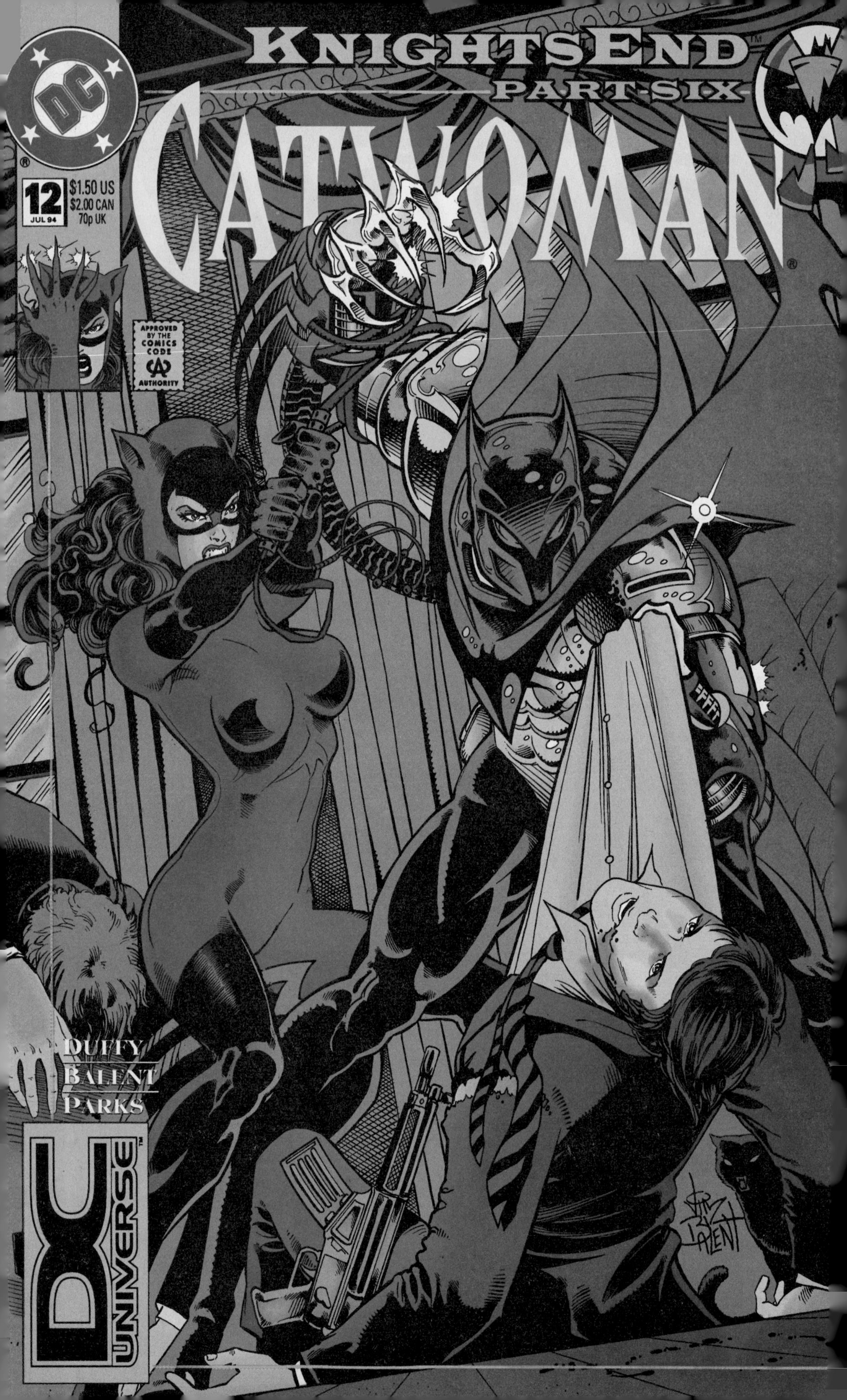

KNIGHTSEND
PART SIX
DC
CATWOMAN
12
JUL 94
$1.50 US
$2.00 CAN
70p UK
APPROVED BY THE COMICS CODE AUTHORITY
DUFFY
BALENT
PARKS
DC UNIVERSE

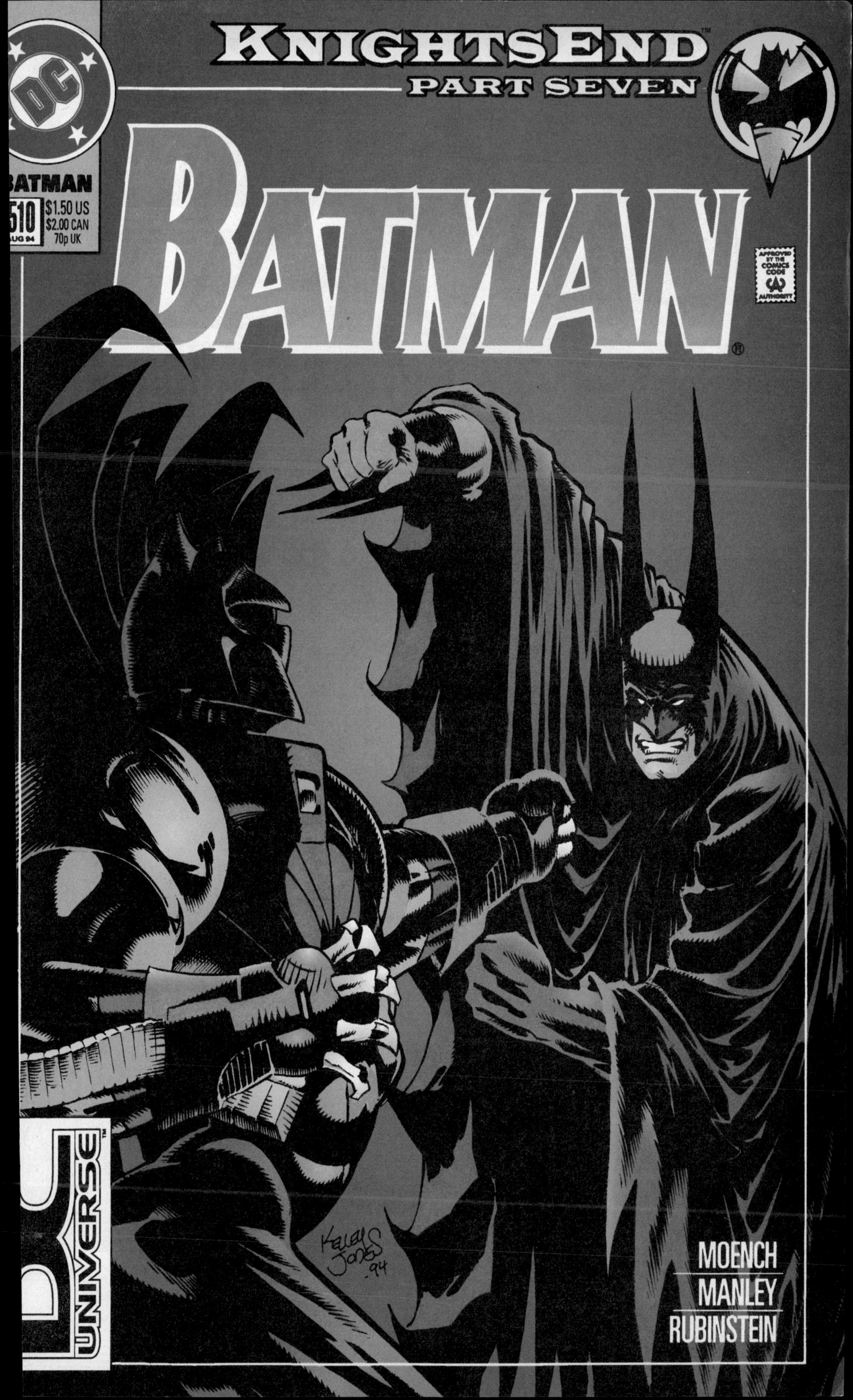

KNIGHTSEND
PART SEVEN
DC
BATMAN
510
$1.50 US
$2.00 CAN
70p UK
AUG 94
BATMAN
APPROVED BY THE COMICS CODE AUTHORITY
DC UNIVERSE
MOENCH
MANLEY
RUBINSTEIN

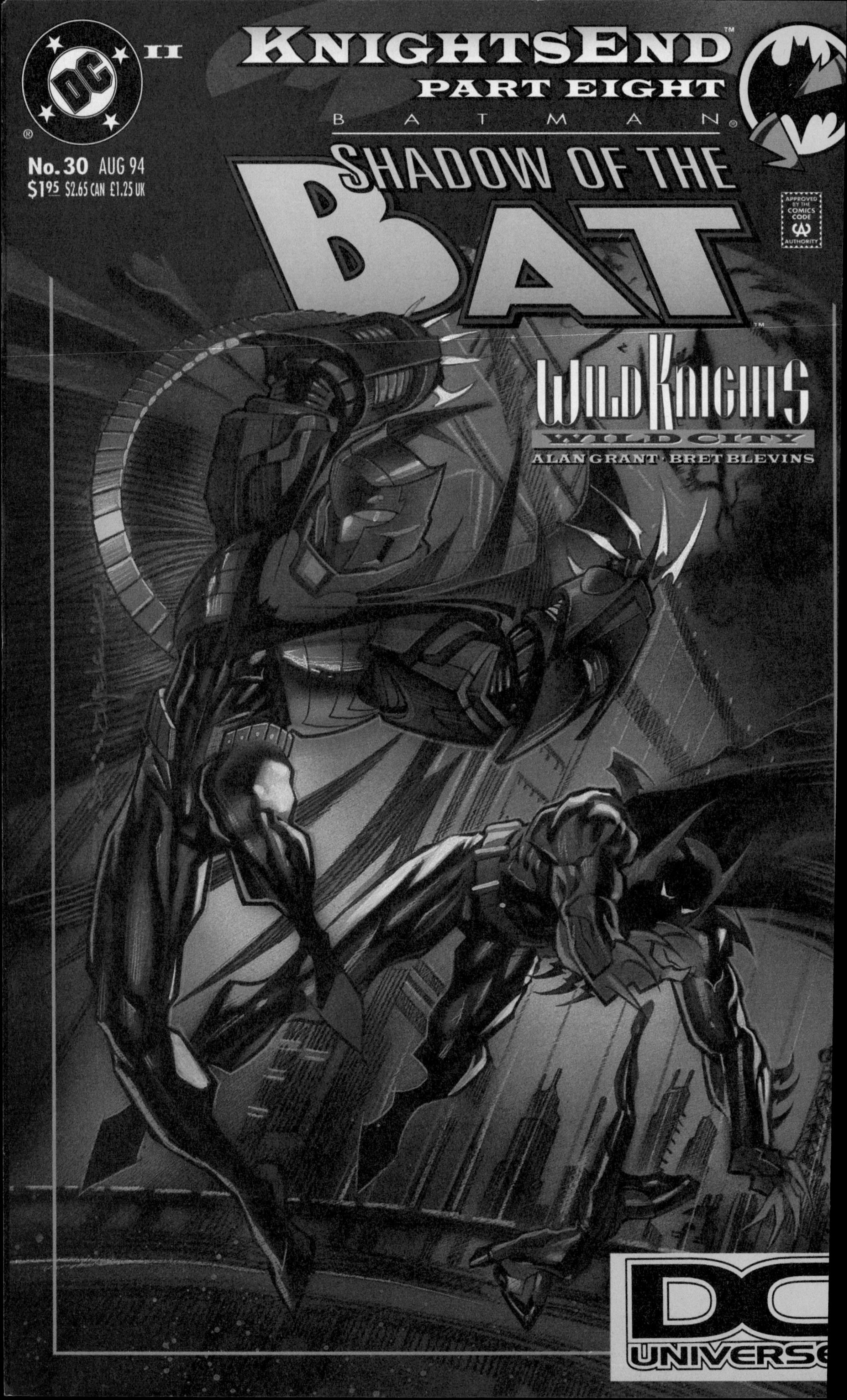
DC
II
KNIGHTSEND
PART EIGHT
BATMAN®
SHADOW OF THE BAT
No. 30 AUG 94
$1.95 $2.65 CAN £1.25 UK
APPROVED BY THE COMICS CODE AUTHORITY
WILD KNIGHTS
WILD CITY
ALAN GRANT · BRET BLEVINS
DC UNIVERSE

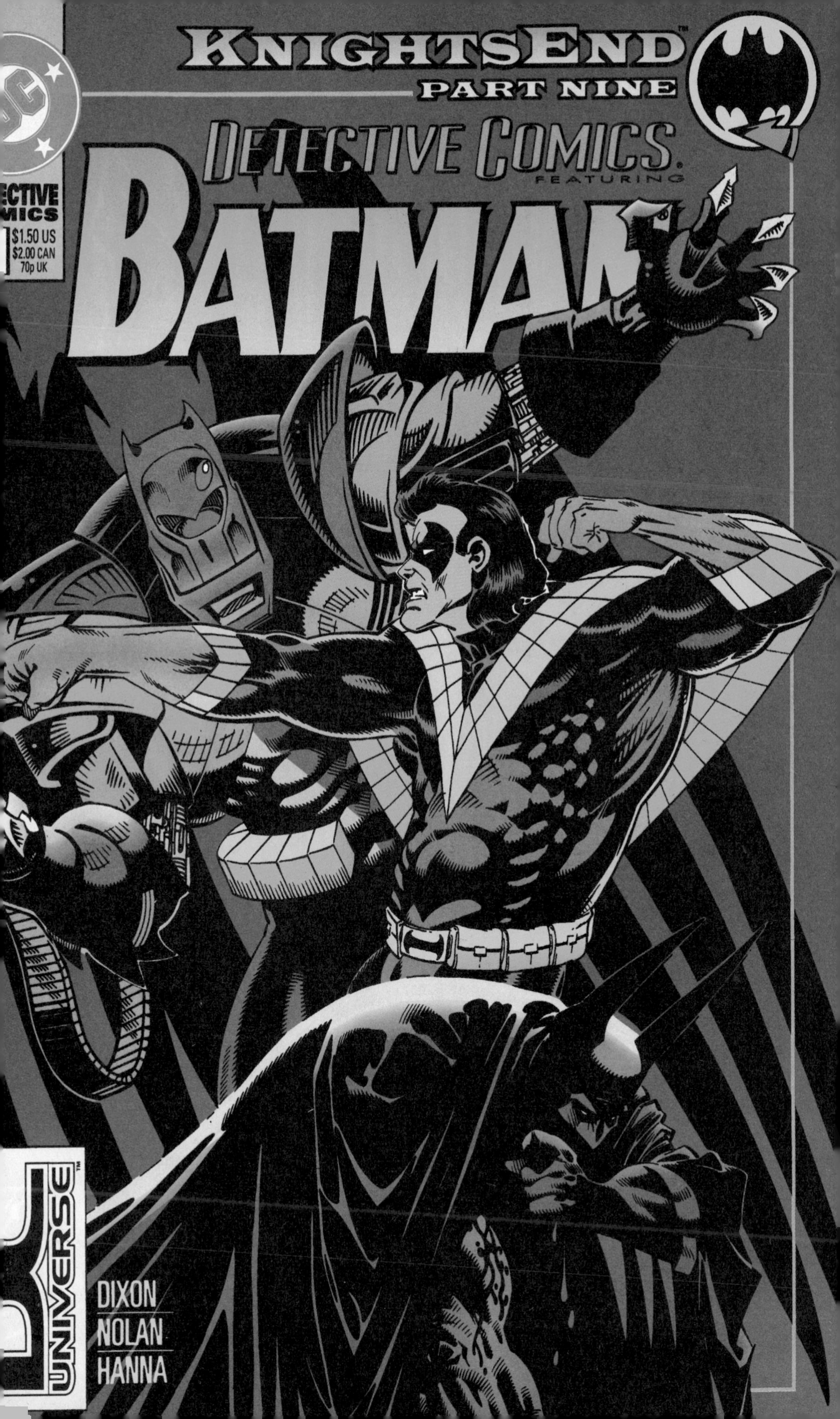
KNIGHTSEND™
PART NINE
DETECTIVE COMICS
FEATURING
BATMA
ECTIVE
MICS
$1.50 US
$2.00 CAN
70p UK
UNIVERSE™
DIXON
NOLAN
HANNA

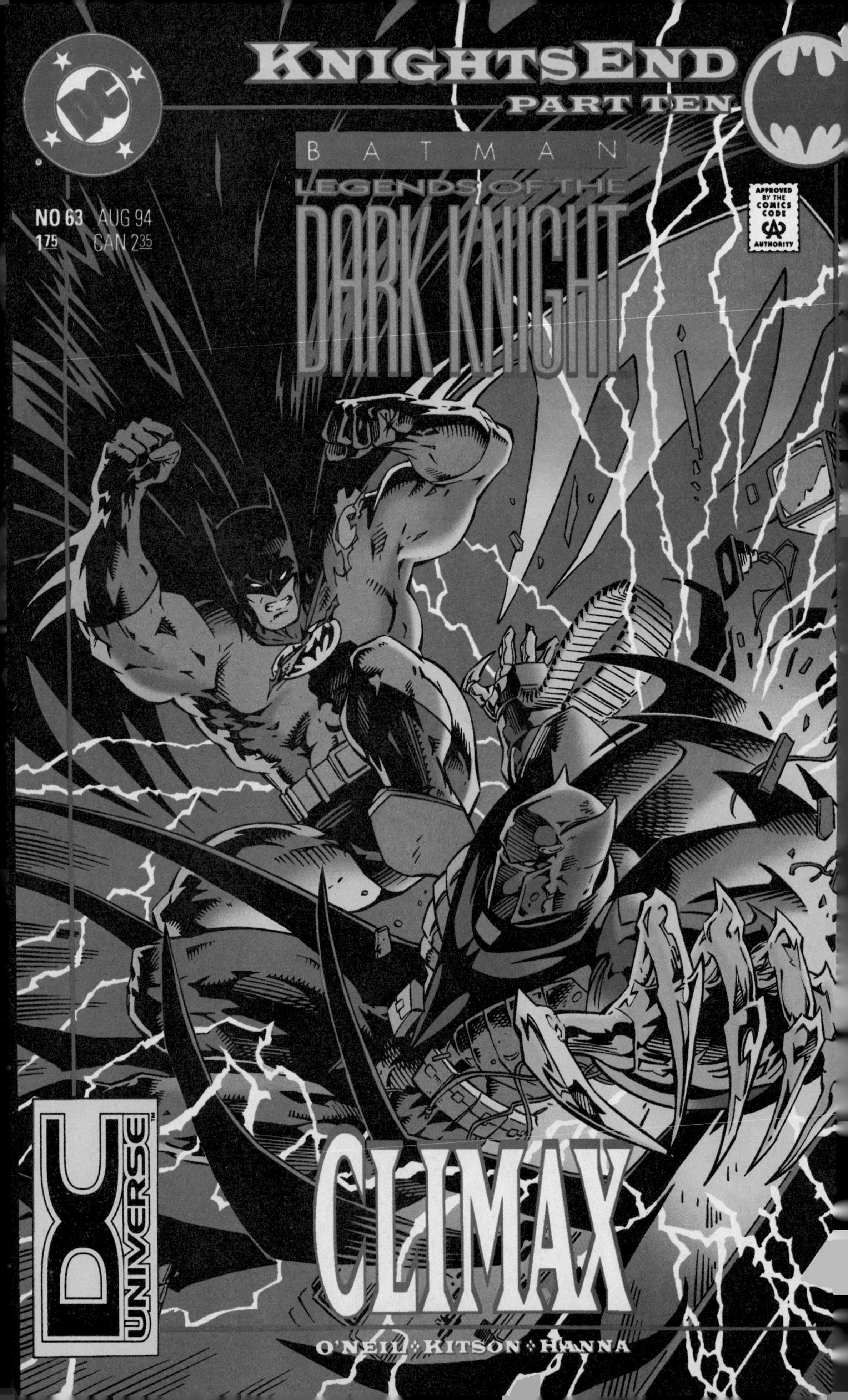

KNIGHTSEND
PART TEN
BATMAN
LEGENDS OF THE
DARK KNIGHT
NO 63 AUG 94
1.75 CAN 2.35
APPROVED BY THE COMICS CODE AUTHORITY
DC UNIVERSE
CLIMAX
O'NEIL KITSON HANNA

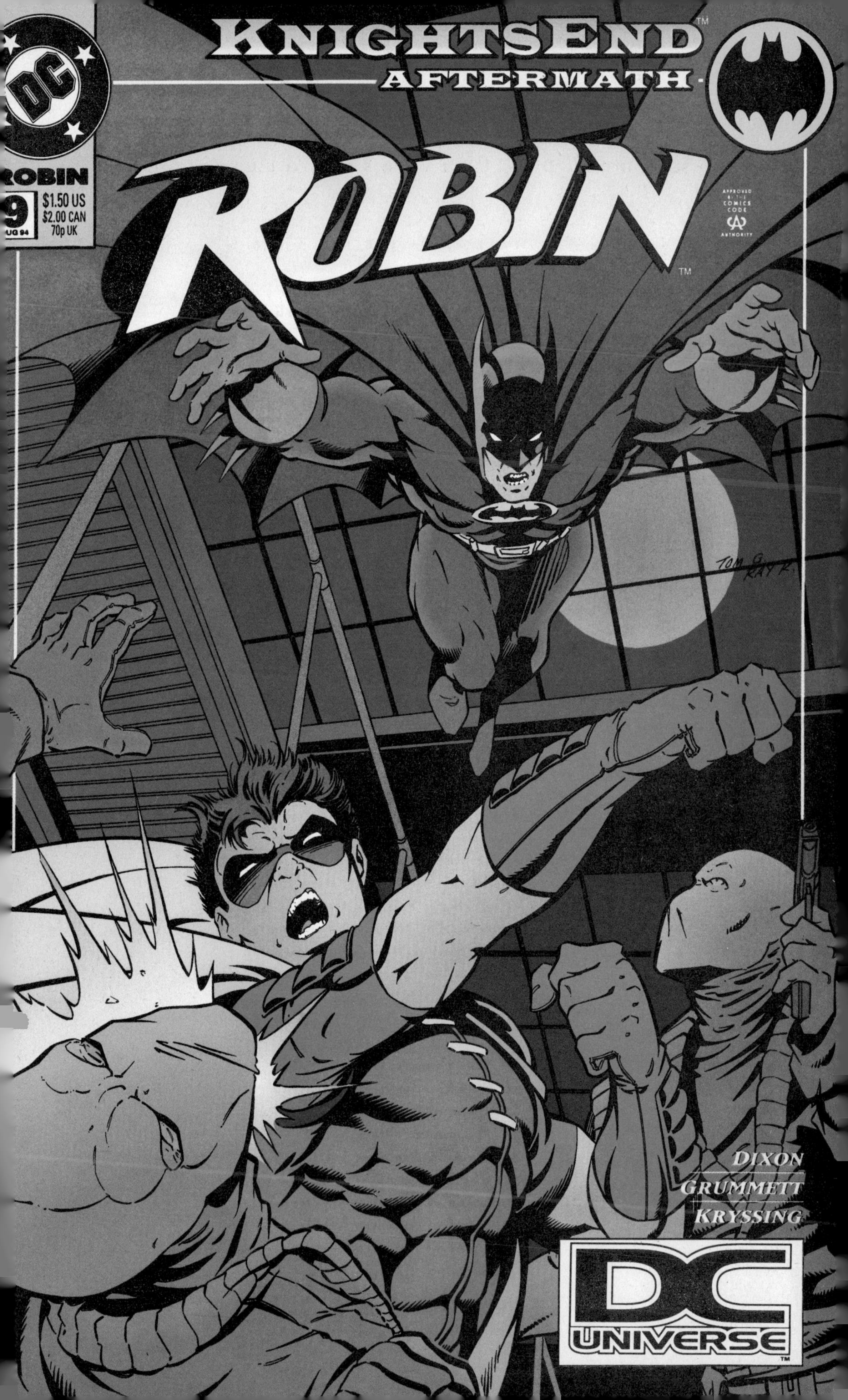
KNIGHTSEND™
AFTERMATH
ROBIN
9
$1.50 US
$2.00 CAN
70p UK
AUG 94
ROBIN™
APPROVED BY THE COMICS CODE AUTHORITY
TOM G. RAY K.
DIXON
GRUMMETT
KRYSSING
DC UNIVERSE™

OTHER DC UNIVERSE COLLECTIONS

TRADE PAPERBACKS

Batman: Blind Justice
Batman: Collected Legends of the Dark Knight
Batman: The Cult
Batman: The Dark Knight Returns
Batman: Gothic
Batman: Knightfall Part 1: Broken Bat
Batman: Knightfall Part 2: Who Rules the Night
Batman: Prey
Batman: Shaman
Batman: Sword of Azrael
Batman: Tales of the Demon
Batman: Venom
Batman: Year One
Batman vs. Predator: The Collected Edition
Green Lantern/Green Arrow: Hard-Traveling Heroes
Green Lantern/Green Arrow: More Hard-Traveling Heroes
World's Finest

STANDARD FORMAT BOOKS

Batman: A Death in the Family
Batman: A Lonely Place of Dying
Green Lantern: Emerald Dawn
Green Lantern: The Road Back
Legends: The Collected Edition
Robin: A Hero Reborn
Secret Origins of the World's Greatest Super-Heroes
Superman: Panic in the Sky
Superman: The Death of Superman
Superman: World Without a Superman
Superman: The Return of Superman

HARDCOVER BOOKS

All Star Comics Archives Vol. 1
All Star Comics Archives Vol. 2
Batman Archives Vol. 1
Batman Archives Vol. 2
Batman Archives Vol. 3
Batman: The Dark Knight Archives Vol. 1
Justice League of America Archives Vol. 1
Justice League of America Archives Vol. 2
Justice League of America Archives Vol. 3